Measuring
Educational
Outcomes
Fundamentals of Testing

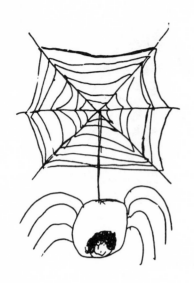

HARCOURT BRACE JOVANOVICH, INC.
New York   Chicago   San Francisco   Atlanta

BRUCE W. TUCKMAN
Rutgers University

Measuring
Educational
Outcomes
Fundamentals of Testing

ISBN: 0-15-557692-5

Library of Congress Catalog Card Number: 75-273

Printed in the United States of America

Cover art by Lisa, Jennifer, and Elena Noa.

To my grandmother, Hattie Goldberg

Preface

The field of tests and measurement is changing at a dramatic rate. The influences of such new developments as criterion-reference testing, accountability, and affective measurement are being seen and felt in classrooms and administrative offices. Educators are becoming more aware of the potentially constructive uses of tests in the decision-making process. Monitoring and certifying student progress are important ingredients in the change, and test publishers and other experts are meeting the challenge.

But for testing to contribute to effective education, its classroom uses must be realized by teachers, because major educational decisions are often based on the scores students get on tests that teachers construct and/or administer. Decisions about admission, guidance, placement, and the awarding of scholarships; diagnosis of student learning; appraisal of new programs, procedures, materials, and equipment; program management; national assessment of educational progress are all based on tests—some of which teachers themselves build and others of which are produced commercially and administered in the classroom.

Measuring Educational Outcomes: Fundamentals of Testing was written in response to this growing and continuing need by teachers and other educational professionals be able to (1) construct their own tests, (2) judge and evaluate the quality of tests, (3) choose from among published tests, and (4) use and interpret test results. Considering the importance of tests, it is amazing that supervisors supervise instructing but not testing, that teacher training focuses primarily, if not exclusively, on curriculum and instruction with little mention of testing, that teachers' lesson plans may be filed although their tests are rarely viewed by anyone except the students who take them. This book should help fill that gap in the training of preservice and in-service teachers.

Because people tend to equate measurement with statistics and to be wary of the difficult and relatively useless concepts they expect to encounter in a course in tests and measurement, this book uses some important techniques to make instruction about testing both comprehensible and useful. Each of the fifteen chapters in this book begins with a list of *Objectives*, that is, intended learning outcomes; each chapter ends with a *Self-test of Proficiency* to enable the student to measure whether he or she has mastered each objective. The objectives have been prepared in shorthand form, and the test items have been built around the objectives (a minimum of two for each) to ensure their fit, or appropriateness. This procedure is itself illustrative of principles of testing described in the text. Readers are encouraged to complete the test at the end of each chapter, score it by using the answers provided at the back of the book, and review those parts of the chapter as necessary to overcome deficiencies.

Teachers will find that different kinds of tests or test interpretations are needed for different situations. Two broad types, *norm-referenced* (interpretation on a relative basis) and *criterion-referenced* (interpretation on an absolute basis), are covered. The latter provides more concrete information about what an individual student can or cannot do and, hence, is more applicable to individualized instruction or any other student-centered approach. Since teachers' own tests are used for criterion-referenced interpretation, a *Criterion-referenced Checklist*, presented in Chapter 11, suggests ways in which teachers can evaluate their tests in terms of appropriateness, validity, reliability, interpretability, and usability.

Writing this book has been an exciting experience for me. I have tried to convey the concepts and practices of this changing and developing field in an open, practical, and comprehensive way. I have tried also to show how important testing is as an educational tool, one which, if used correctly, can reveal much useful information that ultimately will benefit students. By helping teachers to manage the learning process, tests can actually give them more independence and more time to be creative. This book shows teachers how to write objectives and to write items to measure those objectives; to measure students' knowledge as well as thinking skills, attitudes, performance, and behavior; to check the adequacy of their tests and then improve the tests if necessary; to understand and use published tests; and finally, to use the results of tests to become better teachers.

I would like to acknowledge the publishers who let me reproduce their copyrighted materials; my students, who continue to inspire me; my secretary, Sharon Davis, who continues to decipher me; my editors and reviewers, particularly William J. Wisneski and Louise Baer, who continue to assist me; and my family, who continue to tolerate me.

Bruce W. Tuckman

Contents

Author's Foreword

TESTING IN CONTEXT: FROM PAST CREATIONS TO PRESENT CONTROVERSIES

The modern history of testing is the history of testing for intelligence or mental ability. Tracing the origins of testing will help place in context some of the present issues and controversies of measurement. A logical beginning is to examine the phenomenon that tests were invented to measure—individual differences in skills among adults.

Early Measurement of Individual Differences. In January 1796, Maskelyne—the astronomer royal of Greenwich Observatory in England —dismissed his assistant, Kinnebrook, because the latter was recording the movement of stars across the telescope field eight-tenths of a second later than was Maskelyne himself. Maskelyne concluded that Kinnebrook had fallen "into some irregular and confused method of his own" for judging the time it took for a star to move from one hairline marker to the next.

Maskelyne recorded the event in the *Astronomical Observations at Greenwich*, and Bessel—the astronomer at the Königsberg Observatory in Germany—read about it in 1813. In 1820, Bessel compared ten observations of his with those of a fellow astronomer, named Argelander, and found them to differ consistently by a fraction more than one second. A second set of comparisons in 1823 yielded the "personal equation," $A - B = 1.223$ *sec.*, for the difference between Bessel's observations and those of Argelander. By making subsequent comparisons on more than one occasion with the same colleague, Bessel demonstrated the variability in the personal equation, since it fluctuated from occasion to occasion. As a result of Bessel's discoveries, astronomers took to publishing their personal equations along with the results of their observations.

The use of the chronograph simplified the measurement of stellar transit, because the astronomer only had to tap a key at the instant of transit. Hence, the personal equation was reduced to "simple reaction time"—a measure of the time required to react to a simple stimulus.

In 1863, Sir Francis Galton, a half-cousin of Charles Darwin, began his systematic study of human individual differences. His book *Inquiries into the Human Faculty and Its Development*, published in 1883, has been regarded by some scientists as the beginning of mental tests. His tests included the "Galton whistle," a device for determining a person's highest audible pitch; the "Galton bar," a measure of visual acuity and judgment; an instrument with weights to measure muscle sense; and a series of other apparatus-type tests. All these tests were intended to measure sensory or perceptual characteristics.

In 1884, Galton opened his Anthropometric Laboratory to collect the characteristic measurements of people. Data for 9,337 persons were collected, including height, weight, arm span, breathing power, strength of pull and squeeze, quickness of blow, hearing, seeing, color sense, and other personal data (Boring, 1950). These data, however, yielded no noteworthy generalizations about individual differences other than the erroneous one that women are inferior to men in all capacities.

Galton's emphasis on the inventory of human abilities as a means of classifying and understanding "human nature" was perhaps excessive and bore little fruit. His concern with human physical and perceptual characteristics as measures of mental abilities was misplaced and misdirected; we now know that physical and mental properties are often unrelated. His focus on human measurement, though, was an important step in the evolution of testing.

A contemporary of Galton's, J. McKeen Cattell, an American psychologist, was also studying individual differences in primarily physical terms. A list of Cattell's tests is shown below (Cattell, 1890).

(1) Strength of grip, as measured by a device called a dynamometer
(2) Rate of movement: the quickest time in which the hand can be moved through a distance of fifty centimeters
(3) The smallest perceptible distance between two points on the skin, known as "two-point discrimination"
(4) The amount of pressure necessary to cause pain by pressing a strip of hard rubber upon the forehead
(5) The smallest discernible difference in weight, measured by requiring that two weights be lifted in succession
(6) The speed with which an individual can react to a sound
(7) The speed with which an individual can name ten specimens of four different colors arranged in haphazard order
(8) The accuracy with which an individual can bisect a fifty-centimeter line

(9) The accuracy with which an individual can indicate an interval of ten seconds

(10) Immediate rote memory

These tests are considerably more "biological" than today's mental tests.

The Beginnings of Individual Intelligence Testing.   By 1904, Alfred Binet had established himself as France's premier psychologist and expert in human individual differences with his studies of the differences between "bright" and "dull" children. Naturally, when Paris school officials became concerned about nonlearners and decided to set up special schools with simplified curriculums, they turned to Binet. Teachers, the officials reasoned, could not accurately pick out children with mental deficiency; the officials were concerned that the teachers' judgment would be affected by such other factors as the child's general behavior, personality, and social background. For example, troublemakers might be classified as mentally deficient while pleasant children might escape unnoticed. Binet was asked to develop a procedure for identifying the truly dull child. In 1905, he and Théodore Simon produced the Binet-Simon Scale, the first "intelligence test." It consisted of thirty short tasks arranged in ascending order of difficulty.

Binet had discovered that children who were observed to be best in judgment were also superior in attention, vocabulary, and other traits. That is, some children had more general ability than others. Binet chose his thirty tasks to represent the many areas of intelligence that he felt reflected general ability. He refined his idea of intelligence by trial and error, selecting and rejecting tasks on the basis of their correspondence to other indicators of mental ability. He revised the scale in 1908 and again in 1911. The 1908 revision represented the first use of age norms in measurement; scores were determined by comparing a child's performance to the average performance of children his or her own age.

In 1916, Louis Terman and his associates at Stanford University brought the intelligence test to the United States by preparing the Stanford revision of the Binet-Simon Scales, which came to be known as the Stanford-Binet. The revision was so extensive as to constitute, in effect, a new test. In addition, the entire scale was restandardized on an American sample of approximately 1,000 children and 400 adults. For the first time the concept of IQ was used in a test, it being defined as the ratio of mental age divided by chronological age multiplied by 100. The Stanford-Binet was revised in 1937 and again in 1960 and 1972 and is currently in use as an individually administered test of intelligence.

Using the standardized sample, test administrators can determine the age in months of children who, on the average, get a task right. When a child reaches a point on a subtest where he or she cannot successfully complete an item, his or her score is the age in months of children who, on the average (that is, 50 percent of them), also cannot go beyond that item. This age in months of the average child who stops at a particular item is called the *mental age* of the child. If a child's chronological age conforms to his or her mental age, the ratio is one. Multiplying the ratio by 100 gives an *intelligence quotient*, or *IQ*, of 100, considered to be the average, or normal, intelligence quotient for a child.

The Proliferation of Intelligence Testing. When the United States entered the First World War, the government wanted to screen the thousands of men being inducted into the army so that misfits could be rejected and the remainder classified for different kinds of training and different levels of responsibility. To accomplish this, a test known as Army Alpha was developed; it measured simple reasoning, ability to follow directions, numerical reasoning ability, and general knowledge.

Officers were found to score higher on the test than enlisted men; college graduates scored higher than those with only an eighth-grade education. These results led the test's proponents to conclude that the test was valid and caused industrialists and educators to adopt it enthusiastically. Army Alpha was easy to give to large groups, easy to score, and easy to interpret. However, interpreting the Army Alpha as a measure of "native intelligence" independent of prior education is a questionable practice. It seems more reasonable to consider this type of test a measure of general scholastic ability or of verbal and numerical reasoning abilities, as Lee J. Cronbach (1970) has suggested.

To counter the bias of Army Alpha toward language skills and experiences, Army Beta, the first nonlanguage group test, was developed for illiterate soldiers and soldiers who did not speak English. It was given to all men who fell below a certain score on the Alpha and was used chiefly to measure spatial orientation and perceptual speed and accuracy. However, because it emphasized speed and was patterned after the Alpha, it produced results very similar to those of the Alpha. Hence, its nonverbal feature did not eliminate from it all forms of bias.

In 1939, the Wechsler-Bellevue Scale was published. It tests the intelligence of persons from age 10 through 60 (Wechsler, 1944). Like the Stanford-Binet, it is an individually administered IQ test, but it differs from the Stanford-Binet in certain important ways. First, while the Stanford-Binet is standardized primarily on children and is somewhat limited in measuring adult intelligence, the Wechsler-Bellevue is standardized on a more adult population. Second, the Stanford-Binet puts an almost exclusive emphasis on verbal intelligence, but the Wechsler-Bellevue is split between verbal tasks and performance tasks.

A third, and perhaps the most important, difference between the two scales is that the Stanford-Binet subtests are organized by performance of age groups and the Wechsler-Bellevue subtests are organized by item type. Page 314 of this book lists the performances measured on each age-graded subtest of the Stanford-Binet. The Wechsler-Bellevue is made up of the following item-type subtests:

Verbal

(1) Information (general knowledge)
(2) General comprehension (indicating understanding)
(3) Arithmetical reasoning (solving simple arithmetical problems)
(4) Memory span for digits, forward and backward (repeating a series of digits heard once)
(5) Similarities (stating the likeness that exists between two words)
(6) Vocabulary (word meaning)

Performance

(7) Picture arrangement (putting pictures in the correct order to tell a story)
(8) Picture completion (noting and naming the missing parts in pictures)
(9) Block design (putting blocks in a particular order to conform to a given design)
(10) Object assembly (assembling wooden parts to complete a specified object)
(11) Digit-symbol test (recalling the symbol with which a given digit was paired)

The Current Controversies. In 1969, the *Harvard Educational Review* published an article by Arthur Jensen entitled "How Much Can We Boost IQ and Scholastic Achievement?" Although the article was a long, scholarly consideration of intelligence and scholastic achievement, it became famous mainly for one statement:

> ...it [is] a not unreasonable hypothesis that genetic factors are strongly implicated in the average Negro-white intelligence difference. The preponderance of the evidence is, in my opinion, less consistent with a strictly environmental hypothesis than with a genetic hypothesis, which, of course, does not exclude the influence of environment or its interaction with genetic factors.

Naturally, this statement aroused a considerable response in both professional and nonprofessional circles. Jensen seemed to be claiming that whites outperformed blacks on IQ tests primarily because whites were genetically superior, not because they had been reared in more favorable circumstances. To support his claim, Jensen cited findings of performance equal to that of whites by other disadvantaged and minority groups (e.g., Chinese-Americans) on nonverbal IQ tests such as

Raven's Progressive Matrices. His critics contended that his data were poor, his analyses questionable, and his conclusions equivocal.

One benefit of the debate was to make educators more careful in the use of IQ tests. Clearly, blacks and whites as groups do tend to score differently on IQ tests—perhaps, it could be argued, because blacks have had poorer schooling. Possibly, then, we should reconsider how tests should be used. Except for the diagnosis of marked deficiency, we would be wise to focus our testing on what children have learned as a result of school experiences and to draw conclusions on this basis rather than on the basis of variations in native intelligence. Consider the following incident.

The General Aptitude Test Battery (GATB) is a type of broad-based intelligence test that the United States Employment Service uses in screening and counseling job seekers. It is also used as a screening device for apprenticeship training programs. Because blacks tend to score lower than whites on this test, they are eliminated from competition for places in apprenticeship programs.

In the late 1960s, while many civil rights groups focused their efforts on elimination of the test as culturally biased, Ernie Green of the A. Phillip Randolph Institute took a different approach. He developed a program in Brooklyn's Bedford-Stuyvesant section to train potential appreticeship candidates to take the test. Assuming that white candidates have had more specific training in taking such tests as the GATB, he added relevant experience to the culture of minority candidates to overcome the cultural bias. Using mainly self-educated ex-convicts as teachers, he had black candidates spend six to eight weeks learning basic math and English. They practiced on items similar to those found on the current form of the GATB (a review process not unlike the College Board review or the "Regents review" in New York schools).

Their heads filled with vocabulary words, analogies, and math skills, Ernie Green's first group of graduates took the exams. The results were gratifying: virtually all the students in the program were above the cut-off scores. "They're beating the system," shouted their critics, who were trying to maintain the status quo. "It's not fair to teach people to take a test." "But," responded Green, "isn't that what the middle-class school experience is all about?" The courts agreed. Those who have never been taught what the tests measure should be given the opportunity to learn it.

The results on tests may be the cause of school behavior and not just its effect. If children who have higher IQ scores are expected by their teachers to do better in school than children with lower scores (a not unreasonable supposition), and if teachers are nicer to these high IQ test scorers and help them more than they help the low scorers, it is evident that IQ test scores are not only the effect of school experiences but also their cause.

In Summary.   Testing can be helpful if its use increases the learning and performance of children. Envisioning this, Alfred Binet—"the father of intelligence testing"—said:

> A child's mind is like a field for which an expert farmer has advised a change in the method of cultivating, with the result that in place of desert land, we now have a harvest. It is in this particular sense, the one which is significant, that we say the intelligence of children may be increased. One increases that which constitutes the intelligence of a school child, namely, the *capacity to learn*, to *improve with instruction*. (Binet, 1909.)

It is possible that tests have been imbued with more powers than they actually possess and used as an excuse for maintaining the status quo. David McClelland, a psychologist most noted for his work on achievement motivation, has cited findings of a relationship between scores on College Boards and both school grades and occupational status. Test performance and school grades require the same kind of game-playing skills, McClelland claimed, and success in both is a thread in the fabric of conformity to upper- and middle-class values. "Why," asks McClelland, "call experience at these test games intelligence?" (McClelland, 1973.)

While we must acknowledge the shortcomings of tests, we must also overcome their deficiencies. Tests serve a variety of important functions in education. Despite their shortcomings, they are the best means we have for detecting characteristics in a reasonably objective fashion. They help us gain the kinds of information about learners and learning that we need to help students learn.

Bruce W. Tuckman

part one/Planning a Test

chapter one / Putting Measurement and Evaluation in Perspective

OBJECTIVES

1. Identify reasons for giving tests to students in the classroom.

2. Describe, in nontechnical terms, how tests are constructed and evaluated.

3. Identify the meaning of some common terms used in describing tests.

Observations have a highly subjective quality. They often represent what is in the eye of the beholder rather than what actually exists. The teacher and the scientist, however, must obtain information that is accurate or *veridical*—it must reflect what is happening, not what we would like to happen. Tests and other forms of measuring instruments are designed to replace subjective judgment with objectivity to the greatest degree possible. Without the detachment and impartiality of the well-designed, properly used test the teacher is left compounding and confounding judgment with judgment, never having any independent basis for assessing the behavior of students. (However, it must be remembered that even tests can be misused to help make a point.)

Sometimes we are faced with the necessity not of observing a behavior as it tends to happen but of stimulating the behavior to happen or finding out if the person is capable of performing the behavior in question. In these situations, we must not only measure the behavior but, in a sense, sample it from among the individual's total repertoire of behavior. For all of these purposes we use what are commonly called *tests*.

Because teachers are faced with the responsibility of recording, measuring, and evaluating the behavior and performance of their students, they will find tests a valuable tool. With the aid of tests they can monitor student learning and diagnose strengths and weaknesses as they occur in their students.

A few case studies will help illustrate the ways teachers can use tests and give some indication of their importance in the teaching–learning process.

Some Case Studies

• Miss Farragut, a first grade teacher, had a child in her class who was slow in reading and had difficulty in drawing common shapes. Miss Farragut asked the school psychologist to test this girl. He administered the Stanford-Binet Intelligence Scale and the Bender Gestalt Test, and she was found—based on the latter—to have a perceptual difficulty. Because of this diagnosis, the child was given special perceptual activities by her teacher to permit her to learn more easily and to strengthen her performance in this area of weakness.

• Mr. Johns, the chemistry teacher, was concerned about letting his class use acids before they had mastered laboratory techniques and practices. Rather than trying to use his own judgment to determine when the class was ready, he decided to create a test situation. Everyone was assigned two Erlenmeyer flasks, a tripod, filtering equipment, and a burette. Each was also given vials of chemicals marked with the names of acids, bases, and other compounds. (Actually, the vials contained harmless substances.) Instructions for a laboratory experiment were also given. Mr. Johns had prepared a checklist of safe laboratory practices associated with the mock experiment. Each of the twelve statements on his list were essential to laboratory safety. As he walked around the room he wrote the initials of all students who performed a safe practice next to the name of that practice on his checklist. At home that night, he tallied the marks and identified those students who had demonstrated safe practices. Each of these students was awarded a safety certificate and a button and was permitted to use the laboratory. The other students could use the laboratory only when accompanied by a member of the safety group, who would use the checklist to judge their behavior in an effort by them to obtain the safety certificate too.

• Mrs. Thomas was a fifth grade teacher who every spring administered a standardized achievement test battery to her class. During the summer she carefully studied the class list of results that appeared on a computer print-out supplied by the testing company. She noticed that many of her students had done poorly on the language mechanics subtest. Upon further examination of the individual records and a closer look at the test itself (a copy of which she kept in her files), she realized that her students had not clearly understood the principle of using a comma to separate nouns in sequence. She made a note to herself to include this topic in one of her lesson plans so that this deficiency would not reoccur in her next fifth grade class. She also made a note to report this finding to her principal for the benefit of the sixth grade teachers.

• Miss Levine was teaching English to high school seniors and working on her master's degree. She had a theory that the compositions students wrote reflected their needs and orientations toward life, if only in subtle ways. For the research requirements in her master's program and to test her insight as a teacher, she decided to test this hypothesis by collecting data. She asked each of her students to write a composition about the most frustrating experience of his or her life, and scored each composition for the presence or absence of each of six needs that seemed important to students of this age: power, achievement, affiliation, nurturance, succorance, and autonomy. Prior to doing this, she had checked "needs" in the *Mental Measurements Yearbook*.[1] A test called the Edwards Personal Preference Schedule that measured sixteen personal needs and used a short-answer format was described and reviewed. Miss Levine acquired this test and used it to measure students on the same six needs measured on the compositions. To her delight the needs of students as measured on the Edwards test were quite like those measured on the compositions, even when another teacher rated the compositions. Miss Levine had not only substantiated her hunch but now had some insight as well into the needs of her individual students.

MMY

- Mr. Detwhiler, who taught automotive engineering, developed a test he called the Auto Troubleshooters Competency Test. On one of the engines he had on hand Mr. Detwhiler would locate or program in a fault or malfunction. The student was then given the task of locating the fault and was asked to keep track of his or her time and also to keep a written record of everything he or she did. If the student located the fault he or she was given 100 points. One point was then deducted for each minute it took to locate the fault, and ten points deducted for each step taken that a qualified mechanic would not take in locating the fault. Any student who could earn sixty-five points was "certified" as competent on Mr. Detwhiler's test.

- Mrs. Shore was taking part in an experimental program. She was being trained to follow the principles of the British Infant School–Open Classroom approach in her third grade classroom. The experimental program also included an evaluation to determine the extent to which it was meeting its goals. Since one of its goals was to make school a more positive experience for youngsters a measure called the School Sentiment Index was used. All the students in Mrs. Shore's class filled out this instrument so that their attitudes toward school could be determined. Mrs. Shore was pleased to know that children in her class scored high on this instrument relative to children in other classes. It made her feel

---

[1] The *Mental Measurements Yearbook* is a detailed listing of virtually all tests commercially available at its time of publication. It also includes many pertinent test reviews. The *MMY*, currently in its seventh edition (1972), is edited by Oscar K. Buros and published by The Gryphon Press.

that the methods she had been trying out were helping her to relate to her students.

• Mr. Price was a sixth grade teacher. For years he had been complaining about the use of standardized tests to evaluate his students' progress in math, reading, and language arts. "Of what value is it," he was often heard to say in the teacher's room, "to know whether our kids do better than kids in Sante Fe, New Mexico, on tests that measure some things that we don't even teach." Occasionally his arguments were stronger if less rational. One day he decided to build his own test. He made up a list of his teaching goals in math, reading, and language arts and circulated them to all the sixth grade teachers in his district. He also asked some fifth and seventh grade teachers for their opinions of his list of goals. When he had arrived at a sufficiently acceptable list, he began to make up test items to measure each goal. After he had constructed two test items for each objective, he administered the items to students and, based on the results, eliminated the items that didn't seem to be measuring what he intended to measure. For the past two years now, Mr. Price's district has been using his

"You don't think they'd try to slip in something educational on this program, do you?"

test on a district-wide basis at the sixth grade level in place of a standardized test battery and there are plans to try the same approach at other grade levels.

• Miss Rodriguez taught art appreciation in a middle school. She was a new teacher and in her teacher training had not been taught much about testing and had had little interest in learning about it. Now, in her second year of teaching, she became very concerned about what her students were learning and how she could measure their learning. She had thus far depended on her instincts but had come to lose confidence in her informal judgments. She wanted to construct a good test but did not know how. Fortunately for her, her district ran an in-service workshop devoted to testing where it was suggested that she first construct her instructional objectives as a basis for designing a good test. She tried this approach and subsequently found that it was easier for her to write test items.

Based on cases such as those above, we can list the following uses of tests.

Some Reasons for Tests and Measurement

OCCFFGU

(1) To Give Objectivity to Our Observations.   As educators we are used to making observations. Since we are concerned with shaping human behavior, we must constantly be observing it. At times we evaluate the behavior we are observing in terms of a set of criteria or standards that may be unspecified and operate only within our minds. These observations often lack specificity and exactness and in some situations that is not necessarily a problem.

However, there are occasions in all endeavors—education being no exception—when reasonably precise observations are needed. Precision in observation refers to the accuracy with which we are able to capture a particular quality or component of the behavior before us. To measure behavior objectively we need measuring instruments. We need measuring instruments that *record* behavior from a *neutral* vantage point so that we can apply our own standards and values in *evaluating* it.

(2) To Elicit Behavior under Relatively Controlled Conditions. Can we judge student performance from homework? From classwork? Such judgments must be limited by the many variables that operate in these situations. Were there distractions? Was the student given help? Did he or she look up the answer in a book? Did he or she have enough time? Too much time? And so forth. These kinds of variables will not only change for different assignments but will change for different students on the same assignment. How then is a teacher to know about student performance? The testing situation is one that occurs under conditions over which the teacher can exercise reasonable control. By controlling some of the conditions, the teacher can eliminate the influence of many variables that may bias the outcome being sought.

(3) To Sample Performances of Which the Person Is Capable. A person does not demonstrate all of his or her skills and characteristics in all situations in ways that are evident to an observer. To find out certain things about a person, we create a situation in which we can sample specific capabilities or tendencies. Whenever we ask a person, "Can you do this?" or "Do you like this?" or "Do you know this?" we are testing him or her. We could conceivably watch this person for a long time without ever knowing whether he or she could do a particular thing, and if so, how well. It is far easier and more efficient to pose the question or create the situation for him or her, thus providing the opportunity to sample the relevant performance from his or her repertoire. Measuring, therefore, is sampling. To find out what we want to know, we are aided by the test or measuring device.

(4) To Obtain Performances and Measure Gains Relevant to Goals or Standards. It is often less than sufficient to know whether a person can do something or not. The question more typically put is how well can he or she do it, particularly after being instructed in doing it. Simple observation is insufficient here. We must have a performance sample that can be judged in some way as to its appropriateness, accuracy, correctness of fit, timeliness, or some other standard or criterion. For this to happen, the performance must be obtained in a form that makes *evaluation* or comparison possible. Again, the mere observation of behavior does not render it in a form or size suitable for comparison to some standard. We must create a situation that will allow us to evaluate behavior or performance, particularly that which results from learning and instruction.

(5) To Apprehend the Unseen or Unseeable. Biologists long ago abandoned the naked eye in favor of the microscope for detail work. The naked eye can see neither microbes nor molecules, the constructs of science. Similarly the naked eye cannot fully see attitudes or values, developmental levels or social patterns. For these we need instruments—instruments that help us tap what is inside people. The complexities of life force the person to present himself or herself in complex ways. The proper measuring instrument gives us the insight that the naked eye may rarely afford.

(6) To Detect the Characteristics and Components of Behavior. When we are given the opportunity to isolate behavior, to explore the performances of which a person is capable, we can often gain information about behavior in small units, not necessarily differentiable by normal observations. Achievement partitions itself into math, social studies, and so forth, and math into algebra and geometry. Character becomes aggressiveness, warmth, sociability, and frustration tolerance. Classroom climate becomes esprit de corps, openness, support, and structure. Leadership becomes consideration and initiating structure. And so it goes.

(7) To Predict Future Behavior. Certain tests have been found to relate to future outcomes or events thus creating the possibility of being able to predict a person's future performance based on his or her test score. While this is the most controversial aspect of testing, there is some basis for saying that if we can detect characteristics, we can predict related behavior, and in some instances prevent undesirable outcomes.

(8) To Make Data Available for Continuous Feedback and Decision Making. In education we test in order to improve instruction. Testing provides data about outcomes that can serve at least two important functions: to inform students about the quality of their performance, and to help teachers make instructional decisions. For the teacher, all the other reasons for testing feed into this one: to facilitate student learning and growth.

Thus, measurement in education and the social sciences is a *controlled* and somewhat *objective* procedure by which the performances of which a person is *capable* may be sampled and evaluated against *standards*, such performances often being *unseen* and representing the *components* of behavior. It is this procedure that makes possible the availability of data for student feedback; the diagnosis of learning disabilities, of past failures, of present weaknesses; the detection of mastery, of competence, of the acquisition and possession of skills, knowledge, creativity; the discovery of character, of temperament, of values, of attitudes, of interests; that and much more. But the success of any measuring venture by teacher or scientist depends on how well the test, scale, question-naire, checklist, or whatever is constructed, how well it is used, and how reasonably it is interpreted. Such considerations are the subject of this book.

HOW DO WE MEASURE?

Because detailed information on the techniques and procedures of measurement will be presented throughout the book, this section is intended merely as an overview of the measurement process.

The first step in measurement is to decide what it is you want to measure. Measurement requires a fairly precise set of goals or objectives that will guide the measurer in choosing his or her pro-cedures. Trying to measure something that has not been clearly stated is like trying to put together a jigsaw puzzle without first seeing a picture of what it will look like when completed. It is hard to know which pieces to combine unless you know how the end result should look.

Once you have your objectives you are ready for your measur-ing instrument (within the limitation that all of your objectives may not be immediately measurable). You can either construct your own instrument or use one already in existence. (A third pos-sibility is to adapt and modify an existing instrument—a combina-tion of the two primary options.) Since test construction ordi-narily is more time-consuming than stating objectives, it may be advantageous to use an existing instrument if one is available that meets your objectives. We are fortunate in having a compendium like the *Mental Measurements Yearbook,* which lists most if not all of the commercially available tests along with pertinent infor-mation about each and critical reviews of many. A careful scrutiny of the *MMY* will often provide the test user with the names of instruments relevant to his or her objectives. At other times instru-ments may be mentioned in professional journals and magazines; writing to the author will bring you a copy of the instrument in question. Another reliable source of information about existing tests is the literature provided by the major testing companies.[2]

Obviously test construction is more complex than test selec-tion. Starting with objectives the test developer uses a set of rules such as those described in Part II of this book to develop test items. Such items may be short-answer or open-ended (e.g., essay);

[2] A list of major test publishers appears in Appendix D.

they may involve paper and pencil or actual physical performance; they may deal with what we know and think or what we like and how we feel; they may be designed for the student to fill out or for the teacher or other observer to fill out. The test items are the critical mass of the test. They are the controlled situations, each aimed at sampling some aspect of human behavior. Success in sampling will always be determined by how good the items are.

The test user cannot make valid judgments with a test that is imprecise or inaccurate. The worth of a test is measured in terms of its *validity* or *appropriateness* and *reliability*. Validity and appropriateness address themselves to the question of whether the test measures what it is supposed to measure. To establish validity it is often helpful to have some independent way of assessing the property that the test is supposed to measure. Sometimes, in the absence of any such independent criteria, tests must be evaluated in terms of their fit to the objectives of which they are supposed to be a measure. In this book, we will refer to the fit between a test and its objectives as the *appropriateness* of the test. Reliability refers to the test's consistency. Whatever a test measures, it must measure the same thing on each occasion it is used. It must give us as error free an estimate of the property to be measured as is possible. Thus, the test developer must not only write test items, he or she must also evaluate them against certain criteria.

Tests must also have some basis for interpretation. That is, the test must provide the user with a way of evaluating the performance of a person. What does the person's score mean? What does it tell us about him or her? The score itself cannot be considered to be the final product of a test. It must be interpreted. There are two ways of interpreting test scores. One way is in terms of the scores that other people get on the same test. We can talk about the fact that a score is higher than 65 percent of all the scores obtained on a test, or we can talk in absolute terms about how good a score is by virtue of some other criterion. If a test represents what a person should know to become an accountant, then we may demand that a person get 75 percent of it right without regard to how many or how few attain this level of performance. At any one testing, it is possible that no one may attain this predesignated level.[3]

The art and skill of measurement also include test administration. To be able to measure you must be able to give a test

---

[3] We refer to the first kind of test interpretation as *norm-referencing* and the second kind of test interpretation as *criterion-referencing*.

under controlled conditions and you must be able to report the results of a test in an understandable and useful way.

There is also the matter of ethics. The taker of tests must be afforded certain safeguards such as confidentiality so that the power of testing will not be abused. Those of us who give tests to human beings, particularly children, must be aware of and sensitive to their rights and undertake all necessary steps to protect them. This protection is as much a part of testing as the construction of test items.

A CLARIFICATION OF TERMS

Because the terms *evaluation, measurement,* and *testing* are used throughout this book, it is important that their meanings be clear.

Evaluation is a process wherein the parts, processes, or outcomes of a program are examined to see whether they are satisfactory, particularly with reference to the program's stated objectives, our own expectations, or our own standards of excellence. The assessment of a program's outcomes or results is facilitated by measurement. In other words, tests may be used constructively in the process of evaluation. Essentially, tests are *tools* that are useful in a number of *processes* such as evaluation, diagnosis, or monitoring.

The entire field of inquiry with which this book deals can be called measurement. *Measurement* is a broad term that refers to the systematic determination of outcomes or characteristics by means of some sort of assessment device. *Testing* is a less specific term that has typically been taken to mean educational measurement. More specifically, a test can be considered to be a kind or class of measurement device typically used to find out something about a person. Moreover, it is the kind of measuring device in which the person provides samples of his or her own behavior by answering questions or solving problems. Similarly, the words *inventory, questionnaire, opinionnaire, scale,* and the like have been used to label measuring instruments in which a person provides answers to questions.

The word *test* has many unfavorable connotations that will be judiciously avoided in this text. A test is sometimes taken to mean an instrument that is used to obtain data on which a person is "judged," in the most invidious sense of that term. For our purposes a test will be taken to be a common type of measurement device—one that the individual completes himself or herself as

ROTHCO
ORIGINAL

"Pssst! Want to get straight A's?"

contrasted with one completed by an observer, and whose intent is to determine changes or gains resulting from a particular educational experience.

There are also the terms *validity*, *reliability*, and *appropriateness*, which were discussed earlier in the chapter.

The term *objective* will appear with frequency. An objective is an intended outcome for learners as a result of certain experiences. Where possible, objectives are generally stated in observable, hence measurable, terms. When so stated they serve as a description of the intended behavior of the learner rather than that of the teacher.

Norm-referenced and *criterion-referenced* are terms used to describe types of test score interpretation. Scores from norm-referenced tests are interpreted on a relative basis in terms of the performance of a "test" or sample group (called a *norm group*) while scores from criterion-referenced tests are interpreted on the basis of some absolute performance criterion such as, "does she know it," or "can he do it." Criterion-referenced tests are built on the assumption that tests are tools that provide an accurate representation of absolute performance. Often called proficiency tests, they are used to determine which objectives a student has acquired competency in.

ORIENTATION OF THE BOOK

The subject of testing has usually been treated in such a highly technical way as to remove it from the level of understanding of some teachers and thereby render it into the domain of black magic. This situation is bad for at least two reasons, first, that the teacher will miss out on the many benefits of a testing program, and second, that testing programs will be carried out without any degree of teacher control. Moreover, every teacher must do some testing, and testing, like other teaching techniques, requires training. Thus, the first tenet of this book's orientation is that *testing must be presented in a manner that can be understood*—that is, a less technical manner.

Testing must have a purpose. You cannot test nothing; you must test something. The orientation taken in this book is that *the development of measurement instruments of any kind must be preceded by the preparation of objectives.* In other words, before a teacher can prepare a test, he or she must have decided what it is he or she wants to measure, that is, what the objectives are.

The third point to be made is that *testing is a tool that can help teachers help their students.* Thus, usability and ease of interpretation are important criteria in test construction and selection. And, test results should be used as part of the instructional process.

Fourth, *feedback and evaluation as aspects of instruction often require testing as a source of data.* Needless to say, accountability is facilitated by the availability of relevant test data. Instructional approaches that involve individual student progress typically require testing as a means of monitoring student performance. Testing can help teachers identify areas in which more emphasis is needed.

Fifth, *testing need not be restricted to those things that are easy to test.* When this happens, the easy-to-test things tend to become the most important criteria for evaluation to the exclusion of equally or more important criteria. Creativity (that is, the formulation of original yet appropriate solutions) gives way to intelligence; problem solving gives way to simpler forms of achievement based largely on memory; attitudes and feelings about self and school give way to reading level. This need not be the case. Measurement can itself be creative, enabling the more complex and in many cases more meaningful criteria to enter the classroom.

Sixth, *tests need not necessarily be used to compare students to one another* (although sometimes comparative information is useful). Put more positively, tests can be used to determine the

understood

purpose

tool

feedback

not restricted to ease

not always comparison

level and degree of performance of individual students by comparing their performance against independent criteria. For example, if a youngster can add two fractions and get the right answer on two occasions, we might reasonably conclude he or she knows how to add two fractions. We need not always be concerned with the percentage of students nationally who have mastered this skill. It is often sufficient to have determined the degree of mastery of an individual child as a basis for determining whether that child is ready to proceed to new learning.

Seventh, *tests must be consistent with the kinds of instruction and the kinds of learners they are being used to evaluate.* New forms of instruction such as individualized instruction and open education require tests that are consistent with the goals and objectives of these programs. Students with different backgrounds or different learning patterns often require different kinds of tests to measure their capabilities. An hourglass would not be an effective instrument for measuring the acceleration of a jet plane. Modern instruction requires modern testing.

consistent

PLAN OF THE BOOK

The book is organized into four parts. Each is described briefly below.

The first step in testing is to plan the test you will need. This is done by specifying your objectives to be measured and then relating these objectives to specific test items. Before you can write or select test items, you must prepare objectives. Accordingly, the first part of this book deals with the actual procedures for writing objectives and for relating these objectives to test items.

**Part One/
Planning a Test**

Basically there are two ways to obtain a test—construct it or find it. If it is unique to your needs, then you have no choice but to construct it. This section of the book will describe how to construct tests in different areas and of different types: paper-and-pencil tests, performance tests, attitudinal tests, value tests, tests of social structure, short-answer tests, essay tests, checklists, questionnaires, and other types that may find their way into a classroom. Information will be provided on how to build, use, and interpret these different kinds of tests to serve a wide variety of needs.

**Part Two/
Constructing a
Test: Teacher-
built Tests**

Part Three/
Evaluating a Test

AVRIU

A test is a tool for evaluation that must itself be evaluated or "tested" for its suitability as a prerequisite to using it. Within this process of evaluating or judging a test's suitability, the following questions may be asked as aids or tools to assist in the judgment: (1) Does it meet my objectives—is it *appropriate*? (2) Does it measure what I am using it to measure—is it *valid*? (3) Does it measure that consistently and accurately—is it *reliable*? (4) Does it provide results that can be understood and applied—is it *interpretable*? and (5) Is it reasonably easy to administer—is it *usable*? In order to answer these questions, one must understand and be able to apply skills and concepts such as that of appropriateness, types of test validity, standard error of measurement, reliability coefficients, norm-referencing, standard scores, grade-equivalent scores, and criterion-referencing. These and related concepts are presented in Part Three along with their means of implementation not only for teachers to evaluate their own tests but also to understand the evaluation of published or standardized tests that follows.

Part Four/
Using
Published
Tests

The alternative to building a test is finding one. Often teachers are called upon to administer and interpret tests that others have selected. When this is the case teachers may be at a marked disadvantage. To overcome or offset this disadvantage this book will deal with existing tests in a wide variety of areas, such as achievement, intelligence (or mental ability or aptitude), reading, interest, personality, and so on. In addition to describing the major tests available in each area, descriptions of the concepts themselves and what they mean are offered along with some bases for choosing between alternative tests. The administration and interpretation of the major tests in the various areas is also covered.

Testing programs and procedures can be used for a variety of purposes in the school such as assessing student progress, providing student feedback, evaluating instruction, and determining whether the district's program is thorough and efficient. The last chapter of this Part will draw upon materials covered in parts One through Three to deal with such programmatic uses of tests so that their procedures and results can be better understood. Applications by both teachers and administrators will be outlined with respect to test performance of individuals, of groups, and on a district-wide basis.

Because the ideas about testing and test item writing presented in this book are organized around measurable objectives, it will be necessary for the teacher first to understand and be able to write objectives. Therefore, before we turn to test item construction (Part Two), we will deal with the matter of writing objectives.

Additional Information Sources

Barclay, J. R. *Controversial issues in testing*. Boston: Houghton Mifflin, 1968.

Chauncey, H. & Dobbin, J. E. *Testing: Its place in education today*. N.Y.: Harper & Row, 1963.

Ebel, R. L. Measurement and the teacher. *Educational Leadership*, 1962, *20*, 20–24.

Michael, W. B. Prediction. In R. L. Ebel (Ed.) *Encyclopedia of educational research*, 4th ed. N.Y.: Macmillan, 1969, 982–993.

Payne, D. A. *The specification and measurement of learning outcomes*. Waltham, Mass.: Blaisdell Publishing, 1968.

Worthen, B. R. & Sanders, J. R. *Educational evaluation: Theory and practice*. Worthington, Ohio: Charles A. Jones, 1972.

Self-test of Proficiency

(1) Mr. Carlson tests all of his students the first day of class. Which of the following reasons for testing would be unsuitable?
   a. to get an indication of a student's proficiency
   b. to assign grades
   c. to plan class assignments
   d. to diagnose a specific deficiency

(2) Observation is sufficient to judge the extent of a person's knowledge or the depth of his or her feelings.
               TRUE   FALSE

(3) What is the first step in measurement?

(4) The final product of a test is a (an)
   a. series of items.
   b. score.
   c. interpretation of a score.
   d. performance.

(5) In this book, the fit between a test and its objectives is called _____.

(6) Criterion-referenced tests are used to determine
   a. how a student's performance compares to that of a sample group.
   b. whether a student likes coming to class.
   c. how successful he or she will be in college.
   d. which objectives a student has acquired competency in.

(Answers to all Self-tests of Proficiency begin on page 495.)

chapter two / Constructing Objectives

OBJECTIVES
1. Describe a classroom system model and the role of objectives in it.

2. State purposes for objectives in education.

3. Identify the three different parts of an objective, namely: action, conditions, and criteria.

4. Construct measurable objectives containing the three different parts.

5. Identify and describe criteria for evaluating objectives and the application of these criteria.

6. Use cognitive and affective taxonomies to classify objectives.

We can conceive of a simple model of the classroom as shown in Figure 2.1 below.

If we consider the classroom as a system,[1] our description of it must include a statement of its goals and objectives. The following may be some of the goals of the classroom system.

to develop the reading and writing skills of students
to help students gain knowledge of math and science
to enable students to develop and clarify values
to facilitate the development of each student's self-concept
to help students acquire more positive attitudes toward school
to enable students to develop independent study skills

Each of these objectives can in turn be broken down into other, more detailed, objectives, but as they are, they help us define the classroom as a system. If we want to measure the success of the system in meeting these objectives, we need some measurement instruments, but if we select measurement instruments

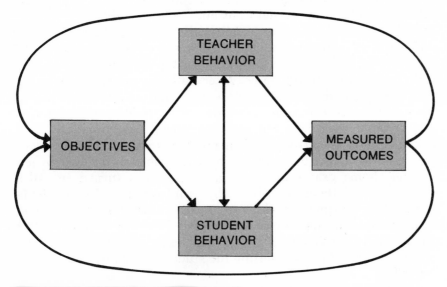

The Classroom As a Simple System.   **Figure 2.1**

---

[1] Churchman (1969) uses the following characteristics to describe a system: its objectives, its performance measures, its constraints or limits, its resources, its components and their functions, and its management.

without regard to the system's objectives, then the information these instruments provide will bear little relation to the system's successes or failures.

Applications of the Model

Consider the following occurrence in the light of the systems model.

- Miss Logan wanted to teach the students in her ninth grade social studies class to be better consumers. She was interested in having them develop the knowledge and skills to be able to identify the characteristics of a product and evaluate the quality of that product. She was also anxious to see them buy items of better quality and greater usefulness and be willing to spend the time shopping around to get something at the lowest price without sacrificing quality. Her last objective was that they would learn to critically evaluate commercials and advertisements. She did not know how to help her students learn these things so she began making inquiries.

Her inquiries brought a unit on consumer education to her attention and a game called Consumer. She was able to convince the high school principal to purchase the consumer education unit and was also fortunate enough to borrow the game. She set aside a portion of each class period to try out the unit and devoted two full class periods to the game. After both the unit and the game had been used, she gave her students a kind of take-home exam. They were to research and evaluate some products and to judge and critique some ads. She also gave them a record sheet and asked them to keep track of their purchases and to evaluate them for cost and quality using a procedure described in the unit. When the take-home exams and record sheets were turned in, Miss Logan studied them carefully. They told her that her students were demonstrating the skills of making critical judgments and evaluations, but that their own buying behavior did not reflect these skills. "I think next time I had better concentrate less on what to do and more on getting the students to do it," she said to herself.

Miss Logan was functioning as a systems analyst without knowing it. She had established some objectives for herself and identified a subsystem that she hoped would meet these objectives Her subsystem had two components: (1) the unit, and (2) the game. As the teacher she managed the system. She developed measures of the system's outcomes that she could then use to tell whether the system had met her objectives. When she saw that some objectives were not met, she decided to make certain changes in the system.

The point to be made here is that measurement occurs in a context; measurement occurs with respect to something; measurement plays an educational role. *Those elements that connect measurement to the classroom system are called objectives.*
Another example may provide further clarification.

• Kitty, a fifth grader, was a poor student in math. She seemed to be falling further and further behind the class. Her teacher, Mr. Washington, tried giving her supplementary material but it was ineffective in altering her performance. Finally, Mr. Washington said, "I had better look at math more systematically." He sat down one day and began mapping out all the things that students must learn before learning to add and subtract sequences of fractional expressions—a skill Kitty couldn't master. He ended up with a list of twelve items:

(1) adding 2 dissimilar fractions
(2) subtracting 2 dissimilar fractions
(3) expressing mixed numbers as improper fractions
(4) expressing improper fractions as mixed numbers
(5) supplying fractional equivalents
(6) identifying the lowest common denominator
(7) identifying common multiples
(8) adding 2 similar fractions
(9) subtracting 2 similar fractions
(10) identifying fractional equivalents of whole numbers
(11) identifying multiples
(12) dividing with a remainder

He then constructed a test which included items to measure each of the twelve competencies in his math system. After school one day he gave Kitty the test and then took it home and scored it. He discovered that Kitty did not know how to identify common multiples (e.g., what number can divide into both 9 and 12 evenly? answer: 3). Kitty's problem in subtraction of fractions was actually based on her difficulties in understanding division. Because she could not identify common multiples, she had difficulty in finding the lowest common denominator of two fractions and hence adding them or subtracting them. Mr. Washington had thus found the weak link in the system, the missing piece so to speak, and could then concentrate on teaching Kitty how to overcome this problem.

In the above example the teacher found it necessary to generate a list of objectives before he could use the techniques of measurement to identify the basis for a learning difficulty. Kitty's teacher could not measure Kitty's mastery of skills in mathematics until he could first specify what these skills should be. Again, objectives served as the link between the learning system and measurement of the characteristics and quality of that system.

This brings us to our next question: What are objectives?

WHAT ARE OBJECTIVES?

Many adjectives have been placed before the word "objectives" including instructional, behavioral, performance, measurable, expressive, terminal, and enabling. An *objective* will be defined here as *an intended outcome stated in such a way that its attainment (or lack of it) can be observed and measured.* We might broaden this definition by saying that an objective can be the statement of an intended or prescribed characteristic although when used in relation to instruction those intended characteristics typically represent intended instructional outcomes. Gagné (1974) considers an instructional objective to be an expression of a learning outcome in terms of human performance including a specification of the situation in which it is to be observed. Bloom, Hastings, and Madaus (1971, p. 20) say that "a statement of an objective is an attempt by the teacher or curriculum maker to clarify within his own mind or communicate to others the sought for changes in the learner." Mager (1962, p. 3) says that "an objective is an *intent* communicated by a statement describing a proposed change in a learner—a statement of what the learner is to be like when he has successfully completed a learning experience. It is a description of a pattern of behavior (performance) we want the learner to be able to demonstrate."

Objectives so defined may be reasonably called instructional objectives since they represent the goals of instruction. (Moreover, such objectives can be labeled as measurable or behavioral[2]

---

[2] It is perhaps more reasonable to say that the outcome will be "measurable" rather than "behavioral" since it may be difficult to think of the writing of test answers as a behavioral demonstration in the usual sense of the word.

—relatively interchangeable terms—since they specify outcomes in observable form.) For the most part, the tests that teachers construct will represent an attempt by them to assess the attainment by students of their instructional objectives. Test objectives represent those performances or characteristics that a test has been designed to measure. When tests are used to evaluate the effects of instruction, test objectives will be represented by the instructional objectives for the units of instruction being evaluated.

Objectives have many values for the teacher as instructor, primary among them being to aid the teacher as tester. Objectives help you to determine **what it is you want students to learn and, hence, what you want to measure,** and suggest further **how to measure what you want to measure, whether students have achieved what is intended, areas in which your instruction has been successful and unsuccessful.**

In the area of teacher-built tests that are used primarily (but not exclusively) to measure achievement, objectives are a necessary starting point. Before preparing test items (in fact, usually before preparing instruction), objectives should be prepared. These objectives help tell you what test questions or items to write and increase the likelihood that the items you write will represent the things you want to measure. It is of little sense to talk about teacher-built achievement tests without talking about instruction since the purpose of the testing is to measure the effects of instruction. *Objectives must serve to guide both instruction and the construction of achievement tests.*

Published tests have, in some cases, explicitly stated objectives and if not these, a detailed content outline. These objectives can help teachers select and interpret published tests by examining them in relation to their own objectives. The teachers' own objectives are thus of assistance even in test selection.

PREPARING OBJECTIVES

When an objective is written in full or detailed form, it has three parts:

(1) **the action or behavior that the learner or test taker is to perform,** *ACTION (verb)*
(2) **the conditions or "givens" under which the action or behavior is to be performed for observation,** *COND (given)*
(3) **the criteria by which the action or behavior is to be judged.** *CRIT (eval)*

Action Statements   Let us concentrate initially on the first component, the action or behavior to be performed—since this is the critical element of the objective and for shorthand purposes may be used as the statement of an objective by itself.[3] The emphasis is on the word *action* or *behavior* since this tells us what to test for. The action or behavior is a descriptive statement of intended student performance. Because measurement requires an active response by the test taker, the statement should include an *action verb* to depict the appropriate behavior. For example, we can observe and measure whether a student can *identify, describe,* or *demonstrate* something; hence, the emphasis on action verbs. From these observations or measurements we can then infer whether he or she understands or appreciates the subject of study. Our measurements are the vehicle for this kind of inference.

Any verb that expresses action will suffice for writing an objective. Figure 2.2 provides a lengthy list of such verbs keyed to the taxonomies of the cognitive and affective domains, which will be described later in this chapter. Note from this figure the large number of usable verbs.

Figure 2.2   *Action Verbs for Writing Objectives based on the Taxonomies of the Cognitive and Affective Domains.*

KCAA SE

I. COGNITIVE DOMAIN

   a. *Knowledge*   define, describe, identify, label, list, match, name, outline, select, state

   b. *Comprehension*   convert, defend, distinguish, estimate, explain, extend, generalize, give examples, infer, paraphrase, predict, rewrite, summarize

   c. *Application*   change, compute, demonstrate, discover, manipulate, modify, operate, predict, prepare, produce, relate, show, solve, use

   d. *Analysis*   break down, diagram, differentiate, discriminate, distinguish, identify, illustrate, infer, outline, point out, relate, select, separate, subdivide

[3] Note that the objectives at the start of each chapter in this book are so written, although it is advisable to write all three components until you have gained considerable experience in stating objectives. In all cases, for measurement purposes the second and third components must be at least implied.

e. *Synthesis* categorize, combine, compile, compose, create, design, devise, rewrite, summarize, tell, write

f. *Evaluation* appraise, compare, conclude, contrast, criticize, describe, discriminate, explain, justify, interpret, relate, summarize, support

II. AFFECTIVE DOMAIN

a. *Receiving* ask, choose, describe, follow, give, hold, identify, locate, name, point to, reply, select, sit erect, use

b. *Responding* answer, assist, comply, conform, discuss, greet, help, label, perform, practice, present, read, report, respond, select, tell, write

c. *Valuing* complete, demonstrate, describe, differentiate, explain, follow, form, initiate, invite, join, justify, propose, read, recognize, report, select, share, study, work, write

d. *Organizing* adhere, alter, arrange, combine, compare, complete, defend, explain, generalize, identify, integrate, modify, organize, order, prepare, relate, synthesize

e. *Characterizing by a value or value complex* act, discriminate, display, influence, listen, modify, perform, practice, propose, qualify, question, revise, serve, solve, use, verify

A second, considerably shorter, list has been compiled by the American Association for the Advancement of Science (1965). This list—with definitions and examples—is shown in Figure 2.3. A third, even shorter list, appears below. This list—based on the second—provides five action verbs, one of which can be used for writing any objective. This list also includes a description of the activity used to measure the attainment of each type of action.

Identify—given a stimulus array, the student can point to (by recognition) the specific stimulus required by instruction.

Distinguish—given two potentially confusable stimuli, the student can point to (by recognition) the one possessing the specific, predesignated property.

Describe—given an object or concept name, the student can state (by recall) those characteristics of the concept or of the object in a manner sufficient to "describe" it in accordance with its defined properties.

Construct—given the name of a "manufacturable" object or concept and sufficient equipment for doing so, the student can produce the object or concept in a way consistent with its defined properties.

Demonstrate—given a problem or performance request and all the necessary elements for completing it, the student can carry out a procedure sufficient for attaining the required performance by virtue of its conformity to defined rules and resulting in the appropriate outcome.

The advantage of working with such a short glossary of verbs as appears above is that once the verb is chosen, the method of measurement follows automatically.

Now that the words to describe measurable action have been presented, it may be helpful also to present the words that describe inferences, hunches, and hopes rather than observable acts. Chief among these are the following.

understand	*be aware of*
know	*be sensitive to*
appreciate	

As instructional goals the above are vital but as outcomes they cannot be directly measured. They must be inferred from some performance or behavioral act. For example, we may want students to understand that many people in the world live in conditions of poverty. We can ask them to *describe* such living conditions or to *demonstrate* through statistics the extent of poverty in the world but we cannot ask them to *understand* it. If they can describe it or demonstrate it, we may infer that they understand it.

Figure 2.3 *Nine Action Verbs for Use in Writing Objectives.**

DEFINITION OF ACTION WORDS

The action words that are used as operational guides in the construction of the instructional objectives are:

(1) *Identifying*: The individual selects (by pointing to, touching, or picking up) the correct object of a class name. For example: Upon being asked, "Which animal is the frog?" when presented with a set of small animals, the child is expected to respond by picking up or clearly pointing to or touching the frog; if the child is asked to "pick up the red triangle"

ICDODENOS

when presented with a set of paper cutouts representing different shapes, he is expected to pick up the red triangle. This class of performance also includes identifying object properties (such as rough, smooth, straight, curved) and, in addition, kinds of changes such as an increase or decrease in size.

(2) *Distinguishing (similarities and/or differences)*: Distinguish between objects or events which are potentially confusable (square, rectangle), or when two contrasting identifications (such as right, left) are involved.

(3) *Constructing*: Generating a construction or drawing which identifies a designated object or set of conditions. Example: Beginning with a line segment, the request is made, "Complete this figure so that it represents a triangle."

(4) *Naming/Listing:* Supplying the correct name or names (orally or in written form) for a class of objects or events. Example: "What is this three-dimensional object called?" Response: "A cone." Or, "list two commonly seen three-dimensional objects." Response: "An ice-cream cone, a block."

(5) *Ordering*: Arranging two or more objects or events in proper order in accordance with a stated category. For example: "Arrange these moving objects in order of their speeds."

(6) *Describing*: Generating and naming all of the necessary categories of objects, object properties, or event properties, that are relevant to the description of a designated situation. Example: "Describe this object," and the observer does not limit the categories which may be generated by mentioning them, as in the question, "Describe the color and shape of this object." The child's description is considered sufficiently complete when there is a probability of approximately one that any other individual is able to use it to identify the object or event.

(7) *Stating*: Makes a verbal statement (not necessarily in technical terms) that conveys a rule or a principle, including the names of the proper classes of objects or events in their correct order. Example: "What is the test for determining whether this surface is flat?" The acceptable response requires the mention of the application of a straightedge, in various directions, to determine touching all along the edge for each position.

(8) *Demonstrating*: Performing the operations necessary to the application of a rule or principle. Example: "Show how you would tell whether this

surface is flat." The individual must use a straightedge to determine flatness by touching of the edge to the surface at all points.

(9) *Explaining*: The child should be able to take two or more pieces of data and describe relationships between or among them. For example, he may describe the relationship between a pencil, a known object, and a pen, an object new to him.

* Adapted with permission from the A.A.A.S. Copyright 1965 by The American Association for the Advancement of Science.

By their very nature, all of our instructional objectives will not be measurable. When unmeasurable objectives are important, they should be retained. However, where possible, objectives should be in observable terms (particularly if they are going to be

Reprinted by courtesy of Medical Tribune and Joseph Farris

"I wonder what I'm driving at."

of any assistance in measurement) even though they are based on or derived from more general goals like "understanding."

Let us consider the action portion of objectives starting out with more general goals. Suppose a chemistry teacher would like students to **understand Boyle's Law.** One manifestation of understanding Boyle's Law should be the ability to use it. Hence, one objective may be students' ability to **demonstrate a procedure for calculating the temperature (or pressure) of a gas.** Suppose an elementary school teacher wanted his or her students to **understand the transitive property of numbers and mathematical sentences.** Students who know a procedure should be able to demonstrate it; hence, students should be able to **demonstrate a procedure for writing a mathematical sentence that illustrates the transitive property.** The third illustration takes us to music appreciation where the music teacher wants students to **appreciate Beethoven's Fifth Symphony.** Perhaps the music teacher would agree that students who have gained the desired appreciation will **describe their feelings toward the symphony in positive terms** (presumably in order to give the teacher feedback as to their appreciation or lack of it). The American history teacher is concerned that students **be aware of the causes of the War between the States.** Since the history teacher is likely to measure this awareness by giving the students a list of statements and asking them to check the ones that represent causes of the War between the States, we might say that he or she expects them to be able to **identify statements that represent causes of the War between the States.** (Note that this objective, as many, can be made measurable by replacing the in-action verb—"be aware of"—with a suitable action verb, in this case, "identify.")

The high school English teacher is teaching students to **know how playwrights create characterizations.** Those who know could be expected to be able to either **demonstrate a process for arriving at a characterization** or **describe one character in writing.** Meanwhile, the teacher of a new vocational program in data processing wants his or her students to **understand the key punch machine.** The teacher may choose to evidence whether they do or do not by their ability to **(demonstrate a procedure for) operating a key punch machine.** And finally, Langston Hughes' admonition to **dig all jive** would probably come out in "objective-talk" as being able to **(demonstrate a procedure for) carrying out a conversation in at least two English "languages,"** (i.e., speak in at least two English languages).

Conditions and Criteria For the teacher as instructor, the action statement by itself suffices as the objective. However, the teacher as measurer will find it important to state both the conditions, that is, when will the behavior occur, and the criteria, that is, how will the acceptability of the behavior be judged for his or her objectives.

The statement of conditions typically appears at the beginning of the objective, preceding the action statement, and begins with the word "given." The statement of criteria typically appears at the end of the objective, following the action statement.

The illustrations used to describe the action statement of an objective in the preceding section have been expanded to include a statement of conditions and criteria and appear below.

Given the pressure and temperature of a gas at time *1*, and its pressure (or temperature) at time *2*, the student can demonstrate a procedure for calculating its temperature (or pressure) at time *2*, accurately to one decimal place in two instances.

Given pairs of related mathematical sentences in the form of $a = b$ and $b = c$, the student can demonstrate a procedure for writing a third sentence that will illustrate the transitive property (if $a = b$ and $b = c$, then $a = c$) in each of three instances.

Given an opportunity to hear Beethoven's Fifth Symphony and asked to write a composition about it, the student can describe his or her feelings in positive terms, as evidenced by the appearance of at least two positive evaluative terms (e.g., enjoy, pleasant, good) and no negative ones.

Given a list of statements, the student can identify those that represent basic causes of the American War between the States by placing a check mark next to every one that had previously been designated as acceptable by the teacher.

Given a play to read, the student can demonstrate a process for creating a characterization, as evidenced by his or her identifying all characters, describing each, and relating each to the play's plot and theme.

or

Given a play to read and instructions to characterize, the student can describe one character in writing, that description to include the character's basic qualities as manifested in the play, his or her relation to other characters, and relation to the play's plot and theme.

Given a sheet of data in proper form, the student can demonstrate a procedure for punching it into proper columns using a key punch and programmed control within ten minutes.

Given ten phrases in "street talk," the student can state the equivalent or translated phrases in standard written English, being completely accurate (to the satisfaction of the English teacher) on nine out of ten.

Even though you may state your own objectives in the abbreviated form of action statements, you will find yourself having to select or identify the conditions under which the action statement is to be measured and the criteria by which the action is to be evaluated.

Unit Objectives

The objectives that represent the end result of an instructional unit are often called *terminal objectives*. Over the course of a school year, a teacher may have twenty or so terminal objectives in a subject matter area. The teacher's testing program will reflect an attempt to determine whether these objectives have been met. There is also another kind of objectives, called *enabling objectives*, that build upon one another like steps and lead to a terminal objective. Teachers who test for the attainment of enabling objectives during the course of each unit are in a position not only to estimate mastery of terminal objectives but to diagnose sources of failure where failure occurs. Thus, enabling objectives form the basis for *diagnostic testing*, that is, testing to diagnose or detect areas in which learning has not taken place.

Unit objectives, therefore, are comprised of both terminal objectives and enabling objectives. Course or curriculum objectives would be a set of terminal objectives. However, because it is often arbitrary where one segment of instruction begins and another ends, what are terminal objectives in one segment, like a unit, become enabling objectives for a larger segment, like a course.

A set of objectives for a mathematics unit on solving equations with one unknown is shown on the next page.

Unit Terminal Objective

Given applied math problems in verbal form, solve equations with one unknown contained within.

Unit Enabling Objectives

Simplify an equation by adding and subtracting terms to both sides.

Simplify an equation by multiplying and dividing both sides by terms.

Clear an equation of fractions.

Simplify an equation by adding and subtracting numbers to both sides.

Simplify an equation by multiplying and dividing both sides by numbers.

Supply product and quotient equivalents to products and quotients (terms).

Identify needed operations in order.

Add and subtract terms in sequence.

Supply sum and difference equivalents to sums and difference (numbers) and terms.

Supply product and quotient equivalents to products and quotients.

Combine fractions with like denominators.

Simplify fractional expressions.

Identify procedural order (left, right, collect, divide).

Recognize equivalent terms.

Recognize equivalence of multiplication and division terms.

Divide parenthetical terms.

Factor.

Identify the order of operations (the use of brackets).

Identify the equivalence of $1x$ and x.

Identify an equation ($=$ sign).

Obtain products with zero.

EVALUATING OBJECTIVES

How can you, the teacher, tell whether you have written the right objectives? How can you tell that these are the outcomes you should be aiming at for your students? Kriege (1971, p. 142) suggests that the teacher judge objectives against the following ten criteria:

Written in terms of *student performance*?
Observable by one or more of the five senses?
Specific enough to be meaningful?
Valid in relation (i.e., relevant) to the major objective or goal?
Measurable in terms of *a*. level of performance and *b*. conditions under which the performance is to take place?
Sequential in relation to prior and subsequent objectives?
Relevant to the student's experience?
Attainable within the time period allotted?
Challenging to each individual student?
Acceptable to the societies of which the student is a member?

A A C M O R S S V (handwritten annotation)

Some of the above criteria refer only to the *form* or *structure* of an objective (e.g., student performance, observable, specific, measurable) and can be applied quite simply. "Did I use an action verb?" "Did I describe conditions and criteria?" "Did I avoid vague, undefinable terms?"

Others of the above criteria refer to the *relation* of the objective to the curriculum and the learning situation (e.g., valid, sequential, attainable). Tuckman and Edwards (1971, p. 22) suggest the three questions shown in Figure 2.4 for validating an objective based on its place in the sequence, that is, its relation to other objectives. An objective may be invalid because it appears too late or too soon in the sequence or because the proper prerequisites fail to precede it. Often, we can tell a great deal about what objectives we need or do not need in terms of where they appear in the sequence. When we cannot make these decisions on a logical basis, we can make them after seeing how students perform on a test based on the objectives. If students uniformly fail an objective (like *B* in Figure 2.4) but uniformly pass the one it presumably feeds into (like *A* in Figure 2.4), then objective *B* has little validity. Failure to pass *A* after passing *B* and *C* often means that an objective is missing (or else that instruction on *A* itself was insufficient). Performance data can be used not only to validate an objective in terms of its relation to other objectives, but to

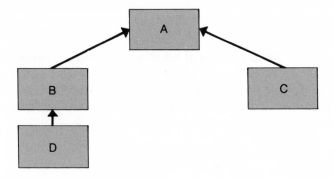

Figure 2.4   *Validating an Objective in Terms of Its Place in the Sequence.*

For example:

(1) Does performance on given objectives (e.g., *B* & *C*) contribute to performance on a subsequent objective (e.g., *A*)?

(2) Does performance on a given objective (e.g., *B*) depend on or require performance on an objective that precedes it (e.g., *D*)?

(3) Is performance on a given objective (e.g., *C*) independent of performance on a parallel objective (e.g., *B*)?

test the attainability of an objective within an allotted period of time.

The remaining three criteria (relevance, challenge, and acceptability) refer to the *reaction* by various audiences to the objectives. These criteria are the most judgmental of the ten. To apply them, the teacher would have to gain the reaction of experts, students, and parents through meetings and discussion groups as well as by questionnaire. One of the positive features of objectives is that they make public scrutiny and public acceptability of the curriculum possible. Indeed, if instruction occurs without thought-out objectives, this kind of public acceptability cannot occur.

All objectives can be evaluated as to form and structure. Enabling objectives in particular can be evaluated in terms of their relation to one another. Terminal objectives can be evaluated not only in their relation to other objectives but perhaps more importantly by the reaction they provoke from various audiences. Not only do students and parents represent potential sources of feedback—other teachers, subject matter experts, and curriculum designers as well can comment on the potential relevance, challenge, and acceptability in terms of students' patterns of development and career goals. The fact that objectives are tangible and visible (at least potentially so) makes them particularly suited to the process of public examination. Their relation to one another and potential for sequencing make them particularly useful for instructional purposes, and their form and structure make them useful for test design since they help the teacher determine what performances to measure for and the conditions and criteria that will be applied in the measurement situation.

Box 2.1

Arguments against Behavioral Objectives

W. James Popham, one of the modern pioneers in the development of behavioral objectives (and director of the Instructional Objectives Exchange at UCLA), probed the validity of eleven arguments against behavioral objectives (Popham, 1968). Critics claim, he argued, that

1. easier to operationalize, trivial goals will be emphasized at the expense of important goals;
2. prespecifying goals prevents the teacher from capitalizing on the unexpected;
3. other educational outcomes equal pupil behavior changes in importance;
4. measurability is mechanistic, hence dehumanizing;
5. planning how students will behave is undemocratic;
6. it's unrealistic to expect teachers to state measurable goals;
7. in certain subject areas, identifying measurable outcomes is difficult;
8. precise statements of educational goals would reveal them as innocuous;
9. measurability implies accountability and is thus threatening;
10. it is a time-consuming and difficult task to state goals in measurable terms;
11. prespecified goals blind evaluators to the important but unanticipated outcome.

Are these arguments valid? Popham proceeds to argue against each. Operationalizing tends to make the triviality of certain outcomes apparent so that we can reject them. Planning need not stifle sponaneity in teachers, students, or evaluators. The primary business of the school is promoting desirable pupil behavior. And so on. Try your own hand at countering the eleven arguments.

THE WHAT AND WHY OF TAXONOMIES

A taxonomy is a device for classifying things in terms of certain of their characteristics; thus, it identifies the relationship of one thing to another in terms of these characteristics. As is generally known, taxonomies exist for classifying plants and animals and for classifying chemical elements. What we are concerned about here are taxonomies of educational objectives, that is, of the goals of our educational system or parts of it. Bloom (1956) suggests that such taxonomies will help teachers *a.* define nebulous terms such as "understand" so that they can communicate curricular and evaluative information among themselves, *b.* identify goals that they may want to include in their own curriculums, *c.* identify directions in which they may want to extend their instructional activities, *d.* plan learning experiences, and *e.* prepare measuring devices. While we are primarily concerned here with the last of Bloom's points, it is unwise to isolate the measurement aspects of taxonomies from their other features.

Taxonomies are devices of human origin that not only help teachers to label objectives in terms of one or more of their properties, but also to get some idea of the sequences in which objectives may best occur, thus contributing to their validation.[4] This latter feature is based on the fact that many taxonomies attempt to be *hierarchical,* that is, organized into levels or ranks. Let us illustrate these points with reference to a taxonomy of the cognitive domain (Bloom, 1956; usually called Bloom's Taxonomy) which is summarized in Figure 2.5.

levels

Cognitive Taxonomy Consider the elementary teacher who is interested in teaching his or her students how to research a social studies topic. The objective might start out vaguely as something like "knowing where to go to get information about a topic." In essence, the teacher is interested in having students acquire knowledge; more specifically, it is knowledge about ways and means of dealing with specifics (rather than knowledge about the specifics themselves). That is, the teacher does not in this objective want the students to learn something about a topic such as "deserts" but to learn ways and means of finding out about that or other topics.

---

[4] It is important to emphasize that taxonomies are the product of human beings, not necessarily of nature. While they help us organize thoughts and observations, they must not be used as rigid strait jackets.

Taxonomy of the Cognitive Domain.*   **Figure 2.5**

1.00 KNOWLEDGE
   1.10 of Specifics
      1.11 of terminology
      1.12 of specific facts

   1.20 of Ways and Means of Dealing with Specifics
      1.21 of conventions
      1.22 of trends and sequences
      1.23 of classifications and categories
      1.24 of criteria
      1.25 of methodology

   1.30 of the Universals and Abstractions in a Field
      1.31 of principles and generalizations
      1.32 of theories and structures

2.00 COMPREHENSION
   2.10 Translation
   2.20 Interpretation
   2.30 Extrapolation

3.00 APPLICATION

4.00 ANALYSIS
   4.10 of Elements
   4.20 of Relationships
   4.30 of Organizational Principles

5.00 SYNTHESIS
   5.10 Production of a Unique Communication
   5.20 Production of a Plan, or Proposed Set of Operations
   5.30 Derivation of a Set of Abstract Relations

6.00 EVALUATION
   6.10 Judgments in Terms of Internal Evidence
   6.20 Judgments in Terms of External Criteria

According to the taxonomy, knowledge of ways and means of dealing with specifics is of a higher order, that is, is more advanced or complex, than knowledge of specifics. Most specifically, the objective in question—knowing where to go to get information about a subject—falls into category 1.25: knowledge of methodology (the most advanced of the knowledge of ways and means categories). By referring to Figure 2.2 and looking under "Knowledge," a teacher could find a set of action verbs that are useful for writing "knowledge" objectives. In this particular instance, the teacher could say, for example, that he or she wanted the students to be able to *describe ways to get information about a social studies topic* (e.g., deserts). Given this objective, the means for measuring it are fairly obvious—although there are undoubtedly a number of different test items that could be written for eliciting the desired behavior.

"Just between us, how can you tell what's arts and what's crafts?"

Now that the teacher has dealt with the task of getting information, he or she will probably become concerned with having students "understand" the information they collect. This moves us into the second level of Bloom's Taxonomy, "Comprehension." Perhaps the teacher's concern for comprehension will fall into the category "2.20 Interpretation." Using an action verb from the list in Figure 2.2, he or she may formulate the objective to *explain why the life styles of desert dwellers throughout the world take a similar form.*

The teacher may feel that comprehension is not a sufficient place to stop and may go on to "Application." He or she may want students to *produce a model of a dwelling that they could use if they were going to spend their summer in the desert.* From here the teacher may proceed to "Analysis"; for example, he or she could read students a short biographical sketch of a child in a desert tribe and then ask them to *point out those aspects of desert life that have caused the child of the desert to be different from them.* Moving on to "Synthesis," the teacher may ask students to *write a poem or an essay describing life on the desert and the feelings of the desert dwellers.* Finally, in the category of "Evaluation," students would be asked to *contrast the things they like about their own life with the things they like about desert life.*

Bloom's taxonomy can be helpful in developing tests to determine students' levels of cognitive skills. It can also help teachers gain more insight into their goals and into the relationship between their goals and instructional activities. Perhaps most importantly, the taxonomy enables teachers to better identify the level of their activities so that they can move to ever increasing levels of complexity. Rather than limiting objectives to the levels of knowledge and comprehension, teachers are encouraged by the taxonomy to extend instruction into application, analysis, synthesis, and evaluation.

Affective Taxonomy
emotions

A second taxonomy of educational objectives has been developed for the affective domain (the term "affective" means believing, emoting, or feeling rather than thinking, perceiving, or doing) by Krathwohl et al. (1964). An illustrative version of this taxonomy appears in Figure 2.6. (Along with each of the categories in the affective taxonomy, an objective has been added using the "desert life" motif.) Like the taxonomy of the cognitive domain, the taxonomy of the affective domain identifies a sequence of levels that may be used for structuring instructional experiences or developing test items, the latter being our concern here. Figure 2.2 also provides action verbs for preparing objectives in the affective domain, the procedure being the same as that outlined for the cognitive domain.

Figure 2.6   *An Illustrated Taxonomy of the Affective Domain.**

1.0 RECEIVING (ATTENDING)
   1.1 Awareness
   Describe the aesthetic factors in the clothing, food, and shelter that desert dwellers use to satisfy basic needs.

   1.2 Willingness to Receive
   Identify books that have been read voluntarily about desert life.

   1.3 Controlled or Selected Attention
   Reply to questions raised by teacher on aspects of desert life.

2.0 RESPONDING
   2.1 Acquiescence in Responding
   Present an assigned report on desert life.

   2.2 Willingness to Respond
   Respond with apparent interest and zeal to assignments on desert life.

   2.3 Satisfaction in Response
   Report pleasure in having studied people of the desert.

3.0 VALUING
   3.1 Acceptance of a Value
   Recognize that children in all cultures have similar basic needs.

   3.2 Preference for a Value
   Demonstrate a desire to study and understand people of different cultures.

   3.3 Commitment
   Write a "letter" to a desert child expressing recognition of your common needs.

4.0 ORGANIZING
   4.1 Conceptualization of a Value
   Identify a continuum or hierarchy of basic human needs that each person must be able to satisfy.

4.2 Organization of a Value System

Prepare a plan for satisfying one's own basic needs and helping others to satisfy theirs

5.0 CHARACTERIZING BY A VALUE OR VALUE COMPLEX

5.1 Generalized set

Display tolerance of human behavior directed toward need satisfaction.

5.2 Characterization

Practice tolerance as part of an operational philosophy of life.

OBJECTIVES, TAXONOMIES, TESTING, AND TEACHER

Why should teachers be concerned with objectives and taxonomies? What does all this have to do with testing? These questions can perhaps be best answered by considering the systems model of the classroom at the outset of this chapter. The classroom is a small system within which a teacher and a group of students operate. The mission of the system is that the students learn and grow. The responsibility for this mission rests largely with the teacher. Thus, the essence of education is that the teacher arranges the conditions of learning (Gagné, 1970) including his or her own behavior so that students increasingly learn and develop. Mission attainment in any system is facilitated when the goals of the mission are spelled out; hence, objectives. Rather than merely representing an exercise in self-discipline, the writing or choosing of objectives provides the teacher with a set of goals or targets toward which to aim in his or her classroom. Whether the goals are formalized or not, most if not all teachers have them. Objectives are merely a way to make those goals more visible.

Why does a teacher give tests? There are three primary reasons: (1) to determine whether and to what degree each student is experiencing learning and development (this is the *monitoring and certification function*); (2) to identify those students who are not learning and growing and in particular the area of their deficiency (this is the *diagnostic function*); (3) to determine

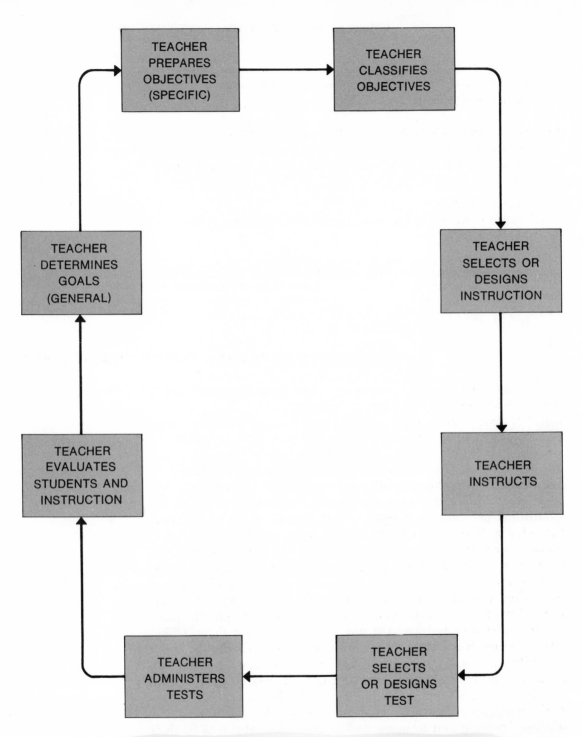

Figure 2.7 *Flow Chart of Teacher Activities in the Classroom System.*

whether instructional inputs are, in general, effective (the *program evaluation* function).

As we have seen, objectives help the teacher evaluate the appropriateness of his or her tests and test items. Objectives also help the teacher know what to test for; they form the basis for the development of tests and test items. Objectives represent a definite point of reference in the classroom system both for instruction and testing. Since tests attempt to measure the attainment of the teacher's goals, and objectives are formal statements of goals, then objectives tell a teacher what to measure. The activities of the teacher with respect to goal-setting, teaching, and testing are shown in Figure 2.7.

The primary purpose of classifying objectives is to gain additional insight about the levels of instruction and the relationship between instructional goals. But classified objectives also facilitate the preparation of test items. If one's instructional goal is knowledge acquisition, measuring for comprehension or synthesis would be inappropriate and unfair. If one's instructional goal is analysis, measuring simply for knowledge would be equally inappropriate. Not only do the taxonomies help you write items at the intended level (as will be seen in Part Two); they help you check on the appropriateness or validity of items for the intended purpose (as will be seen in Part Three).

Additional Information Sources

Armstrong, R. J. et al. *Development and evaluation of behavioral objectives.* Belmont, Calif.: Charles A. Jones Publishing, 1970.

Gerhard, M. *Effective teaching strategies with the behavioral outcomes approach.* Nyack, N.Y.: Parker Publishing, 1971.

Johnson, R. A., Kast, F. E., and Rosenzweig, J. E. *The Theory and management of systems,* 2nd ed., New York, McGraw-Hill, 1967.

Kibler, R. J., Barker, L., & Miles, D. *Behavioral objectives and instruction.* Boston: Allyn & Bacon, 1970.

Mager, R. F. *Preparing instructional objectives.* Palo Alto, Calif.: Fearon Publishers, 1962.

McAshen, H. H. *Writing behavioral objectives.* N.Y.: Harper & Row, 1970.

Vargas, J. *Writing worthwhile behavioral objectives.* N.Y. Harper & Row, 1972.

Self-test of Proficiency

(1) Define an objective and give three reasons why the classroom system needs objectives.

(2) Think of a kitchen as a system. List four goals or objectives of that system.

(3) State two activities of teachers for which objectives can serve as a guide.

(4) If you were a student, what are two ways that knowledge of the teacher's objectives would be of help?

(5) Which one of the following is part of an objective?
    a. knowledge to be understood
    b. appreciation to be felt
    c. action or behavior to be performed
    d. awareness or sensitivity to be developed

(6) The conditions of an objective represent the standards by which performance on the objective is to be judged.
                TRUE   FALSE

(7) Write a full (three-part) objective for the goal: *to know the location of the longest river system in the United States.*

(8) Write a full objective for the goal: *to be able to add two 3-digit numbers.*

(9) Which of the following is *not* a criterion of a good objective?
    a. measurable
    b. reliable
    c. specific
    d. challenging

(10) In evaluating an objective, explain what is meant by the criterion "sequential" and how this criterion would be applied.

(11) Into which one of the categories of the Taxonomy of the Cognitive Domain would the following activity be best classified: *producing a unique plan for enlisting community support*?
    a. comprehension
    b. application
    c. analysis
    d. synthesis
    e. evaluation

(12) Which one of the following objectives would best be classified in the "valuing" category of the Taxonomy of the Affective Domain?

a. *Prepare an outline for helping other people meet their needs.*

b. *Name five books that deal with characters who are emotionally supportive of one another.*

c. *Demonstrate by your actions the desire to help other people.*

d. *List your ten best friends in the order of their importance to you.*

chapter three / Basing Test Items on Objectives

OBJECTIVES

1. Identify an appropriate test item for measuring a given objective.

2. Identify three areas into which objectives can be usefully classified, namely: knowledge and comprehension, higher cognitive processes, and the affective domain.

3. Classify given test items into each of the three areas.

4. Prepare objectives in shorthand form (that is, in action part only).

5. Prepare a content outline for a given topic or objective as the first step in test construction.

It has been emphasized before, and will be again throughout this section, that tests are constructed to measure whether objectives have been met. A test is defined as a sample of student performance on items that have been designed to measure preselected objectives. Even if objectives are not explicitly stated, tests still measure the performance of students. In order to insure that your tests and the performances they require are related to (i.e., measure) the objectives you want them to measure, it is important to state them objectively, if only in "shorthand" form (that is, action portion only). The objectives, once stated, will help you determine the test items you need to construct to measure student mastery of those things you intend for students to master. The use of objectives in instruction or in communication of aims are also important purposes that justify their preparation.

You are now ready to begin learning how to construct your own tests, most of which will be used to measure achievement or mastery of the material you teach. In this book, we will show that test construction includes three steps: (1) preparation of objectives, (2) preparation of test items, and (3) evaluation of test items. Each step is important; none should be omitted. The purpose of this chapter is to (1) illustrate the relationship between objectives and test items through the use of sample tests, (2) show how different domains or areas of objectives relate to test items, and (3) demonstrate how to complete the first step in test construction—the development of objectives—referred to here as a content outline.

Some Illustrations of Objectives and Tests

• Miss Hart teaches math in the seventh grade. She had just finished a unit on sets and was ready to give her students a test to see how much they had learned. As a first step, she sat down and thought about what she had been trying to teach them. She went over her lesson plans and wrote the following objectives.[1]

(1) Given a statement of the elements or nonelements of a set, use mathematical symbols to represent the statement.
(2) Given a set in roster form, use set-builder notation to represent the set.

[1] It would have been better pedagogy, of course, had Miss Hart written her objectives before instruction rather than after.

49

(3) Given terms used to describe sets and their relationship, that is, equal, empty, sub-, and proper, identify the correct definition of each.

(4) Given two or more sets, identify those that are equal.

(5) Given a set and the empty set, identify their relationship and distinguish between them.

(6) Given two or more sets, identify those that are subsets of and those that are proper subsets of one of the given sets.

(7) Given a set, state the number of elements in it.

After further consideration, she decided *a.* that objectives *1, 2, 6,* and *7* were equally important and that they were more important than the others; *b.* that objectives *3* and *4* were of equal but intermediate importance; and *c.* that objective *5* was least important. The greater importance of objectives *1, 2, 6,* and *7* is based on their greater complexity and the fact that they form the basis for subsequent performance. She then decided on ten exercises with a total value of twenty-eight points: five points to measure each of the objectives *1, 2, 6,* and *7*; three points to measure objectives *3* and *4* respectively; and two to measure objective *5*. Her next task was to write the ten exercises. Because the objectives gave her a strong clue as to what each item should be like, writing the test was not difficult. Miss Hart's test is shown in Figure 3.1.

Figure 3.1   *Miss Hart's Seventh Grade Math Test.**

(1) Use mathematical symbols to indicate the following:
 a. C is equal to the set whose elements are 5, 10, and 15.
 b. 5 is a member of set C.
 c. 7 is not an element of set C.
 d. The set of all elements x such that x is an even integer.
 e. The set of all elements y such that y is an odd number greater than 7.

(Objective 1; 5 points)

(2) Use set-builder notation to indicate each of the following sets:
 a. {1,2,3,4,5,6,7,8,9,10}
 b. {1,3,5,7,9}
 c. {4,6,8,10,12}
 d. {a,b,c,d,e,f,g}
 e. {s,t,u,v,w,x,y,z}

(Objective 2; 5 points)

(3) Connect each term at the left with the correct definition at the right.

a. equal sets

b. the empty set

c. subset

d. proper subset

i. every element of the set is also an element of the other set

ii. every element of the set is also an element of the other set and vice versa

iii. every element of the set is also an element of the other set but the reverse is not true

iv. the set contains no elements

(Objective 3; 3 points)

(4) Which of the sets listed below are equal?

A = {1,3,5,7}

B = {2,4,6,8}

C = {x/x is an odd number and x is less than 9}

D = {5,3,7,1}

(Objective 4; 1½ points)

(5) Which of the sets listed below are equal?

A = {1,2,3,4}

B = {5,6,7,8}

C = {y/y is an even number and y is less than 9}

D = {2,4,6,8}

(Objective 4; 1½ points)

(6) Given A = {a,b,c,d} and the empty set ϕ:

a. Is every element in ϕ in A?

b. Is every element in A in ϕ?

c. Is ϕ a proper subset of A?

(Objective 5; 1 point)

(7) Explain the difference between ϕ and {ϕ}.

(Objective 5; 1 point)

(8) Which of the following sets are subsets of (a,b,7,$\triangle$)?

a. {a,□}

b. {7}

c. {5,7}

d. {a,b,7,$\triangle$}

e. ϕ

f. {ϕ}

g. {$\triangle$,a,7}

h. {$\triangle$,b,7,a}

i. {a,b,ϕ}

j. {   }

(Objective 6; 3 points)

(9) Which of the sets in item 8 are proper subsets of the given set?

(Objective 6; 2 points)

(10) State the number of elements in each of the following sets.

a. {7,a,□,ϕ}   *d.* {ϕ}

b. {a,□,ϕ}   *e.* ϕ

c. {□,ϕ}

(Objective 7; 5 points)

* Reprinted and adapted by permission of the publishers from *Modern Elementary Mathematics* by Malcolm Graham, Copyright © 1970 by Harcourt Brace Jovanovich Inc.

• Mrs. Morris teaches first grade. The greatest amount of her time is spent in teaching reading. A school-wide achievement test is administered once a year to assess children's overall reading performance, but in order to provide continuous monitoring of reading performance she finds it necessary to test about once every two weeks. Before beginning a unit that stressed reading comprehension, she listed for her own use the following aims for student accomplishment.

(1) Given a picture, name its contents and describe the activity going on (as a way of explaining it).

(2) Given a sequence of story facts, draw a conclusion based on it.

(3) Given the names of characters in a story, list the characteristics they have in common.

(4) Given two stories, list the characteristics on which their settings differ.

(5) Given the behavior of characters in a story, distinguish between those behaviors that are realistic and those that represent fantasy.

Answers

(1) *a.* C = {5,10,15}; *b.* 5εC; *c.* 7εC; *d.*{x/x is an even integer}; *e.* {y/y is an odd number greater than 7}

(2) *a.* {x/x is an integer greater than 0 and less than 11}

b. {x/x is an odd integer less than 11}

c. {x/x is an even integer greater than 2 and less than 14}

d. {x/x is a letter of the alphabet coming before h}

e. {x/x is a letter of the alphabet coming after r}

(3) *a.* ii; *b.* iv; *c.* i; *d.* iii

(4) A = C = D

(5) C = D

(6) *a.* yes; *b.* no; *c.* yes

(7) ϕ is a symbol used to indicate the empty set which contains no elements; {ϕ} indicates a set containing one element, the empty set.

(8) *b, d, e, g, h, j*

(9) *b, e, g, j*

(10) *a.* 4; *b.* 3; *c.* 2; *d.* 1; *e.* 0

Although the five objectives were only a portion of Mrs. Morris' goals, she felt that they were representative of the reading comprehension skills that her students should possess. At the completion of the unit she made up a short test based on the five objectives. It is shown in Figure 3.2.

*Mrs. Morris' First Grade Reading Comprehension Test.**   **Figure 3.2**

Tell me whom and what you see in this picture. Tell me what is happening.

(objective 1)

(2)

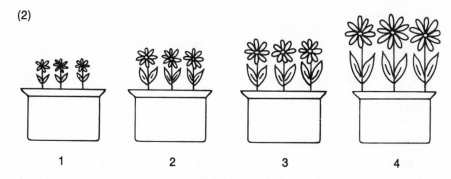

| 1 | 2 | 3 | 4 |

Tell me the reason that picture 4 comes after pictures 1, 2, and 3 and not before them or in the middle.

(objective 2)

(3) You have read three stories: *Angus and the Ducks, Blueberries for Sal*, and *Michael Who Missed His Train.* In each story there were animals. Tell me three ways that the animals in each story were like one another.

(objective 3)

(4) You have read the story, *City Streets and Country Roads*, about life in the country and life in the city. Tell me three ways that life in the city is different from life in the country.

(objective 4)

(5) You have read the story, *The Three Bears.* Tell me three things that the bears in the story were doing that real live bears cannot do (like talking).

(objective 5)

* Adapted from Instructional Objectives Exchange, Reading K–3.

• Mr. Emerson teaches English to eleventh graders in a course primarily devoted to poetry. His objectives for the first half of the course are shown below.

(1) Explain the *meaning* of a poem on the
   a. literal level in terms of what the poem actually describes,
   b. figurative level in terms of what the poem's underlying message is—using the poem's symbols for evidence, and
   c. personal level in terms of how you relate to the poem.
(2) a. Identify the *tone* of a poem (attitude conveyed toward subject matter and audience), and
   b. describe in a short essay the means by which the poem's tone is revealed.
(3) Demonstrate understanding of a poem's diction:
   a. identify words that connote multiple associations, and
   b. describe in a short essay the value and effect of these words.

Answers

1. Two girls, two frying pans, one with fried eggs, one with pancakes, table, pitcher; two girls in kitchen making pancakes and eggs; probably cooking breakfast; wearing aprons to keep their dresses clean. 2. Because the flowers are blooming a little more in each picture. 3. All have mothers, all can walk, all like to eat, all get into trouble, all like to play games. 4. Noisier, few trees, lots of houses, few animals, no farms, little grass. 5. Sleeping in beds, sitting on chairs, eating from bowls.

(4) Demonstrate an understanding of the *relationship between figurative language and meaning* in poetry:
  a. identify figures of speech in poetry,
  b. describe the feelings and ideas contained in each, and
  c. describe in a short essay their importance to the meaning of the poem.
(5) Demonstrate an understanding of the *function of repetitive sound* in poetry (meter or rhyme):
  a. identify regular and irregular patterns of meter and rhyme in a poem, and
  b. describe in a short essay the contributions of the regularities and irregularities to the poem's meaning.

"How do you expect to read when you can't even tell the sun from a mastodon?"

Mr. Emerson's exam is shown in Figure 3.3.

Figure 3.3 *Mr. Emerson's Eleventh Grade Poetry (English) Exam.**

(1) a. State briefly the literal level of the poem "Oh Who Is that Young Sinner" by A. E. Housman; that is, describe the story that the poem tells.

b. "The color of his hair" is symbolic; explain what it symbolizes. What is the symbolic meaning of the poem?

c. Briefly describe an instance in which you witnessed or experienced or heard of a person being discriminated against or put down for "the color of his/her hair" or skin.

(objective 1)

(2) What is the tone of the poem "In Just—" by e. e. cummings? How is the tone revealed?

(objective 2)

(3) Describe the connotations that the following words from "Richard Cory" by Edward Arlington Robinson have in common. What is their function in the poem?

crown (line 3)   imperially (line 4)   arrayed (line 5)
glittered (line 8)   King (line 9)

(objective 3)

(4) Name three figures of speech that are used in "Is Heaven a Physician?" by Emily Dickinson. What attitude is conveyed by each of these figures of speech?

(objective 4)

(5) Is the meter of the poem, "Fife Tune" by John Manifold, well-suited or poorly-suited to its meaning? (Justify your response with illustrations from the poem.)

(objective 5)

(Each item is worth 20 points)

* Adapted, Instructional Objectives Exchange, English Literature 10–12.

• Mrs. Dorfman teaches high school biology to a class made up of tenth and eleventh graders. She just finished a unit on reproduction that included the following objectives.

(1) The student will be able to define and describe each of the following processes in terms of *a*. when and *b*. in what exact manner it occurs:

    1. mitosis

    2. meiosis (sexual reproduction)

    3. asexual reproduction

    4. natural selection

    5. Mendelian heredity

(2) The student will be able to describe and explain how each of the above six processes in its own way maintains the continuity of life, that is, makes it possible for certain forms of life to survive.

(3) The student will be able to contrast the above six processes in terms of their

    a. simplicity–complexity,

    b. dependence on the environment,

    c. speed,

    d. predictability, and on any other dimensions that seem relevant, showing how each varies on each dimension.

(4) The student will be able to describe and present in an essay or poem personal feelings related to

    a. the transitoriness of "individual" life and

    b. the continuity of "class" life.

Mrs. Dorfman composed the test shown in Figure 3.4 below to determine whether the students had learned the matter covered in the unit.

Mrs. Dorfman's High School Biology Unit Test on Reproduction.* **Figure 3.4**

(1) Show, *using pictures only and no words*, the process of

    a. mitosis

    b. meiosis

                                    (objective 1)

(2) Imagine that you were a ball point pen. How do you think you might go through the process of asexual reproduction?

                                    (objective 1)

(3) Imagine that you were a string bean. According to Mendelian heredity principles, how would you compare to your "mother" and "father"?

                                    (objective 1)

(4) Suppose that you were a big strong dinosaur. Explain how natural selection might have operated to put you out of existence.

(objective 1,2)

(5) Describe two things that the processes of reproduction all have in common. Describe two things that the processes don't have in common (that is, in which they differ).

(objective 3)

(6) Write a short essay or poem on the difference between the "short" life of an organism and the "long" life of a "class." The essay or poem should suggest how you feel about this difference.

(objective 4)

* Adapted from Instructional Objectives Exchange, Biology 10–12.

Tests Measure Objectives; Objectives Facilitate Test Construction

It can be seen from the preceding examples that teacher-built achievement test items are written to reflect a set of objectives and that the existence of objectives is an important asset in test construction. If one were to ask any of the teachers in the illustrations what they considered their tests measure, they would point out the relationship between their objectives and their test items. Some teachers attempt to link goals and tests in a highly informal and imprecise way, an approach that does not necessarily help them measure what they want to measure. If you look closely at the objectives and test items in each of the four illustrations, you will be able to see their relationship with reasonable clarity.

Recall from Chapter 2 that an objective is divided into conditions, behavior, and criteria. (Most of the objectives in the preceding illustrations have left the criteria unstated. In many instances, these criteria are implicit; for example, performing an operation or task correctly where correctness can be judged objectively.) The core of the objective is the behavior. Take the behavior, "identify an elephant." We would probably give a student a picture containing four or more animals and ask him or her to indicate which was an elephant since "pointing to" is the behavior called for by the action verb "identify." The mechanics of item writing will be discussed in the succeeding chapters, but the point here is that the objective accomplishes two purposes: (1) *it reminds the teacher what he or she wants to measure* (or helps him or her to focus on it) and (2) *it provides some guidance on how to measure it* (provided that the teacher has built such information into the objective in the first place). Naturally, the more detailed the objective, the more information it provides for the "how to meas-

measures
guides

ure" question. Look closely at the objectives and corresponding items in the preceding examples and you will begin to appreciate the extent to which objectives facilitate item writing.

The preceding examples are also intended to illustrate types of tests and test questions that involve paper and pencil to answer. Paper-and-pencil is the test medium in which most tests are written. (The medium of performance testing will be covered in a subsequent chapter.) We can distinguish between short-answer questions and essay questions, each representing a different question–answer format. Finally, we can roughly distinguish among (1) the measurement of knowledge acquisition and comprehension, (2) the measurement of the higher mental processes—application, analysis, synthesis, evaluation, and (3) the measurement of affective outcomes such as attitudes, to use the terms from the taxonomies described in Chapter 2 (pages 38–43).

essay measures: knowledge, high mental proc, affective

Box 3.1

CRITERIA APPLIED TO OBJECTIVES

Charles Granger, writing in the *Harvard Business Review* (1964), cited the following six criteria to be applied to an objective in the business context:

1. *Is it, generally speaking, a guide to action?*
   In educational terms, we might ask: does the teacher use it as a basis for instruction?
2. *Is it explicit enough to suggest certain types of action?*
   Educationally, does it help the teacher know how to proceed in order to facilitate its achievement?
3. *Is it suggestive of tools to measure and control effectiveness?*
   For the teacher: does it help him or her to construct tests for measuring the attainment of his or her teaching goals? (This is the subject of this chapter.)
4. *Is it ambitious enough to be challenging?*
   In the classroom: are students motivated to attain it?
5. *Does it suggest cognizance of external and internal constraints?*
   In constructing it, does the teacher take into account his or her instructional resources and the capacities of the students?
6. *Can it be related to both the broader and the more specific objectives at higher and lower levels in the organization?*
   Educationally, does it fit into the sequence of objectives?

AREAS OF OBJECTIVES

Knowledge Acquisition and Comprehension   The most common use of tests in the classroom is measuring knowledge acquisition and comprehension. Basically, tests constructed for this purpose measure the degree to which students have acquired information and can understand what it means. If you reexamine Bloom's Taxonomy summarized on page 39 you will see that the first two levels are "knowledge" and "comprehension." These two levels refer to the acquisition, incorporation, and recall of factual information. The acquisition of knowledge and comprehension of facts are major goals in education and considerable effort has been contributed to their measurement.

Two of the four tests presented as illustrations at the beginning of this chapter measure knowledge and comprehension. These are the ones in reading and math; the last two largely measure higher cognitive processes. The most common and efficient measurement approach for measuring knowledge and comprehension is the short-answer item.[2] Although essay items may be used for this purpose, short-answer items are well-suited to the measurement of fact understanding and recall and, of the two types, are the easier to score objectively.

objective test

Some examples of short-answer knowledge and comprehension items appear in Figure 3.5. These items range from those clearly measuring direct recall, such as the first, to those measuring some form of interpolation, such as the last. All attempt to measure what the student knows and can understand on the basis of his or her ability to identify the correct response choice. The particular types of short-answer items that may be used and their construction will be discussed in the next chapter.

Higher Cognitive Processes   In the domain of cognitive or mental processes, there are important educational goals that deal with more complex forms of mental activity than knowing or understanding facts. These higher cognitive processes can be thought of as *thinking* or *using knowledge* and have been labeled as application, analysis, synthesis, and evaluation by Bloom (1956) in the taxonomy of the cognitive domain (see page 39).

---

[2] This is sometimes referred to as an *objective* or *objective-type* item, meaning that it is scored on a reasonably objective basis in contrast to the more subjective scoring of essay items. To avoid confusing the name of these items with the previously used term "objective," meaning goal or purpose, we will refer to these items throughout as short-answer (a reasonably descriptive term that distinguishes them from the essay type).

Short-answer Items That Measure Knowledge Acquisition (Recall) **Figure 3.5**
and Comprehension.*

(1) About what proportion of the population of the United States is living
on farms?

    a. 5%   *b.* 15%   *c.* 35%   *d.* 50%   *e.* 60%

(2) The primary germ layer, from which the skeleton and muscles develop, is known as the

    a. ectoderm.   *d.* endoderm.
    b. neurocoele.   *e.* mesoderm.
    c. epithelium.

(3) According to Daniel Webster, that which is most inseparable from
"union" is

    a. "country."   *c.* "the North."
    b. "liberty."   *d.* "welfare."

(4) If the volume of a given mass of gas is kept constant, the pressure
may be diminished by

    a. reducing the temperature.   *d.* decreasing the density.
    b. raising the temperature.   *e.* increasing the density.
    c. adding the heat.

(5) Which of the graphs below best represents the demand schedule of
a commodity for which there is a perfectly inelastic demand?

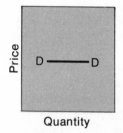 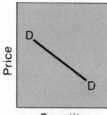 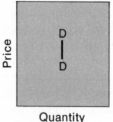 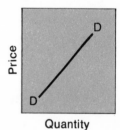

(6) "Milton! thou shouldst be living at this hour: England hath need of
thee; she is a fen of stagnant waters."—Wordsworth
The metaphor "she is a fen of stagnant waters," indicates that Wordsworth felt that England was

    a. largely swampy land.
    b. in a state of turmoil and unrest.
    c. making no progress.
    d. in a generally corrupt condition.

(7) A scientist cultivated a large colony of disease-producing bacteria.
From them, he extracted bacteria-free material referred to as substance X. A *large* dose of substance X was then injected into each

animal of group A. These animals promptly developed some of the symptoms normally produced by infection by the bacteria in question. Then, into each animal of group B, the scientist made a series of injections of *small* doses of substance X. Animals in a third group, C, received no injections. Three weeks after this series of injections, and continuing for two years thereafter, group B could be made to develop the disease by injecting them with several thousand times the number of bacteria that was fatal to group C. Substance X acted upon the animals of group A as if it were a

a. poison.

b. destroyer of poison.

c. stimulator of destroyer of poison.

With reference to its effect upon the animals of group B, small doses of substance X appeared to act as

a. a means of counteracting the effects of the disease-producing bacteria.

b. a means of stimulating the production of the bacteria or of their poisonous products.

c. if it were a poisonous product of the bacteria.

* Adapted with permission of the David McKay Company, Inc., from B. S. Bloom, *Taxonomy of Educational Objectives*: Cognitive Domain, 1956.

It is far more difficult to measure improvement in these higher cognitive areas than in the preceding ones; the greater difficulty in measuring is probably what has accounted for the lesser degree of attention paid the higher cognitive areas. This neglect has manifested itself in the use of teacher-built achievement tests to measure knowledge and comprehension with the assessment of students' higher mental processes left to the teacher's judgment based on class participation. Difficulties inherent in the measurement of thinking skills have led some educators to condemn testing as a factor responsible for limiting the curriculum to the more mundane goal of information transmission. The limited use of testing in the higher parts of the cognitive domain is not an inherent failing in testing but one that has been prompted by the difficulty in measuring the use of the thinking process. By improving their test-construction skills, teachers will be able to feel more

---

Answers

(1) *a* (2) *e* (3) *b* (4) *a* (5) *c* (6) *d* (7) *a, a.*

comfortable in aiming some objectives at the attainment of thinking skills, hence increasing the application of instruction to the development of thinking. The improvement of thinking may be ultimately facilitated rather than inhibited by the science and art of testing.

Sample paper-and-pencil test items for the higher cognitive processes appear in Figure 3.6. However, it must be pointed out that thinking skills need not necessarily be measured only by a paper-and-pencil test. They are often measured accurately by a test requiring an active, observable performance on the student's part. (Performance tests will be described in Chapter 7.) For illustration here, written items have been used. Note that the first item in Figure 3.6 requires that the student *apply* what he or she has learned in algebra and geometry to the solution of a real problem. The second involves the *analysis* of a position or opinion into those arguments that do and do not support it. The third requires that the student *synthesize* what he or she knows about desert life into the drawing of a suitable picture. The fourth calls for the *evaluation* of clothing materials in terms of criteria that the student must have already learned.

The higher mental processes are oriented more to the process by which an answer or solution is obtained than to the answer or solution itself. Consequently, test items that measure outcomes or responses based on these processes are usually more difficult to score since answers are not necessarily completely right or wrong; their degree of correctness is based on how they were obtained. The teacher, therefore, must have access to the solution process or the logic or justification behind it in addition to the solution itself. Perhaps it is this characteristic that accounts for the rarity of such tests and which requires that attention be paid not only to test item writing but to answer key or criterion writing as well.

*Items That Measure Thinking Skills.**   **Figure 3.6**

(1) The length of a rectangular lot exceeds its breadth by 20 yards. If each dimension is increased by 20 yards the area of the lot will be doubled. Find the shorter dimension of the original lot. Show your work below.

    a. 20   *c.* 35   *e.* none of the above

    b. 30   *d.* 40

(2) Resolved: *That the term of the president of the United States should be extended to six years.*

Mark each statement (a–e) below

A—if you feel that it could be meaningfully used by the affirmative side in a debate on the resolution.

N—if you feel that it could be meaningfully used by the negative side.

X—if you feel that it has no bearing on either side of the argument.

(NOTE: You are not asked to judge the truth or falsity of the resolution or the statements.)

a. Efficiency increases with experience.

b. According to the principles upon which the United States was founded, the people should have a frequent check on the president.

c. The party system has many disadvantages.

d. During most of a presidential election year the economic life of the nation is depressed by the uncertainty of the outcome.

e. The people should have the opportunity to keep a satisfactory president as long as they wish.

(3) Draw a picture of a desert scene that shows different aspects of desert life and what the people who live there are like.

(4) Jane is going to make a dress for school. The dress will receive heavy wear through most of the year, and will be laundered frequently. She has chosen dacron polyester over wool or cotton. Identify at least six criteria, such as convenience in washing and durability, that can be used for evaluating the chosen material, as well as the alternatives Jane considered. Indicate how your criteria apply to the three materials, and whether they lead you to make the same choice as Jane. Be as specific as possible in stating and applying criteria.

* Adapted with permission of the David McKay Company, Inc., from B. S. Bloom, *Taxonomy of Educational Objectives*: Cognitive Domain, 1956.

The Affective Domain   The affective domain refers to the attitudes, feelings, and values of students. The description of this domain is shown on pages 42–43 and includes receiving, responding, valuing, organizing, and characterizing by a value or value complex. We attempt in education to contribute to student development of awareness, attention, motivation, self-concept, satisfaction, aspiration, tolerance, interest, value

---

Answers

(1) *d.* (2) *a.* A, *b.* N, *c.* X, *d.* A, *e.* X.

(3) drawing should reflect awareness of topography, climate, dwelling places, dress, living habits, animal life, and so forth. (4) Response should use criteria such as the following to evaluate given materials: colorfastness, crease resistance, softness, durability.

"The reason you have to take exams, Blake, is that even though *you* consider this place to be a think tank, we don't."

clarification, self-direction and the like but seldom attempt to systematically determine whether such affective outcomes are being achieved. When teachers are called upon to make these judgments, they often proceed in a casual manner by considering their opinions of students. However, more systematic measurement within the affective domain is possible as shown by the illustrative items in Figure 3.7.

Unlike most cognitive items, affective items do not have right or wrong answers. Scoring is based on a key that indicates the direction of the item reflecting the orientation chosen by you as desirable. If one were scoring the first item in Figure 3.7 to reflect interest in engineering, for example, all four statements would be keyed to the *dislike* response whereas for music interest, all four statements are keyed to the *like* response.

Many contemporary educational strategies are aimed at the affective domain. Teachers and program developers must carefully consider their affective objectives and then seek adequate ways to measure these objectives. Where suitable tests do not exist, such tests will have to be developed or existing ones modified. Such test development, as will be described in later chapters, calls for the generation of items that reflect such things as opinions, attitudes, and values for which absolute right and wrong answers do not apply; responses are scored in terms of their correspondence to a scoring key representing "desirable" responses. Affective items must also be subtle enough to avoid provoking contrived or distorted responses.

Figure 3.7   *Items That Measure the Affective Domain.**

(1) As you read each item below, underline one of three letters
   L if you *would like* to do what the item says.
   N if you *neither like nor dislike* what the item says but you would still be willing to do it.
   D if you *dislike* what the item says and would not want to do it.
   L N D   *a.* Sing songs at parties.
   L N D   *b.* Sing in a glee club, chorus, or choir.
   L N D   *c.* Play in an orchestra or band.
   L N D   *d.* Make up tunes to hum, or compose music.

(2) You read short stories or novels (other than for school)
   a. 1. never (if you choose this answer, omit items *b* and *c*).
      2. occasionally.
      3. frequently.
   b. 1. with little or no enjoyment.
      2. with a fair amount of enjoyment.
      3. with great pleasure.
   c. 1. just for the story.
      2. paying some atttention to plot and characterization.
      3. making a detailed examination of the idea and structure of the work.

(3) The following statements represent opinions about various phases of school life. Since there are no right or wrong answers, you are to express your own point of view about the statement. Underline
   A if you *agree* with the *whole statement.*
   U if you are *uncertain* how you feel about the *whole statement.*
   D if you *disagree* with the *whole statement.*
   A U D   *a.* It is better for seniors and freshmen to eat at different lunchroom tables.
   A U D   *b.* Seniors and freshmen should not dance with each other at school dances.
   A U D   *c.* A capable freshman would make just as good a student council president as a capable senior.
   A U D   *d.* Senior men and freshmen women should not have dates with each other.

(4) A person who works all week might spend Sunday engaging in the activities described below. Arrange these answers in the order of your personal preference by writing *1* next to the statement that describes the activity you would like most to do, *2* next to the one that is next most attractive, *3* next to the third most, and *4* next to the least attractive.

   a. trying to educate himself or herself by reading serious books.

   b. trying to win at golf or tennis.

   c. going to an orchestral concert.

   d. hearing a really good sermon.

* The items were adapted with permission of the David McKay Company, Inc., from D. R. Krathwohl, *Taxonomy of Educational Objectives*: Affective Domain, 1964.

DEVELOPING A CONTENT OUTLINE

The purpose of this chapter is to help you see the relationship between objectives and test items. Before test items are written, objectives should be prepared. A shorthand list of objectives forms the basis for a *content outline.* Once the content outline is prepared, it can serve as the basis for determining what test items must be written. We shall talk here about the procedure for developing a content outline; the procedures for preparing test items will be presented in the next chapters. The examples given at the beginning of this chapter illustrate the kinds of tests that can result from content outlines based on objectives.

Some teachers develop lists of objectives to guide their development of lessons and others do not. Those that do not are encouraged to develop objectives at least as a basis for developing a content outline, that is a list of the concepts or tasks to be mastered in a shorthand form, rather than proceeding to write test items without any formal content structure. Where instructional objectives already exist, they should be summarized or listed in the shorthand form of a content outline.

In summary, then, a content outline is a list of concepts or tasks to be mastered in shorthand form. Sample content outlines

list of tasks

Answers

(1) [on music interest key] *a.* L, *b.* L, *c.* L, *d.* L (2) [on reading interest key] *a.* 3, *b.* 3, *c.* 3 (3) [on being pro "integration"] *a.* D, *b.* D, *c.* A, *d.* D (4) [on "intellectual" key] *a.* 1, *b.* 4, *c.* 2, *d.* 3

for the subjects of reading and mathematics appear below. Note that each statement in the content outline represents a statement of an objective only in the form of the desired behavior or action. The statement of the conditions and the criteria have been left off, as they are typically in a content outline, for purposes of brevity.

Reading Content Outline
    (1) Recognizing the sound of final consonant digraphs
    (2) Recognizing the sound of initial consonant blends
    (3) Recognizing the sound of final consonant blends
    (4) Identifying vowels modified by r in words
    (5) Identifying vowel diphthongs in words
    (6) Classifying singular and possessive nouns
    (7) Classifying adjective endings
    (8) Classifying irregular verbs and verb endings, present tense
    (9) Classifying compound words·
  (10) Classifying contractions
  (11) Identifying synonyms and antonyms
  (12) Identifying personal pronouns
  (13) Identifying words using context and configuration clues
  (14) Restating sequence of details
  (15) Inferring main idea

Mathematics Content Outline
    (1) Identifying place value (1's, 10's, 100's)
    (2) Adding columns of numbers without carrying
    (3) Recognizing applications of the associative principle
    (4) Subtracting two-digit numbers without borrowing
    (5) Recognizing applications of the distributive principle
    (6) Identifying common fractions
    (7) Identifying improper fractions
    (8) Identifying place value (1,000's, 10,000's)
    (9) Identifying decimal fraction values to (hundredths)
  (10) Reading and writing decimals
  (11) Converting decimals to fractions
  (12) Converting fractions to decimals
  (13) Adding two- and three-digit numbers with regrouping
  (14) Stating multiplication facts
  (15) Determining the product of two-digit numbers

Thus, test construction (to be described in the following chapters) begins as a first step with the preparation of a content outline (or list of objectives in brief form) that tells you what it is you want to measure. The following steps ordinarily occur in the preparation of a content outline.

(1) Identify the segment of instruction for which testing will be done. Your test may be a unit test following completion of a unit, or it may cover a week of instruction, a half a year, a year or any other segment. Your test should be based on the chosen segment if it is to accurately reflect achievement in that segment.

I SRI

(2) Specify the concepts, ideas, or skills covered in the segment. What are the areas in the segment in which learning was to have taken place? These concepts, ideas, or skills to be learned should be stated in any form that has most meaning to you. It is entirely likely that you have already stated these prior to offering instruction.

(3) Restate the concepts, ideas, or skills in behavioral terms. What you will ultimately measure are performances that reflect the concepts, ideas, and skills to be learned. The preparation of test items is facilitated by the availability of objectives stated in behavioral or measurable terms. (For a review of these procedures, refer to Chapter 2.) To restate concepts, ideas, or skills in measurable terms requires that each statement include an action verb. (See Figures 2.2 and 2.3 on pages 26–28 and 28–30 for a list of action verbs.) Decide upon the appropriate action verb in each instance and restate the concept, idea, or skill accordingly. You need not include statements of conditions and criteria; these will be supplied, at least implicitly, when preparing the test items. However, it will simplify the subsequent development of test items and suggest certain content areas that will not prove measurable if conditions and criteria are at least considered.

(4) Indicate any difference in relative emphasis of the various objectives. Each of the objectives in the outline may or may not be of equal emphasis. Where unequal emphases occur, objectives may be weighted using a system like the following: least emphasized objectives are weighted *1*, the objectives of intermediate emphasis are weighted *2*, and the most emphasized objectives weighted *3*. Where all are of equal emphasis, weightings need not be added.

You are now ready to consider the conditions and criteria of measurement and then to prepare items. You must write items for each and every objective in your content outline. Where objectives are equally weighted, the same number of items should be written for each objective. Where weightings occur, the number of items per objective must be proportional to the weighting of the objective. In other words, an objective with a weighting of *3* should have approximately three times as many items as one with a weighting of *1*.

Using a content outline to construct a test is a procedure aimed at insuring the appropriateness of that test. (The concept of "appropriateness" is covered in Chapter 8; the development of test item specifications is described in Appendix B.)

Once the content outline is finished, conditions and criteria are ready to be embodied into test items. The chapters in Part Two deal with the preparation of tests and test items.

Box 3.2

STATING THE CRITERION FOR SUCCESS

Robert Mager, in his book *Preparing Instructional Objectives* (1962), emphasizes the importance of stating a criterion for success in an objective—the criterion representing the *minimum acceptable performance*. Some of the more common ways of defining acceptable performance are indicating

1. a time limit within which performance must occur,
2. the minimum number of correct responses,
3. the minimum percentage or proportion of correct responses (e.g., eight out of ten),
4. the important characteristics of performance accuracy (e.g., the acceptable deviation from some standard).

He also offers the following example of a complex objective that is replete with criteria for success:

> The student must be able to write a musical composition with a single tonal base. The composition must be at least sixteen bars in length and contain at least twenty-four notes. The student must demonstrate his or her understanding of the rules of good composition by applying at least three of them in the development of his or her score. The student is to complete his or her composition within four hours.

Additional Information Sources

Ammons, M. Objectives and outcomes. In R. L. Ebel (Ed.), *Encyclopedia of Educational Research*, 4th ed. N.Y.: Macmillan, 1969, 908–914.

Krathwohl, D. R. & Payne, D. Defining and assessing educational objectives. In R. L. Thorndike (Ed.), *Educational measurement*, 2nd ed., Wash., D.C.: American Council on Education, 1971, Chap. 2.

Mager, R. F. *Measuring instructional intent*. Palo Alto, Calif.: Fearon Publishers, 1973.

Tinkelman, S. N. Planning the objective test. In R. L. Thorndike (Ed.), *Educational measurement*, 2nd ed., Wash., D.C.: American Council on Education, 1971.

Self-test of Proficiency

(1) Listed on the left are three map-reading test items. Match each one with the shorthand form of the map-reading objective on the right that it measures.*

a. To go from the post office to the school (as shown on a map) would you go north then west or north then east?

b. On this map of the schoolroom, point out the fire alarm, piano, and chalkboard.

c. With a set of blocks, construct a model of the street on which your school is located and then position your school on it.

i. Use a given material to create a representation of a specified area.

ii. Identify map symbols on an outline map.

iii. Use geographical directions to designate the route between given locations on a map.

iv. Identify objects that correspond to symbols on a map.

(2) If you had the objective: *Describe the balance of power between the three branches of the United States government*, which one of the following items would best measure it?

a. The legislative power of the government is constituted in the _____.

b. Construct a chart that illustrates the balance of power.

c. What does the term "balance of power" mean and how is it carried out within the United States government?

d. In the United States system of "balance of power," the judicial function is carried out by the Supreme Court.
                     TRUE   FALSE

(3) For which one of the following areas is it possible to prepare test items with answers that are completely right or wrong?

a. affective domain

b. higher cognitive processes

c. knowledge acquisition and comprehension

d. creative processes

---

* These items and objectives were adapted from *Social Science (Geography) K–9*, distributed by the Instructional Objectives Exchange.

(4) *a.* In the classroom, tests are most often used to measure the area of higher cognitive processes.

TRUE   FALSE

b. To score an answer to an item that measures evaluation, the teacher needs access to the logic behind the answer.

TRUE   FALSE

(5) Into which one of the areas (knowledge acquisition, comprehension, application, analysis, synthesis, or evaluation) would the test items *a, b,* and *c* in number 1 above be best classified?

(6) Into which of the areas listed in item 3 above would you classify the following test item?

	strongly			strongly
I like this textbook very much.	agree	agree	disagree	disagree

(7) Write an objective in shorthand form for the goal: *to know who the United States senators are from your state.*

(8) Write a shorthand version of the following objective: *Given a familiar melody, the student will create an accompaniment for the melody, such accompaniment having the quality and mood of the melody, using the appropriate instruments.*

(9) Given the shorthand form objective, *change a flat tire on a car*, prepare a content outline with at least three tasks.

(10) Given the shorthand form objective, *define, describe,* and *compare facism and democracy*, prepare a content outline with at least three tasks.

part two/Constructing a Test: Teacher-built Tests

chapter four / Short-answer Items to Measure Knowledge and Comprehension

OBJECTIVES

1. Identify six types of short-answer items: unstructured, completion, true–false, other two-choice, multiple choice, and matching.

2. Identify and state rules and recommendations associated with the construction of each of the six item types.

3. Construct sample items for a given objective using each of the six item types in accordance with the rules and recommendations.

4. Distinguish between the different characteristics or features of the six item types and the testing situations in which each of the item types is best used.

This chapter deals with the measurement of knowledge acquisition and comprehension—areas of primary interest to the classroom teacher. The teacher typically monitors, by means of tests, the extent to which knowledge and the understanding of that knowledge have been transmitted to students. The majority (but not all) of a teacher's objectives probably fall into this area and thus it becomes an important area for testing. Such testing enables the teacher to evaluate students' learning progress, diagnose their weaknesses, and get some idea of the effectiveness of the instruction.

We will assume at this point that the teacher has completed the first three steps in test construction; that is, he or she has (1) specified the goals, (2) put them in the form of a content outline, and (3) written them as expanded objectives. In originally specifying his or her goals, the teacher should also have decided which objectives required knowledge acquisition and comprehension, which required thinking and problem-solving, which involved attitudes and values, and which involved behavior change. In this and the subsequent three chapters, the construction of test items— the next step in the process—will be covered. This chapter, in dealing with knowledge acquisition and comprehension, will focus exclusively on short-answer items, which are the type of items most commonly used for the measurement of these processes.

Spec. goals
Cont. Outl.
Exp. Obj.

Short-answer items have either free or fixed choices. There are basically two free choice formats. One is the unstructured format, the other the fill-in or completion format. Fixed choice formats include true–false, other two-choice, multiple choice, and matching. Both free choice and fixed choice items have previously determined correct responses. However, in the free choice type, the student is not given choices from which to select the correct response as he or she is in the fixed choice type. In this chapter each type of short-answer item will be described and illustrated and some guidelines for the construction of each will be offered.

free choice –
student's choice

Short-answer items typically ask students to identify, distinguish, state, or name something. Such items may also, particularly in math, ask them to demonstrate something. In the free choice format, the measurement basically involves asking students a question that requires that they *state* or *name* the specific information or knowledge called for (that is, *recall* it), indicating acquisition of that knowledge. In the fixed choice formats, the measurement basically involves giving students two or more alternative responses and asking them to *identify* the correct one or *distinguish* between correct and incorrect ones (that is, to *recognize* the correct response). The act of identifying can be taken as an indication that the students have acquired the particular piece of information or knowledge called for in the item.

Keep in mind that objectives that call for students to identify, distinguish, state, or name something—and hence demonstrate knowledge acquisition or comprehension—are most readily measured by means of one of the various types of short-answer item formats that will be described on the following pages.

UNSTRUCTURED FORMAT

The unstructured short-answer format utilizes a question that can be answered by a word, phrase, or number. Some examples are given below.

Examples
- Who was the seventeenth president of the United States?
- What gland of the body secretes the hormone ACTH?
- What phrase did Hamlet use to describe Yorick?
- Which state in the United States produces more copper ore than any other?
- $\frac{1}{8} + \frac{1}{4} - \frac{1}{16} =$
- Who wrote the poem, "Ode on a Grecian Urn"?

one word answers

no guessing, clues

easy to write

Pros and Cons.   The most attractive features of the unstructured format are that (1) it minimizes the likelihood of guessing, (2) the student is not given clues as, for example, in a multiple choice item, (3) it represents a reasonably easy type of item to write (the test maker does not have to think of alternative answers to present), and (4) it can be accommodated quite easily to the kind of item where a map, figure, or graph is given and the student must answer questions such as: "What is the name of the part labeled *A*?"

Most notable of the undesirable aspects of this format has to do with scoring (that is, keying and correcting). Some unstructured items invite any number of answers, many of which may

Answers

Andrew Johnson, pituitary, a fellow of infinite jest, Arizona, 5/16, Keats.

resemble the correct one to some degree. Consider the item, "What chemical is often added to drinking water to help prevent tooth decay?" Students may answer fluorine, fluoride, sodium fluoride, stannous fluoride, fluride, among others. In scoring, the teacher will have to decide what the student had in mind. Mind-reading adds a difficult dimension to item scoring.

The unstructured response format works best for the *measurement of specific knowledge,* most commonly in math, science, and history.

Writing the Item. In writing an unstructured response item, the first point to keep in mind is *to write the item so that the correct response will require the fewest words possible.* Reducing response possibilities, which obviously simplifies the task of scoring, is often facilitated by *keeping the item itself brief and to the point,* and of such nature that *one response and only one will suffice as the correct response.* Scoring is further aided by *supplying students with an answer blank identified by numbers with the items.*

The items themselves should be *written in the simplest language possible* so that the act of understanding the item does not become a task in itself. Consider the two examples below written for the objective: distinguish between a ratio scale and interval scale in terms of the unique zero point feature of the former.

- A ratio scale has a principal feature that distinguishes it from an interval scale. What is that feature? _____
- What does a ratio scale have that an interval scale does not have? _____

Though the answer to both items would be "a zero point" the second item is simpler and clearer than the first and more clearly illustrates one major characteristic of an unstructured response item, namely that it is *written in question form* rather than statement form.

COMPLETION FORMAT

The completion or fill-in item format is also a free choice format in that the students must construct their own response rather than choose from among given choices. It differs from the unstructured item by requiring that they fill in or complete a sentence from which a word or phrase has been omitted.

Examples

- The man who discovered Florida while searching for the "fountain of youth" was _____.
- Boyle's Law states that pressure of a gas multiplied by its _____ is equal to a constant.
- "Give me liberty or give me _____" was the pronouncement of a famous American revolutionary.
- Among the hormones secreted by the pituitary gland, two are: _____ and _____.
- A fixed zero point is the characteristic that distinguishes a _____ scale from an interval scale.
- _____ produces more copper ore than any other state in the Union.

Pros and Cons.   The completion format has many of the same advantages and disadvantages as the unstructured response format while being somewhat more difficult to write. Because the item must give sufficient clues so as not to be ambiguous but not so many to be unchallenging, the wording of completion items is particularly critical. Completion items when properly written are easier to score than unstructured ones but they do have the disadvantage of being quite constrained by their own grammar. However, by requiring that the students formulate their own answers, this type of item poses a challenge for them. Completion and unstructured items can both be included in the same test to offer the student a change of pace in situations where specific fact learning is to be tested.

Writing the Item.   In writing completion items, the key is *to strike a balance between leaving out so much that the item becomes ambiguous and leaving out so little* (or otherwise providing so many clues) *that the item becomes too easy.* Consider the three examples below.

- The evolutionary theory of _____ is based on the principle that _____.
- The evolutionary theory of _____ is based on the principle that the fittest will survive.
- The evolutionary theory of Darwin is based on the principle that the _____ will survive.

Answers

Ponce de Leon; volume; death; ACTH, pitocin, vasopressin, TSH; ratio; Arizona.

The first example suggests a variety of answers. There the answer will depend on which theorist the student chooses for the first blank, thus making the item indefinite by inviting a wide range of possible responses. The third illustration provides a very strong clue; students are likely to remember the phrase "survival of the fittest" and quickly realize that the word "fittest" should be applied. The second item is best. Completion items should be used to measure simple factual recall and not to measure more complex thinking processes.

To write items that have neither too many nor too few clues, you should *try to avoid instances where the grammar of the sentence helps determine the answer.* Grammar is most often a problem with respect to the plural number and to the indefinite article (a, an).

- A subatomic particle having a negative unit charge and negligible mass is an _____.
- A subatomic particle having a negative unit charge and negligible mass is a (an) _____.

By using "a (an)" the second illustration avoids indicating to the student that the answer, *electron*, begins with a vowel.

As a final point, *completion items should have a single correct answer, preferably a word or short phrase.* Those items that prompt students to give a range of responses are much more difficult to score than those items that tend to elicit the same correct response from many students. It may be helpful to write an item originally as an unstructured item and then rewrite it as a completion item. Remember that completion items are only useful in measuring the acquisition of specific knowledge. Consider the following examples.

- Ebbinghaus, an Austrian psychologist, did experiments on human _____.
- Ebbinghaus, an Austrian psychologist, did experiments to discover the conditions under which human beings would _____ best.

Although both illustrations are aimed at eliciting the same general answer (in the first case, *memory*, and in the second, *remember*), a student might be tempted to write the word *beings* in answer to the first, an answer that would have to be considered acceptable. For either illustration, *learning* or *learn* might be chosen as answers but could legitimately be considered incorrect.

If you are having difficulty writing a completion item, consider the following two suggestions. The first is to include only a single blank in any item, thus avoiding the ambiguity that may occur with multiple completions. The second is to consider offering from two to four response choices—in effect making the item into a multiple choice item. Consider the following.

- That branch of government charged with making the laws is the _____. (executive, legislative, judicial)
- Argon, neon, and xenon have something in common. They are all considered _____. (radiant metals, biological vapors, inert gases, rare earths)
- Boyle's Law states that the pressure of a gas multiplied by its _____ (volume, temperature, weight) is equal to a constant.

Substituting multiple choice items for completion items represents a reasonably effective strategy for limiting the ambiguity and scoring difficulty that often accompany completion items. Multiple choice items are discussed in detail beginning on page 90.

TRUE–FALSE (YES–NO) FORMAT

Some short-answer items provide two response choices. This differs from the unstructured or completion modes, which provide no response choice, and the multiple choice type, which provides three or more response choices. These two-choice items often include the options "true–false" or "yes–no."

Examples

• Australia, the island continent, was discovered by Columbus.	TRUE	FALSE
• Most Australians live along the east coast of Australia.	TRUE	FALSE
• Much of Australia is a cold desert.	TRUE	FALSE
• Wheat is imported by Australia.	TRUE	FALSE
• Sydney is the capital of Australia.	TRUE	FALSE
• Uranium and bauxite have been found in Australia.	TRUE	FALSE

Answers

Legislative; inert gases; volume.

- Below are a list of plural animal words. Circle YES for those that have been done properly and NO for those that have been done improperly.

oxes	YES	NO
deer	YES	NO
mouses	YES	NO
bear	YES	NO
monkeys	YES	NO

Pros and Cons.   One big advantage of true–false items is the fact that they are perhaps the easiest type of item to write and can be answered quickly by students. Their easiness to write is due to to their simplicity—just a single statement that is either accurate or inaccurate. Their easiness to answer is due to the fact that the student need only read the statement and circle "true" or "false." But what about the false statements? Are we teaching students information that is false by having them read these items? Another difficulty is the significant amount of ambiguity that may be contained in these items.

- When a plane crashes exactly on the
  Canadian-American border, half of the
  survivors are buried in each country.   TRUE   FALSE

How many of you read that item and answered it without realizing that it contained the word *survivors*, and survivors are characteristically not buried. Thus, the correct answer is *false*. Or,

- Early in his career, Will Rogers said:
  "I never met a man I didn't like."   TRUE   FALSE

Did Will Rogers make that statement or did someone else? Was it exactly what was said or has the statement been altered? If Will Rogers did say it, did he say it early in his career? Here are three questions in one causing ambiguity about what the student has or has not learned. Thus, although true–false items are easy to write and quick to take, they may be ambiguous in their interpretation.

True–false items are best used for measuring the recognition of fact. Free choice items deal with facts also but require the student to *recall* them. In the true–false item the fact is given to the student in either accurate or inaccurate form and he or she need

---

Answers

False, True, False, False, False, True, No, Yes, No, No, Yes.

only *recognize* it. True–false items are considered to work well in the measurement of objectives that call for discrimination between absolutes, requiring the student to distinguish or discriminate between statements of correct and incorrect fact or interpretation.

Finally, there is the matter of guessing—perhaps the biggest weakness in true–false items. When students guess, they have a fifty-fifty chance of being right. Given all the clues in the item, they may be able to improve those odds. The purpose of a test is to measure what students are capable of, not how lucky they are. The large element of luck can usually only be controlled by using a great many items. Keep in mind, then, that good guessing can account for a considerable number of points on a true–false test, particularly for the brighter students whose adept use of clues leads them to make "educated guesses."[1] This weakness can be

---

[1] Such guesses can be a reflection of "test-wiseness" and not of knowledge in the specific area.

compensated for, in part, by imposing a penalty for guessing wrong; for example, deducting a half or a quarter of a point for each incorrect answer.

Writing the Item. In writing true–false items be careful neither to give too many clues nor to build in tricks. One useful rule is to *avoid the use of absolute terms like "always" and "never."* First of all, absolute facts are hard to find, and secondly, you may fall into the habit of using absolutes to make items false —a habit students may come to recognize. Learn not to telegraph your intentions as does the fighter who touches his nose before throwing a punch or the pitcher who turns his glove before throwing a curve.

- The market value of gold always exceeds the market value of silver.   TRUE   FALSE
- The market value of gold exceeds the market value of silver.   TRUE   FALSE
- Today, the market value of gold exceeds the market value of silver.   TRUE   FALSE

The first illustration is too broad and sweeping while the second is ambiguous—not telling the time to which it refers. The third illustration is the most accurate of the three as a true statement because of its specificity. The first and second would not be recommended as either true or false items. The suitable false item then might be:

- Today, the market value of silver exceeds the market value of gold.   TRUE   FALSE

A helpful practice in writing true–false items is *to write only true items and then afterward turn about half of them around* to make false items. This system guarantees the items a certain degree of uniformity of form and structure and also produces a test on which half of the items are true and half are false (thus minimizing the effect of guessing). In turning items around, it is better to do so as in the above examples (that is, switching *gold* and *silver* to say that the "market value of silver exceeds gold") than by adding the word "not" (e.g., "the market value of gold does not exceed the market value of silver"). Adding the word "not" does turn an item around (that is, switch it from a true to a false) but often also adds either a clue or an ambiguity.

Also, *the items should be placed in a random order* with respect to one another[2] to avoid response patterns that serve as strong guessing clues.

To construct the test as clearly and unambiguously as possible *include only a single major point in each item*, that point being the relationship between two facts, and write the item so that it is the truth or falsity of that relationship that the student must judge. For example:

- Maid Marion, Little John, and Brother
  Tuck are all characters in *Robin Hood*,   TRUE   FALSE

is a bad item because its truth or falsity is not based on the relationship between characters and book but on the replacement of *Friar Tuck* with *Brother Tuck*. It would have been fairer to say

- Maid Marion, Little John, and Friar Tuck
  are all characters in *Ivanhoe*,   TRUE   FALSE

in which case it would have been the relationship between characters and book that was false.

An important basis for structuring an item is the objective that is being measured. If the objective were "to distinguish between the petal and the sepal of a flower," in terms of the former being part of the corolla, and the latter being part of the calyx, the following item might be written:

- The petals of a flower are the parts of the
  flower's calyx.   TRUE   FALSE

TWO-CHOICE CLASSIFICATION FORMAT

There are a variety of two-choice formats other than true–false and yes–no. In most cases, these formats ask the student to apply classification to a set of stimuli, as shown in the examples below.

Examples
- Underline the words that could be used as verbs and draw a line through ones that could not.

  | *a*. eat | *c*. wrist | *e*. flew | *g*. myself |
  | *b*. cat | *d*. knit | *f*. helps | *h*. were |

[2] A table of random numbers such as appears in Tuckman (1972) is recommended for this purpose. Number your items in the order they are written; then choose a column in the table of random numbers and re-order the items. The resulting order will be suitably random.

- Use *a* or *an* before each word:

  ———oak   ———hour

  ———ear   ———mountain

  ———uniform   ———orange

  ———umbrella   ———letter

- Teddy hasn't got $\left\{ \begin{array}{c} \text{any} \\ \text{no} \end{array} \right\}$ money.

Pros and Cons. Two-choice formats such as those illustrated above provide teachers with an opportunity to use ingenuity in fitting test items to their specific needs, and also add a little variation to a test. These formats are less pat than the true–false format and may require less forcing and artificiality than multiple choices (meaning three or more choices). Moreover, the task of classification can normally be cast into at least two categories—the presence of a quality versus its absence. Thus, we have a European country versus a non-European country, gas versus a nongas, and so on. As you add classification categories, your item becomes a multiple choice item and eventually a matching item. However, the contrast between that which fits into a category and that which does not calls for the two-choice format.

- Below are the names of eight cities in the United States. Mark a check next to each city that is a state capital.

  a. Atlanta   *e.* Lansing

  b. Birmingham   *f.* Madison

  c. Chicago   *g.* New York

  d. Denver   *h.* Pittsburgh

Thus, a two-choice format most conveniently fits the task of a one-variable, two-level, classification.

As with all the other short-answer formats, the limitations of the two-choice format must be recognized. It works best for factual knowledge, is susceptible to guessing, and is invalidated by ambiguous items. However, it is easier to avoid ambiguity with this format than with the ones described thus far, and the guessing problem is often less severe since the students must react to stimuli presented in a series.

Answers

Underline *a, d, e, f, h*; all "an" except uniform, mountain, and letter; any; check *a, d, e, f.*

Writing the Item. Remember that the two-choice format works well in a classification situation. *Make sure that the category to be used is clear and distinct from other potentially confusable categories.* Also, *make the stimuli to be classified clear instances or noninstances of that category.* Clarity is clearly illustrated in a field such as mathematics.

- Circle those numbers that are prime numbers.
  4, 5, 6, 7, 8, 9, 10, 11, 12

Ambiguity can arise when dealing in situations where right and wrong are more relative.

- Which of the following can be considered causes of the War between the States?

slavery	farm economics
states' rights	industrial vs. agrarian interests
personal conflicts	foreign interference

Some of the stimuli above are vague in their meaning (e.g., personal conflicts) while others seem to overlap. This criticism is not meant to suggest that the two-choice format should not be used in potentially confusing areas but that care must be taken to make each stimulus clear and understandable in its own right.

Those stimuli or instances that fit the given category are called *exemplars* of that category while those that do not fit are called *nonexemplars. There is no need to have the same number of exemplars as nonexemplars.* In fact, the numbers of each should vary each time the format is used to avoid giving an extra clue. Moreover, the order of each should be as random as possible so that each may fall at any point in the order and no pattern emerges.

It is often easiest to write an item of this type by *identifying the classification category first and then thinking of exemplars and nonexemplars.* For example, if your instructional objective deals with identifying ductless glands in the body, then "ductless glands" becomes the classification category. It becomes the explicit basis for choosing a stimulus as an exemplar or nonexemplar. Obviously, correct choices or exemplars would be the various ductless glands such as the pituitary, thyroid, adrenal cortex, gonads, etc. Then decide what category you want students to dis-

---

Answers

5, 7, 11; all are correct except the last.

tinguish ductless glands from. Is this nonglands or duct glands or both? This decision will form the basis for the choice of non-exemplars. The item might come out as follows:

- Circle those parts of the body that are ductless glands.

  pituitary   thyroid   kidney
  thymus   parathyroid   adrenal cortex
  liver   spleen   lymph nodes

Finally, item difficulty can be manipulated by the range of the nonexemplars based on the objective you are trying to measure. Remember that the exemplars or correct choices fit the given category, for instance "ductless glands" in the above example. The alternative to the given category can itself be a given specific category or can simply be the absence of a given category (depending on your objective). Thus, ductless glands can be contrasted with glands having ducts or with any part of the body that is not a ductless gland (i.e., glands vs. nonglands). When the categories are broader, the list of nonexemplars will also be broader and hence more difficult to deal with. Consider the following two examples.

- Which of the following are nineteenth century poets?

  Keats   Hemingway
  Frost   de Maupassant
  Stevens   Wordsworth
- Which of the following are nineteenth century poets?

  Keats   Whitman
  Frost   Baudelaire
  Stevens   Wordsworth

In the second example the stimuli have been limited to poets. The student must therefore only distinguish between nineteenth century poets and twentieth century poets. In the first example he or she must also distinguish between poets and nonpoets (novelists and short story writers). *Choices for categories and nonexemplars should be based on the distinctions that you are trying to teach students to make* (which in turn should be reflected in your objectives).

Answers

Pituitary, thymus, thyroid, parathyroid, adrenal cortex; Keats, Wordsworth, Baudelaire.

The two-choice format can be a useful and stimulating means of measuring knowledge acquisition. It challenges teachers to be reasonably creative in item writing (particularly in choosing non-exemplars) and particularly demands that teachers be aware of what they are trying to measure (i.e., the objective).

MULTIPLE CHOICE FORMAT

Perhaps the most commonly used short-answer format is the multiple choice, although its ubiquity is probably more true in published than in teacher-built tests. A multiple choice item typically offers from three to five alternative answers of which one is correct; the rest are incorrect choices.[3]

Examples
- *John, shy as he was of girls, still managed to marry one of the most desirable of them.*

Directions: Substitute *John's shyness* for *John, shy* and then rewrite the sentence, keeping its original meaning. Your correct rewritten sentence might contain which of the following?
   a. him being married to
   b. himself married to
   c. him from marrying
   d. was himself married to
   e. him to have married

- Which of the graphs could represent the velocity–time relationship of a box containing a weighted disk fastened solidly to it that is set in motion on a horizontal plane with no external friction between it and the plane?

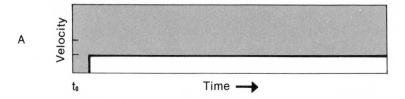

---

[3] These incorrect choices are sometimes called distractors.

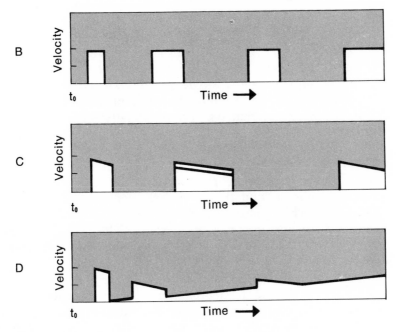

e. None of the above.

- "In a flash it came upon me that *there* was the reason for advancing poverty with advancing wealth. With the growth of population, land grows in value, and the men who work it must pay more for the privilege. In allowing one man to own the land on which and from which other men live, we have made them his bondsmen in a degree which increases as material progress goes on. This is the subtle alchemy that in ways they do not realize is extracting from the masses in every civilized country the fruits of their weary toil."

The person most likely to have written these words is[4]
- *a.* John Jacob Astor
- *b.* William Jennings Bryan
- *c.* Thorstein Veblen
- *d.* Lincoln Steffens
- *e.* Henry George

[4] This and the two preceding illustrative items are from *Multiple-choice Questions: A Close Look* (copyright © 1963 by Educational Testing Service. All rights reserved. Reproduced by permission).

Answers

c, a, e.

Pros and Cons. The correct answer to the first illustrative item, choice *c* (*him from marrying*) was chosen by about 60% of the test group. Using this phrase, the given sentence would be rewritten as follows: *John's shyness with girls did not prevent him from marrying one of the most desirable of them.* Choice *a* would result in a sentence that was grammatically incorrect. Choices *d* and *e* result in sentences that change the meaning of the original. Choice *b* results in a wordy sentence with a somewhat inappropriate tone. In order to successfully complete this item, a student would have to rewrite the given sentence five times, once for each alternative phrase, and then compare them to find the best one. Obviously, such an activity requires more than mere retention of facts; comprehension is clearly elicited. *Well-constructed multiple choice items have the potential to measure comprehension and application.*

Almost all the students in the test group gave the correct answer, a, to the second illustrative item. This high degree of success is based partly on the simplicity of the question and partly on the implausibility of most of the choices, particularly *c* and *d*. A shortcoming of multiple choice questions as used in achievement tests is that *the correct answer can sometimes be determined without any prior knowledge or instruction*—possibly because there are too many clues or too many implausible options or because an item tests the aptitude of the student to deal with it as a novel situation rather than testing for knowledge.

Choice *e*, the correct answer to the third illustrative item, was chosen by only about a quarter of the test group, probably because the correct source of the given quote is the most unfamiliar person of the five given. However, *a certain degree of success on multiple choice items can be obtained through guessing.* Guessing can sometimes be minimized by a built-in penalty, such as scoring the test as number right minus one-quarter number wrong so that wrong answers lose points while omitted items do not.

Multiple choice items are unquestionably *easier to score and easier to analyze* in terms of patterns of incorrect responses[5]—both of which features have undoubtedly reinforced their commercial use—than are other forms of objective items. They are, however, difficult items to write because (1) *they demand plausible response options*, and (2) *they usually require some preliminary*

---

[5] Analyzing patterns of incorrect responses as a way of understanding the nature of students' difficulty can only be done if the response choices are initially constructed to provide for this feature.

testing, analysis, and refinement in order to sharpen the contrast between the correct answer and incorrect choices. Both of these requirements have tended to limit their use by teachers, and, unfortunately when teachers have used them, the items often have not undergone the kind of scrutiny and refinement required for maximum effectiveness.

Writing the Item. Perhaps the most critical part of the construction of a multiple choice item is the selection of the response alternatives—the correct answer and the incorrect choices. The difference in difficulty between writing any other type of objective item and writing a multiple choice item is the selection of incorrect choices. These wrong answers must be plausible to someone who does not know the answer, yet distinctly different from the correct answer. They should tap the kinds of errors that students are likely to make if they have incorrect knowledge or faulty comprehension. Obviously such care in writing items is a tall order. Item analysis, as will be illustrated in a subsequent chapter, can help considerably and the process can also be facilitated by keeping in mind the suggestions offered below.

(1) Consider the kinds of mistakes a student is likely to make and use them as a basis for writing the incorrect response choices.

Not only should incorrect choices separate correct performance from incorrect performance, they should also help diagnose the kinds of incorrect notions that students have acquired. Wrong answers or distractors that tap common errors best accomplish these purposes; those that students never choose are useless and simply serve to reduce the number of effective or working response choices provided. For example:

- The lowest common denominator of ½, ¼, and ⅙ is

good	*a.* 6	or	**poor**	*a.* 4
	b. 24			*b.* 5
	c. 12			*c.* 12
	d. 8			*d.* 2

The choices to the left are better because all four choices represent a common denominator for at least two of the fractions, and two choices represent a common denominator for all three. The wrong choices on the right are too obviously wrong. (The correct choice is *c.*)

(2) Construct incorrect choices that are, in fact, incorrect.
It is equally undesirable for all or nearly all students to select a
particular wrong answer as it is for no one to choose it. If an incorrect choice is over-chosen that means it is probably too close to
being correct itself or that the entire item or one or more answer/
choices are ambiguous. When this occurs, either the particular
incorrect choice or the whole item must be rewritten. Consider
the following examples.

poor • *Twenty Thousand Leagues under the Sea* is considered to be
  a. an adventure story.
  b. a science-fiction story.
  c. an historical novel.
  d. an autobiography.

better • *Twenty Thousand Leagues under the Sea* is considered to be
  a. an adventure story.
  b. a tragedy.
  c. an historical novel.
  d. an autobiography.

In the "poor" example, while *a* is the correct answer, *b* might also
be considered accurate by modern-day students. In the "better"
example, choice *b* is changed to *a tragedy*.

(3) Construct incorrect answers that are comparable in
length, complexity, and grammatical form to the correct
answer.

It is important to avoid giving clues in the construction of response
alternatives. The purpose of an item is to measure what a student
knows and understands and not how clever a test taker he or she
is. Some students have a tendency to choose the longer, more complex, or grammatically different form as the correct one. Equally
long and complex alternatives of comparable structure neutralize
this tendency. Consider the examples below.

poor • When we say that a court possesses appellate juris-
diction we mean that it
  a. must have a jury.
  b. has the power or authority to review and decide appeals.
  c. can conduct the original trial.
  d. can declare laws unconstitutional.

better • When we say that a court possesses appellate juris-
diction, we mean that it
  a. must have a jury.
  b. can review the decisions of other courts.
  c. can conduct the original trial.
  d. can declare laws unconstitutional.

Choice *b*, the correct one, is longer and more complex than the
other choices in the first example and also contains the word "appeals" that can be connected with the word "appellate" in the question. These clues have been eliminated in the second example.

 (4) Write the questions and choices in language that your
   students can understand.

Construct a reading test only if that is your purpose. Do not introduce the various forms of bias described on pages 220–23 and 248
by writing items that measure general intelligence, test-wiseness,
reading comprehension, or knowledge based on a selective interest.
Consider the examples below.

poor • Which of the following is a statement of the Yerkes-
Dodson Law?
  a. The rate of acquisition of habit strength is a
   nonlinear decreasing function of delay of reinforcement.
  b. The relation between intensity of noxious
   stimulation and acquisition of habit strength
   is U-shaped.
  c. The relation between stimulus intensity and
   maximum mean physiologic response is positive and linear.
  d. The response extinction rate is more rapid following ratio scheduling than following interval scheduling.

better • Which of the following is a statement of the Yerkes-
Dodson Law?
  a. Learning occurs more slowly when rewards
   are delayed than when they are immediate.
  b. Learning is greatest when pain or stress is
   intermediate rather than absent or intense.
  c. The more intense a stimulus, the greater the
   bodily response.
  d. Forgetting or unlearning occurs more quickly
   when previous rewards have occurred regu-
   larly rather than intermittently.

In both examples *b* is the correct answer, but in the first the excessive use of complex jargon clouds the purpose of the item. Good measurement is not pedantic. Its purpose is to measure objectives of instruction rather than vocabulary.

>   (5) State your items so that there can be only one interpretation of their meaning.

It is important to be specific as the examples below illustrate.[6]

poor   • The shortest day of the year is in
>   *a.* March.
>   *b.* June.
>   *c.* September.
>   *d.* December.

better   • The shortest day of the year in the Northern Hemisphere is in
>   *a.* March.
>   *b.* June.
>   *c.* September.
>   *d.* December.

By indicating Northern Hemisphere, the second question quite clearly requires *d* as the correct response.

>   (6) In constructing response choices, avoid the use of such words as "always," "never," and "all" whenever possible.

The above kind of extreme words are *specific determiners*. Their use often increases the likelihood of correct guessing by disqualifying an otherwise plausible choice. Test-wise students in particular have learned that things rarely occur either "always" or "never" and that many test builders are using these words to try to throw them off the track. In fact, their use serves as a clue to avoid choices that contain them.

poor   • The theme of Wordsworth's poem, "Composed upon Westminster Bridge," is
>   *a.* a city is always most beautiful in the morning.
>   *b.* the countryside is more beautiful than the city.
>   *c.* the city shares in the natural beauty of all created things.
>   *d.* the city is never an attractive sight.
>   *e.* all the people of the city believe in its natural beauty.

---

[6] Taken from *Making the Classroom Test. A Guide for Teachers* (copyright © 1959 by Educational Testing Service. All rights reserved. Reproduced by permission).

better • The theme of Wordsworth's poem, "Composed upon Westminster Bridge," is
  a. a city is more beautiful in the morning than at night.
  b. the countryside is more beautiful than the city.
  c. the city shares in the natural beauty of created things.
  d. the city is not an attractive sight.
  e. the people of the city believe in its natural beauty.

The presence of "always," "all," and "never" in a distractor often serves to make the choice obviously wrong, thereby reducing its value as a plausible distractor. In the "better" example, these words have been eliminated from both the distractors and from *c*, the correct response.

(7) Do not provide extra clues to the correct answer within the item statement itself.

The items below illustrate this point.

poor • The Missouri city most often referred to as the "Gateway to the West" is
  a. Topeka.
  b. Kansas City.
  c. Chicago.
  d. St. Louis.
  e. Des Moines.

better • The city most often referred to as the "Gateway to the West" is
  a. Topeka.
  b. Kansas City.
  c. Chicago.
  d. St. Louis.
  e. Des Moines.

The poor example provides the clue—*a Missouri city*. In the better example, only the "Gateway" city, *St. Louis*, is asked about.

(8) Do not test more than one point in a single item (except as noted in point 9).

If there are two points you want to test, use two items. Testing for multiple points in a single item makes an item confusing because the student does not know which point to answer.

poor   • The principal value of a daily program of exercises
is to
    a. eat less.
    b. develop musculature.
    c. increase intelligence.
    d. keep fit.
    e. use up extra time.

better   • The principal value of a daily program of exercises
is to
    a. eat less.
    b. develop musculature.
    c. increase intelligence.
    d. help make friends.
    e. use up extra time.

In the "poor" example, either *b. develop musculature* or *d. keep fit*
can be considered the correct answer. Two acceptable answers
make it impossible to key the item. The item is improved by replacing one of the acceptable choices, *d. keep fit*, with a clearly unacceptable one, *help make friends*.

(9) However, multiple points can be made in a single item,
where appropriate, by providing choices that specifically
include two or more of the choices already given.

The so-called multiple multiple choice item uses options such as
"both *a* and *b*," "all of the above," "none of the above," "both *b*
and *c*." The following is an example.

• The principal value of a daily program of exercises is to
    a. maintain optimum weight.
    b. develop musculature.
    c. keep fit.
    d. improve self-image.
    e. all of the above.

Here, the correct answer, *e*, includes all the other choices as well.
There is no reason to avoid multiple or combination answers as
long as they are clearly indicated, unambiguous, and where all or
more than one choice is correct. However, the repeated use of
combination answers as incorrect answers but not as correct answers (or vice versa) quickly leads the student to be clued in to
their relevance or irrelevance.

(10) After the test items are written, vary the location of the
correct choice (between the options *a* to *d* or *e*) on as
random a basis as possible.

It is only natural for test takers to seek whatever clues a test might offer. A response pattern is one such clue. They might note that *e* had not occurred in ten items and use that as a basis for guessing *e* on the eleventh item. By being as random as possible in choosing the location or letter designation of the correct choice, you render this kind of pattern studying a superstitious behavior.

(11) Be careful not to let one question on your test reveal the answer to another or depend on the answer of another.

This is not an uncommon pitfall. To avoid it, read your test over, looking for instances of clues from one item to another. For example:

- *Rien* means
  - *a.* nothing.
  - *b.* something.
  - *c.* laughing.
  - *d.* otherwise.
  - *e.* then.
- *Rien n'est parfait* means
  - *a.* all's well that ends well.
  - *b.* nothing is perfect.
  - *c.* reading is fun.
  - *d.* everything is lost.
  - *e.* ice cream is good.

When a student sees two such questions on the same test, he or she can use one to figure out the answer to the other. In these examples, he or she could observe the word *rien* in each to get answers *a* and *b* respectively.

(12) Response alternatives should be short, unique from one another, and not specifically clued by the question.

The "poor" example on page 94 concerning appellate courts illustrates a question cluing the correct response by means of the connection between the words *appeal* and *appellate*. The "better" example overcomes this deficiency by substituting *decisions* for *appeals*. Following is an example of answer choices that overlap in their degree of correctness.

poor   • An isosceles right triangle contains
  - *a.* a pair of equal sides.
  - *b.* three equal sides.
  - *c.* a 90° angle.
  - *d.* a pair of equal sides and a 90° angle.
  - *e.* three equal sides and a 90° angle.

better • To be labeled an isosceles right triangle, a triangle must contain
  a. a pair of equal sides.
  b. three equal sides.
  c. a 90° angle.
  d. a pair of equal sides and a 90° angle.
  e. three equal sides and a 90° angle.

In the "poor" example, *a*, *c*, and *d* are all correct. This overlap is eliminated by changing the question or stem. The use of the word *must* in the "better" example provides the specificity that enables the student to discriminate between partially correct (*a* and *c*) and completely correct (*d*) choices.

The reader is also referred to Berg (1961) for additional multiple choice item writing rules.

MATCHING FORMAT

Matching items require that the student deal with multiple questions or stems and multiple responses at the same time. Primarily this type of test is used to determine whether the student can distinguish between similar ideas or facts. Matching items are typically considered to be the most difficult type of short-answer item to construct.

Examples
 • (1) was the "father of our country."
   (2) was son of a president.
   (3) was the first secretary of the treasury.
   (4) killed a cabinet member in a duel.
   (5) wrote the Declaration of Independence.
   (6) chaired the Constitutional Convention.
   (7) won the Battle of New Orleans.
   (8) regretted having only one life to give his country.

   a. Aaron Burr
   b. Nathan Hale
   c. James Madison
   d. Andrew Jackson
   e. John Quincy Adams
   f. Alexander Hamilton
   g. George Washington
   h. James Monroe
   i. John Adams
   j. Thomas Jefferson

- (1) The argument   *a.* synthesis
  (2) The opposing argument   *b.* prethesis
  (3) The resolving argument   *c.* thesis
                               d. antithesis

Pros and Cons.   Matching items are fun to take because they are like puzzles and the student has the task of putting the pieces together. They also *enable the teacher to cover a lot of ground* in a single item. In essence they are many items rolled up into one and therefore represent a certain degree of efficiency. A third big plus is that matching items *require students to distinguish or discriminate between things*.

Matching items also have shortcomings, principal among which is that *they are difficult and time-consuming to write well* because writing one matching "exercise" (as they might more appropriately be called than "items") is like writing a half a dozen of another type of short-answer item. They are also hard to write because all the "pieces" must fit together yet each must be clearly distinguishable from every other. It may also be pointed out that matching exercises *cannot be used for eliciting all types of information.* There are certain situations, particularly those involving lists of potentially confusable things, where matching exercises work well and other situations, involving individual pieces of information, where they do not work as well. Finally, matching exercises *have a tendency to provide clues within the items themselves.* Like all puzzles, guides exist to help fit pieces together and every time a correct fit is made, fewer pieces remain and are, therefore, easier to fit. Students usually first match the stems and responses they know go together (assuming no option can be reused), thus immediately reducing the difficulty of the remaining matching tasks because the number of available responses has been reduced. Then, too, stems often contain clues as to the correct response (e.g., the shortest response fitting the shortest stem). Effective writing of matching exercises can minimize these problems.

Writing the Item.   The first rule for writing a matching exercise is that *each item must deal with common elements of a single category* (e.g., all leaders, all parts of a flower). Because cluing is a

---

Answers

(1) *g,* (2) *e,* (3) *f,* (4) *a,* (5) *j,* (6) *c,* (7) *d,* (8) *b;* (1) *c,* (2) *d,* (3) *a.*

Drawing by Dana Fradon, copyright 1974, The New Yorker Magazine, Inc.

Why does a fireman wear red suspenders?
A.☐ The red goes well with the blue uniform.
B.☐ They can be used to repair a leaky hose.
C.☐ To hold up his pants.

principal area of difficulty in a matching exercise, then the second rule for writing this type of exercise has to be: *avoid cluing where possible.* (This, in fact, is a rule for writing any type of test item, particularly those where response options are given.) Some suggestions are: *Keep the responses short, make the responses distinct and nonoverlapping, provide plausible incorrect responses that do not match with any stem.* These extra incorrect response choices will prevent answers from becoming obvious toward the end of the question.

Another very important suggestion is to *select stems and responses that focus on those things between which the student is required to distinguish.* Consider the examples below, in which students are asked to match items in the right-hand column with items in the left-hand column.

poor • (1) ubiquitous   *a.* harmful
     (2) enigmatic   *b.* equivalent to
     (3) deleterious   *c.* widespread
     (4) tantamount to   *d.* purposeful
                             e. puzzling

better • (1) prosthetic   *a.* predictive
　　　　 (2) pathetic   *b.* itinerant
　　　　 (3) prophetic   *c.* artificial
　　　　 (4) peripatetic   *d.* abundant
　　　　　　　　　　　　　　e. pitiable

In the "poor" example the stem words bear little relation to one another; hence, little or no discrimination is required. Secondly, stem *4* and response *b* are clued to one another by the additional word "to." Finally, the one incorrect option is just a random choice and does not relate to the list other than by virtue of being an adjective. In the "better" example, the words all are potentially confusable (at least in appearance), which may affect their discriminability in meaning (since associations tend to become blurred in memory). No clues are inadvertantly provided and the distractor is a synonym for "prolific," another "look-alike" word to those provided.

In fairness to the student it is imperative that you *include all the necessary information within the matching exercise.* Matching exercises, by virtue of their size and complexity, can contain an entire situation with which a student must deal and can be used to measure sequencing, classifying, and analyzing. Consider the following example.[7]

- Read the statements below, carefully paying attention to their relation to one another. Then next to each statement mark *a*, *b*, *c*, or *d*, as indicated.
    - *a.* If the statement contains the central idea around which most of the statements can be grouped.
    - *b.* If the statement contains a main supporting idea of the central idea.
    - *c.* If the statement contains an illustrative fact or detailed statement related to a main supporting idea.
    - *d.* If the statement contains an idea or ideas which are irrelevant.

[7] Taken from *Making the Classroom Test. A Guide for Teachers* (copyright © 1959 by Educational Testing Service. All rights reserved. Reproduced by permission).

Answers

To both exercises: (1) *c*, (2) *e*, (3) *a*, (4) *b*.

(1) The Roman roads connected all parts of the Empire with Rome.

(2) The Roman roads were so well built that some of them remain today.

(3) One of the greatest achievements of the Romans was their extensive and durable system of roads.

(4) Wealthy travelers in Roman times used horse-drawn coaches.

(5) Along Roman roads caravans would bring to Rome luxuries from Alexandria and the East.

(6) In present-day Italy some of the roads are original Roman roads.

Responses should quite clearly relate to a particular stem. When matching items focus on facts, they are much more likely to satisfy this requirement than when they involve interpretation such as is the case in the preceding example; however while the recall of "hard facts" is less ambiguous, it is also less challenging than the more complex process of interpretation.

Matching exercises—like all objective items—*should not contain systematic response patterns.* Do not trust your own ability to scramble the order from one matching item to another. You are more systematic than you may think. Use a table of random numbers (as suggested earlier) or number slips in a hat or a pair of dice.

Finally, *do not mix stems and options in a matching question.* An option may fit many stems (e.g., George Washington in the example on page 100 was many things besides the "father of our country" but the only person referred to as the "father of our country" was George Washington). Keep the stems on the left and the response options on the right with the stem normally being the longer and more specific of the two.

Generally in matching exercises, options (that is, responses) are used only once and that is a good strategy to follow *except* in those instances where you want to make an item particularly difficult or to elicit a pattern or classification (as in the preceding illustration).

Answers

(1) *b*, (2) *b*, (3) *a*, (4) *d*, (5) *c*, (6) *c*.

CHOOSING AMONG SHORT–ANSWER FORMATS

The six types of short-answer items are summarized on a comparative basis in Figure 4.1 While each has certain unique features that make it useful for specific testing needs there are occasions when the types can be used interchangeably. In deciding which type of test to use consider item writing difficulty, item scoring difficulty, and specific measurement purposes (i.e., objectives). Tests that are used extensively or repeatedly generally utilize multiple choice questions because repeated use justifies their difficulty in preparation while their ease in scoring and wide range (i.e., to measure knowledge acquisition, comprehension, and occasionally more complex processes) clearly recommend them. They also lend themselves better to item analysis and hence can be refined and improved.

For the one-time/one-class test, unstructured and completion item types might be recommended because of their ease of construction and because scoring may not be a major problem with a small group. These item types seem to work better with elementary school children who have not developed the test-taking sophistication of their older counterparts. For older students, these free choice item types may yield too great a range of responses. (Some teachers may prefer to avoid altogether the arguments that can ensue from scoring free choice items and thus use more structured formats with any age students.)

True–false items can be used under a wide range of circumstances as a substitute for either multiple choice or free choice items although good "false" items can be very difficult to write. This difficulty plus the great susceptibility of true–false items to guessing, makes them one of the less generally useful short-answer types.

Matching items are time consuming to score particularly on a large-scale basis. They are best used on an occasional basis for variation or a change of pace. In certain situations, however, matching items are the best format to measure recognition of knowledge or comprehension.

Other two-choice item types most readily measure the student's ability to classify and are quite useful in the same context as the free choice types. They lend themselves quite well to worksheets as a way of aiding students in learning classification tasks (within the instructional process). These points are summarized in Figure 4.1.

Figure 4.1   *An Overview of Types of Short-answer Items.*

Type	Format	Sample Item	Difficulty in Writing	Difficulty in Scoring	Measure of	Recommended Use
Unstructured	Free Choice	What form of economic system is most often instituted in African and Asian countries following independence?	Easiest (6)	Can be difficult	Recall of knowledge	One-time/ one-class testing
Completion (Fill-in)	Free Choice	The form of economic system most often instituted in African and Asian countries following independence is _____.	5	Can be difficult	Recall of knowledge	One-time/ one-class testing
True–False (Yes–No)	Fixed Choice	The form of economic system most often instituted in African and Asian countries following independence is socialism. TRUE FALSE	3	Easy	Recognition of knowledge	Multi-group/ repeated testing
Other Two-Choice	Fixed Choice	Circle those African and Asian countries that have introduced socialism upon achieving independence. INDIA GHANA ZAÏRE CHINA SOMALILAND LIBYA	4	Easy for small groups but more difficult for larger ones	Classification of facts	One-time/ one-class testing
Multiple Choice	Fixed Choice	Upon achieving independence, the majority of Asian and African countries turned economically to (A) capitalism. (B) laissez-faire. (C) socialism. (D) mercantilism.	2	Easy	Recognition of knowledge or comprehension (or occasionally of higher levels)	Multi-group/ repeated testing
Matching	Fixed Choice	Match the countries to the economic systems. (1) Capitalism (2) Communism (3) Socialism (4) Isolationism _a._ South Africa _b._ Seilanka _c._ Ghana _d._ Madagascar	Most difficult (1)	Easy for small groups but more difficult for larger ones	Recognition of knowledge or comprehension	Change of pace

Additional Information Sources

Gerberich, J. R. *Specimen objective test items.* N.Y.: Longmans, Green & Co., 1956.

Gerberich, J. R., Green, H. A., & Jorgensen, A. N. *Measurement and evaluation in the modern school.* N.Y.: David McKay Co., 1962.

Green, J. A. *Teacher-made tests.* N.Y.: Harper & Row, 1963.

Scheier, I. H. What is an "objective" test? *Psychological Reports*, 1958, *4*, 147–57.

Schoer, L. A. *Test construction: A programmed guide.* Boston: Allyn & Bacon, 1970.

Wesman, A. G. Writing the test item. In R. L. Thorndike (Ed.), *Educational measurement*, 2nd ed., Wash., D.C.: American Council on Education, Chap. 4.

Wood, D. A. *Test construction: Development and interpretation of achievement tests.* Columbus, Ohio: Charles E. Merrill, 1960.

Free choice
_____
unstructered - ques then 1 word
answer
fill-in, completion   blanks

Fixed choice
_____
TF
other two choice
multiple choice
matching

Self-test of Proficiency

(1) *a.* In a free choice format, students are asked to _____ (*state, identify, evaluate*) the correct response.

    b. In a fixed choice format, students are asked to _____ (*state, identify, evaluate*) the correct response.

(2) Match each item on the left with its type of item from the list on the the right.

    a. The capital of Maine is

1. Bangor.	*i.* other two-choice
2. Portland.	*ii.* unstructured
3. Augusta.	*iii.* multiple choice
4. Bath.	*iv.* completion

    b. The capital of Maine is _____.

    c. What is the capital of Maine.

(3) Which one of the following is *not* a recommendation to follow in writing multiple choice items?

    a. Vary the location of the correct choice.

    b. Make sure that incorrect choices are implausible.

    c. Avoid letting the item clue the correct choice.

    d. Make correct and incorrect choices about the same length.

    e. Make sure that incorrect choices are completely wrong.

(4) Indicate whether each of the following statements is true or false.

    a. Completion items should have a single correct answer, preferably a word or short phrase.

    b. Answers to earlier items should help clue students to answers for succeeding items.

    c. In writing true–false items, one useful rule is to include absolute terms like *always* and *never*.

(5) Given the objective, *Name the first three presidents of the United States in the proper sequence*, write an unstructured, a completion, a true–false, an other two-choice, a multiple choice, and a matching item, to measure this objective.

(6) Given the objective, *Add two 1-digit numbers*, write one of each type of short-answer item to measure it.

(7) Which one of the types of items listed below is the easiest to score?

a. completion	*d.* unstructured
b. matching	*e.* other two-choice
c. true–false	

(8) Which one of the types of items listed below is most frequently used for repeated testings with large groups?

    a. multiple choice

    b. other two-choice

    c. completion

    d. matching

    e. unstructured

chapter five/Essay-type Items to Measure Thinking Processes

OBJECTIVES

1. Describe the meaning of four thinking processes, namely: application, analysis, synthesis, and evaluation.

2. Identify the component parts of essay-type items written to measure each of the four thinking processes.

3. Construct essay-type items to measure the student's ability to use each of the four thinking processes individually and in combination.

4. Name and describe the criteria and procedures for reliably scoring an essay item response.

In the preceding chapter we focused on the use of short-answer items to measure knowledge acquisition and comprehension. However, we are often as concerned with the ability of students to *think about* and *use* what they know as we are with their simply knowing it. In these instances, types of items are needed that allow greater latitude in the form of the response; the response cannot be restricted to a word or phrase. *Essay items provide test takers with the opportunity to structure and compose their own responses within relatively broad limits.* Essay tests enable them to demonstrate their ability to apply knowledge and to analyze, to synthesize, and to evaluate new information in the light of their knowledge. Avoid using essay items when your *only* purpose is to have the students demonstrate that they have acquired certain knowledge.

The process of scoring essay tests is characteristically a more difficult one than the process of constructing the item, one reason being that the answer to the item will usually be many times longer than the item itself. Considerable space in this chapter will be devoted to scoring of essay items.

Again, as in the preceding chapter, we will assume that objectives have already been prepared and a content outline developed and that you are ready to sit down and construct and subsequently score essay tests. Essay items will be subdivided, for presentation purposes only, into those that measure (1) application, (2) analysis, (3) synthesis, and (4) evaluation. (Note that the types of essay questions used for these four purposes are similar; the subdivision is primarily for organizational purposes.)

We will now consider procedures for constructing essay items that can be used for the four different purposes listed above.

ITEMS TO MEASURE APPLICATION

Application refers to the use of knowledge in the solution of problems. As set forth by Bloom (1956), application involves

> . . . the use of abstractions in particular and concrete situations. The abstractions may be in the form of general ideas, rules of procedures, or generalized methods. The abstractions may also be technical principles, ideas, and theories which must be remembered and applied. (p. 205.)

Examples[1]

- You are in charge of planning meals and ordering food at a small summer camp. There are 100 campers—boys aged 12–15 years—and a staff of fifteen adults. You must be concerned both with cost and nutritional value since these will be the criteria for judging your menus. Write out menus for five days of breakfasts, lunches, and suppers and explain why you made the choices you did.

- When a geyser begins to erupt, hot water overflows at the orifice and this is followed by a rush of steam, mingled with hot water. Explain how the first overflow of hot water aids in the production of steam. Show how the principle of the geyser is used in the production of energy (that is, how it applies to one or more of the energy-producing techniques described in class).

- You have just bought a thermometer to measure the temperature in your house and the strip of metal that contains the degree markings has been left off. How would you go about making a set of degree markings so that you could read the temperature using your thermometer? (Do not use more than one side of a page to write your answer.)

Writing the Item.   An essay item intended to measure application must require that the student use knowledge that has been acquired (probably in school) to describe a way of dealing with a concrete situation. Thus the first rule in the measurement of application is that *the item must present a concrete situation*—one that can somehow be included in the reality of the students being tested and one to which they can relate. The second rule in the measurement of application is that *the item must require that some action be taken or choice be made in the situation in order to accomplish a given task*. The third rule is that *the action or choice should be based on knowledge that has been transmitted*. (However, the specific problem itself that measures the application of previously acquired knowledge must be new and unfamiliar to the student.)

The relationship between the required solution and school-based knowledge may be a close one or one that is not so obvious. The likelihood that application will occur increases as the relationship between the task and what has been learned increases. *The*

---

[1] A number of examples in this chapter have been adapted with permission from the David McKay Company, Inc., from Bloom (1956).

teacher can increase the likelihood that application will occur by increasing the salience of the relationship between the knowledge and the task. For example, the item might be: To arrive at a solution, apply the knowledge you have gained in the unit on interest rates. Such a direct instruction establishes the degree of application of school knowledge as a criterion for evaluating performance and is likely to increase the degree of application. The salience of the relationship between acquired knowledge and the task solution can also be increased in more subtle ways within the problem statement itself—often by the inclusion of cue words. In the first example on page 112 the term "nutritional value" may provide a strong cue to the materials that formed the basis for the preceding weeks of instruction. Thus, application can be prompted by directly instructing the students to do it (that is, explicitly making it a performance criterion), or by cuing them toward it by the inclusion of terms dealt with in classwork.

Essay questions are not to be thought of as being entirely without structure. *The greater the clarity and detail provided, the more likely the item is to measure what you intend it to.* In the application item, clarity and detail must be sufficiently present in the two major parts—*the statement of the situation* and *the statement of the problem* or choice—to enable all students to work within a common, understandable context. The less the detail, the greater is the required interpretation simply to understand what is required, a situation that produces a greater range of responses and makes scoring difficult.

In addition to the (1) *situation* and (2) *problem* parts, there is also a part of essay items to measure application called (3) *response instructions*, which represents an attempt to structure responses to some degree. Response instructions include such things as *a.* minimum or maximum lengths, *b.* specific points to be covered or performances required, such as explaining a solution in addition to describing it or stating the number of suggested solutions required, and *c.* various *criteria* for evaluating performance such as organization of material, neatness, and spelling.

Very often in writing an essay item to measure application, one thinks first of the problem and then builds a situation around it. This approach is most common since our objectives usually contain problem statements. Typically, response instructions are added last. Suppose, for example, that your objective dealt with writing skills. First try to think of a practical demonstration of writing skills, for example, writing a letter to apply for a job. Now create the appropriate situation and compose the item.

- You are interested in a summer job and have learned of one as a camp counselor that interests you. Write a letter in proper form to the director of the camp describing yourself and why you want the job. You will be graded on the basis of how clear, interesting, and well-written your letter is, on its neatness, form, and spelling, and how convincing you are.

It is important to realize that measuring application is in a gray area between multiple choice items and essay items. To choose between the multiple choice format and essay format, consider the basic requirements of your objective.

ITEMS TO MEASURE ANALYSIS

According to Bloom (1956),

> Analysis emphasizes the breakdown of the material into its constituent parts and detection of the relationships of the parts and of the way they are organized. It may also be directed at the techniques and devices used to convey the meaning or to establish the conclusion of a communication. (p. 144.)

Typically, analysis is undertaken to identify the elements or parts of concepts or objects, relationships between the parts, or organizational principles among the parts. Once these elements or principles have been identified through analysis, the same problem presented again will only require recall of facts. Thus, analysis requires the student to be accomplishing the process on the specific problem for the *first* time; accordingly, none of the sample essay questions below should have been discussed in class before the test.

Examples
- Galileo was interested in investigating the problem of acceleration of freely falling bodies but had no means of measuring the very short intervals of time over which acceleration occurred. Instead he studied the problem by rolling balls down very small planes inclined at increasing angles, and used the data to extrapolate for the case of free fall. Implicit in the extrapolation was a number of assumptions. Identify two, explain why they were necessary, and comment on their validity.

- Identify four reasons why Hamlet did not kill King Claudius until the end of the play despite his commitment to do so at the beginning. Describe how you determined what these reasons were.
- You have just seen a movie about the United Nations. What are some of the reasons that the U.N. was founded in the first place? Can you think of any other organization in your community that attempts to contribute to the betterment of humanity? What are some of its activities?
- You have just heard a story about a girl who was severely and unfairly punished. Describe some of the feelings that such punishment might have aroused in her. Can you think of times in your own life when you had these feelings? Describe one such time.

Writing the Item.   Similar to application items, analysis items typically include a *situation* or *setting* and *response instructions*. Unlike application items analysis items do not contain *problem* parts. The situation is one with which the student presumably is familiar and that contains elements, relationships, or organizational principles which can be analyzed. Such items often ask the student to make comparisons and contrast, as seen in the example below.

- Consider the ways A. S. Neil and B. F. Skinner might teach a child to swim. In what ways would their techniques be different? In what ways the same? How can you tell?

As in the case of application items, the clearer and more detailed the description of the situation, the less the variability in response and the easier the scoring. Of course, detail can be carried to the point where so few different answers might result that it would be more like a free choice, short-answer item.

The response instructions in analysis items usually call for the student to *identify* certain elements, relationships, or organizational principles. However, the mere act of identifying or listing is basically short-answer performance of the type called for by unstructured or free choice items. To utilize the vehicle of the essay item, it is useful to ask the student to *describe* the basis by which the analysis was accomplished. Another invitation to expand upon an identification is to ask the student to *compare* or *contrast*. (This instruction may also yield evaluation or application. Since the distinction between essay item types in this chapter is made primarily for instructional purposes, there is no reason why multiple objectives and hence multiple thought processes cannot be measured by a single essay item. Most of the examples in this chapter are limited to single processes only for the sake of avoiding instructional confusion.)

Analysis items can be used very effectively in conjunction with students' intellectual, emotional, and aesthetic experiences and provide a basis for determining whether the student can analyze component ideas and feelings contained in and provoked by the experience. This ability to analyze or differentiate the component parts of an experience is according to Harvey, Hunt, and Schroder (1961) an important prerequisite for producing unique thoughts and solutions and hence is worthy of measurement.

While Bloom (1956) suggests the use of multiple choice short-answer items for measuring analysis, the essay approach is recommended here for teachers who want to build their own tests. It is extremely difficult to write plausible distractors for multiple choice analysis items since to do this one must first analyze a situation thoroughly and know many of the pitfalls and cul-de-sacs of faulty thinking. Then, item testing must be done to check out one's choices of right and wrong answers. All of this preparation represents considerable impracticality for the working classroom teacher who will find the use of essay items in this instance an expedient despite the difficulty of scoring them. As was mentioned in the last chapter, the multiple choice item is the raw material for the often used test and is characteristically most effectively employed in published tests.[2]

ITEMS TO MEASURE SYNTHESIS

In describing synthesis, Bloom writes:

> Synthesis is here defined as the putting together of elements so as to form a whole. . . . This is the category in the cognitive domain which most clearly provides for creative behavior on the part of the learner. However, it should be emphasized that this is not completely free creative expression since generally the student is expected to work within the limits set by particular problems, materials, or some theoretical and methodological framework. (p. 162.)

---

[2] However, for those cases where you prefer to use multiple choice exercises to measure analysis, it is recommended that you construct them as free choice items initially and use the incorrect responses to collect plausible distractors.

Bloom (1956) subdivides synthesis into production of *a.* a unique communication (like a story), *b.* a plan or proposed set of operations (like a machine), and *c.* a set of abstract relations (like a theory).

Examples

- Add a second verse of four lines to the verse written below.

  > Men cannot swim
  > As fishes do
  > They only slave
  > A hard way through.

- Draw and describe a design for a mechanical lung. Label all parts in the drawing and explain how the mechanical lung would work and how it would be made.[3]
- Develop and describe a new plan for succession to the vice-presidency of the United States in the event the vice-president leaves his or her position. Give the reasons behind your choice. (Do not simply describe the current constitutional procedures for vice-presidential succession.)
- Suppose you have been put in charge of raising money to build a clinic aimed at providing health services for the poor people in your community. Plan and describe a promotion campaign for soliciting donations.

Writing the Item. Bloom (1956) warns us against limiting the creativity required in synthesis items by making instructions and situations too detailed.

> If the effort is to be rather creative, the student should also have considerable freedom of activity—freedom to determine his own purposes, freedom to determine the materials or other elements that go into the final product, and freedom to determine the specifications which the synthesis should meet. (p. 173.)

As in items measuring application, items measuring synthesis present a problem to be solved. The difference lies in the fact that the application problem requires the direct use of knowledge already acquired while the synthesis problem requires that the

---

[3] This biology item is predicated on the students having just completed units on *a.* the lungs, and *b.* the design of a mechanical heart. Here, they are called upon to synthesize the information on function and structure of the lungs with information on mechanical organ substitution. The idea of a mechanical lung would not have been discussed in class.

"I'm not learning anything. I'm developing cognitive skills."

© Punch

student go beyond his or her existing knowledge to the creation of new and, if possible, unique thoughts and productions. (These new thoughts and productions based on the synthesis of learned information need not be new for society but they should be new for the student formulating them.) Thus, the problem statement in an essay item intended to measure synthesis should be *outside of the range of the familiar or the practical and require the production of a novel solution.* Writing a creative piece, formulating a theory, designing a novel piece of equipment, proposing a new procedure are among the problem statements of synthesis items.

Moreover, *the particular problem itself must also be novel for the student.* That is, he or she should have neither seen the exact problem or a close parallel nor had direct experience with the specific solution through instruction (although the knowledge to be synthesized must have already been acquired). Since synthesis represents or requires original thinking, problems to measure it must be completely *original* from the student's frame of reference.

Bloom (1956) is also concerned about response instructions in essay items for measuring synthesis. With regard to the variable of time, he writes the following.

> Many synthesis tasks require far more time than an hour or two; the product is likely to emerge only after the student spends considerable time familiarizing himself with the task, exploring different approaches, interpreting and analyzing relevant materials, and trying out various schemes or organization. (p. 173.)

It may well be that the procedures a teacher uses for measuring synthesis should themselves have a creative quality. A take-home exam, for example, may provide more of the conditions described above than would a conventional classroom test. Perhaps students should be encouraged to seek inputs from other sources that can be synthesized into their solutions. In some cases the teacher might provide resource material that can contribute to the synthesis task.

It is important to keep in mind the thought that synthesis *should be measured under conditions favorable to creative work* and that testing is usually done under conditions that are perhaps antithetical to creative work. Response instructions should be designed to break the mold of the conventional test and put the student more at ease. Wallach and Kogan (1965) have provided clear empirical evidence on this point at least relative to the measurement of creativity (if not learning). Untimed tests, instructions reinforcing the idea that creativity or novelty or originality is to be strived for, a statement that there are no "right" or "wrong" answers are appropriate kinds of instruction for items aimed at measuring synthesis.

ITEMS TO MEASURE EVALUATION

Of evaluation, Bloom (1956) writes:

> Evaluation is defined as the making of judgments about the value, for some purpose, of ideas, works, solutions, methods, material, etc. It involves the use of criteria as well as standards for appraising the extent to which particulars are accurate, effective, economical or satisfying. (p. 185.)

Bloom (1956) further distinguishes between (1) evaluations based on internal standards such as consistency, logical accuracy, and the absence of internal flaws (more subjective criteria), and

(2) evaluations based on external standards such as efficiency, economy, utility of means for ends, and standards of excellence.

- Write an essay of 250–500 words, evaluating the poem given below. The evaluation should include, for example, the poem's structure, meter, organization, form, meaning, and symbolism. Your principles of evaluation should be made clear—although they need not be elaborately described or defended.[4] Take time to organize your essay carefully. Save time for revisions and proofreading so that the essay as it appears in your examination booklet represents your best intention. It is suggested that you give twenty minutes to planning, eighty to writing, and twenty to revising your essay. *Please try to write legibly* (although handwriting will not be counted against you).

Since there's no help, come let us kiss and part;
Nay, I have done, you get no more of me,
And I am glad, yea glad with all my heart
That thus so cleanly I myself can free;
Shake hands forever, cancel all our vows,
And when we meet at any time again,
Be it not seen in either of our brows
That we one jot of former love retain.
Now at the last gasp of love's latest breath,
When, his pulse failing, passion speechless lies,
When faith is kneeling by his bed of death,
And innocence is closing up his eyes,
Now if thou wouldst, when all have given him over,
From death to life thou mightst him yet recover.[5]

- An important function of the United Nations is to help settle disputes among nations. Describe how one such dispute was handled successfully, pointing out how the settlement illustrates a general strength of the United Nations. Your essay should be about 300–400 words in length (2–3 pages in longhand).[6]

---

[4] The requirement for evaluation in terms of formal characteristics involves analysis in addition to evaluation.

[5] The poem was written by Michael Drayton (1563–1631).

[6] Adapted from *Making the Classroom Test. A Guide for Teachers* (copyright © 1959 by Educational Testing Service. All rights reserved. Reproduced by permission). To do an adequate evaluation, it will be necessary for the student also to analyze.

- Above is a diagram of an electrical circuit in the starting mechanism of a machine. [In the actual problem a diagram is supplied.] Do you think the circuit is sufficient to start the machine? [The specifications of the machine are also provided.] Write a short report stating your evaluation of the capacity of the given circuit to start the given machine. Be as specific as possible in your evaluation and provide as much evidence or support for your evaluation as possible. Keep your report to within two pages.

Writing the Item.   Evaluation items contain two parts: (1) *that which is to be evaluated*, and (2) *response instructions*. Response instructions also include information about the *criteria* that are to be used in the evaluation.

The student must be given something to evaluate. As illustrated in the examples, that "something" may range from a poem to an organization to an electrical circuit. Anything that is subject to rational examination can be submitted to evaluation. Thus, evaluation items can range widely across subject-matter areas.

Students must also have available to them a criterion or criteria on which their evaluations are to be based. Will the "something" work? Is it successful in keeping the peace? Does it conform to the acceptable internal structure? Have its effects been positive? These are some of the criterion questions that can be asked. Beyond this, additional and more detailed criteria must be supplied by the students themselves. Students may be expected to supply the specific evaluative criteria as well as to use them in evaluating that which is given. In some cases these criteria may be objective and universal; in other cases they may be more individual in quality. Usually, there are some of each—some criteria that the student has learned and others that he or she has invented.

Finally, there may be in evaluation items, as there are in all the essay items, specific response instructions about length, detail, and so on. Admonitions for detail or for defending one's point of view are perhaps most frequent in evaluation items since evaluation is intended to solicit judgments and it is the use of argumentation and justifiable supporting evidence that distinguishes between whimsical opinion and responsible judgment. (If only an opinion were necessary, the short-answer format could be used.) It is in defending and supporting an evaluative position that students demonstrate the breadth and depth of their thinking relative to the teacher's objectives and criteria.

Thus, an essay item intended to measure evaluation provides the student with something to be evaluated, a general criterion for evaluating it (at the minimum, and occasionally more specific criteria as well), and general response instructions with a usual admonition to provide detailed support for one's evaluative position or judgment.

An important difference between essay items and the short-answer items described in the previous chapter is that essay items produce responses that may be quite noncomparable and thus difficult to score. (Short-answer items, of course, produce more directly comparable responses particularly in the case of fixed-choice items.) In order to further the likelihood of comparable essays (not equivalent essays but ones that can be *compared*), the types of judgments or evaluations required must be set forth in the item. It is hoped that such detail will eliminate the tendency for some students, when asked to evaluate the poem in the first example, to write, "I liked this poem because . . . ."

A last point in understanding the use of essays for measuring higher cognitive processes is an important one. These processes build on and hence include the "lower" ones of knowledge and comprehension. Where the underlying processes are deficient, the higher-order ones cannot be expected to operate to their maximum level of capability.

ITEMS TO MEASURE COMBINATIONS OF PROCESSES

At times a teacher will have objectives that require a student to demonstrate more than one process in dealing with a problem situation. For example, an essay item might require that a student use synthesis to generate a problem solution and then critically evaluate his or her own solution (e.g., construct a solution to a problem in social management and then evaluate that solution according to given criteria). Another common possibility is for a student to have to analyze a performance and then to evaluate it. For example, the first two sample assignments under evaluation (page 120) require both analysis and evaluation, in the first example of a poem, and in the second example of the operation of the United Nations.

As the following examples show, by combining processes, a single essay item can be used to measure the attainment of two or three objectives.

Examples

- Look at the poster at the front of the classroom. (Posters could deal with any one of a number of subjects; for example, a fund drive, a clean-up campaign, a political campaign, alcoholism.) *a.* Describe what you think the artist was trying to say and how he or she made use of form, texture, color, etc., to say it. Try to be brief and to the point. *b.* How successful would you say the artist was in getting the point across? On what do you base your opinion? *c.* How would you change the poster to better make the point you think the artist was trying to make?
- Write a one-page composition describing the kind of work your mother or father does for a living. In your composition, discuss all the different aspects of the job. For example, does he or she wear a uniform, a suit? Does he or she work indoors or outdoors? Does the job require physical strength? Does it require an ability to deal with details? Does it offer opportunity for advancement? Then, evaluate each part of the description you have given in terms of how well that aspect of the job would fit your idea of the perfect job for you. Defend your judgments.
- Describe ten possible uses for a horseshoe magnet. Then consider each use you have named and decide whether there would be a better way to accomplish that particular purpose. If so, describe the better way.

Writing the Item.   Analysis, synthesis, and evaluation can all be combined in a single, multiple-part item as illustrated by the first example. Giving students an object, an organization, an occurrence, and asking them to *analyze* its parts or workings is the first step. *Evaluating* the parts or workings is the second step and redesigning or improving upon it through *synthesis* is the third step. The major shortcoming of this combination approach is that each part is contingent on the preceding parts: a failure in analysis will serve to affect the subsequent evaluation and the subsequent synthesis. However, since evaluation and synthesis items often leave the responsibility for prerequisite analysis to the students (at least implicitly), the combination item has the advantage of *requiring* explicit analysis before evaluation and synthesis in order to open up the total thinking process.

It would be wise for a teacher to contrast performances of synthesis and evaluation items: (1) those that make no mention of analysis and thereby leave its requirement implicit, (2) those that explicitly require analysis first (i.e., combination items), and (3) those that provide the students with the analysis so they do not have to do it themselves.

The second example on page 123 illustrates the combination of analysis and evaluation. Again the prototype is for the students to analyze a given situation, phenomenon, or object and then evaluate its components against a set of criteria. Often the students themselves must determine the criteria: in this illustration, the various aspects of a particular job in terms of the students' own job ideals.

The third example combines synthesis (or possibly application—depending on how creative the solutions are) with evaluation. The value of this particular combination is that it provides students with the opportunity for creativity but influences that creativity to be functional by virtue of the requirement for self-evaluation. However, it must be made clear to students if they are to generate their own criteria for evaluation, as in the item on the horseshoe magnet. (In some items, the criteria for evaluation are provided.) Also, the teacher must recognize the fact that when students generate their own evaluative criteria their essay responses will not be comparable in terms of content. In such instances the teacher must be prepared to react *primarily* to the process illustrated by the response (as we shall see below) rather than to the content alone.

CRITERIA FOR SCORING ESSAY ITEMS

In essence, scoring an essay item confronts the teacher with the task of evaluation, a process that requires criteria. It is important that these criteria be predetermined and if possible prespecified as part of your objectives. (Criteria can form the basis for constructing a model response at least in outline form.) Following is a discussion of various criteria as they apply to scoring.

Content Criterion   Although the reason for using essay items is not to elicit facts as much as to measure the thinking process, within an essay a considerable amount of information is likely to be presented. The content criterion deals only with the presence of knowledge and its accuracy and not with its application, analysis, synthesis, or evaluation use. All you are trying to judge is whether the content that the student provides leads you to conclude that he or she is knowledgeable in the area of the essay. Since knowledge is the underpinning for thinking and problem-solving skills, some knowledge will be needed as a prerequisite to solving the problem. In essence the content criterion reflects the prerequisite knowledge that the student has acquired in a particular area.

Organization and other writing skills are important components of essay performance and of many other sorts of academic performance as well. If they become criteria for essay response scoring, their importance is likely to become more formally recognized by students.

Organization Criteria

"A composition such as 'My Trip to the Zoo' will cost you 30¢."

What do you look for as evidence of organization? Initially look to see if the problem has been set up or introduced. When recommendations are made, they should be accompanied by supporting evidence. It should be possible for the reader to tell which statements are the recommendations and which supporting statements go with which recommendations. The traditional organization of an essay includes three parts: an introduction, a body, and a conclusion.

An essay response is not intended to be merely thinking out loud, for such a procedure tends to result in rambling. Students should be encouraged to prepare outlines for their responses before writing. A strategy of organization for communicating thoughts reflects a logical mind; thus the kinds of progressions and sequences that are the vehicles of organization should be looked for and evaluated by the scorer of essay questions. In addition, spelling and grammar should be evaluated since they are aids in the communication process. Response instructions should alert students that these various aspects of essay organization will be evaluated.

Process Criteria   Since the major purpose of essay-type items is to measure application, analysis, synthesis, and evaluation skills, or some combination of them, the most important criteria for scoring are those that reflect the adequacy with which these processes were carried out. Each of these processes results in a *solution* or *recommendation* (often with details of its implementation) and *reasons for justifying or supporting that solution or recommendation.* Hence, essay response scoring must evaluate the adequacy of the solution and the adequacy of the reasons behind it.

In essence the scoring of process must focus on the problem-solving behavior that the response is intended to represent. Let us consider problem-solving behavior to include the five steps shown below.

(1) Define the problem.
(2) Generate alternative solutions.
(3) Weigh alternative solutions and choose among them.
(4) Implement the choice.
(5) Evaluate the outcome.

It should be possible to find evidences of some or all of the steps in every essay response, depending on the nature of the task to be done. In general, the first three steps should always be present, and, if the first step has clearly been provided in the item itself, the second and third step should be a minimum performance requirement. Within the second and third step, it may be that only a single solution need be generated (step 2) and that its defense or support would constitute the weighing process. (The teacher would have to predetermine the minimum number of solutions necessary and may or may not communicate this number to the students.)

The evaluation of a problem solution and reasons to support it can be made on the basis of (1) accuracy or reasonableness in terms of external criteria, (2) completeness and consistency in terms of internal criteria, and (3) originality or creativity. *Accuracy* or *reasonableness* refers to the extent to which the proposed solution is judged to be workable, that is, to yield a satisfactory outcome. Will the proposed application work? Have the correct analytical dimensions been identified? Is the synthesized product appropriate? Has the given object been correctly evaluated? Since there are rarely absolute and objectively correct answers to essay items, the decision of solution accuracy is one based on the judgment of the scorer.

Beyond these kinds of suggested criteria, only procedural recommendations can be made for scoring. In the final analysis, scoring decisions are judgmental. The teacher must formulate in his or her own mind those solutions that he or she deems accurate but still must be prepared to consider open-mindedly unanticipated solutions. Criteria of reasonableness and accuracy should also be applied to the reasons cited in support of the solution. Again, judgment must be used in weighting these arguments.

The question of *completeness* and *internal consistency* refers primarily to the extent to which the supporting material is appropriate for and fits the proposed solution, and the degree to which it suffices in dealing with the problem posed. Obviously, partial and incomplete responses will not receive as high scores as complete ones. Obviously, too, the teacher must have a preconceived idea of what constitutes the complete answer to use as a basis for judgment.

Originality and *creativity* both in proposed solutions and in arguments to support them are important components in an unstructured testing format such as the essay. Again, the judgment of the scorer is called upon to recognize the unexpected and to credit it.

Criteria and the Student   It is important to recognize that essay items are intended to measure discreet objectives that have been prespecified in a content outline and that students should be informed of these objectives so that they may engage in goal oriented learning. Objectives, as you may recall, include mention of criteria. Consider the following one.

- Given an impressionist poem, the student will be able to evaluate the effectiveness of its symbolism and defend that evaluation in an accurate, complete, and creative manner.

The point here is that the students should know the criteria that will be applied to the evaluation of essay responses so that they may goal-direct their behavior toward those criteria as part of the learning experience. Rather than being a private and mysterious set of judgments, the bases for scoring essay responses, i.e., the criteria, should become themselves a subject for learning. Moreover, performance feedback to students should contain more than a grade. Students can learn from performance if they are shown how their behavior fit the criteria, and, more importantly, how it did not. The result will undoubtedly be an increased tendency by students to generate essay responses that can be judged successful in terms of scoring criteria.

Three Kinds of Scoring Scales   There are three kinds of scoring scales that can be used for assigning grades to essay responses. These are an interval scale, an ordinal scale, and a nominal scale.

Interval Scale.   An interval scale is made up of a series of numerical scores that can be considered to be equidistant. A useful one for scoring is the one to ten scale shown below.

Note that the distance between numbers is a constant. There is nothing magic about the number ten; it is simply a convenient scale to work with. In using it the teacher would first of all identify all of his or her criteria as shown in Figure 5.1 and his or her weightings for each. As shown in Figure 5.1, process criteria taken together have a weighting of thirty as compared to ten for each of the other two criteria, content and organization. These weightings of course are only for illustrative purposes. You may set any

A Sample Essay Response Scoring Sheet   **Figure 5.1**

STUDENT_____   TEST_____
DATE_____   ITEM_____

CRITERION	WEIGHT	POINTS POSSIBLE	(JUDGE A) POINTS OBTAINED	(JUDGE B) POINTS OBTAINED	(AVERAGE) POINTS OBTAINED
CONTENT	1	10			
ORGANIZATION	1	10			
PROCESS					
SOLUTION					
ACCURACY	½	5			
CONSISTENCY	½	5			
ORIGINALITY	½	5			
ARGUMENT					
ACCURACY	½	5			
CONSISTENCY	½	5			
ORIGINALITY	½	5			

TOTAL POINTS POSSIBLE=50
TOTAL (AVERAGE) POINTS OBTAINED=

$$\text{PERCENT SCORE} = \frac{\text{TOTAL POINTS OBTAINED}}{\text{TOTAL POINTS POSSIBLE}} \times 100 =$$

COMMENTS:

weightings you please as you decide the relative importance of each of the criteria. (For fairness, the scoring system should be explained to students before they write their essays.)

After the scoring sheet has been made up, a useful second step in scoring the essay is to write an outline of the correct essay response in terms of the categories of the scoring sheet (content points, organization points, and the various process points). Your outlined answer should reflect the aspects the student must mention and evaluate in each category in order to earn *full credit*. The value of outlining these aspects is that it gives you a standard model of acceptability against which each student's essay response can be compared.

Now you are ready to read each essay response. The following rules must be established.

(1) hide the name of the student who wrote the essay; read every essay *blind*;

(2) read each essay once (Judge A), shuffle the order and hide your first scores, and read each essay again (or have a second person read them—Judge B);[7]

(3) after you read an essay, use your best judgment (and your outline or model answer) to assign it a numerical score of 1 to 10 (10 being the highest or best) on each criterion.

The importance of *blind* scoring is to avoid introducing a bias based on expectations for student performance. Some teachers have a tendency to evaluate the work of the better students higher (or sometimes harder) because they have come to view them as more likely to produce. The double reading is done in an effort to establish scoring reliability (discussed on page 131) in order to overcome some of the subjectivity of essay response scoring. The interval 1–10 scale is then applied as a best judgment within the structure of the scoring sheet. Note that the scoring sheet forces the teacher to make eight judgments, rather than to allow the entire scoring outcome to be based on a single judgment. The scores from the two judgments or two judges are now averaged, the averages summed to give a total score, and the total score converted into a percentage score by dividing into it the maximum possible score and multiplying by 100.

It seems like a lot of work, and it is! But it is important to guard against subjecting students to the tyranny of a subjective, undisciplined scoring system. The use of a proper scoring system and an outline or model response plus the use of detailed feedback (give the student back a copy of his or her scoring sheet including detailed comments) makes the essay item a constructive and authentic part of the schooling process.

Ordinal Scale.   The ordinal scale simply substitutes overall rankings of the total essay response for scores on each criterion. (Rather than assigning performance on each criterion a score between 1 and 10, the ordinal procedure involves evaluation of total worth of responses on a comparative or relative basis.) First, all responses to an essay item are read through quickly, and then, upon a second, more intensive reading, are placed in a sequence or order from best to worst—considering all the scoring criteria together. The best essay response would then end up on top of the pile, the second best would be second on the pile, the third best, third, and so on until the worst essay response which would end up at the bottom of the pile. You then make a note on a separate

---

[7] Or, if two sets of judgments are impossible because of time, at least read every fourth or fifth essay (chosen at random) a second time.

sheet of paper of the order or ranking and then reread and rerank the responses or have them read and ranked by another person. All judgments should be made blind, that is, without an awareness of who wrote the response. Each essay would then receive the average of the two ranks. The last step is to convert ranks to grades which can be done by assigning the top so many percent an *A*, the next so many percent a *B*, and so on.

Nominal Scale. If you wish to end up with five grades or categories of scores such as *A*, *B*, *C*, *D*, *E* or outstanding, good, acceptable, marginal, and unacceptable, you would read each essay response and then assign it to one of the five categories. (You may first choose to read all the essay responses to give yourself an idea of their relative quality and then read them again and assign each to the category judged to be of best fit.) Like the ordinal approach, the nominal approach is a global one in which criteria are applied in total as a basis for judging performance rather than discreetly and independently as is true in the interval approach. As with the other approaches, judgments should be made blind and either done twice or once each by two readers. In each case the judgment is a categorical one—deciding which of the five categories each essay response belongs in—relative *not* to one another but to the scoring criteria that have been established.

Summary. The interval scoring system represents more work than the ordinal or nominal systems but it is also more systematic, more objective, and more closely related to the kinds of criteria of mastery normally specified in instructional objectives. It is recommended that teachers use the interval method in the expectation that its use will improve their scoring consistency.

INTER-RATER RELIABILITY

The general concept of *test* reliability will be covered in Chapter 10. Here we are dealing with that aspect of reliability known as *inter-rater reliability* or *inter-judge agreement*. The teacher as an essay response scorer is an imperfect measuring instrument, subject—as any human being is—to fatigue, biases, expectations, and other sources of influence. However, because the teacher is functioning as a measuring instrument steps must be taken to insure the greatest degree of objectivity (or consistency or accuracy) or reliability. To this end, multiple judgments are recommended. A second independent judgment will compensate for some of the subjectivity in the first judgment. This second judgment can be made by the same teacher who made the first or by another person. Using the average or mean of the two judgments increases the reliability of the scores.

It is possible to compute the degree of inter-rater reliability by determining the degree of correspondence or overlap between the two sets of scores.[8] What is recommended is that (1) each essay be scored twice by the teacher or once each by two teachers, (2) each set of judgments or scorings be as independent of the other as possible, (3) teachers work on the blind, i.e., not know whose response they are scoring or what score it has already received, and (4) separate judgments be made for each criterion as illustrated in Figure 5.1.

Sometimes reading essay questions twice becomes a prohibitive task, and it is not always possible to find a second reader. When such is the case, randomly select one-fifth to one-quarter of the essays for a second reading to help make some judgment about your scoring reliability.

Example

Two sample essay items, the responses, and the teacher's notations and scoring appear in Figure 5.2a. Figure 5.2b contains the teacher's objectives and criteria along with the scoring rules. By giving back the student his or her essay with the teacher's markings on it (i.e., check marks, underlinings, item scores) along with a copy of the information shown in Figure 5.2b, the student will have sufficient feedback to be able to identify the nature of the information required and of the errors made.

Figure 5.2a   *Two Sample Essay Items from a Tenth Grade Anthropology Course and the Actual Responses of a Student.* *

(1) Name and describe five of the most important features of human beings that make them very adaptable to different environments. (5 pts.)

(2) Briefly describe the everyday life of a typical man of the Australopithecus genus. (5 pts.)

* The markings are those of the teacher.

[8] Technically, this may be accomplished by computing a correlation coefficient between the two sets of scores but for practical purposes it can be judged by eye.

Men and women have been pretty generalized, so they can adapt to almost any environment here on earth. The ✓ most important feature is their <u>brain</u>. Because of our brain we are capable of developing instruments to help us cope with our environment. We are both
✓ <u>vegetarians or <s>carnibars</s></u> carnivores. Therefore, the type of food in our environment doesn't necessarily bother us. We can swim but also dwell on land. We can ✓ <u>survive in the cold</u> with technology, etc., but can <u>withstand the heat</u>. We pretty much can survive through
③ any environmental change. Our brain, leg and arm muscles pretty much help to generalize us.

The everyday life of Australopithecine was based around his searching for food and shelter. He probably woke ✓✓ up went out <u>hunted or gathered his food</u>, <u>slept</u> a little maybe spent
✓ some hours <u>drawing in the ground or counting his toes</u>, and then
⑤ probably went to sleep again. He ✓ didn't <u>need to do much</u> of anything else. Therefore slept and ate ✓ like all wild <u>animals</u>.

Figure 5.2b *The Teacher's Objectives (Including Criteria) and Scoring Rules for the Two Essay Questions Shown in Figure 5.2a.*

Question 1: Objective—The student will be able to name and describe at
(analysis)   least five important features that contribute to human adaptability to environment, drawn from among the following:

> brain—leads to tools, shelter, creativity, etc.
>
> stereoscopic vision—helps us see clearly
>
> eat meat or vegetables—helps us live more completely off the land
>
> delineate hand control—to make things
>
> warm-bloodedness—live in wide range of temperatures, climates, and humidities—lets us tolerate land and water
>
> social cooperativeness—helping one another to survive
>
> long period of caring for young—increases likelihood of survival

Scoring rule—One point will be awarded for each of the above points covered up to five.

Question 2: Objective—The student will be able to describe (drawing from his or her own imagination) the daily life of a typical man of the genus Australopithecus, his or her descriptions dealing with the areas of
> getting food
> sleeping
> culture

and emphasizing the
> routineness of life
> animal-like existence
> primitiveness of culture.

Scoring rule—For each of the above points mentioned by the student in creating the description, one point will be awarded up to five.

Box 5.1

HOW ACCURATELY CAN ESSAY QUESTIONS BE SCORED?

In a classic study of the scoring of essay questions (few, if any, of which have been done so comprehensively since), Ashburn (1938) asked his colleagues in the History and English Departments at West Virginia University to write essay questions for a test to be administered to seventy-five students in the general humanities course. The history professors wrote the following.

Compare or contrast in approximately 400 words life in a medieval castle and life in a medieval town in regard to the following points:

    a. security or the lack of it
    b. sanitation or the lack of it
    c. training of boys for knighthood or industry
    d. recreations or diversions

The English professors wrote the following.

Answer any two of the following questions, in paragraphs or short compositions of 150–200 words each. Wherever possible, support the statements you make by reference to the parts of *The Canterbury Tales* that you have read.

    a. What was Chaucer's plan and purpose in *The Canterbury Tales*?
    b. Show that Chaucer had a sense of humor.
    c. Show that the *Prologue* affords a good picture of medieval society.
    d. Are the characters in the *Prologue* and the *Tales* individuals or merely types?

Three history professors read each of the seventy-five essay responses independently and their scorings were compared. Three English professors also read all seventy-five essays and their scorings were compared. Two weeks later the professors reread and rescored all the essays and these scorings were compared to their first scorings.

How consistent were the professors considering the exceptional care given to the preparation of items and scoring? The degree of agreement was about fifty *percent*. About six percent of the students failed and forty-four percent passed regardless of who scored or when. About forty percent varied from *passing* to *failing* or vice versa depending on which professor did the scoring while ten percent varied between passing and failing depending on when the papers were read.

Judge for yourself. Are you willing to settle for fifty percent?

A Final Point.   We have now covered the two most common types of classroom test items, short-answer and essay. Reasons for use of essay items should not be that (1) they are the easier to write of the two types, and (2) fewer of them need to be written. Essay items should be chosen when and if the objectives to be measured call for the types of processes best measured by essay items, and then only if the teacher is serious enough about objectivity and consistency to use the kind of scoring outline, form, categories, and procedure described and illustrated in this chapter.

Additional Information Sources

Coffman, W. E. Essay examinations. In R. L. Thorndike (Ed.), *Educational measurements*, 2nd ed., Wash., D.C.: American Council on Education, 1971, Chap. 10.

Green, J. A. *Teacher-made tests*. N.Y.: Harper & Row, 1963.

Solomon, R. J. Improving the essay test in the social studies. In H. D. Berg (Ed.), *Evaluation in social studies*. Wash., D.C.: National Council for Social Studies, 1965, 137–153.

Stalnaker, J. M. The essay type of examination. In E. F. Lindquist (Ed.), *Educational measurement*. Wash., D.C.: American Council on Education, 1951.

Self-test of Proficiency

(1) The left-hand column lists the four thinking processes measured by essay items. Match each of these items with its particular characteristic listed in the right-hand column.

a. application.

b. analysis.

c. synthesis.

d. evaluation.

i. puts elements together to form a whole.

ii. applies criteria to judge an idea, a work, a solution, a method, or a material.

iii. measures knowledge acquisition and comprehension.

iv. uses abstractions to solve concrete problems.

v. breaks down material into constituent parts and determines the relationship of the parts.

(2) Essay items to measure the higher cognitive processes should present situations that are novel for the student.

TRUE   FALSE

(3) Construct an essay item to test whether the student can *apply* knowledge gained from a unit on economic theories to a specific situation.

(4) Construct an essay item to test whether the student can *analyze* four potentially confusable animals (birds, plants) to show what characteristics they have in common and others in which they differ.

(5) Construct an essay item to test whether the student can, through *synthesis*, describe a procedure for making a useful object out of materials not normally used for that purpose.

(6) Construct an essay item to test whether the student can *evaluate* a solution to a political problem.

(7) You are about to score essay question responses for your class. List criteria that you would use for scoring.

(8) Check each statement below that represents a recommendation for reliable scoring of essays.

a. read as quickly as possible.

b. use a scoring sheet.

c. score separately by categories.

d. read no more than half the essay at one time.

e. score blind.

f. score twice.

g. read between the lines.

h. construct a sample response.

chapter six / Scales and Procedures to Measure Affective Processes

OBJECTIVES
1. Construct sample affective goals for the classroom.

2. Identify five approaches to the measurement of attitudes, namely: Likert scale, two-choice scale, adjective checklist, bipolar adjective scale, and nominations.

3. Identify and explain rules for writing attitude statements.

4. Prepare a topical outline for use in constructing an attitude scale.

5. Construct four types of attitude measuring items, namely: Likert, semantic differential, adjective checklist, and nominations.

6. State cautions and identify uses for attitude measurement in the classroom.

The affective domain[1] refers to the *emotional* or *feeling* aspects of human functioning in contrast to the thinking or performing aspects (although in many respects, feeling and thinking are interrelated). Of course we are all aware that major portions of our lives and energy are devoted to feeling and that many of our everyday tasks and activities include or provoke feelings to some degree. In other words, it would be extremely shortsighted to exclude the area of feelings from our definition of those behaviors and capacities that are important in dealing with and teaching human beings.

Perhaps the most widely studied of the affective states is attitudes. *Attitudes are systems of positive or negative evaluations, emotional feelings, and pro or con action tendencies with respect to social objects* (Krech, Crutchfield, & Ballachey, 1962). Thurstone (1946) has defined an attitude as the degree of positive or negative affect (i.e., feeling) associated with some object. People have attitudes toward themselves, toward groups of others, toward things, toward experiences, and so on. Attitudes definitely influence the tendencies of people to behave in particular ways in particular situations.

The role and place of the affective domain (and its components such as attitudes) in the classroom is an emergent one. Affective and moral education, value clarification, and other related approaches represent an attempt to formalize an already existing teaching function. Acknowledging the legitimacy of affective goals (e.g., students should like themselves, students should like school) introduces the requirement for some measurement of goal attainment, hence measurement in the affective domain (under proper conditions).

Then there is the matter of classroom behavior such as the ability to work with others; this affective area (call it affective behavior) is of considerable interest to the teacher and has typically been subjected to evaluation albeit of the subjective variety. Many school districts have recently developed systems for measuring affective behavior. Whether or not such systems are currently in the use in the district, the classroom teacher may be interested in the measurement of these behaviors as part of the overall individual student assessment. This behavioral aspect of the affective domain will be dealt with in the next chapter.

[1] The taxonomy of the affective domain was described on pages 41–43.

Box 6.1 _____

SHOULD TEACHERS MEASURE STUDENTS' ATTITUDES?

Many years ago John Dewey's advocacy of the education of the whole child formed the basis for the progressive education movement. However, it has really been only very recently that affective or humanistic education has found its way into the classroom. Many people, professional and lay alike, view the areas of feelings, attitudes, and values as educational dynamite.

Don't you think that it's time for us to forthrightly recognize that all children and all teachers bring their feelings, attitudes, and values with them to school each day and, as a result, much unintended "affective education" takes place? Wouldn't it be better to acknowledge this and provide teachers with the training to carry out intended affective education with a high degree of competence and self-confidence than to let it happen by accident? When a child's feelings are hurt, we can't put our head in the sand and pretend not to notice. We can't depend on all the other institutions in society to make children alert consumers, participating citizens, self-fulfilling adults, and good neighbors. We have to help them learn about their own inner worlds. To do this, we may find it useful from time to time to measure some aspects of those inner worlds so that the measurement can serve as a personal mirror for each child. When this time comes (and it has come), wouldn't you feel more comfortable knowing how to measure attitudes?

_____

While the teacher may have acknowledged the affective domain, and perhaps dealt with it informally, no attempt was made to measure it. The purpose of this chapter is to give the teacher the information and skills necessary for measuring those affective outcomes or states we commonly refer to as attitudes.

Cautions People have a tendency to be more sensitive about disclosing what they feel than what they know. For this reason affective measures tend to produce stronger reactions than cognitive ones. While many adults tend to overreact to or be defensive about the measurement of feelings, children's reactions may be overly naive or nonprotective. In measuring children, then, the task of exercising cautions often falls to the teacher. Here are some suggestions to keep in mind when using or designing affective measures.

(1) Use or adapt existing measures where possible. It is usually reasonable to assume that published or researched tests have taken into account issues of sensitivity. Screen them before using them, however, regardless of source. (Existing tests are described in Chapter 14.)

(2) Do not have the students write their names on their papers if your purposes can be served without knowing individual identity.

(3) Let the students decide what they want to share with their classmates rather than requiring total disclosure.

(4) Do a briefing and a debriefing (before and after) to defuse anxiety.

(5) In constructing your own measure, be aware of and sensitive to the fears and anxieties of students and how your measure might affect them.

(6) Get feedback from your students on their feelings about your measure and modify it where appropriate.

(7) Try your measure on some of your colleagues in order to anticipate student reaction.

Keep these points in mind as you read the ensuing pages.

SOME GOALS OF AFFECTIVE EDUCATION

The classroom is alive with affective behavior, and everything that happens reflects an underlying affective state. Students' moral attitudes influence their inclination to follow directions and their inclination to cheat or not to cheat; their attitudes toward achievement influence their concentration and effort; their interest in what is being taught influences their tendency to behave in an "orderly" or "disorderly" fashion.

Do you as a teacher have goals that you can apply to affective education? John Dewey (1895) talks about techniques to ". . . elevate the school to a vital, effective institution in the greatest of all constructions—the building of a free and powerful character." In other words, Dewey saw the development of character, an affective state, as one of the primary goals of education. It would be fair to say that:

- the student should like school;
- the student should like himself or herself;
- the student should want to learn;
- the student should be willing to work;

- the student should be respectful to other people and property;
- the student should be able to work independently without constant supervision;
- the student should be willing to help others;

and undoubtedly a whole host of other similar goals, are reasonable to apply to the classroom. Moreover, Kohlberg (1973) suggests that there are values or ethical principles that we want to inculcate in children. Thus, he would establish some of the following as classroom goals:

- the student will believe in the value that all people are entitled to fair and just treatment regardless of who or what they are.
- the student will believe in the equality of human rights.
- the student will believe in the inherent dignity of persons as individuals.
- the student will believe in reciprocity (that is, behaving toward others as you would have them behave toward you).

From these kinds of general affective goals, many teachers have evolved more specific ones, such as:

- the student will have positive attitudes toward work.
- the student will be able to think and behave in a flexible way.
- the student will believe that he or she can control his or her own fate.
- the student will take pride in his or her work.
- the student will believe in the essential dignity of physical labor of any sort.
- the student will not hold prejudiced attitudes toward groups.

The classroom is alive with feelings and beliefs; these are transformed into behavior with the teacher, implicitly or explicitly, attempting to increase certain behaviors and beliefs and decrease others. Because the manipulation of feelings and beliefs can involve certain dangers, be sensitive to the possibility of dangers and impose the safeguards that the situation requires. Encourage all students to establish an ethical system that can be used to evaluate behavior, and have them seek universal ethical principles, but be broad in your conception of the attitudes and beliefs that follow thereupon. Remember that the teacher as measurer—as well as the teacher as instructor—bears a responsibility to the student.

ROTHCO

"I feel there's more to education than mere marks. There's the relationship of teacher to pupil, the personal interest and understanding that helps a person mature and grow. . . ."

CONSTRUCTING SCALES

Attitudes and beliefs are typically measured by the use of scales. *A scale is a continuum marked off into numerical units that can be applied to some object or state in order to measure a particular property of it.* We are all familiar with the bathroom scale that provides us with a scale of weight based on the force that our bodies offer in opposition to a spring. In order to measure such intangible things as attitudes, beliefs, or values, we have to construct a numerical scale that can be used to subjectively assess the degree of presence of something, although the social scales that are described below lack the precision of physical scales or of cognitive scales. While scales that measure attitudes and beliefs provide useful information that may not be otherwise accessible, they yield results that cannot be considered exact. (We will consider the issue of test evaluation further in Part III.)

Likert Scale   In the measurement of attitudes the most frequently used scale is the *Likert Scale.* It looks like this:

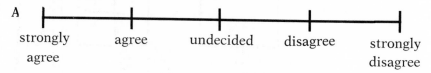

In response to a given statement the student checks that option that most closely represents his or her feeling about the statement. Each student attaches his or her own value to the points on the scale and the statement to which it applies. (We cannot assume that the scale points have an absolute or uniform meaning for all students.) Consider the following example.

- This class was interesting. **SA   A   U   D   SD**

or

- This class was boring. **SA   A   U   D   SD**

Note that the line that represented the scale has been omitted and the words have been replaced by their first letters; for convenience, the student is instructed to circle the letter that best reflects his or her opinion.

Scoring a Likert Scale requires the following: on a positive item (e.g., this class was interesting) score SA=5, A=4, U=3, D=2, SD=1; on a negative item (e.g., this class was boring) score SA=1, A=2, U=3, D=4, SD=5. Add the item scores to get a sum that tells you how positive the attitudes are toward the object or experience being rated.

Two-point Scale[2]   The two-point scale is the simplest form of scale. It has one point labeled *yes* and one labeled *no.* On a two-point scale the sample item above might appear as the following item.

- This class was interesting.   YES   NO

or

- This class was boring.   YES   NO

Although the two-point scale may be somewhat easier for the student to use, and eliminates the middle category (e.g., undecided), it has the disadvantage of forcing the student into a position that might not really reflect his or her attitude. In general, the Likert

---

[2] Two-point response formats are often called checklists. The term will not be used in this instance in order to avoid confusion with its use in "adjective checklist."

Scale is recommended for older students (high school, college) and the two-point scale for younger students.

To score a two-point scale, give +1 for positive answers (*yes* or *true*) to positive items and negative answers (*no* or *false*) to negative items, and −1 for negative answers to positive items and positive answers to negative items. The resultant sum represents the positiveness of the attitude.

The adjective checklist provides the student with a list of adjectives for describing or evaluating something and instructs him or her to check those that apply. For example:

Adjective Checklist

- This class was   _____ interesting
                             _____ informative
                             _____ worthwhile

Unless the adjectives chosen are quite simple and the procedure is explained in detail, the adjective checklist may be too complex for young children. The advantages of this approach are that it cuts down on extra verbiage, is easy to interpret, and helps students to learn about the use of adjectives to describe feelings, thus becoming a useful part of the instructional process.

Scoring is accomplished by counting the number of adjectives checked that are indicative of a positive evaluation and subtracting from it the number of adjectives indicative of a negative evaluation. The result is the positiveness of the attitude.

A bipolar adjective scale is usually a seven-point scale linking an adjective to its opposite and is used to evaluate or describe a particular object or experience. An example appears below.

Bipolar Adjective Scale

THIS CLASS

```
interesting____:____:____:____:____:____:____boring
        bad____:____:____:____:____:____:____good
   pleasant____:____:____:____:____:____:____unpleasant
```

The bipolar adjective approach was pioneered by Osgood, Suci, and Tannenbaum (1953) and is often referred to as the *semantic differential*. Although it is complex, its uses for attitude measurement are widespread, and it has a far greater potential for classroom use than present practice would suggest.

Those pairs with the positive pole at the left are scored by labeling the spaces 7,6,5,4,3,2,1 where 7 is the positive and 1 is the negative end. Those pairs with the positive pole at the right are scored 1,2,3,4,5,6,7. The scores for each adjective pair are then summed, the result representing the positiveness of the attitude toward the object or experience in question.

Nominations Procedure

The nominations procedure can be used as a form of scaling[3] to help measure, for example, students' feelings toward peers or events. In this procedure, the student is asked to name one or more things, people, or experiences that best fit a given category of attitude. Its most common use is to measure liking or friendship patterns. Questions such as Who are the three students you like best? Who are the three you like least? are asked. In response to each question, the student would write in the names of three classmates. This information is then used to plot a picture of friendship patterns called a *sociogram*. Used in the context of assessing attitudes toward classes, the following example would apply.

- Name the three courses that you have taken so far that you felt were the most interesting.

  _____   _____   _____

- Name the three courses that you have taken so far that you felt were the most boring.

  _____   _____   _____

Scoring for this procedure is done as follows: a course gets one point for every student who nominates it as "most interesting" and loses one point for every student who nominates it as "most boring." The final score for each course is the number of "interesting" nominations minus the number of "boring" nominations.

The nominations procedure works particularly well in making relative evaluations. It also has the advantage of being very concrete (students know what it means to name their favorite and least favorite things when asked) and hence can be used with confidence with students of most ages. However, the user must make sure the context of the nominations is clear. For example, a student might not nominate the same three students to do a project with as he or she might choose to play with. For the procedure to be valid, the student must know specifically what it is that he or she is nominating someone for.

---

[3] If one counts up the number of nominations something or someone receives, the result can be considered a scale score on the frequency scale.

WRITING ATTITUDE STATEMENTS

An *attitude scale* contains a series of statements or stimuli each of which is responded to by using a scale. *Attitude statements* are statements about an object, person, or experience to which the test taker responds by using the Likert or two-point scale format. *Stimuli* are the objects, persons, or experiences themselves that can be responded to by using one of the adjective scale formats, or, with slight adaptation, can be used with the nomination procedure. Since (1) attitude statements are somewhat more difficult to formulate than stimuli, and (2) attitude scales containing attitude statements are of more specific use, we will concentrate our greater attention on guidelines for writing attitude statements.

Guidelines for Writing Attitude Statements

Edwards (1957) in his book, *Techniques of Attitude Scale Construction*, suggests criteria to be used in the construction of attitude statements. These will be offered here along with some additional elaboration.

(1) *Avoid Factual Statements.*

An attitude statement should require a student to speculate or to project, rather than to report on the truth or falsity of facts. Factual statements fit into cognitive measurement and should be excluded from affective measurement. Consider some examples.

poor	• Career education programs require considerable developmental funds to begin.
better	• The price tag for starting up career education programs is too high to be warranted.
poor	• My teacher punishes children when they misbehave.
better	• I am frightened of being punished by my teacher.

(2) *Avoid Reference to the Past.*

Attitude statements should be written in the present or future tense rather than the past tense since attitude measurement relates to the current state of attitudes that are held and their anticipated effects. Consider the examples below.

poor	• I have always gotten good grades when I wanted to.
better	• I can get good grades when I want to.
poor	• Last year when I got a poor report card, my mother got mad.
better	• If I get a poor report card, my mother will get mad.

Items that refer to the past measure self-reports of behaviors that have already occurred. While such reported behaviors may be quite legitimate for measurement, they do not reflect the attitudes of the student. Attitude measurement requires that the student project himself or herself into a situation rather than reporting on what has happened in that situation. It is the speculative nature of that judgment that provides a means of finding out what a student's attitudes are.

(3) *Avoid Multiple Interpretations.*
An attitude statement must be interpretable in only a single way. If it provokes more than one interpretation, students will not know how to respond to it; that is, which interpretation to respond to. Some examples may help clarify this point.

poor	• My teacher demands high levels of performance.
better	• My teacher assists and encourages students to perform well.
poor	• I am my own worst enemy.
better	• I have a tendency to get myself in trouble in many situations.

For example, "my teacher demands high levels of performance" could be interpreted as representing a positive expression of motivation and support or a negative one of excessiveness and overbearing, and thus not lead a student to know how to use the statement to reflect his or her true attitude.

(4) *Avoid Irrelevancies.*
Attitude scales are written to measure attitudes toward a specific object, be that object a person (like "oneself"), a thing (like "a book"), an idea (like "freedom"), or an experience (like "school"). All of the attitude statements in that scale must refer to that object and to no other. Statements that refer to any object other than the one under consideration are irrelevant. Some examples appear below.

poor	• My morning walk (or ride) to school is a pleasant one.
better	• I look forward each morning to going to school.
poor	• The principal in this well-designed building is very supportive of teachers.
better	• The principal of this school is very supportive of teachers.

Naturally, what is irrelevant on one instrument may be relevant on another depending on what the object of measurement is. Check your items against the object toward which you intend to measure attitudes in order to be sure they all are relevant.

(5) *Avoid Nondistinguishers.*
Do not include statements that every student is likely to agree with or that no student is likely to agree with. The purpose of an attitude scale is to distinguish between people holding favorable attitudes and those holding unfavorable ones. Items that fail to distinguish between various attitude positions are of no use whatever on an attitude measure.

poor	• I would rather go to school than do anything else.
better	• School is one of my more pleasant experiences.
poor	• The United Nations has an important responsibility in the world.
better	• The existence of the United Nations makes me feel confident about the future of the world.

(6) *Cover the Full Range.*
The set of attitude statements should reflect the full range in which an object, person, or experience can be conceived rather than just one or two facets. To insure full coverage it is best to begin with a content outline that identifies the areas in which the attitude will be measured. Consider the task of measuring *attitudes of educators toward the open classroom.* A content outline might look like this:

student benefits from open classroom	philosophical appeal
maximal use of resources	positive British results
turnover costs to system	"too much" freedom
building limitations	

By constructing an attitude scale that contains several statements for each of the above areas the full range of the attitude will be covered rather than restricted to a limited aspect.

Suppose the attitude scale were to measure *attitudes toward school.* The content outline might include:

effects of other students	parental demands
effects of the teacher	the total school climate
—interpersonal	meeting self needs
—instructional	

(7) *Write Simply, Clearly, Directly.*
Do not use big, confusing words when they can be avoided. Attitude statements must be clear and easy to understand. Remember, attitude tests are not intended to be measures of intelligence; they should not tax the student's ability to understand. Below are examples:

poor • As a subject, chemistry provokes my strong involvement.

better • I like to study chemistry.

poor • People's treatment of other people should reflect a reciprocal concept of justice.

better • People should treat others the way they would like to be treated.

(8) *Write Short Statements.*
Attitude statements should rarely if ever exceed twenty words. Long attitude statements are much more likely to break one of the other rules than are short statements. Witness below:

poor • When a person finds himself or herself in a situation in which he or she can take advantage of another person, he or she can usually be expected to do so.

better • Basically, people can't be trusted.

poor • In any kind of choice situation, we are likely to find that different people will react in ways that are idiosyncratic to them, and we should be willing to tolerate different kinds of behavior.

better • People have a right to do things their own way.

(9) *One Thought per Statement.*
If an attitude statement contains two thoughts (such as people are different, and differences are tolerable), how will a student know which to respond to (to both? or if to one, which one?) and how will you know which he or she has responded to? This problem is best avoided by restricting statements to a single thought as illustrated below:

poor • A good teacher knows his or her subject matter and treats all students fairly.

better • A good teacher treats all students fairly.

poor • Although I am often very lonely, I am easy to like.

better • I am easy to like.

If you write an item that has two thoughts, convert it into two items with each item containing one of the thoughts. In this way, each item will elicit only a single reaction from a person.[4]

(10) *Avoid "All," "Always," "None," and "Never."*
These universal words often introduce ambiguity into a statement or else render it automatically acceptable or unacceptable. At best these words add nothing; at worst they add either confusion or certainty.

poor	•	I never met a person I didn't like.
better	•	I find that I like most people I meet.
poor	•	I always feel I'm acting rather than being true to myself.
better	•	I often feel I'm acting rather than being true to myself.

When you are tempted to use one of the universal words, try to substitute words like "often," or "rarely," or "most." These words avoid the pitfall of eliciting universal agreement or disagreement.

(11) *Use "Only," "Just," "Merely" Sparingly.*
These words also introduce ambiguity and can often be eliminated. It is not that they must be entirely avoided; the rule is that an entire attitude scale not contain this kind of qualifier word in *every* statement.

poor	•	Organized religion is the only way that people can express their faith.
better	•	Organized religion is the best way that people can express their faith.
poor	•	Teachers just can't be trusted to be fair.
better	•	Teachers can't be trusted to be fair.

In the first example, the use of the word "only" would not necessarily invalidate the item unless it had been used in many of the items contained in the total scale. Its use, however, poses the problem of making an attitude statement too universal in its acceptance or rejection. Changing or eliminating words such as "only" or "just" helps minimize this problem.

---

[4] Many of these rules (such as this one, for example) can also be applied to the writing of short-answer type cognitive items such as true–false items. (Refer to Chapter 4 for a description of writing true–false items.)

(12) *Use Simple Sentences.*

The "one thought" approach is also the simple sentence approach. By avoiding sentences with clauses attached and by avoiding sentences replete with commas, attitude statements can usually be kept simple, direct, and to a single point.

poor • All other things being equal, a person's fate can be determined by how hard he or she works.

better • Hard work insures a person's fate.

poor • Vocational education programs, particularly those that lead to immediate employment, are highly desirable for the local school to offer.

better • Local schools should offer vocational education programs.

(13) *Avoid Double Negatives.*

The use of two negative words (e.g., *no, not, none*) in one sentence serves only to make the sentence more difficult to understand. Such sentences can often be written with no negative words since the negative words can be thought of as cancelling each other.

poor • No teacher in this school does not respect student rights.

better • Teachers in this school respect student rights.

poor • Nothing I could say about myself would not be good.

better • I can only say good things about myself.

Figure 6.1 *Summary of the Thirteen Guidelines for Writing Attitude Statements.**

(1) Avoid factual statements.
(2) Avoid reference to the past.
(3) Avoid multiple interpretations.
(4) Avoid irrelevancies.
(5) Avoid nondistinguishers.
(6) Cover the full range.
(7) Write simply, clearly, directly.
(8) Write short statements.
(9) One thought per statement.
(10) Avoid "all," "always," "none," and "never."
(11) Use "only," "just," "merely," etc., sparingly.
(12) Use simple sentences.
(13) Avoid double negatives.

* Edwards, 1957.

In summary, then, (see Figure 6.1) one should try to write attitude statements that are quite simple and readable, that relate to a single point, and that are not likely to be agreed with or disagreed with by everyone (although students' responses may tend to be similar if students come from similar backgrounds). Such statements should be clear and understandable and register as wide a range of attitudes as are present in the group of respondents.

CONSTRUCTING A LIKERT AND TWO-POINT ATTITUDE SCALE

The purpose of this section is to describe the procedures to be used in constructing the Likert and two-point types of attitude scales. Typically this category of scales is revised following its first use to eliminate poor items. The revision is based on item analysis, which will be explained in Chapter 10.

Before starting construction of the scale, the teacher or other test designer must decide what the purpose or objective of the attitude scale is, that is, the area toward which attitudes are to be measured (e.g., self, school, teacher, chemistry, team teaching). The first step assumes that you have identified the attitude area to be measured.

(1) Preparing a Topical Outline. The topical or content outline was described briefly on page 149. It is a delineation of the attitude area into topical or subareas that, taken together, constitute the various aspects of the attitude area to be measured. Suppose, for example, that you are trying to measure high school students' attitudes toward the emerging and changing role of women in conjunction with a program dealing with male–female relationships. The categories offered below would serve as a useful outline of topics contained within this particular attitude. (Item numbers refer to Fig. 6.2.)

- Topics to measure attitudes toward the emerging and changing role of women:
  (1) relative superiority (items 1,3,13)
  (2) division of labor (items 2,7,20)
  (3) claim to education (items 11,12,19)
  (4) social roles (items 8,14,17)
  (5) career stereotypes (items 15,18,21)
  (6) in school (items 5,6,10)
  (7) clothes and styles (items 4,9,16)

In other words, the outline provides specific targets or topics around which to write items; having such an outline avoids writing them haphazardly on a global theme (such as attitudes toward the emerging and changing role of women). The more detailed the outline, the easier it will be to generate appropriate attitude statements. In the above example, attitudes toward women's changing role were essentially defined as being the collective result of attitudes toward various aspects of a woman's role in relation to a man's role: relative superiority, division of labor, education, social interaction, career, stereotypes, school activities, clothes and styles.

Figure 6.2 *A Sample Attitude Scale To Measure Students' Attitudes toward the Emerging and Changing Role of Women.**

ATTITUDE SURVEY

Instructions: Below are 21 statements with which you should indicate your agreement or disagreement. Read each statement carefully and then circle a letter below each to indicate your feelings about that statement. If you *strongly agree* with the statement, circle SA; if you *agree* with it, circle A; if you *disagree*, circle D; and if you *strongly disagree*, circle SD. This is not a test. There are no right or wrong answers. This is a measure of how you *feel* about some things. *You will not have to put your name on your paper.* Any questions?

(1) Boys are superior because they are physically stronger than girls.

SA   A   D   SD

(2) If there are both boys and girls in a family, only the girls should do jobs like dishwashing and cleaning.

SA   A   D   SD

(3) Girls can be leaders just as well as boys can.

SA   A   D   SD

(4) The trend toward unisex styles of dress is a good one.

SA   A   D   SD

(5) Physical education classes should be coeducational.

SA   A   D   SD

(6) It's unfeminine for a girl to play the drums in the band.

SA   A   D   SD

(7) It's all right for a boy to do some of the cooking for the family.

SA   A   D   SD

(8) The boy should pay the cost of a date.

SA   A   D   SD

(9) Girls should wear dresses or skirts unless they are doing something that really requires them to wear slacks.

SA   A   D   SD

(10) Boys should be allowed to study home economics or early childhood education if they want to.

SA   A   D   SD

(11) Parents should make as much effort to give their daughters as good an education as their sons.

SA   A   D   SD

(12) Colleges and universities should not have quotas based on sex for accepting students.

SA   A   D   SD

(13) Girls are the weaker sex.

SA   A   D   SD

(14) A girl shouldn't destroy a boy's ego by winning games like chess or golf.

SA   A   D   SD

(15) Girls who want to study engineering are not feminine.

SA   A   D   SD

(16) A boy who has his hair styled by a men's stylist must be a bit odd.

SA   A   D   SD

(17) It's all right for a girl to ask a boy for a date.

SA   A   D   SD

(18) It's better for society if men and women have clear-cut work roles and people know what careers they may or may not select in life.

SA   A   D   SD

(19) If a couple wants to get married while they are in college, the girl should quit school and get a job so that the boy can finish his education.

SA   A   D   SD

(20) A man who stays home to take care of the children while his wife goes out to work is losing his masculinity.

SA   A   D   SD

(21) Men should get higher pay because they have to support families.

SA   A   D   SD

* This scale was developed by the Educational Evaluation Group of Highland Park, N.J., © 1974, and is reproduced here with their permission.

(2) Writing Pro and Con Statements. Once the topical outline is complete, you are ready to begin writing attitude statements. Write about half of your attitude statements in a pro or positive direction with respect to the topic and half in a con or negative direction, to avoid what has been referred to earlier as *acquiesence* or *response bias* (page 221). If a student checks "yes" or "strongly agree" on every item because he or she is lazy or hostile or asleep or misunderstands, he or she will convey the misleading impression of being quite favorably inclined toward the topic. If, however, about half of the items go in each direction, such students will just cancel themselves out, being half positive and half negative. Morever, the change of pace—from pro to con items—may be stimulation enough to keep students alert.

Start with your first subtopical area, which in the illustration (positiveness of attitudes toward changing roles of women) is "relative superiority." Think of a good positive statement and a good negative statement and then write one of each adhering to the thirteen rules presented in the preceding pages. Below is one positive and one negative item on the subtopic of relative superiority of the sexes.

(+)   • Girls can be leaders just as well as boys can.
(−)   • Girls are the weaker sex.

In constructing the test do not put all the positive items together. Randomly locate positive and negative items with respect to one another to produce a good mix.

(3) Selecting a Response Format.   After all the items have been written you must decide which response format to use, the Likert, the yes–no, or some variant of either. Consider the level of maturity of your students. For elementary and middle school students, generally the simpler yes–no approach is recommended. For secondary school students or adults, the Likert approach yields more information. (Users of the Likert scale occasionally leave the middle "undecided" response category off the scale to insure that all responses will reflect a directional opinion. The illustration in Figure 6.2 uses a Likert scale so modified.) Once you have chosen your format and have written your items, you are ready to try out your attitude scale. (Procedures for revision based on student responses to improve validity and reliability will be discussed in Part III.)

If you have followed the instructions for test development described here and utilized a topical outline based on your objectives, your resulting instrument should have a high degree of *appropriateness* for meeting your objectives. After trying it out (see the cautions on page 141) you will have a better idea of its worth.

The attitude scale for measuring the positiveness of students' attitudes toward the emerging role of women, from which the previous examples of a content outline (see page 153) have been drawn, appears in Figure 6.2 as an illustration of the Likert approach. The illustrative scale has been given the innocuous title of "Attitude Survey" rather than "The Emerging Role of Women Scale" (although that is its topic) in order not to oversensitize the students to the scale's topic and thereby influence their judgments.

A Sample Attitude Scale

CONSTRUCTING ADJECTIVE ATTITUDE SCALES

An adjective scale is composed of (1) a stimulus word or phrase for the students to react to and (2) a list of adjectives by which to react. The list of adjectives can be used over and over again for different stimulus words; only the stimulus words or object to be rated needs to be changed.

To construct such a scale, decide on the stimulus words or object first. (A sample list of stimuli appears in Figure 6.3.) Then select a list of adjectives. Osgood, Suci, and Tannenbaum (1953) have found that when adjectives are used that do not relate exclusively to the stimulus to be rated (such as rating "behavioral objectives" as "clean" or "dirty"), they generally fall into the following areas of meaning: (1) evaluative (e.g., good–bad), (2) potency

Sample Stimuli for Measuring Attitudes in a Variety of Attitude Areas.   **Figure 6.3**

Attitude Area	Sample Stimuli		
Self-appraisal	I am	Myself	Me
School sentiment	School	My class	My teacher
Specific experiences	Today's field trip	This movie	Today's speaker
Values	Helping others	Hard work	Independence
Current events	The U.N.	Organized labor	Common cause
Educational programs	Career education	Open classroom	Team teaching
Interests	Baseball	Science	Birdwatching
Other people	Classmates	My group leader	My friends
Activities	Doing homework	Watching T.V.	Helping Mom

(e.g., strong–weak), and (3) activity (e.g., active–passive). An example of the use of an adjective scale of the Osgood et al. variety appears in Figure 6.4. An example of the use of an attitude scale (and its scoring) of the more specific type appears in Figure 6.5. These types of scales are called *semantic differentials*.

Semantic Differential   The major task in constructing a semantic differential is in selecting adjectives. Osgood, Suci, and Tannenbaum (1953) provide a lengthy list of adjectives for general use from which the twelve adjective pairs shown in Figure 6.4 are taken. Of the twelve, those five that provide an *evaluation* of the stimulus (i.e., "behavioral objectives") are dirty–clean, good–bad, unpleasant–pleasant,

Drawing by Frank Modell, copyright 1972, The New Yorker Magazine, Inc.

"Just because the painting doesn't happen to appeal to Marvin doesn't necessarily mean it stinks."

A Sample Semantic Differential.   **Figure 6.4**

Behavioral Objectives

(1)	DIRTY	_____:_____	:_____	:_____	:_____	:_____	:_____	CLEAN
(2)	SHARP	_____:_____	:_____	:_____	:_____	:_____	:_____	DULL
(3)	GOOD	_____:_____	:_____	:_____	:_____	:_____	:_____	BAD
(4)	STRONG	_____:_____	:_____	:_____	:_____	:_____	:_____	WEAK
(5)	RUGGED	_____:_____	:_____	:_____	:_____	:_____	:_____	DELICATE
(6)	UNPLEASANT	_____:_____	:_____	:_____	:_____	:_____	:_____	PLEASANT
(7)	HONEST	_____:_____	:_____	:_____	:_____	:_____	:_____	DISHONEST
(8)	PASSIVE	_____:_____	:_____	:_____	:_____	:_____	:_____	ACTIVE
(9)	BEAUTIFUL	_____:_____	:_____	:_____	:_____	:_____	:_____	UGLY
(10)	LIGHT	_____:_____	:_____	:_____	:_____	:_____	:_____	HEAVY
(11)	LARGE	_____:_____	:_____	:_____	:_____	:_____	:_____	SMALL
(12)	SLOW	_____:_____	:_____	:_____	:_____	:_____	:_____	FAST

Scoring:

Evaluation = (item 3 + item 7 + item 9) − (item 1 + item 6)

Potency = (item 4 + item 5 + item 11) − item 10

Activity = item 2 − (item 8 + item 12)

honest–dishonest, and beautiful–ugly. *Potency* is measured by strong–weak, rugged–delicate, light–heavy, and large–small; *activity* by sharp–dull, passive–active, and slow–fast.

You will note on the instrument shown in Figure 6.4 that some of the adjectives have been written with the positive end on the left, some with the positive end on the right. This is the counterpart of positive and negative attitude statements on the Likert Scale. Since people read from left to right in English, those adjective pairs with the positive pole on the left are considered positive items (e.g., GOOD–BAD) while those pairs with the negative pole on the left are considered negative items (e.g., DIRTY–CLEAN). Like the Likert Scale, an approximate balance and random order of positive and negative items are sought. For ease of scoring, positive and negative items can both be scored 7 : 6 : 5 : 4 : 3 : 2 : 1,[5] and then the score on negative items subtracted from scores on positive items to arrive at a total score. This approach is used in Figures 6.4 and 6.5.

[5] Previously, the scoring of a semantic differential was explained by having positive and negative items scored in opposite directions. The approach here yields the same result but is quicker.

For the semantic differential, you should (1) use the adjective pairs given in Figure 6.4, or (2) use others on the Osgood, Suci, and Tannenbaum (1953) list, or (3) make up your own pairs. A single pair or two will not suffice in assuring adequate reliability; a dozen adjective pairs is generally a good number to work with.

The semantic differential is a quick and fairly easy way of assessing attitudes. The use of the kind of general adjectives shown in Figure 6.4 often disguises the desirable response thereby reducing the tendency toward conscious distortion. It is a recommended way for teachers to put themselves in frequent contact with their students' attitudes on a variety of issues, particularly for feedback purposes.

Figure 6.5a shows a more specific semantic differential, one that is used for description of a teacher's behavior by students, colleagues, or other observers. The purpose of this description is primarily to supply the teacher with feedback. The adjectives have been specifically chosen to fit the four factors or clusters shown in the scoring instructions[6] (Figure 6.5b).

Figure 6.5a *Tuckman Teacher Feedback Form (TTFF)**

Teacher Observed _____ Date _____

Observer _____

Class _____

Place an X in that one space of the seven between each adjective pair that best indicates your perception of the teacher's behavior. The closer you place your X toward one adjective or the other, the more you think that adjective better describes the teacher than the other.

(1)	ORIGINAL	____:____:____:____:____:____:____	CONVENTIONAL
(2)	PATIENT	____:____:____:____:____:____:____	IMPATIENT
(3)	COLD	____:____:____:____:____:____:____	WARM
(4)	HOSTILE	____:____:____:____:____:____:____	AMIABLE
(5)	CREATIVE	____:____:____:____:____:____:____	ROUTINIZED
(6)	INHIBITED	____:____:____:____:____:____:____	UNINHIBITED
(7)	ICONOCLASTIC	____:____:____:____:____:____:____	RITUALISTIC
(8)	GENTLE	____:____:____:____:____:____:____	HARSH

[6] Actually a statistical procedure called factor analysis was used to confirm the clusters shown on the scoring sheet. For more information about this statement, see Tuckman (1974).

(9)	UNFAIR	___:___:___:___:___:___:___	FAIR
(10)	CAPRICIOUS	___:___:___:___:___:___:___	PURPOSEFUL
(11)	CAUTIOUS	___:___:___:___:___:___:___	EXPERIMENTING
(12)	DISORGANIZED	___:___:___:___:___:___:___	ORGANIZED
(13)	UNFRIENDLY	___:___:___:___:___:___:___	SOCIABLE
(14)	RESOURCEFUL	___:___:___:___:___:___:___	UNCERTAIN
(15)	RESERVED	___:___:___:___:___:___:___	OUTSPOKEN
(16)	IMAGINATIVE	___:___:___:___:___:___:___	EXACTING
(17)	ERRATIC	___:___:___:___:___:___:___	SYSTEMATIC
(18)	AGGRESSIVE	___:___:___:___:___:___:___	PASSIVE
(19)	ACCEPTING (people)	___:___:___:___:___:___:___	CRITICAL
(20)	QUIET	___:___:___:___:___:___:___	BUBBLY
(21)	OUTGOING	___:___:___:___:___:___:___	WITHDRAWN
(22)	IN CONTROL	___:___:___:___:___:___:___	ON THE RUN
(23)	FLIGHTY	___:___:___:___:___:___:___	CONSCIENTIOUS
(24)	DOMINANT	___:___:___:___:___:___:___	SUBMISSIVE
(25)	OBSERVANT	___:___:___:___:___:___:___	PREOCCUPIED
(26)	INTROVERTED	___:___:___:___:___:___:___	EXTROVERTED
(27)	ASSERTIVE	___:___:___:___:___:___:___	SOFT-SPOKEN
(28)	TIMID	___:___:___:___:___:___:___	ADVENTUROUS

* Copyright 1971 by Bruce W. Tuckman.

Tuckman Teacher Feedback Summary Sheet   **Figure 6.5b**

The scores on those items are written with the negative pole on the left are subtracted from those with the positive pole on the left. To avoid having the resulting score for a factor be a negative number—which will happen if the sum of scores to be subtracted (on the right) exceeds the sum from which they are subtracted (on the left)—a number (either 18 or 26) that is greater by one than the maximum possible negative score is added.

(1) Item Scoring
    a. Under the last set of dashes on the sheet of 28 items write the numbers *7-6-5-4-3-2-1.* This will give a number value to each of the seven spaces between the 28 pairs of adjectives.
    b. Determine the number value for the first pair, *original–conventional.* Write it into the formula given below on the appropriate line under Item 1. For example, place an *X* on the first dash next to *original* in item 1, then write the number 7 on the dash under item *1* in the summary formula on the next page.

     c. Do the same for each of the twenty-eight items. Plug each value into the formula.

     d. Compute the score for each of the four dimensions in the summary formula.

(2) Summary Formula and Score for the Four Dimensions

     a. Creativity

         Item $(1+5+7+16)-(6+11+28)+18$

            $(|+|+|+|)-(|+|+|)+18 = \underline{\hphantom{xxxxx}}$

     b. Dynamism (dominance and energy)

         Item $(18+21+24+27)-(15+20+26)+18$

            $(|+|+|+|)-(|+|+|)+18 = \underline{\hphantom{xxxxx}}$

     c. Organized Demeanor (organization and control)

         Item $(14+22+25)-(10+12+17+23)+26$

            $(|+|+|)-(|+|+|+|)+26 = \underline{\hphantom{xxxxx}}$

     d. Warmth and Acceptance

         Item $(2+8+19)-(3+4+9+13)+26$

            $(|+|+|)-(|+|+|+|)+26 = \underline{\hphantom{xxxxx}}$

The Adjective Checklist

The adjective checklist features a list of adjectives to be applied to some stimulus or object in order to reflect a person's attitudes toward that stimulus or object. Typically, both positive and negative adjectives are used and the student is asked to rate the applicability of each adjective to the object rather than simply checking those that apply. An example of this type of instrument for measuring self-concept appears in Figure 6.6. As was true for the other types of attitude instruments, this instrument is scored by scoring the negative items in the opposite direction from the positive items.

Figure 6.6 *The I AM Form.*

Below is a list of words. These words can be used to describe people. For example, "she is a *smart* person" or "you are a *happy* person," or "I am a *mean* person." Think about each word, one at a time. Think about how well each word describes you. Think about how well each word describes you COMPARED TO YOUR CLASSMATES. If you think a word fits *your classmates better than it fits you*, do not write anything in the space next to it. If you think a word fits *you and your classmates to the same degree*, make a check in the space. If you think a word fits *you better than your classmates*, make two checks in the space.

Here are some examples:

My classmates are *smarter* than I am.   (no check)
I am as *smart* as my classmates.   (one check)
I am *smarter* than my classmates.   (two checks)
My classmates are *meaner* than I am.   (no check)
I am as *mean* as my classmates. (one check)
I am *meaner* than my classmates.   (two checks)

smart_____	nice-looking_____	impolite_____
happy_____	annoying_____	caring_____
mean_____	neat_____	generous_____
friendly_____	moody_____	snobbish_____
jealous_____	talkative_____	honest_____
fun_____	pushy_____	responsible_____
noisy_____	bad_____	lazy_____
likeable_____	nice_____	sneaky_____
troublesome_____	popular_____	important_____
helpful_____	lively_____	witty_____

CONSTRUCTING A NOMINATIONS FORM

Our last type of instrument for measuring students' attitudes is the nominations form, an approach in which each student names or nominates fellow students, teachers, subject matters, events, and so forth, that are perceived as fitting into certain categories. This procedure is most commonly used for determining popularity, friendship, or liking preferences in conjunction with a technique called sociometry. Sociometry is the measurement of classroom social patterns based on nominations of liking preferences. Sample questions for use with the nominations procedure appear in Figure 6.7.

Sample Questions for Use with the Nominations Procedure.   **Figure 6.7**

My three best (worst) friends are . . .

The three people I like most (least) to eat lunch with are . . .

The three people who are best (least) liked by their fellow students are . . .

The three student leaders in this class are . . .

The three classmates I would most (least) like to bring home are . . .

The three classmates I would be most (least) willing to stay after school to help with their school work are . . .

The three teachers I like best (least) are . . .

The three most (least) liked teachers in this school are . . .

The three things we did in this course that I liked best (least) are . . .

A sample nominations form for measuring preferences of students for classmates is illustrated in Figure 6.8. This form is scored by counting the number of times each nominee is named. Students were asked to name most chosen rather than least chosen in order to identify possible social "stars." In this case the form is measuring preferences or liking rather than avoidance or dislike.

Figure 6.8   *A Sample Nominations Form for Measuring Preferences.*

Do *not* write your name on this paper. Please answer each question as carefully as possible by writing the names of five *classmates*. Use only the names of children in your homeroom class. Use first names and last initials in your answers.

List five boys or girls with whom you would *most* like to eat lunch.

_____   _____   _____   _____   _____

List five boys or girls whom you would *most* like to elect class leader.

_____   _____   _____   _____   _____

If you were having a party, who are the five boys or girls you would *most* like to invite?

_____   _____   _____   _____   _____

USING AN ATTITUDE SCALE

The formal introduction of the affective domain into the classroom has not been without controversy. To sensitize teachers to some of the problems that may arise and help them avoid them, some cautions were provided early in the chapter, including a briefing and debriefing.

Although a teacher cannot give students very much information in advance about the purposes of an attitude measurement test without unduly influencing their responses, a teacher should inform students of the safeguards that will be used to protect their privacy. Then, once the test has been completed, the teacher can provide a full explanation, or debriefing. Students should be told, for example, what the instrument measured, why it was given, and how the results will be used. In addition, when the results are available, they should be shared with the students who took the test.

Some of the purposes for which a teacher might construct and use an attitude scale are the following.

(1) To help students acquire more knowledge about and insight into themselves (which, in turn, should facilitate maturation). Students can be helped to more clearly see their own feelings about people and events.

(2) As part of an affective education experience. If the teacher engages students in an experience dealing with attitudes, it may call for attitude measurement as part of its procedure or in order to evaluate its result.

(3) To provide students with feedback relative to an event. Students may be helped to clarify their feelings about an event (for example, a national political occurrence or a specific school event such as a field trip) by completing an attitude instrument and having the teacher report the total class results.

(4) To provide the teacher with feedback for self-improvement. Knowing how students feel about specific events or instructional experiences may help the teacher improve them or consider dropping them from further use.

(5) To gain information upon which to base interpersonal decisions. As a person responsible for the education of the whole child, the teacher may find information about friendship patterns or self-concept or school sentiment highly useful in guiding his or her interaction with students. A teacher may be helped to discover which students need greater support and encouragement to bolster their image of themselves, for instance. (It must be pointed out that this last use is probably the most delicate of the five. The teacher would do well to consult the school psychologist or seek additional training before embarking on this venture.)

There are other aspects of feelings and emotions manifested in the classroom beyond attitudes. Much *behavior* is a reflection of students' feelings toward the school setting and their ability to function in it. The next chapter will describe the measurement of student performance and behavior.

Additional Information Sources

Edwards, A. L. *Techniques of attitude scale construction.* N.Y.: Appleton Century Crofts, 1957.

Lake, D. G., Miles, M. B., & Earle, R. B. *Measuring human behavior: Tools for the assessment of social functioning.* N.Y.: Teachers College Press, 1973.

Miller, D. C. *Handbook of research design and social measurement* (2nd ed.). N.Y.: David McKay Co., 1970.

Robinson, J. P. et al. *Measures of occupational attitudes and occupational characteristics.* Ann Arbor, Mich.: Institute for Social Research, University of Michigan, 1969.

Robinson, J. P. et al. *Measures of political attitudes.* Ann Arbor, Mich.: Institute for Social Research, University of Michigan, 1968.

Robinson, J. P. & Shaver, P. R. *Measures of social psychological attitudes.* Ann Arbor, Mich.: Institute for Social Research, University of Michigan, 1969.

Shaw, M. E. & Wright, J. M. *Scales for the measurement of attitudes.* N.Y.: McGraw-Hill, 1967.

Self-test of Proficiency

(1) Write two goals that deal with students' attitudes toward school.

(2) Write two goals that deal with students' interpersonal behavior in school.

(3) Match the sample item at the right with the type of attitude scale it is illustrative of at the left.

a. Likert Scale.
b. Adjective checklist.
c. Bipolar adjective scale.
d. Two-point scale.

i. Math is my favorite subject.
        Yes   No

ii.   Math
exciting _:_:_:_:_:_tedious

iii. Name your favorite subject.
_____

iv. Of all my courses, I like math best.
SA   A   U   D   SD

v. Math is _____ exciting.
_____ tedious.
_____ unpleasant.

(4) The instrument that uses the bipolar adjective approach to measure attitudes is called the _____.

(5) Below is a list of sentences. Check those that are rules for writing attitude statements.

_____ a. Avoid reference to the past.
_____ b. Avoid nondistinguishers.
_____ c. Avoid statements of opinion.
_____ d. Write simply, clearly, and directly.
_____ e. Have two or more thoughts per statement.
_____ f. When possible use compound sentences.
_____ g. Cover the full range.
_____ h. Write short statements.

(6) Consider the following attitude statements.

a. Classrooms in an open educational system often are without physical walls.
b. Mathematics in my school is fun to take and my teacher teaches it well.

Explain, in a sentence, what is wrong with each statement and why you should avoid using it.

(7) Suppose you wanted to determine students' attitudes toward your course. Name three aspects or categories of this attitude area about which you could ask questions.

(8) Prepare a topical outline with at least three categories (each of which refers to a different aspect) for measuring positiveness of attitudes toward the object: FIELD TRIPS.

(9) Construct six Likert scale items, three positive and three negative, to measure positiveness of attitudes toward the object: FIELD TRIPS. Use the topical outline prepared in item 8 and write one positive and one negative item per aspect or outline category.

(10) Construct two semantic differential items, two adjective checklist items, and two nominations questions to measure positiveness of attitudes toward the object: FIELD TRIPS. Again use the topical outline from item 8.

(11) Which one of the following would *not* ordinarily be thought of as a use for attitude measurement in the classroom?
   a. to provide student with feedback
   b. to provide the teacher with feedback
   c. to increase student's sensitivity to others
   d. to find out whether a student's attitudes are acceptable
   e. to help student gain self-insight

(12) You have been asked to lead a discussion in a faculty meeting regarding the use of affective measures in the classroom. Prepare an outline of your presentation to include a statement of the precautions necessary in testing in this area.

chapter seven / Checklists and Scales to Measure Performance and Behavior

OBJECTIVES

1. State criteria for choosing to do performance testing.

2. Specify desired performance outcomes and testing situations for performance testing.

3. Prepare a performance checklist containing process and product criteria.

4. Specify and describe classroom behaviors to be evaluated.

5. Prepare a behavior rating scale.

6. State uses for behavior measurement in the classroom.

Although some people see the teacher's role in measurement limited to paper-and-pencil testing administered on a group basis, teachers frequently say that they do not rely on such tests alone as the basis for student assessment. In addition, they observe students' performance and behavior on a day-to-day basis and use these observations as part of their student assessments; indeed in certain situations such evidences may be more real than paper-and-pencil test performance for both the teacher and students.

Thus, the need arises to provide teachers with ways of measuring that can be applied to a specific performance or to ongoing behavior so that this real and relevant evidence of student capabilities can be utilized. Such measurement must be designed without totally compromising the standards on which good measurement is based, namely that the measurement procedure be appropriate, valid, reliable, interpretable, and usable (see Part III). The procedures described in this chapter are aimed at making the assessment of *cognitive performance* and *affective behavior* possible within the limits of these five criteria.[1]

MEASURING PERFORMANCE

The prototypic situation for the measurement of performance is an individualized testing setting in which a student is given a task, that task being to solve a problem, to identify a malfunction, to make a decision, or to implement a decision or solution. Typically, performances are associated with either solutions (that, in some cases, are products) or implementations or both. While the student is operating in a hands-on manner to achieve a solution or implementation, he or she is observed by one or more judges who use a checklist to record or evaluate each step in the performance. In a school setting, of course, the teacher would be the judge. (The student may or may not be aware that the performance is being observed, but usually he or she is.)

---

[1] The term *performance* is used to label the observable manifestations of knowledge, understanding, ideas, concepts, skills, and so on (that is, the cognitive and psychomotor domains), while the term *behavior* is used to label the observable manifestations of feelings, attitudes, values, personality orientations, and so on (that is, the affective domain).

Measuring Skills and Competencies

To measure skills and competencies a student is asked to solve a problem and/or perform a task. For example: *a.* Where is the malfunction in the system? *b.* Get all the washers on a peg in decreasing order of size without ever putting a larger washer on top of a smaller one. *c.* Of this series of cards, which one has been preselected as the correct one? *d.* What would be the fastest and safest way to get across the island shown on the map assuming that there were eight of you and two were so injured that they had to be carried? *e.* Act out a skit that illustrates the reason why Francis Scott Key wrote the "Star Spangled Banner." In each instance the individual student or group of students is asked to perform in order to produce a solution. Evaluation focuses on the procedures or steps undertaken to achieve the solution as well as on the quality of the solution.[2] Let us consider some specific illustrations in more detail.

Some Illustrations. In a high school program in data processing one of the objectives was the following:

> Given a data sheet containing 1200 pieces of business data, the student will be able to use a key punch and programmed control to punch these data onto cards in thirty minutes with no uncorrected errors while following the correct procedure.

To evaluate attainment of this objective a performance test was used. Each student was given a sheet of data and a deck of key punch cards, was seated at a key punch, and was told to punch the data onto cards. The teacher observed and timed the performance and then examined the finished product. The *product* was evaluated in terms of *a.* the number of errors that it contained and *b.* the time that was required to complete it. The *process* or procedure was evaluated in terms of the checklist shown in Figure 7.1 (described by Tuckman, 1967).

Brown (1970) implemented a procedure for the evaluation of performance in commercial food processing courses at the secondary level. He developed, with the help of experts, a list of the performances that would be required of people employed as salad mixers, grill cooks, or short order cooks. He then had this list of performances validated by employers of people in these occupa-

[2] When the performance being judged is a group performance, each student is usually given whatever evaluation the group receives, unless individual contributions can be separated, in which case each student is evaluated individually.

*Checklist for Evaluating Key Punch Performance in Data Processing.** **Figure 7.1**

	YES	NO
(1) Student was capable of activating all three of the proper functional control switches at the proper times.		
(2) Student used the correct procedure for punching numeric data.		
(3) Student used the correct procedure for punching alphabetic data.		
(4) Student correctly marked up the given data sheet to indicate column punching designations, field sizes, and program card layout.		
(5) Student prepared the proper program card from his or her own designations and any given punching and verifying instructions.		
(6) Student correctly mounted the program card on the drum.		
(7) Student punched cards (other than those punched automatically) in consistent and proper fields.		
(8) Student proofed the first card in each series.		
(9) Student properly verified all cards.		
(10) Student functioned in an efficient and smooth manner.		

* Each step is given equal weight. All must be performed.

tions and developed the performance checklist, part of which is shown in Figure 7.2. (The first six task areas shown apply to salad mixers and the last two to grill cooks.)

Tuckman (1970) reported on the measurement of performance in electronics by the United States Army in the training of signalmen. The students were given a piece of electronics equipment with a fault or malfunction programmed in. Equipment to locate the fault was available. The test administrator evaluated not only whether the fault was located but how the student went about locating the fault—particularly in terms of his use of test equipment and troubleshooting procedures. A sample administrator's instruction sheet for the test appears in Figure 7.3.

Figure 7.2 *Part of a Checklist for Evaluating Performance in Commercial Food Processing.**

Experienced _____ Inexperienced _____ Pilot Student _____ Vocational Student _____

THE SEQUENCE
_____Read entire order upon receipt
_____Checked equipment for proper temperature setting
_____Checked the supply of vegetables
_____Made the Italian dressing first
_____Made the tossed salad next
_____Made the other cold dishes next
ITALIAN DRESSING
_____Was able to read and understand the recipe provided
_____Measured the correct quantity
_____Used all the proper ingredients
_____Placed dressing in refrigerator
_____Mixed the dressing before using
_____Used a reasonable amount on each salad
_____Cleaned up station after making dressing
THE SALADS (tossed)
_____Used all three greens provided
_____Removed cores before chopping
_____Cut greens uniformly
_____Did not chop excessively large or small chunks
_____Washed greens thoroughly
_____Drained greens well
_____Mixed greens uniformly
_____Filled bowls to a reasonable level
_____Covered excess greens with damp cloth
_____Refrigerated excess greens

THE SALADS (Continued)
_____Wedged tomatoes, or chopped them
_____Placed tomatoes on top of salad
_____Cleaned up station
TUNA SALAD
_____Used commercial opener correctly to open can of tuna
_____Drained can of tuna
_____Broke up tuna before adding mayonnaise
_____Diced celery uniformly
_____Used appropriate celery size
_____Used less than half as much celery as tuna
_____All ingredients were thoroughly mixed adding mayonnaise as needed
_____Consistency of final product was smooth and firm enough to retain shape when formed
_____Excess salad was covered and refrigerated
_____Cleaned up station
TUNA SALAD PLATE
_____An appropriate amount of crisp clean greens was used as a bed
_____Salad was neatly formed with a scoop and placed on bed
_____A reasonable portion was used
_____Selected five or six garnishes from those provided
_____Arrangement was neat and colorful
_____Cleaned up station

SOLE FISH PLATTER

_____Used a six to eight ounce portion

_____Cooked fish to a golden brown crisp appearance

_____Removed fat by placing fish in a pan lined with a towel

_____Wedged lemon

_____Garnished with tartar sauce and lemon wedge

_____Final appearance of the dish was acceptable

_____Cleaned up station

CHOPPED SIRLOIN

_____Started with clean utensils

_____Used a six to eight ounce portion

_____Formed a smooth oblong patty

_____Cooked the meat to the right degree of doneness

_____Started the meat before the fish or omelette

_____Cleaned up station

* Reproduced from Brown, 1970 by permission of the author.

Instructions for Administering a Performance Test in Electronics.   **Figure 7.3**

STRATEGIC MICROWAVE REPAIR COURSE PHASE VIII
ADMINISTRATOR'S INSTRUCTION SHEET

Purpose:

To measure the student's ability to: (1) Select and operate test equipment associated with the AN/FRC-109 receiver; (2) Develop and apply a logical procedure in locating malfunctions in the AN/FRC-109 receiver.

Equipment:

The AN/FRC-109 receiver training facility and Simpson 260 VOM, Hi-Band test set, Frequency Selective Voltmeter Sierra 128A, Oscilloscope Tektronix Type 561A, Oscillator H/P 651B, Miscellaneous matching transformers, Aids-Block Diagrams, level diagrams.

Procedure:

(1) All equipment will be warmed up and in proper operating condition before the test is administered. A problem will be inserted into two different radio receivers at the same time.

(2) The testing procedure will be described to the students.

    a. All test equipment necessary will be at the test position. You will be required to select and then calibrate the proper test equipment to be used.

    b. There will be one fault in each of two receiver racks. You will be required to locate the fault in each rack using the correct troubleshooting procedure.

    c. The time limit for each problem is six minutes.

d. You will be graded on the following items: (1) Selection, calibration, and application of test equipment. (2) Procedure used in locating the faults. (3) Localization of the faults.

e. If you have any questions, ask them before you begin one problem; talking will not be permitted during the test.

Scoring:

The test administrator will assign scores in accordance with the following:

(1) Completing correctly problem 1	5 points
(2) Completing correctly problem 2	5 points
(3) Selection and use of test equipment	5 points
(4) Troubleshooting procedure	5 points
Total Points	20 points

Good examples of performance tests can also be drawn from science and mathematics. A sample performance test in science dealing with units of force appears in Figure 7.4. In this test intended for fourth graders, the student is given a spring scale, weights of known force, and graph paper, and is asked to calibrate the spring. He or she is then asked to determine the magnitude of an unknown force using the calibration developed in the first test exercise. Note that the performance test includes (1) a list of the materials required, (2) instructions for the test administrator in terms of both what to do and what to say, and (3) scoring instructions, including a description of acceptable performance.

Figure 7.4   *A Performance Test in Science for Fourth Graders.**

UNITS OF FORCE

(Objective 1)   1–3. Provide the child with four containers, each of which weighs one newton; a spring that he has not seen before mounted on a tripod (e.g. Macalester Tripod Spring with centimeter tape on plastic cylinder); a pencil and some graph paper. Tell him: EACH ONE OF THESE CONTAINERS WEIGHS ONE NEWTON. USE THEM AND THE GRAPH PAPER TO CALIBRATE THE SPRING SO THAT YOU CAN USE THE STRETCH OF THE SPRING TO MEASURE FORCES. One check should be given in the acceptable column for task one if the child plots one point correctly, one check in the acceptable column for task two if he plots two points correctly, and one check in the acceptable column for task three if he plots three or more points correctly.

(Objective 2)   4. Using your hand, pull on the spring until it is stretched to some length within the range of calibration. Tell him: MEASURE THE FORCE THAT I AM EXERTING ON THE SPRING WITH MY HAND. DRAW AN ARROW ON YOUR GRAPH TO SHOW ME WHERE YOU ARE READING THE FORCE, AND TELL WHAT THE READING IS. One check should be given in the acceptable column for task four if the child indicates the correct point on the graph with an arrow and states the measure of the force in newtons. If he merely gives a value (say 3.5), it is allowable to prompt with the question: 3.5 what? Allow an error of 0.2 newtons.

* Adapted. From *Part E* of *Science—A Process Approach*, Copyright © 1968, by American Association for the Advancement of Science, published by Ginn and Company (Xerox Corporation).

Figure 7.5 is a teacher-built performance test in mathematics on the fifth grade level. (One could argue that all testing in mathematics is performance testing since math-related behavior is essentially of a problem-solving nature. Even where multiple choice items are used in math, essentially problem-solving behavior must occur to make a correct choice. The most useful distinction may be that in performance testing, as opposed to short-answer testing, the tester gains access to the problem-solving process as well as or in addition to the problem solution.) In this test, the student is asked to measure an angle, label others, and make a determination of an angle that would be produced by reflected light.

In English an example of a performance test would be an assignment for high school seniors to write a letter to the Acme Employment Agency, 100 Main Street, Centerville, N.Y. 10345 to try to obtain a job for the following year. The students are told that the letter should include a description of their background and capabilities and the kind of jobs they would be interested in. They are also told that the form of their letter (proper business form), spelling, punctuation, and neatness will be evaluated as well as content. There is a time limit of thirty minutes.

The above performance test illustrates the less-than-exact line that separates the different kinds of tests. This test seems much like an essay test primarily because the materials are paper and pencil or typewriter. The major distinction between an essay test and a performance test is that the end result of a performance test is an actual product rather than a set of thoughts or ideas.

Figure 7.5 *A Sample Performance Test in Mathematics for Fifth Graders.*

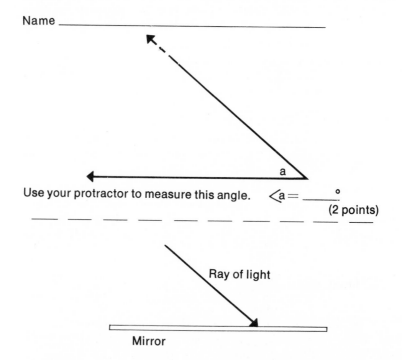

Name _____

Use your protractor to measure this angle. ∠a = _____°

(2 points)

Ray of light

Mirror

Imagine the ray of light hitting the mirror as shown. Draw a line showing the path of the ray of light reflected by the mirror at the correct angle.

(2 points)

Label the *angle of incidence* with the letter *a*. (1 point)
Label the *angle of reflection* with the letter *b*. (1 point)

You might say that performances have a functional quality in that their outcome usually has some potential use for the performer. Beyond this, these distinctions may have their primary value in teaching and learning about test construction rather than in the construction of tests themselves.

DECIDING ON A PERFORMANCE TEST

A performance test is usually given on an individual basis; hence it is a time-consuming form of testing. Before engaging in performance testing, the teacher should examine these criteria:

Essential Considerations (Criteria)

(1) Real Performance Requires a Hands-on Situation. Certain performances can occur only if the student can handle actual materials or equipment. In such cases, abstracting the performance on a paper-and-pencil basis will rob it of its essential validity, i.e., you will be measuring something other than your objective. Where an objective requires a hands-on demonstration or construction, performance testing is required (including performances for which paper and pencil are the equipment, as in letter writing).

(2) Access to the Solution Process Is Essential. Group paper-and-pencil testing often prohibits the teacher from having access to the process or procedure by which the outcome or product was arrived at. In order to see how a student solves a problem or makes a product or implements a solution, the teacher must observe the performance of that student. If the process is itself as worthy of measurement and evaluation as the product, then a performance test is needed to allow the teacher to witness and judge the process.

(3) The Final Outcome or Product Has a Material Form. Often we try to get students to produce decisions or ideas. These can usually be measured by paper-and-pencil tests, but the situation is completely different if the final outcome of the test has a material form. Asking a student how to make something is not always a valid substitute for having him or her make it. If your purpose is to measure both knowledge of process and skill in performance, a performance test is needed.

(4) You Are Trying to Assess Psychomotor Learning (i.e., Skills). While cognition (what you know) and affect (what you feel) can often be measured by paper-and-pencil tests, skill acquisition cannot. To demonstrate skills, a student must physically do them. Hence, a performance test is required.

(5) You Are Trying to Assess Individual Effectiveness in a Group Setting. Where the purpose of the test is to measure one person's effect on another (for example, leadership skills), actual performance testing is needed. (That is, you have to observe the person in a leadership situation that you may have contrived in order to see how effectively he or she could help the group to solve a problem.) A person might be able to solve a problem individually or to describe in writing the desired behavior but be incapable of actually working in a group. Performance tests require the test taker to demonstrate performance rather than describe it.

(6) You Are Trying to Measure Understanding by Its Application. You can use a performance test to measure understanding but only in terms of the concrete application of that understanding. The outcome is still a concrete product but its construction may well be a reflection of certain cognitive processes. (Habitual performances like riding a bike soon become automatic, and hence no longer reflect cognition.)

CONSTRUCTING A PERFORMANCE TEST

A performance test, as we have seen, is a test initiated by the teacher and involves the student in a performance under a controlled set of conditions. It is usually given on an individual or one-to-one basis although it is possible sometimes to utilize group administration for part or all of it, and some testing—leadership skills, for example—requires group administration. Typically performance testing involves both a product and a process—the process being the manner by which the product was produced or arrived at. It does, in all instances then, deal with the ability of

Box 7.1

PASS/FAIL!

The final exam in paratrooper training is a test jump. Trainees are taken up in a plane wearing parachutes they have packed themselves and jump from a height of 8,000–10,000 feet. The next day is graduation. Any trainee who shows up for graduation receives a diploma.

Unfortunately, there are few such performance tests where the criteria for success can be so objectively applied.

the student to do something rather than simply to know something, identify something, or describe something, and it usually involves the use of materials or equipment. What is important to emphasize is that this kind of test is not simply an informal, casual, or happenstance appraisal of actions. It is a test that is planned, designed, and carried out to sample a person's ability to use a process and produce a product under a *given* set of conditions.

The rules to follow in constructing a performance test are listed and explained below.

(1) Specifying Desired Performance Outcomes. The first step in constructing a performance test is to specify desired performance objectives. Since performance objectives state actions by the learner under given conditions (and ultimately include criteria for evaluation), they represent a set of desired performance outcomes. For performance test purposes, teachers should focus on those objectives that use such verbs as *demonstrate* and *construct* because these verbs specify hands-on performance (i.e., demonstrations and constructions); if such objectives do not exist, the teacher should write them. Below are examples of performance objectives.

- Demonstrate a procedure for measuring the volume of a liquid.
- Demonstrate a procedure for bisecting an angle.
- Construct a poem that describes personal feelings about some aspect or aspects of nature.
- Demonstrate a procedure for tuning a car.
- Demonstrate a procedure for conducting an interview.
- Construct a model of an American Indian village.
- Demonstrate the ability to take shorthand at the rate of twenty-five words a minute.
- Construct a cubic meter out of cardboard.
- Demonstrate a procedure for staining pine.
- Construct a display for teaching about different leaves and their characteristics.

(2) Specifying the Test Situation. A test situation is a set of givens with which the student attempts to produce the desired performance. It is the conditions of the objective or what the student must be given in order to perform the objective. (Recall that conditions, performance, and criteria were described in Chapter 2 as the components of an objective.) While a performance test can be a sampling of ongoing behavior, it usually is an examination of a *prespecified* performance using a set of givens and following a set of instructions. Hence both conditions and instructions must be specified. Consider the examples below.

- Demonstrate the use of a balance for weighing objects of unknown weight.
  Givens: (1) a balance, (2) a metal cylindrical prism of unknown weight, (3) a set of known weights as follows: ten 1 milligram weights, nine 100 milligram weights, five 1 gram weights, and three 5 gram weights.
  Instructions: Here is an object of unknown weight, a balance, and a set of weights. Use the balance to determine the weight of the unknown to within one milligram. You will have five minutes to do this.
- Construct a rock display.
  Givens: (1) information in advance so that you can bring all the material you need (including rocks that you have gathered) to class. The minimum number and the types of rocks that are needed are included in the advance information.
  Instructions: Make a rock display that is clear and interesting and that contains at least seven rocks with some of each type that we learned about. The rocks should be mounted so that the display can be stood up on a table in the classroom. You will get up to 10 points for the accuracy of your display, up to 10 points for its completeness, and up to 10 points for its attractiveness of presentation.
- Install an electrical outlet in an open wall.
  Givens: access to a standard set of tools and wire, an outlet fixture, a mounting box, an open wall, an accessible live power source.
  Instructions: Here is an outlet fixture and box. Install the outlet on one of these studs and connect it to the classroom power source so that it can be used.

The instructions should be very clear, whether they are written or oral. The givens should be sufficient for successful task completion although all need not be specifically supplied by the teacher; the student may be required to supply some. When part of the requirements is to choose or to find necessary tools, materials (such as the rocks in the example), or information, the teacher should insure that these are uniformly accessible to the students. The teacher is not interested in measuring the adequacy of the conditions—they should be adequate; he or she is interested in

"If he *really* knew his stuff, he wouldn't make the chalk screech like that."

measuring the skills of the student. A test that is inadequate in its givens or instructions will not measure a student's skills with any validity. Proper test construction includes suitable preparation of givens and instructions.

(3) Specifying Process (or Procedure) and Product Criteria. Performance tests give the teacher access to the product and potential access to the process or procedure undertaken to attain that product, but obviously access to the process, when it occurs, is very temporary.[3] Once the procedure is complete, the observer no longer has access to it unless it was filmed or videotaped or unless the student is asked to do it again. Consequently, the teacher must prepare a set of criteria in advance to apply to the process or procedure. Criteria are necessary, too, to try to make the judgments as objective as possible, for the performance test—like the essay test—has a certain amount of subjectivity built into it. The teacher

---

[3] Also, when the process occurs in the student's mind the teacher will be limited to only those aspects that can be verbalized or acted out.

is the judge. On what basis does a teacher decide what steps the student should take and whether these steps are done correctly? To answer this question, he or she must list the necessary steps in the procedure. The occurrence of these steps then constitutes a criterion for evaluating performance. Consider the following criteria for demonstrating the use of a balance, constructing a rock display, and installing an electrical outlet.

- Demonstrate the use of a balance for weighing objects of unknown weight.
    a. Place object of unknown weight on one tray of balance.
    b. Place objects of known weight on the other tray.
    c. Add or subtract known weights when underbalance or overbalance occurs.
    d. Use lesser weights as balance is approached.
    e. Try a minimum number of different weight combinations to achieve balance within additions and subtractions, always bringing the scale closer to balance (rather than combining weights on a hit-or-miss basis).
    f. Add the weights that produce balance to determine the weight of the unknown.
- Construct a rock display.
    a. Collect different kinds of rocks to include at least three of the igneous class, three sedimentary, and one metamorphic. (These proportions are based on the general availability of these three types of rocks.)
    b. Clean and polish rocks.
    c. Mount attractively.
    d. Label (including name, class, and where found).
- Install an electrical outlet in an open wall.
    a. Select proper tools.
    b. Determine and prepare amount of material needed (e.g., wire).
    c. Decide whether or not (and when) to cut power.
    d. Mount box on stud.
    e. Connect wires with proper polarization to fixture.
    f. Install fixture in box (and put on cover if needed).
    g. Connect to power source.
    h. Test to see if it works.[4]

[4] In skill performances, the steps are usually more accurately described as procedures rather than processes. That is, the steps represent what one must do to produce the product rather than necessarily revealing what one must *know* (other than knowing the procedures).

Recall that an objective includes a statement of criteria for evaluating either the process or the product or both. In essence this third step is simply an elaboration of the criteria that will be used to evaluate the performance. These criteria should be spelled out in sufficient detail so that the teacher can adequately evaluate the performance in as systematic a way as possible. They should also be presented to the students, either as part of the test or during the instruction related to the task. Detailed criteria reduce the subjectivity of the judgment.

(4) Preparing the Performance Checklist.   The performance test is made up of a set of instructions and givens that are presented to the student and a performance checklist that is used by the teacher or judge. The performance checklist is just a format for listing the criteria that were developed in the preceding section. If a criterion on the list is met, it is checked; if it is not met, it is not checked. Consider the examples below.

- Performance checklist: Bisecting an angle.
  - ———— *a.* compass is used
  - ———— *b.* point placed on vertex; arc is made between sides
  - ———— *c.* point placed on each intersection between arc in (b) and side; equal arcs are made
  - ———— *d.* line is drawn from vertex to intersection between arcs in (c)
  - ———— *e.* two resulting angles are equal when checked with protractor
  - ———— overall quality of performance on a 0–5 scale
- Performance checklist: Drawing a realistic nature scene.
  - ———— *a.* a sketch (or outline or layout or some sort of plan) is made first
  - ———— *b.* materials are used properly
  - ———— *c.* drawing is completed neatly
  - ———— *d.* elements of nature can be seen in the drawing
  - ———— *e.* colors are realistic
  - ———— overall quality of drawing on a 0–5 scale

The performance checklist reflects both the steps undertaken in arriving at the product and the quality or acceptability of the product itself. It is a set of instructions and procedures by the teacher to himself or herself in terms of what to look for in evaluating a performance. It also provides a basis for giving students useful performance feedback and attempts to make the evaluation of performance as objective and quantitative as possible.

Obviously, not all performances are equally susceptible to this treatment and hence all performance checklists are not equally detailed. The checklist is a way for the teacher to take those criteria that are in his or her head and to externalize and systematize them by writing them down. The performance checklist can be considered the scoring key for a performance test. The criteria listed as *a* to *e* form the basis for the overall evaluation of the performance shown at the bottom of the checklist.

SCORING THE PERFORMANCE TEST

There are, unfortunately, no absolute rules for teachers to use in scoring a performance test. By considering their own requirements (that is, the requirements as set forth in their objective), the relative importance of the different criteria in an absolute sense, and the extent to which they can differentiate degrees of performance, teachers can build their own appropriate scoring procedures. However, some guidelines may be helpful and are offered below.

It is not necessarily true that all criteria must be checked for the total performance to be judged acceptable or that fifty percent or some other arbitrary number must be checked. (However, if some arbitrary number is demanded, seventy or eighty percent is probably the most reasonable.) Examine your checklist and ask yourself questions such as: Are all of the components in the checklist equally important? Are some absolutely essential for acceptable performance? What degree of success constitutes mastery? Your answers to these questions will lead you to decide whether you want to use a weighting system or to follow the somewhat arbitrary *eighty percent success = acceptable proficiency* rule. Or you may simply want to assign an overall rating to the performance based on the checklist entries and record this rating as an indication of the student's degree of proficiency or quality of performance. Consider the checklist below.

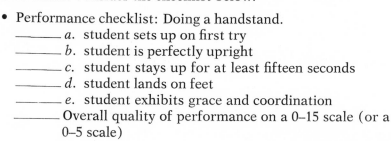

- Performance checklist: Doing a handstand.
    - _____ *a.* student sets up on first try
    - _____ *b.* student is perfectly upright
    - _____ *c.* student stays up for at least fifteen seconds
    - _____ *d.* student lands on feet
    - _____ *e.* student exhibits grace and coordination
    - _____ Overall quality of performance on a 0–15 scale (or a 0–5 scale)

Box 7.2

A DIVING CHECKLIST

Have you ever attended a diving, gymnastics, or figure skating competition or seen one on television? They constitute performance tests. Have you noticed how, after a performance, judges hold up cards with numbers on them (7, 7½, 8, and so forth) to indicate their evaluation of the performance? We can presume that the judges are all using a similar checklist, based on their expertise and judgment, although the checklist is often unwritten. Here is an example of what a checklist for the triple sommersault dive might look like:

Performance checklist: Completing a triple sommersault dive from a three meter board (tuck position)

_____ *a.* shows balance in approaching jump
_____ *b.* jumps evenly, erectly, and high
_____ *c.* goes smoothly into tuck position (i.e., initial entry into tuck position describes an arc)
_____ *d.* completes three complete sommersaults
_____ *e.* doesn't roll while sommersaulting
_____ *f.* comes out of tuck position in three motions
_____ *g.* is out of tuck position before entering water
_____ *h.* body is straight in entering water
_____ *i.* entering splash is small and quiet
_____ *j.* entire motion from start to finish is smooth
_____ Overall performance on a 0–10 scale

Note that there are ten criteria. If each criterion that was met with minimal acceptance were scored ½ point, each criterion met "perfectly" scored 1, with a 0 for each failed, the addition of points would represent a final judgment.

Suppose that you felt that each criterion was equally important but that you wanted to reflect the degree of performance. You might give a student one check for a category if the performance was minimally acceptable. (A student who, for example, got up on the second try might get one check on criterion *a.*) Clearly acceptable performance (such as getting up on the first try—wavering—but staying up) might earn two checks while outstanding performance (e.g., getting right up the first time) might earn three checks.

The student's score for the total performance of doing a handstand then would be the number of checks he or she earned ranging from zero to fifteen. Teachers desiring a simpler scoring procedure could give one check or no checks and require four checks out of five as an indication of acceptable performance. A third possibility would be to consider criterion c to be most essential and to require that it be met as a requirement of mastery with three out of the remaining four needed in addition as a basis for "passing."

MEASURING BEHAVIOR

How does a student behave in class? Does he or she exhibit a tendency to work willingly and capably with others toward the achievement of a common goal or would he or she be more likely characterized as nonconstructive in the area of interpersonal relations? Is he or she the kind of student who works beyond required goals or one who can barely keep up with the class? Is he or she on time or usually late? Is assigned work completed on time or is it consistently late? Does the student continue to perform and work well with others in a high stress situation or does he or she seem to lose composure? These are some of the things that teachers look at and consider important in their assessments of the *personal attributes* of students.

Why Measure Behavior? We have talked about measuring what students know, how they think, how they feel, and how they perform. Clearly, all of these are important goals in education. Now we are talking about their class behavior (which, in turn, forms the basis for judging their personal attributes). Are classroom behaviors and personal attributes also relevant and important educational goals? Should teachers be concerned about them? The answer must surely be *yes*. Part of an education is developing the kinds of personal attributes that enable one to behave in a constructive manner—not in an automatic, robot-like way but in a way that reflects concern and consideration for others, self-discipline, morality, drive, and other qualities generally considered desirable.[5] Part of the learning task involves developing constructive behavior patterns (and the underlying personal attributes) both for the present and the future.

[5] Needless to say, a teacher who does not believe that the role of school is to improve the personal attributes and hence the behavior of its students would not be inclined to measure these characteristics.

Do teachers currently evaluate student behavior and the personal attributes that this behavior reflects? Again, the answer is *yes*. In some form or another teachers observe, record, and often report student behavior, and judge personal attributes. In doing so, they are at least implicitly acknowledging performance objectives such as:

- The student will demonstrate *self-control* by attending to an activity without constant supervision.
- The student will demonstrate the *ability to work constructively* with classmates and share things with them.
- The student will demonstrate the *tendency to do the work* that is expected of him or her in the time available.
- The student will demonstrate *maturity* through socially acceptable behavior and not engage in fights, shouting matches or other forms of acting out.

If such behaviors are to be developed, then there is value in determining whether and to what degree they are being formed. In other words, if we are interested in enhancing or changing the personal attributes of students and the behaviors they prompt, it makes sense to measure them.

The key to the question: Do we test behavior? is the word "test."[6] If you were asked: Do you observe behavior? you would quickly answer *yes*. When you are asked: Do you or should you test behavior? you may not be sure of what to answer. Clearly, you would not be inclined to test behavior in the sense in which the word "test" is commonly used. You would not be inclined to construct a specific test situation into which students would be placed and their behavior observed. In this kind of formal test situation, moreover, students would be likely to perform at their maximum, that is, manifest their "best" behavior, because of their high motivational state. If your interest is to measure "typical" behavior, you would not want to create an obvious test situation that might alter the "typicalness" of behavior. However, you might leave the classroom on purpose to see if students would control themselves,

Do We Test Behavior?

---

[6] Our interest in measuring *behavior* is based on our interest in making inferences about the *personal attributes* that underlie it, just as in measuring *performance* our interest is based on making inferences about the *skills* that underlie it. Similarly, our interest in measuring *recall* is based on our interest in making inferences about the *knowledge acquisitions* that underlie it, and in measuring *attitudes* we are concerned with the *feelings* that underlie them.

or give an independent study assignment to see if students could generate self-initiative. For the most part though, behavior is an ongoing stream without the clear starting and ending points that characterize a test.

There is an important sense, however, in which we do want to "test" behavior and that is the sense in which a test is systematic and reasonably objective. We need a vehicle for describing typical behavior (and not the usual test vehicle that measures intended performance) so that we can refer to it, report upon it, study its improvement, and determine the effects of specific experiences on it. Thus, we need a methodology and more particularly instruments for measuring behavior that will have some of the characteristics of a "test" though not necessarily all of them. We will be specifically concerned with a system for describing behavior that can be used with consistency and some degree of objectivity. For this purpose, we will find that scales or checklists (basic measurement procedures that have been described before in other contexts) are most suitable.

Examples[7]

To illustrate ways of measuring behavior, some examples follow. These examples are of instruments that have been used before (but are not for sale in the usual sense of published tests). They are presented here to serve as a guide for teachers in constructing their own instruments to measure the behavior of students (and students' personal attributes) both individually and collectively.

The first sample behavior measure appears in Figure 7.6. It is called the *Maturity Index* and represents an attempt to quantify student behavior on six dimensions. Teachers are given further guidance on the meaning of the numerical ratings that are assigned to each dimension. While this example illustrates a system-wide procedure, it represents the kind of behavior ratings that teachers can develop on their own. Notice that this measure summarizes all results.

---

[7] A distinction is worth making between the measurement of students' behavior and the personal attributes that underlie it based on the *teacher's observation* and measurement of similar variables based on *students' self-reports* or self-descriptions. It is only the former we are discussing here. Many scales for students' self-reporting are currently available and will be discussed in Chapter 14.

Sample Maturity Index.   **Figure 7.6**

```
                    Trenton, N.J., Public Schools
                         MATURITY INDEX

Name.........................................................................
           Last        First       Initial      H.R.       Adv.Gr.
Address..............................Date of Birth.........Date...............
```

Teacher's Signature	Relia-bility	Work Habits	Self Control	Initia-tive	Sensi-tivity	Punct-uality
Home Room Teacher: Pupil's Estimate						

THE RATING GUIDE APPEARS BELOW

Indicate the <u>degree</u> to which this student measures up to the goals described below.

    4 - Exceptional
    3 - Above average
    2 - Average
    1 - Below Average

Reliability   - Does he work willingly and capably with others toward the achievement of a common goal? Is he truthful, honest, dependable, conscientious? Does he assume responsibility for his actions?

Initiative   - Does he work beyond required goals? Does student assume leadership? Is he creative, original, exploring?

Work Habits   - Does the student complete assigned work?

Self Control - Does student remain emotionally poised and physically restrained under stress?

Sensitivity   - Is student sensitive enough to be thoughtful about his attitudes and responses? Is he considerate of the rights of others?

Punctuality   - Is student on time?

All results are summarized. A cluster of good ratings will offset one poor rating.

"It hasn't helped their reading, but they've become very proficient with computer hardware."

The second example appears in Figure 7.7 and has been adapted from *Pygmalion in the Classroom* by Rosenthal and Jacobson (1968). Unfortunately, some of the labels used to describe student "behavior" in this measure (e.g., "interesting, appealing, needing approval") sound more like indications of teacher attitudes toward a student than the way he or she is seen to behave. In order to use the instrument as a behavioral measure, specific instructions would need to be given to teachers to make the meaning of the terms clear. They should be instructed to respond to observable indications of behavior (and underlying personal attributes) rather than manifestations of attitudes toward particular students (see Box 7.3). For example, "curious" behavior might be described in the instructions as trying to find out how things work, asking frequent questions, looking up information, taking objects apart, and generally taking an active role in the learning and exploring process.

A Classroom Behavior Rating Scale to Measure the Student Behav- **Figure 7.7**
iors Studied by Rosenthal and Jacobson, 1968.

Name of Child _____

Name of Teacher _____

(1) To what extent can the child's behavior be described as CURIOUS?

    NOT AT   1   2   3   4   5   6   7   8   9   EXTREMELY
    ALL   CURIOUS
    CURIOUS

(2) To what extent can the child's behavior be described as INTERESTING?

    NOT AT   1   2   3   4   5   6   7   8   9   EXTREMELY
    ALL   INTERESTING
    INTERESTING

(3) To what extent can the child's behavior be expected to lead to FUTURE SUCCESS?

    NO   1   2   3   4   5   6   7   8   9   EXTREME
    EXPECTATIONS OF   EXPECTATION OF
    FUTURE SUCCESS   FUTURE SUCCESS

(4) To what extent can the child's behavior be described as ADJUSTED?

    NOT AT   1   2   3   4   5   6   7   8   9   EXTREMELY
    ALL   ADJUSTED
    ADJUSTED

(5) To what extent can the child's behavior be described as APPEALING?

    NOT AT   1   2   3   4   5   6   7   8   9   EXTREMELY
    ALL   APPEALING
    APPEALING

(6) To what extent can the child's behavior be described as HAPPY?

    NOT AT   1   2   3   4   5   6   7   8   9   EXTREMELY
    ALL   HAPPY
    HAPPY

(7) To what extent can the child's behavior be described as AFFECTIONATE?

    NOT AT   1   2   3   4   5   6   7   8   9   EXTREMELY
    ALL   AFFECTIONATE
    AFFECTIONATE

(8) To what extent can the child's behavior be described as HOSTILE?

    NOT AT   1   2   3   4   5   6   7   8   9   EXTREMELY
    ALL   HOSTILE
    HOSTILE

(continued on next page)

(9) To what extent does the child behave in such a way to indicate that he (she) NEEDS APPROVAL?

NO INDICATION   1   2   3   4   5   6   7   8   9   EXTREME
OF   INDICATION OF
NEEDING APPROVAL   NEEDING APPROVAL

Box 7.3 —————————————————————————————

PYGMALION

Rosenthal and Jacobson (1968) describe an experiment in their book *Pygmalion in the Classroom* in which teachers were given a list of students who were expected to bloom academically, presumably because they had scored high on an IQ test. In fact, the students whose names appeared on the list had been chosen *randomly* from the student body. What happened to those students whose names were on the list? The researchers found that the expected "bloomers" bloomed: their IQ scores increased over the course of the school year to a greater extent than did the IQ scores of students not on the list.

Teachers were also asked to make behavioral ratings of the students at the end of the school year, using an instrument similar to the one shown in Figure 7.7. What happened? Teachers rated students on the list of expected bloomers as being more curious, more interesting, happier, and in line for greater success than students not on the list. Apparently the classroom behavior of students was affected by teachers' expectations of them; perhaps also the teachers' judgments were affected by their own expectations for students. *It is important for teachers, when completing rating scales, to react to and record what they actually see, not what they expect to see.*

Although certain aspects of the research design for this particular study have been questioned, the basic conclusions of the study have been substantiated by other researchers.

—————————————————————————————

The third example appears in Figure 7.8. It is called the *Student Self-discipline Scale* and can be used for describing the behavior of individual students or of a class of students. It is a series of descriptions of student behaviors in the task area (e.g., moved to a new task without teacher intervention) and in the social area (e.g., did not treat others violently). It represents both the forces urging the student to perform (e.g., carried a task beyond its given requirements) and those restraining him or her from performing improperly (e.g., "behaved" for an adult other than the teacher). This kind of instrument can be profitably used by either the teacher or by an observer to describe student behavior (either individually or collectively) in terms of self-discipline or self-controlled activity.

Student Self-discipline Scale.*   **Figure 7.8**

Degree of Occurrence

Student:	BEHAVIOR ABSENT							BEHAVIOR PRESENT	
Moved to new task as required without teacher intervention	1	2	3	4	5	6	7	8	9
Worked on a task without the teacher's presence	1	2	3	4	5	6	7	8	9
Engaged in task behavior without the teacher's prompting or maintaining it	1	2	3	4	5	6	7	8	9
Carried a task beyond its given requirements	1	2	3	4	5	6	7	8	9
Made accurate evaluation of the quality and completeness of his/her work	1	2	3	4	5	6	7	8	9
Used or assisted classmate(s) as a source of information about doing or correcting his/her work	1	2	3	4	5	6	7	8	9
Used interest center as integral part of work activity	1	2	3	4	5	6	7	8	9
Organized his/her work schedule such that teacher's task requirements are met	1	2	3	4	5	6	7	8	9
Initiated teacher information-giving behavior as resource for on-going activity	1	2	3	4	5	6	7	8	9
Did not treat others violently	1	2	3	4	5	6	7	8	9
Did not attempt to interfere with another's activity	1	2	3	4	5	6	7	8	9
Did not press for the teacher's attention and affection	1	2	3	4	5	6	7	8	9
Maintained work areas	1	2	3	4	5	6	7	8	9
"Behaved" for an adult other than the teacher	1	2	3	4	5	6	7	8	9
When asked by peers, contributed effort or material to their activity	1	2	3	4	5	6	7	8	9

* Developed by Tuckman, 1973.

CONSTRUCTING A BEHAVIOR RATING SCALE

The construction of a behavior rating scale,[8] that is, a measure of the quality or style of ongoing behavior, involves three steps: (1) specifying the behaviors to be evaluated, (2) describing these behaviors, and (3) designing the specific scale or yardstick.

(1) Specifying the Behaviors to Be Evaluated. What behaviors will you choose to evaluate? This will depend on those that you deem important and relevant primarily in terms of the underlying personal attributes you are trying to enhance. In essence, whether you have formalized them or not, you have objectives regarding student behavior and personal attributes. These probably involve such things as self-control, self-direction, adjustment, and the like. You may have some highly specific behavior goals in areas where you are consciously and systematically trying to affect student behavior. The first step in constructing a behavior scale is to make a list of the behaviors you want to evaluate.

Let us say for illustrative purposes that your list appears as follows:

- The student will
  (1) complete his or her work.
  (2) cooperate with the teacher.
  (3) work harmoniously with classmates.
  (4) exhibit an interest in learning.
  (5) utilize the resources of the classroom and school.
  (6) be neat and organized.
  (7) participate freely in the classroom process.

No one can make up a complete list for every teacher. Each teacher has his or her own specific objectives when it comes to classroom behavior although there is probably a common pool from which teachers can draw. Feel free to borrow bits and pieces from the various sources you come in contact with in constructing your own list. The above list emphasizes minimal rule-following (e.g., completing work, cooperation, neatness, and organization) and involvement (e.g., learning interest, resource use, classroom participation).

---

[8] The term "scale" is used here as a numerically-scored continuum or yardstick that serves as the basis for quantifying the degree of presence of a behavior. This does not imply, in the more technical sense, that the numerical properties of the scale or yardstick have first been established empirically.

(2) Describing the Behaviors.   The behaviors to be evaluated must be more than named. They must also be described as operationalized so that they can be judged with reasonable objectivity, reliability, and consistency. (The determination of reliability will be discussed in Chapter 10.) Some behaviors will be easier to describe than others but all must be described at some level. These descriptions constitute the criteria with which to evaluate.

Let us continue with our six sample behaviors and attempt to describe each.

(1) *Completion of work*: *a.* classwork is completed on time, *b.* homework is handed in when due, *c.* classroom performance indicates that assignments have been done, *d.* things once begun are finished in the form required.

(2) *Cooperation*: *a.* helps teacher when asked (and often when not asked), *b.* maintains proper classroom decorum, *c.* helps classmates, *d.* shares with classmates.

(3) *Interest in Learning*: *a.* exhibits knowledge not acquired in school, *b.* exhibits curiosity about new things to be learned, *c.* pays attention to information being presented, *d.* tries to learn about the why and how of things rather than just accepting them.

(4) *Resource Utilization*: *a.* uses specific resources when instructed to do so, *b.* uses specific resources on own initiative, *c.* uses resources (including people) outside of the classroom, *d.* uses resources to best advantage (e.g., in library consults card catalogue).

(5) *Neatness and Organization*: *a.* keeps desk and work area organized and neat when not in use (stores things neatly), *b.* keeps self neat, *c.* helps keep classroom neat, *d.* organizes work and materials in a systematic way.

(6) *Participation*: *a.* asks questions in class, *b.* answers questions posed by teacher, *c.* volunteers for activities, *d.* contributes materials and information to the class and classroom.

Although the above criteria still involve to some extent a teacher's subjective reactions, they do provide specific cues for the teacher to use in making judgments. Four points of reference provide greater help in structuring a judgment than a single one.

If your value for each of the behaviors is not the same, weight them to reflect their differential importance. Suppose, for example, you think that sample behavior (3) is the most important behavior in the list and sample behavior (5) the least important. To reflect this you could assign behavior (3) a weight of *2* and behavior (5) a weight of ½. All other behaviors would have a weight of *1*. Of course, if you had no interest in the total score but simply in recording each individual behavior, weighting would be unnecessary since weighting is used to reflect *relative* importance.

(3) Designing the Scale. As we have seen before, a scale is a numbered continuum where each number represents the degree of a particular quality such as acceptance or rejection, presence or absence. Scales may have as few as three points or as many as 100. The most common rating scales are three-, five-, seven-, and nine-point scales. More scale points introduce greater variations while fewer points limit the possibilities of response. The odd number of scale points has the advantage of providing a middle point to reflect an undecided or down-the-middle judgment.

For illustrative purposes let us cast our six behaviors into five-point rating scales.

(1) STUDENT COMPLETES WORK

1	2	3	4	5
never	*rarely*	*occasionally*	*frequently*	*always*

(2) STUDENT COOPERATES WITH TEACHER AND CLASSMATES

1	2	3	4	5
never	*rarely*	*occasionally*	*frequently*	*always*

(3) STUDENT EXHIBITS AN INTEREST IN LEARNING

1	2	3	4	5
never	*rarely*	*occasionally*	*frequently*	*always*

(4) STUDENT UTILIZES EDUCATIONAL RESOURCES

1	2	3	4	5
never	*rarely*	*occasionally*	*frequently*	*always*

(5) STUDENT IS NEAT AND ORGANIZED

1	2	3	4	5
never	*rarely*	*occasionally*	*frequently*	*always*

(6) STUDENT PARTICIPATES IN CLASSROOM ACTIVITIES

1	2	3	4	5
never	*rarely*	*occasionally*	*frequently*	*always*

The five-point scale is a convenient size and frequency ratings are reasonably easy to structure. Armed with such an instrument, teachers can include the realm of classroom behavior as part of their total evaluation of students and of their own educational effectiveness.

USING A BEHAVIOR RATING SCALE

Following are examples of the use of a behavior rating scale.

(1) Including classroom behavior as part of the overall basis for student evaluation. We grade students on what they know and how they perform. If we want to include students' behavior as part of our evaluation of them, we must measure it.

(2) Diagnosing and documenting behavioral difficulties. Some students present what has been referred to as "behavioral problems." Such students often require special services and parental consultation. Behavioral measurement helps in the diagnosis and documentation of such cases. However, we must be careful not to create a stigma for a student that will influence the expectations of that student's future teachers and hence their treatment of him or her.

(3) Altering, improving, and enhancing particular behaviors. Changing and enhancing certain behaviors and inhibiting others is part of growing up. Teachers often attempt to take some responsibility for this process. In order to give feedback and to try different programs and interventions with different students, the teacher must keep track of and monitor behavior. Hence, the measuring instrument.

(4) Teacher self- and program evaluation. Teachers may be trying certain strategies, such as the open classroom approach, that aim to change the behavior of students (and teachers) in certain specific ways. To determine whether these interventions are producing the desired effect, evidence about student behavior is needed—evidence not focused on individual students but on the overall behavior of the class as a reflection of the outcome of the teacher's approach. An illustrative scale to gather such evidence is shown in Figure 7.9. In this case the observations are made by a department chairman or principal rather than by the teacher.

Figure 7.9   *Sample Classroom Observation Scale To Measure Implementation of Learning Unit Plan and General Teaching Effectiveness.*

Degree of Occurrence

Classroom Climate   ABSENT   PRESENT

Students:

(1) Maintain a conversational noise level	1	2	3	4	5
(2) Move freely and purposefully about the classroom	1	2	3	4	5
(3) Involve themselves in creative activities to capitalize on their talent and/or interest	1	2	3	4	5
(4) Interact with one another in meaningful ways	1	2	3	4	5
(5) Seek help from teacher when in need of assistance	1	2	3	4	5

Subtotal _____

Motivation

Students:

(1) Are aware of learning unit goals as they apply to themselves	1	2	3	4	5
(2) Establish some of their own priorities and objectives	1	2	3	4	5
(3) Make choices and select from among options and alternatives relative to unit objectives	1	2	3	4	5
(4) Work at their own pace within approximate time intervals	1	2	3	4	5
(5) Self-assess and record their work and progress per objective	1	2	3	4	5
(6) Move from one learning activity to another with minimum teacher intervention	1	2	3	4	5

Subtotal _____

Interaction

Teacher:

(1) Asks provocative questions that lead students to participate in class	1	2	3	4	5
(2) Accepts, clarifies, and supports students' feelings and ideas	1	2	3	4	5
(3) Provides for student interaction in a variety of positive ways	1	2	3	4	5
(4) Gives students direction and provides structure as needed	1	2	3	4	5
(5) Uses varied grouping patterns to achieve learning objectives	1	2	3	4	5
(6) Moves from student to student and from group to group	1	2	3	4	5

Subtotal _____

Specific Teaching Variables	Degree of Occurrence				
	ABSENT			PRESENT	

Teacher:

	ABSENT				PRESENT
(1) Engages in continuous evaluation of students' progress on objectives	1	2	3	4	5
(2) Confers with students on goals and use of materials	1	2	3	4	5
(3) Prescribes learning procedures on the basis of individual student diagnosis	1	2	3	4	5
(4) Focuses instructional content on the objectives of the unit	1	2	3	4	5
(5) Implements instructional strategies geared to the objectives of the unit	1	2	3	4	5
(6) Makes available a variety of instructional media and materials to facilitate individualized learning	1	2	3	4	5
(7) Provides instructional sequences to fit different learning styles and rates	1	2	3	4	5
(8) Evaluates each student relative to unit objectives	1	2	3	4	5

Subtotal _____

Some Suggestions

When the scale is used by an outside observer, it is best to do it when the class is in session. Although the scale is best used by the teacher when he or she is not directly engaged in the instructional process, he or she may want to jot down critical incidents as they occur. To increase the objectivity of the entire process, the teacher should try to focus on actual observed behaviors.

To increase the reliability of judgments, particularly when they are made of individual students, the judgments should be made twice, each time independently. Making two judgments helps the teacher become more aware of his or her own internal judgment process; this awareness can then be applied to overcome bias and to increase consistency. When outside observers are employed, observations should be made by two persons, observing independently but at the same time. (The discussion of reliability will be continued in Chapter 10.)

The most important quality required for rating the behavior of people is objectivity. Sufficient work in the development of the scale, adequate understanding of the meaning of scale terms, and time and patience in practicing with the scale (trying it out, for example) will help the teacher develop techniques for rating behavior objectively.

Additional Information Sources

Amidon, E. J. & Hough, J. B. (Eds.). *Interaction analysis: Theory, research, and application.* Reading, Mass.: Addison-Wesley, 1967.

Boyd, R. D. & DeVault, M. V. The observation and recording of behavior. *Review of Educational Research*, 1966, *36*, 529–551.

Flanders, N. A. *Analyzing classroom interaction.* Reading, Mass.: Addison-Wesley, 1969.

Lien, A. J. *Measurement and evaluation of learning.* Dubuque, Iowa: Wm. C. Brown, 1967, Chapter 6.

Simon, A. & Boyer, E. G. (Eds.). *Mirrors for behavior: An anthology of classroom observation instruments.* Philadelphia, Pa.: Research for Better Schools, 1967–70.

Weick, K. E. Systematic observational methods. In G. Lindzey & E. Aronson (Eds.), *Handbook of social psychology*, vol. 2 (2nd ed.). Reading, Mass.: Addison-Wesley, 1968, 357–451.

Self-test of Proficiency

(1) State three criteria teachers should examine and consider before engaging in performance testing.

(2) State two objectives that you would use a performance test to measure and give the reason why you would use a performance test in these cases.

(3) You are interested in testing to find out whether students know how to construct an equilateral triangle. Specify the *test situation* and *desired performance outcome.*

(4) Prepare a *checklist* that can be used to evaluate student performance in constructing an equilateral right triangle.

(5) You have just finished teaching a unit on space relations and want to find out whether students can visualize a spatial arrangement such as a floor plan. Specify a *test situation* and *desired performance outcome.*

(6) Prepare a *checklist* that can be used to evaluate student performance in drawing a floor plan.

(7) You are interested in measuring the extent to which each student in class is motivated to learn. Specify the behavior to be measured and describe it by listing four observable criteria for its detection.

(8) Prepare a behavior rating scale that can be used to measure the extent to which a student is motivated to learn.

(9) You want to measure the extent to which a teacher is prepared to teach a lesson. Specify the behavior to be measured and describe it by listing four observable criteria.

(10) Prepare a behavior rating scale that can be used to measure the extent to which a teacher is prepared to teach a lesson.

(11) You are at a faculty meeting that is devoted to the construction of educational goals and objectives. Cite one argument you might use in favor of the rating of student behavior.

(12) Your school is experimenting with a program in which students engage in discussions of values relative to the issues and problems that they are facing. How might the measurement of student behavior be used in conjunction with such a program?

part three/Evaluating a Test

chapter eight / Test Appropriateness

OBJECTIVES

1. Define appropriateness, a criterion of achievement tests, as the consistency between test items and objectives.

2. Describe and illustrate the use of a content map for building appropriateness into an achievement test.

3. List and apply checklist procedures for evaluating the appropriateness of a test by determining its *a*. overall fit to objectives, *b*. correspondence to intended behavior, *c*. correspondence to conditions, and *d*. correspondence to criteria.

4. Define domain-referencing and its use as a means of increasing test appropriateness.

5. Identify and list factors based on instructional and student characteristics (rather than objectives) that can make test items inappropriate, namely: testing what was never taught, response sets, and cultural bias.

A test is a device for sampling behavior or performance related to the skills, competencies, attitudes, or other characteristics of people. It is in essence a performance sample constructed by the test maker to be representative of a student's proficiency or character and whose results have some credibility. Just as we evaluate the appropriateness of instruction based on objectives, we can evaluate the appropriateness of tests based on objectives. The parallels between the two types of evaluation are strong.

An Example of an Inappropriate Test. **Figure 8.1**

Introduction to Psychology   Spring 1973
    830:121
FINAL EXAM

(1) The Whorfian hypothesis suggests that
    a. the implicit, unverbalized values of a culture affect the behavior of its members.
    b. the structure of perception and thought is dictated by the structure of the language one speaks.
    c. a part of speech is defined by the role the word plays in a sentence rather than by what it stands for.
    d. the agreement between cultures about the meaning of words is high.
(2) The Zeigarnick effect specifies a superior retention of incompleted over completed tasks in the ratio of
    a. 3 to 1.   *c.* 2 to 1.
    b. 2.5 to 1.   *d.* 1.5 to 1.
(3) A transactional view of perception is most clearly associated with the work of
    a. Ames.   *c.* E. Gibson.
    b. J. J. Gibson.   *d.* Riggs.
(4) Nafe's model of thermal sensitivity of the skin is usually referred to as the
    a. concentration theory.   *c.* local generator theory.
    b. gradient theory.   *d.* vascular theory.
(5) The Freudian concept of *reversal of affect* is most clearly illustrated in the case of
    a. The Wolf Man.   *c.* Dora.
    b. Little Hans.   *d.* Leonardo da Vinci.

(6) The earliest piece of psychological laboratory research on memory was conducted by

  a. Ebbinghaus.   *c.* William James.

  b. Hering.   *d.* Wundt.

(7) In establishing test validity, the *standard error of estimate* is found by which of the following formulas?

  a. $\sigma_y^2 \sqrt{1 - r_{xy}^2}$ *c.* $n\sigma_y \sqrt{1 - r_{xy}^2}$

  b. $2 \dfrac{(1 - \sigma_x^2 + \sigma_y^2)}{\sigma_t^2}$ *d.* $\sigma_y \sqrt{1 - r_{xy}^2}$

(8) The *comparison level* as a concept influencing choice of social behavior has been defined as a standard for evaluating the rewards and costs of a given relationship based on the model value of all the outcomes known to the person. This definition was stated by

  a. Thibaut and Kelley.   *c.* Jones and deCharms.

  b. Homans.   *d.* Heider.

(9) A positive conditioned stimulus is firmly established in a dog by means of the usual repetitions with reinforcement. A new stimulus is now occasionally added, and whenever the combination is applied, which may be at intervals sometimes extending to hours or even days, it is never accompanied by the unconditioned stimulus. In this manner the combination is gradually rendered ineffective, so that the conditioned stimulus when applied in combination with the additional stimulus loses its positive effect, although when applied singly and with constant reinforcement it retains its full powers. Pavlov named this phenomenon

  a. external inhibition.   *c.* experimental extinction.

  b. conditioned inhibition.   *d.* deconditioning.

(10) Piaget has labeled the process by which the young infant makes interesting spectacles last as

  a. reproductive assimilation.   *c.* generalizing assimilation.

  b. recognitory assimilation.   *d.* accommodation.

Suppose you were a student in a college course called introduction to psychology and your instructor gave you the examination shown in Figure 8.1. When this exam was given to the faculty and graduate students of a psychology department (a total of forty people) the following results were obtained.

Answers

(1)*b*, (2)*c*, (3)*a*, (4)*d*, (5)*c*, (6)*b*, (7)*d*, (8)*a*, (9)*b*, (10)*c*.

No. Correct	Frequency (No. of People)	No. Correct	Frequency (No. of People)
0	5	6	0
1	9	7	0
2	12	8	0
3	7	9	0
4	4	9	0
5	3	10	0

Most of the faculty and graduate students were able to get only two of the ten items right; none got more than half right. If 65% correct had been set as the passing grade (that is, 6.5 right out of 10), the entire faculty and graduate student group who took the test would have failed, even though it was in their area of expertise! Is this, then, a suitable test for measuring a student's competence in introductory psychology? No! Why not? Because it is too hard? Is it too hard because no one could answer more than half of the questions? This is not the reason for it being too hard; this is the *evidence* for it being too hard. The *reason* for it being too hard is that people who are subject-matter specialists did not have the information required to answer the questions. If subject-matter specialists are unfamiliar with this information, it is unlikely that an introductory psychology course would cover it. In other words, we need to *evaluate* a test and we need *criteria* for evaluating the quality of that test. Without test evaluation in terms of criteria, we might be building or selecting tests that have nothing to do with what we want to measure and therefore are likely to be too hard or too easy.

APPLYING THE CRITERIA OF A GOOD TEST

The first two parts of this book were devoted to test construction. Once you have constructed your own measuring instrument, you are confronted by the practical problem of evaluating and, if necessary, revising it. This part of the book will provide a set of guidelines for assessing the adequacy or suitability of a test in terms of five criteria, namely: *appropriateness, validity, reliability, interpretability,* and *usability.*

Before the testing criteria can be applied, two practical assumptions must be met.

(1) You, as a teacher, are interested in and willing to take the time to evaluate and improve your tests.

(2) Once you have given a test, you are willing to consider the results not only as a way of evaluating your students but also as a way of evaluating your test.

This and the succeeding three chapters will deal with the five test criteria mentioned above and illustrate how each can and should be applied to the process of evaluating a test. At the end of Chapter 11 (the last in this sequence on evaluating a test), the criteria covered in all four chapters will be summarized in the form of a checklist. The five criteria will be covered both for tests that are designed for predicting future outcomes (such as intelligence tests) and for tests designed for measuring current gains (such as achievement gains). The distinction between the two types of tests is described in Box 8.1.

Box 8.1

TWO DIMENSIONS OF TESTS

Carver (1974) distinguishes between *psychometric* and *edumetric* tests in terms of the following purposes: a test is

psychometric . . . if the primary purpose of a test is to measure individual differences, for example, a general aptitude, ability, or trait;

edumetric . . . when the primary purpose of the test is to measure the gain or growth of individuals, for example, the measurement of knowledge, skill, or achievement. (p. 513.)

The same test may be used in either way depending on the purpose. If an aptitude test in mathematics is used to predict achievement in a variety of mathematical tasks, then it would be considered a psychometric test. If, however, the same test were used to determine how much math a student had learned as the result of instruction, it would be classified as an edumetric test.

Psychologists use their tests primarily in a psychometric way, intelligence testing being a prime example (that is, for predictive purposes). Educators use their tests primarily in an edumetric way, achievement testing being a prime example (that is, to assess gains). Test development and evaluation must be done in a way that is consistent with the psychometric or edumetric purpose of the test.

A TEST SHOULD BE APPROPRIATE

A test is of no use if it does not measure what we want it to measure. If we call what a test is supposed to measure its *objectives* and what it does measure its *outcomes*, then one criterion of a good test *is that it measures outcomes that are consistent with its objectives*. A test that measures what we intend it to measure has a special kind of suitability that we will refer to as *appropriateness*.[1]

If a test lacks a purpose or objective, it will be impossible to assess its appropriateness, that is, to evaluate it on this particular criterion. The purpose of a test is to measure some characteristic of people: what they have learned, what they are like, what they like, and so on. The first thing we try to find out about a test (if we are considering selecting it) or should specify about a test (if we are about to construct it) is what its objectives are, that is, what we intend it to measure. Once we have decided what a test is intended to measure, we can determine whether it measures what we want it to, that is, whether it is appropriate.

We should say two more important things about the concept of appropriateness. First of all, it is applied primarily to the evaluation of achievement or gains resulting from instruction. It represents an important way to judge achievement tests but it is not as helpful in judging predictive or psychological tests such as intelligence tests or personality tests. Second, appropriateness (or content validity) is usually not given much coverage because of its limited value for evaluating psychological tests. However, because of its value for evaluating the kinds of tests most typically used by teachers, it is distinctively labeled here and given a full chapter.

The various questions for applying the appropriateness criterion are listed below.

Is My Test APPROPRIATE?

    (1) Does It Fit My Objectives:
        a. Are there at least 2 items for each and every objective and 0 items that fit no objectives?
        b. Do the number of items per objective accurately reflect the relative importance of each objective?

---

[1] In this book, we will distinguish between validity in terms of meeting objectives and validity based on predicted or concurrent outcomes. The former type of validity that is usually referred to as *content validity* will be labeled *appropriateness*, and the term validity reserved for the other type.

(2) Does It Reflect the Action Verbs:
   a. Does each item for a given objective measure the action called for by the verb in that objective?
   b. Have I used the item format most appropriate for each action?
(3) Does It Utilize the Conditions:
   a. Does each item for a given objective employ the statement of givens or conditions set forth in that objective?
(4) Does It Employ the Criteria:
   a. Is the scoring of each item for a given objective based on the criteria stated in that objective?

The Importance of Objectives

Having spent a large portion of preceding chapters dealing with objectives, it will now be seen again how the specification of objectives[2] is important for test construction. If a test's appropriateness is based on the extent to which it measures its own objectives, we must first specify the objectives of the test. If a test fails to measure some of its objectives or measures things that are not part of its objectives then its value will be limited.

Suppose the objective of a test is to determine a child's mental ability. Because this is a gross objective it will be hard to assess appropriateness in terms of it. It would be helpful to say that the purpose of the test is to measure logical reasoning, spatial relationships, numerical reasoning, verbal concepts, and memory (as is true, for example, of the California Test of Mental Maturity).

Remember that appropriateness *represents the extent to which the test content is representative of the content or skills* (i.e., objectives) *that it is intended to sample.* If a teacher gives a test after two weeks of instruction, then the appropriateness of that test will be based on the extent to which the test items represent or reflect the material that was covered (and hence that students were expected to learn) during those two weeks. Appropriateness is like a *mapping* or matching of what is being measured to what is intended to have been learned (and hence presumably taught) in order to see if what is being measured is what was taught. Appropriateness has its time reference in the past, that is, it refers to what *was* intended, and can be applied particularly to achievement tests.

---

[2] The notion of objectives has produced some controversy in terms of prerequisites to instruction. The reference here is to objectives as necessary prerequisites to evaluation. You may be able to instruct without a set of objectives, but you cannot establish the appropriateness of a test without them.

Content Map for a Unit and Test on the Deserts of Africa (Social   **Figure 8.2**
Studies, Fourth Grade).

Objectives for Unit on Deserts of Africa	Units of Importance*					
Given a map of North Africa students can:	1	2	3	4	5	6
(1) Mark in the location of the three major deserts.	◉	◉				
(2) Recall and write in the names of these deserts	◉					
(3) Identify indigenous plant life	◉					
(4) Identify indigenous animal life	◉	◉				
(5) Describe how humans satisfy their basic needs there	◉	◉	◉			
(6) Describe what it is like to grow up there	◉	◉	◉	◉		
(7) Describe the culture (that is, rules of getting along together) there	◉	◉	◉			

* Based on time spent on each

◉ Single test item or point of credit on a test item

For purposes of illustration, let us take a unit of instruction and prepare such a map. The map must tell us what was covered— that is, a *list of objectives* (sometimes referred to as a content outline), and to what degree each part was covered—that is, how much time was devoted to each part (presumably, though not necessarily, a partial indication of importance). Figure 8.2 shows a *content map* for a unit in fourth grade social studies, this particular unit dealing with the deserts of Africa. The unit contains seven objectives that have been listed down the left-most column. Units of importance (a judgment by the teacher of the relative importance of each objective) have been listed across the top.

The test for this unit has been constructed so that a student can obtain a number of points for performing each objective to the degree indicated by its units of importance. Thus, the test not only represents each of the objectives (no more, no less!), but it represents each in proportion to its importance or emphasis. Importance is reflected in test points either by having more items or by having more complex items for which more than a point may be obtained.[3] Importance, thus, is represented by the number of performances required for each objective.

The more accurately a test's content and coverage reflect its content map made up of objectives and their relative importance, the more appropriate a test. If you build your content map before you teach your unit or construct your test, and then teach your unit and construct your test based on your content map, the appropriateness of your test will be high (given properly written items). If your test items are written to be good reflectors of your objectives, a test based on these objectives should attain as high a level of appropriateness as can be expected.

When you are using a test constructed by someone else, such as a published achievement test, you can determine its appropriateness for your purposes based on the correspondence between the content outline of the test and your objectives. Construct a content map for your class and then examine the test items and see whether their content and number reflect your content map. Put in a dot for each item as shown in Figure 8.2 and see how well the test fits your map. Examples of a good fit and a poor fit are shown in Figure 8.3.

Keep in mind that the appropriateness of a test may not be the same for any two teachers; each teacher determines his or her own content map. One teacher's objectives and hence instruction may be more closely related to what the test was designed to measure than another's. Thus, the same test does not always display the same degree of appropriateness.

Applying the Appropriateness Criterion

To test for appropriateness you need two things: (1) the test itself, and (2) the list of objectives of which that test is presumably a measure. Place these two side by side; then ask yourself if you have measured performance on each objective. There should

[3] Scoring may be done by item or by objective. The number of items per objective reflects not only the importance but also the complexity of the objective: the more complex the objective, the more items required to measure it.

A Content Map Compared for Two Tests: One High and One Low in   **Figure 8.3**
Appropriateness.

Objectives	Units of Importance					
	1	2	3	4	5	6
1	●	●				
2	●	●	X			
3	●	●	●	X		
4	●	X				
5	●	●	●			
6	●	●	●	●	X	X
7	⊗					
8						

HIGH APPROPRIATENESS

Objectives	Units of Importance					
	1	2	3	4	5	6
1	●	⊗	⊗			
2	X	X	X			
3	●	●	X	X		
4	●	●	⊗	⊗		
5	●	X	X			
6	●	X	X	X ·	X	X
7	⊗	⊗				
8	⊗	⊗				

LOW APPROPRIATENESS

● Test item that measures a given objective.

⊗ Test item that does not measure a given objective.

X Given objective for which a necessary test item is missing.

Bold line indicates outline of content map.

be no objective for which there are no items on the test (unless you are using some other measurement strategy for one or more of the objectives). There should be no items on the test for which there are no objectives. If you find items on the test for which you have no objective, then either remove those items or rewrite them so that they conform to an objective on your list. (You may also consider modifying your list.) It is important to try to achieve consistency.

Correspondence to Intended Behavior. You will notice from the list of questions on page 212 that the three components—action verbs, conditions, and criteria—have been set forth for evaluating the extent to which your items are consistent with your objectives. Of these three, action verbs typically cause the greatest difficulty. Often, the action verb in the objective will specify one kind of performance and the corresponding item will measure a different kind of performance. For example, the action verb requires the student to *demonstrate* something and in fact the test item asks him or her to *identify* something. Because a student can identify something does not necessarily mean he or she can demonstrate it. If the objective deals with demonstration, the corresponding test item must provide for such an operation.

The best strategy would seem to be to specify your objectives and then design, through the use of content mapping, a test and testing situation appropriate for measuring those objectives. *Let the objectives be the elements that are fixed and the test items the elements that are flexible enough to be fitted to the objectives, rather than the other way around.*

Correspondence to Conditions and Criteria. The same kind of matching of objectives and test items must be demanded in terms of conditions and criteria. Those conditions set forth in the objective as the conditions under which the action or performance must occur should be the conditions provided in the items to measure that objective. If the objective specifies that the student is to be given a "map of the United States," then such a map must be provided in the items to measure that objective. Criteria must be handled in the same manner. If the objective specifies that the student's description of topography will include mention of at least six of the mountain ranges present, then the item measuring that objective should be a free response or essay-type of item and should be scored in terms of the criterion as it was stated in the objective.

"If this machine isn't out of whack, reading is going to be even harder than I expected."

DOMAIN-REFERENCING

As we have seen, a test's appropriateness is dependent on the consistency between the conditions specified in each objective and the manner in which that objective is measured. As the items written to measure an objective become more representative of that set of performances that the objective calls for (otherwise known as the objective's *domain*), the test on which these items appear becomes more appropriate.

Writers of achievement tests are encouraged to engage in domain-referencing to increase the appropriateness of their tests and to improve their interpretability. (See Chapters 11 and 13 for a discussion of criterion-referenced tests—the by-product of domain-referencing.) The problem the item writer faces is that objectives, even good ones, are not item specific; that is, given an objective, a rather large number of items can usually be written. How does the writer know which one to write so that his or her resulting test will be high in appropriateness and have clear interpretability? The answer to this question according to Hively et al. (1973) is to define and describe the domain or class of items that might be written in terms of the range of characteristics that these items might have.

Box 8.2 ──

THE ITEM FORM

Hively (1973) has designed an approach called the Item Form that can be used for constructing appropriate test items for given objectives. The item form allows the test item to be referenced to the objective's domain.

The item form has six categories that provide the basis for constructing one or more items for a given objective. These categories are:

1. response description.
2. content limits.
3. item format.
4. criteria.
5. test directions.
6. sample test item.

Response description refers to the *action part* of the objective and *criteria* to the *criteria* part. *Item format* refers to the *conditions* part of the objective and the type of test item to be used. *Test directions* and *sample test item* are obvious in meaning. Most difficult of the six parts of the form to construct is the *content limits*, which refers to the range of instances of the conditions or givens that will be accepted as suitable for the objective. Content limits specify the objective's *domain*. Putting all the parts together yields the following example.

1. *Response description*: To be able to add fractional expressions in sequence.
2. *Content limits:* No more than four fractional expressions; mixed numbers and fractions will be used; only denominators to be used are between 2 and 8, inclusive, except 7 which is excluded; all answers are greater than one and reducible.
3. *Item format*: One sequence of fractional expressions per item. Students should show their work and fill in their answers in the spaces provided.
4. *Criteria:* All fractional answers should be reduced and converted to mixed numbers. Conversion of fractions to lowest common denominator form should be shown.
5. *Directions*: Below is a list of fractional expressions. Add them up. Show all your work. Express your answer as a mixed number with lowest denominator possible.
6. *Sample item:* $7/8 + 1 1/8 + 3/4 + 1/2 = $ _____.

──

If we have an objective such as determining the volume of an irregular solid using a water displacement procedure, we could develop a statement of the item domain or item form by specifying in detail the characteristics of the irregular solid, the equipment provided, the instructions given to the student, the form of his or her response, and the possible different outcomes that the student might encounter within the range or domain of the objective. Using this kind of detailed information about the conditions under which the performance will be measured, the item writer can know and precisely describe the population of items (that is, *all* the items) that might be written to measure the objective. The item writer can then randomly or representatively select items from this population of items in order to insure that the items chosen are representative of that population and hence that (1) the items are appropriate, and (2) the performance of students on those items can be interpreted to reflect their likely performance on the whole population of items and thereby the degree of proficiency on the objective itself.

Domain-referencing as described by Hively et al. (1973) and others is a considerable undertaking, probably well beyond that which can normally and reasonably be expected of teachers. What is reasonable to expect is that teachers will exercise care and devote effort to describing the conditions of the objecitve so that they will have at least a conception of the domain from which items may be drawn. By being sensitive to at least the major dimensions of that domain, teachers can write items with sufficient levels of appropriateness to allow them to justify the interpretations they make based on them. (See Appendix B.)

WHAT MAKES TESTS INAPPROPRIATE?

If basing tests on objectives makes them appropriate, then lack of an objective base leads them to be inappropriate. However, lack of appropriateness comes in guises other than a lack of correspondence of test items to objectives. Consider three of the more important ones:

(1) You never provided suitable instruction on the objective.
(2) Students are responding to their own sets rather than to the items.
(3) The test items and the students are on different cultural wavelengths.

Testing What Was Never Taught

At the two extremes of achievement testing we have "teaching for the test" and "testing what was never taught." An appropriate achievement test represents testing for what was taught (assuming, of course, that instruction has been geared to the objectives). However, in some respects the test must be independent from what was taught; the student must be able to transfer or apply his or her learning to unfamiliar material. The learning must have been provided for, but the situation in which it is to be manifested must be new in that test items have not been singled out for practice during instruction.

Sometimes when you sit down to construct a test you may feel a mischievious urge to spring some surprises on your students. If you spring too many surprises, you will end up with a test that has little to do with what you taught. This situation is shown in Figure 8.4. A test need not be mundane; the students should not be told in advance what the test items will be; but their instructional experiences should bear directly on the material to be covered in an achievement test or it cannot be considered an appropriate measure of what students *should have learned*.

Figure 8.4 *Relation between Testing and Teaching.*

SIMILARITY BETWEEN TEST AND INSTRUCTION

New Objectives New Items	Same Objectives New Items	Same Objective Same Items
Test of Something Else	Appropriate	Part of Instruction (Practice)

Response Sets

On some kinds of tests students can decide what conclusions they want you, the test maker, to draw about them or they can figure out what you want to hear. This practice is known as *faking*.

Sometimes, however, students distort their responses in the "desired" direction without even realizing that they are doing so. This distortion is called *social desirability bias* since the basis for answering the questions is the social desirability of the respective answer choices. Without being aware of it, most people endorse positive things about themselves and reject negative things. To overcome this potential bias, tests should not be too superficial or obvious in nature. Where multiple choices are given, each must be of nearly equal social desirability.

A third form of distortion is called *acquiesence.* This occurs when students respond with a pattern, such as true-false-true-false, or true-true-true . . . , rather than actually attempting to identify the correct response choice in each and every case. Such a response pattern is often prompted by disinterest or hostility or by test items that are consistently too difficult to answer. Students who have the tendency to overselect the "true" response choice are referred to as "yeasayers."

Asch (1958) identified three kinds of distortions in reporting. Distortions of *perception* occur when we actually see things differently due to social pressure. Distortions of *judgment* are instances when social pressures cause us to alter our responses from what

---

Box 8.3

"TEACHING-TO-THE-TEST" PREVENTION: APPROPRIATE TESTS SHOULD REFLECT INSTRUCTION BUT NOT BE A PART OF IT!

The former U.S. Office of Economic Opportunity was roundly criticized on its evaluation of performance contracting (an approach where an educational technology company contracted to teach "disadvantaged" students and was to be remunerated based on the reading and math gains attained by these students in a given time period) in Texarkana because the contractors had presumably introduced the actual final exam as a part of their instructional program. In their second, larger experiment OEO made arrangements, reports Page (1972), to have

> the identity of pretests and posttests kept secret from everyone . . .
> any attempt by the contractors to discover the identity of the test
> would be sufficient cause for termination of the contract . . . even
> the instructional content was to be spot checked to make sure that
> no testing material was used in the conduct of instruction . . . tests
> were to be administered by outsiders so that there would be neither
> identification of tests nor aid to students in taking them . . . the
> evaluation of the data was to be done by a responsible and
> disinterested corporation.

No question that the new procedures insured that the contractors could not teach to the test. That possibility was adequately safeguarded, but the question of whether the test used was appropriate still remains to be answered.

---

we actually believe to be so because we have come to rely on the judgment of others. Distortions of *action* occur when social pressures cause us knowingly to conform; we consciously compromise what we believe in order to convey the desired impression. Such types of distortion introduce bias into the answers to test items. It may or may not be a conscious bias; in many cases its perpetrator is unwitting in its use—suffering a distortion of self-perception or judgment.

Box 8.4

CULTURAL EXPERIENCE VS. ACTUAL INTELLIGENCE

When is a test a measure of intelligence (that is, mental ability) and when is it a measure of one's exposure to or reinforcement by a culture? If a test is supposed to be an intelligence test and in fact is biased in favor of members of a particular culture, then its *appropriateness* as an intelligence test is questionable.

Many of our commonly-used IQ tests have been criticized for cultural bias, in many instances justifiably.

The following items taken from *The Bitch Test** illustrate the effect that culture might have on test performance.

(1) *Alley Apple*
   a. Brick
   b. Piece of fruit
   c. Dog
   d. Horse

(2) *Black Draught*
   a. Winter's coldwind
   b. Laxative
   c. Black soldier
   d. Dark beer

(3) *Blood*
   a. A vampire
   b. A dependent individual
   c. An injured person
   d. A brother of color

(4) *Boogie Jugie*
   a. Tired
   b. Worthless
   c. Old
   d. Well put together

(5) *Boot* refers to a:
   a. Cotton farmer
   b. Black
   c. Indian
   d. Vietnamese citizen

*Taken from the *Black Intelligence Test of Cultural Homogeneity* by permission of its author, Robert L. Williams. (Ans. (1) *a*, (2) *b*, (3) *d*, (4) *b*, (5) *b*.)

Culture is, among other things, a wavelength of communication. **Cultural Bias**
Teachers communicate largely in their cultures to students whose
cultures overlap to greater or lesser degrees with their own. Tests
also reflect a culture, usually that of the test maker. We may say
that a test always measures two things: a set of objectives, and
an ability to function in the culture in which it is written. If students are in a different culture or on a different wavelength from
that of the test, the test may lack appropriateness for them as a
measure of its objectives. However, we may also say that the
greater the appropriateness of a test based on its representing its
objectives, the greater the likelihood of its overall appropriateness. Hence, cultural bias is potentially a greater threat to the
appropriateness of broader, more general tests, such as standardized achievement tests, than it is to good teacher-built tests. Test
publishers usually screen their achievement tests to try to minimize the chance of culturally biased items. Teachers should be
careful not only to screen their own test items but their objectives
as well.

Where achievement items are not based on the known opportunity to learn (i.e., the availability of school-based instruction),
they may be measuring more culturally-based opportunities to
learn, thus introducing cultural bias. By virtue of their generality,
published tests may often be measuring outcomes that are tied in
their likelihood of occurrence to cultural experience. Items about
sports, for example, may be biased against girls. Tests with cultural
bias lose appropriateness accordingly unless their purpose is to
measure outcomes related to culture.

APPROPRIATENESS AND THE TEACHER

The kind of appropriateness most often considered by the teacher
is whether the test "looks" as if it measures what the teacher
intends to measure with it. We don't usually credit enough importance to this kind of informal judgment, which ironically and
confusingly, is called *face validity.*

If the students taking a test feel that it is inappropriate, this
may affect the way they respond to the items. If teachers feel that
a test is "unfair," they may reduce its value by indirectly communicating their misgivings to the students. If parents feel that a test
is not appropriate, they may successfully push to have the test
removed.

While the "naked eye" is thus an important judge of a test's appropriateness, it is not ultimately the best judge. We might say that appropriateness, a measure of a test's fit to its objectives, is really a *structured* form of face validity. Appropriateness is judged by "eye" rather than by statistics, but the judgment is aided by the application of stated objectives.

In choosing or using published tests, teachers should check the test manual to see whether objectives are available and whether they are the desired ones. (Since test manuals are often difficult to interpret, teachers may want to seek the assistance of a staff member with testing experience, a school psychologist, for example.) Teachers should question the appropriateness of standardized achievement measures for their own use in much the same way they should challenge and subsequently demonstrate (at least to themselves) the appropriateness of their own tests.

It is virtually impossible to judge the appropriateness of any achievement test, teacher-built or published, *unless you know the purpose or objectives that the test is intended to measure.* An achievement test should reflect what a teacher wants a student to have learned and thus presumably has taught. (Reexamine Figures 2.1 and 2.7 in Chapter 2 showing the systems approach—it is relevant to the point being made here.)

We might simplify the relationship between objectives, teaching, and tests as follows:

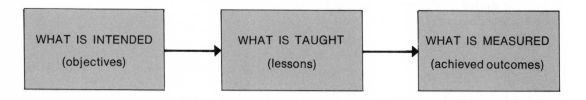

If a test is a measure of what is intended, and what is intended is actually taught, then achievement on the test will tell you the extent to which students have profited by instruction. If the test results indicate that many students have profited from instruction, those that did not may have been inattentive, poorly motivated, ill-prepared, or unable to relate to the instruction. You can also use test results to evaluate your teaching; if test scores indicate that few students profited from instruction, the instruction itself may have been at fault.

Additional Information Sources

Ebel, R. L. Obtaining and reporting evidence on content validity. *Educational and psychological measurement*, 1956, *16*, 269–282.

Lennon, R. T. Assumptions underlying the use of content validity. *Educational and psychological measurement*, 1956, *16*, 294–304.

Millman, J. Passing scores and test lengths for domain-referenced tests. Review of Educational Research, 1973, *43*, 205–216.

Popham, W. J. and Baker, E. *Writing tests which measure objectives.* Englewood Cliffs, N.J.: Prentice-Hall, 1973.

Self-test of Proficiency

(1) The most important consideration in determining a test's appropriateness is
   a. the vocabulary level of the test items.
   b. whether its purpose is psychometric or edumetric.
   c. whether it measures outcomes that are consistent with its objectives.
   d. the extent to which students have improved from pretesting to posttesting.

(2) List four questions that can be used to determine the appropriateness of a given test item.

(3) You have three objectives that you want to measure. Describe how you would use a content map to build an appropriate test of these objectives.

(4) Draw a diagram of a content map for a test of four objectives with total appropriateness. (Use a dot with a circle around it to indicate a test item that measures a given objective.) Make two of the objectives twice as important as the others.

(5) In most cases the minimum number of items necessary to measure each objective is _____.

(6) On the left are listed four standards for judging the appropriateness of a unit test in a high school humanities course. On the right are listed questions for applying these standards. Match each item on the left with an appropriate question on the right.
   a. Fits objectives.
   b. Reflects action verbs.
   c. Utilizes conditions.
   d. Employs criteria.

   i. Does the number of items reflect the relative importance of each part of the unit?
   ii. Does each item reflect the "given" in its corresponding objective?
   iii. Would this test be suitable for a similar humanities course in another school?
   iv. Is the item format appropriate for what the student is asked to do?
   v. Are the answers judged to be correct or incorrect according to terms stated in the objectives?

(7) Determine the appropriateness of the first seven items of this test for measuring the first three objectives of this chapter, listed on page 206.

(8) Domain-referencing requires as its primary prerequisite that
   a. objectives have been labeled as to cognitive or affective area.
   b. behavior to be measured by a set of test items has been specified.
   c. items have been classified as knowledge, comprehension, application, analysis, synthesis, or evaluation.
   d. items have been written to be representative of that set of performances an objective calls for.
   e. the acceptable level of performance has been defined in absolute terms.

(9) Domain-referencing helps insure that the items chosen are not too difficult for students to answer correctly.
TRUE   FALSE

(10) Check those factors below that can affect a test's appropriateness.
   a. response bias.
   b. student motivation.
   c. conditions of test administration.
   d. testing for skills not in the objectives.
   e. specific cultural factors.
   f. how much sleep a student has had the night before.

(11) You have just finished teaching a unit on oceans and have covered the names, descriptions, locations of the oceans, and the resources they provide. Your students are third graders in a small school in rural Tennessee. You are now constructing your end-of-unit test and have written the items below. Unfortunately, some of these items are inappropriate. Match those that are inappropriate on the right with the reason for inappropriateness on the left.

   a. different cultural wavelength.
   b. testing what you never taught.
   c. acquiesence response bias.

   i. What are the names of the five oceans?
   ii. Write a poem describing your feelings as you watch the sun rise over the ocean.
   iii. Which ocean is the largest?
   iv. What is the southernmost land mass on the planet Earth?
   v. The weight of all the water in the oceans is 100 million tons.　(TRUE　FALSE)

chapter nine / Test Validity

OBJECTIVES

1. Define validity, a criterion of predictive tests, as the relation between test outcomes and purposes.

2. Identify the relative size of correlation coefficients associated with different scatter plots.

3. Identify and contrast four different types of test validity, namely: *a*. concurrent, *b*. predictive, *c*. construct, and *d*. criterion.

4. Describe how the four different types of validity are determined.

5. Describe four checklist procedures that teachers can use for applying the above types of validity, namely: *a*. determining the ability of a test to discriminate, *b*. determining the ability of a test to relate to an external standard, *c*. obtaining consensus by colleagues, and *d*. minimizing invalidity based on reading level and other biases.

The question of validity is different from the question of appropriateness, for validity cannot be satisfied only on the basis of a test meeting its own objectives. While appropriateness uses internal criteria, i.e., the test's own objectives for evaluation, validity requires criteria external to the test itself. Hence, a test can be appropriate but not necessarily valid, although the reverse cannot be true. In other words, the fact that a test measures its own objectives may not, in the final analysis, be enough. It may be necessary to validate the objectives themselves to be sure that the test can be used to predict student performance in the area for which the course learning is intended to be a prerequisite. If we simply want to record educational gains (the *edumetric* function), then appropriateness is sufficient. But if we want to predict subsequent outcomes (the *psychometric* function), validity is essential.

Test validity refers to whether a test measures what we intend it to measure. If a test's objective is to measure aptitude for mathematics, how are we to determine whether the outcomes it measures really represent this aptitude? How can we tell whether students who score high on a test of attitudes toward school really like school more than those who score low? Can we assume that students who score higher on an intelligence test are really brighter than low scorers? To answer these questions, we may consider three points of reference for evaluating the outcomes of a test— the past, the present, and the future.

Do Outcomes Reflect Purposes?

The objective of many tests is to measure the effect of certain experiences that have occurred prior to the test. Teacher-built achievement tests and standardized achievement tests share this point of reference. Their purpose is to find out the extent to which the objectives of the prior experience have been met. As such, they are used to *monitor* or *assess* an experience that has already occurred or to determine student learning based on that experience.

Other tests have their point of reference in the future. They aim to *detect* the presence of a quality that will *predict* a person's future behavior. Some companies, for example, use tests in the process of screening job applicants. The objective of these tests is to find out whether an applicant possesses a particular characteristic that, it is assumed, will lead him or her to succeed in the future on the job. The test outcome is expected to be predictive of

Figure 9.1   *Testing for Validity: How We Can Tell Whether the Outcomes of a Test Reflect the Purposes for Which It Is Used.*

Time Referent of Test Outcome	Validity Question	Type of Validity	Kind of Tests
Past	(1) Does the test content reflect what was intended to be taught?	Appropriateness (content)	Achievement Tests
	(2) Do persons who have been taught do better on the test than persons not taught?	Criterion	Achievement Tests (Criterion-referenced)
Present	(1) Do persons who already show other evidence of the quality do better on the test than persons who do not?	Concurrent	Intelligence Tests Competency Tests
	(2) Do scores on the test relate to other qualities with which they are expected to be related?	Construct	Personality Tests
Future	(1) Do scores on the test predict success in a subsequent, related area?	Predictive	Aptitude Tests Personnel Tests College Boards

future success with the company. Colleges and universities similarly use tests for screening purposes. These tests aim to detect the presence of abilities that will help the individual to succeed in his or her future education. While outcomes on these tests may be based somewhat on past experience, the major objective of such tests is to predict future success.

Finally, some tests have their principal point of reference in the *present*, focusing on the concurrence of other presumably related qualities to the one being measured. It may be said, for example, that students with greater achievement motivation will be found to volunteer for more bonus assignments. Finding a relationship between the outcome of a test of "achievement motivation" and "volunteering behavior" would support the conclusion that the test outcome reflects the test objective, that is, that the test is a measure of achievement motivation.

The different respects in which a test may be valid are summarized in Figure 9.1. Each of the procedures for determining the degree to which a test is valid, that is, determining whether the test measures what it is intended to measure, will be described in the remaining sections of this chapter. (Procedures for assessing a test's appropriateness were described in the preceding chapter.)

What happens when you use a test whose validity has not been demonstrated by either you or its publisher? You may be using a test that is unsuitable for your purpose; that is, you may be using a test whose outcomes do not empirically relate to its purpose. Such a test does a disservice to the test taker since conclusions based on it may reflect on some characteristic of the test taker other than the one that you intend to measure. Suppose, for example, you had administered a test intended to measure reading ability and after you scored it you noticed that a student whom you knew to be an excellent reader had gotten a low score. It may be that the test is measuring qualities other than reading ability. If the test is invalid, you will be reaching erroneous conclusions not only about that particular student's ability but about all the students who take the test. You need evidence that a test is measuring what its title says it is measuring.

Failure to Validate

Consider a test used by a large company to hire machinists; on the basis of scores, predictions are made regarding the test taker's subsequent success as a machinist. However, because the test requires a greater degree of reading skill than that required by a machinist, it discriminates against poorer readers, an outcome that does not relate to the objective of the test, namely, to select persons with those skills to be good machinists. Obviously, the company should select a more valid test of machinist aptitude.

There are many tests that are difficult to validate but are used nevertheless to make important decisions. Mental ability (i.e., intelligence) tests are typically validated by comparing them to other mental ability tests. That is not an unacceptable strategy if the comparison test itself can be considered to have a high degree of validity.

Many factors may enter into a person's performance on an intelligence test (or any other test, for that matter). Some of these factors may be based on the fact that the test is a measure of something other than what it is intended to be a measure of. Intelligence tests may be tests of academic motivation or of prior intellectual experiences rather than of potential for learning. Without some acceptable evidence of the validity of a test for the time, place, and group with which it will be used, it is unwise to use it for the purpose of decision-making.

Teachers are not ordinarily called upon to validate tests other than those they themselves construct. However, when teachers use a published test and make judgments based on its scores, they should be able to evaluate that test based in part on the evidence of its validity. Thus, teachers must know not only how to validate their own tests but how to evaluate a published test. Fortunately, most published tests provide evidence of their validity in the test manual.

CONCURRENT VALIDITY

Concurrent validity tells whether the degree to which persons show evidence of a quality on a given test is reflected in or paralleled by their scores on another test of presumably the "same" characteristic. Often, for example, the concurrent validity of a test of mental ability is based on its relation to other tests of mental ability. As we can see from Figure 9.1, concurrent validity has its time reference in the present since the two tests must be given contemporaneously.

Concurrent validity is expressed as the relationship between two sets of test scores. Because this relationship is expressed as a correlation coefficient, to discuss and explain the concept of concurrent validity, we must first understand how to interpret correlation coefficients. Following a discussion of correlation coefficients we will return to the matter of concurrent validity.

Interpreting Correlation Coefficients A correlation coefficient can range from $+1.00$ to -1.00. A coefficient of $+1.00$ indicates that two sets of test scores are perfectly related; a coefficient of 0.00 indicates that two sets of test scores are totally unrelated; a coefficient of -1.00 indicates that two sets of test scores are perfectly related in the opposite direction (as scores on one increase, scores on the other decrease). Figure 9.2

Scatter Plots Showing Test Correlations.   **Figure 9.2**

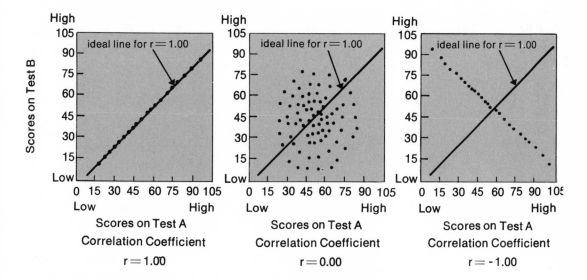

graphically displays some correlation coefficients. A correlation coefficient is displayed by plotting the scores of one test on one coordinate of the graph and the scores for the same persons on the second test on the other coordinate. The resulting set of points, called a *scatter plot*, illustrates by virtue of its spread the size of the correlation coefficient relating the two sets of scores.

Let us examine some actual correlation coefficients between scores on tests intended to measure the same quality to illustrate what is meant by a correlation coefficient and its use in establishing concurrent validity.

Illustrations
Concurrent validity is perhaps best illustrated for mental ability (so-called intelligence) tests. For the Peabody Picture Vocabulary Test (PPVT; presumably a measure of verbal intelligence), median correlations of 0.71 are reported with mental age scores on the Stanford-Binet Intelligence Scale (Dunn, 1965). This test is also reported to correlate at a median level of 0.67 with the Verbal score on the Wechsler Intelligence Scale for Children (WISC). Consistent with its purpose and hence validity, the median correlation of the PPVT (a verbal test) with the nonverbal Performance score on the Wechsler scale is only 0.39 (Dunn, 1965) as contrasted to the 0.67 above.

Figure 9.3   *Correlation of the Culture Fair with Other Tests.**

Mean IQ	Test		(1)	(2)	(3)	(4)	(5)	(6)
96	Culture Fair IQ	(1)	1.00	.49	.69	.62	.63	.72
87	Otis Beta IQ	(2)		1.00	.80	.69	.45	.66
90	Pintner IQ	(3)			1.00	.81	.55	.79
92	WISC Verbal IQ	(4)				1.00	.53	.89
93	WISC Performance IQ	(5)					1.00	.86
92	WISC Full Scale IQ	(6)						1.00

* Reproduced with permission from the Technical Supplement for The Culture Fair Intelligence Test, © 1973 by IPAT, Champaign, Ill.

Another illustration of concurrent validity is shown in Figure 9.3. The correlations between the Culture Fair Scales and other measures of intelligence tend to be high and at least in the same range as the correlations between each of these tests and one another. (Note that the correlation between each test and itself in Figure 9.3 is indicated as 1.00 representing a ceiling or point of reference. Correlations between specific pairs of tests are located by referring to their numbers.)

Concurrent Validity and Correlations

If a test manual reports high correlations between scores on that test and scores on another test presumably of the same quality, we may conclude that the given test has some degree of concurrent validity. If the comparison test is a well-reputed one, high correlations and hence high concurrent validity will constitute a good reason for using that test.[1] The reasonably high correlations reported between the Culture Fair Scales and other intelligence tests provide evidence of its concurrent validity. It tends to correlate as highly with other tests as they do with one another. Its correlation of .72 with the WISC Full Scale is strong positive evidence for its concurrent validity. However, we would expect it to correlate higher with WISC-Performance than with WISC-Verbal since it is a *nonverbal* test. Its correlations of .63 and .62 with WISC Performance and Verbal respectively, raise some question of its concurrent validity as a nonverbal and hence "cultural fair" test.[2]

[1] You might ask: "Why not use the well-reputed one?" The answer may be that it contains features undesirable for your use, e.g., it may require individual administration.
[2] Note, however, that WISC-Verbal and WISC-Performance have an intercorrelation themselves of .53.

CONSTRUCT VALIDITY

Like concurrent validity, construct validity has its time referent in the present (see Figure 9.1) and refers to *the extent to which a test's scores correlate with other scores to which we can expect it to be related.* The correspondence in purpose between two tests used in establishing concurrent validity is quite direct—both presumably measuring exactly the *same* quality. For example, mental ability test #1 and mental ability test #2 should be related because they purport to measure the same qualities. That is concurrent validity. Construct validity, on the other hand, is an attempt to relate tests that measure different, but conceptually connected, qualities. For example, aptitude tests measure the concept or construct of potential for achieving, which presumably would affect a student's degree of achievement in reading; hence, relating an aptitude test to a reading test represents an attempt to establish construct validity. (The differences between concurrent validity and construct validity are illustrated in Figure 9.4).

Another example of construct validity would be to take scores from a test of sociability (which presumably measures the construct: sociability) and show that students possessing more of this construct will have more friends than students possessing less of this construct. By comparing the number of people who report to be friends of high test scorers with the number reporting

Illustrations of Concurrent and Construct Validities.   **Figure 9.4**

CONCURRENT VALIDITY

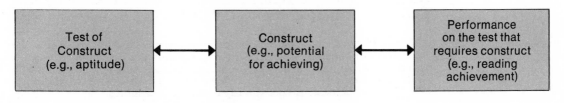

CONSTRUCT VALIDITY

Figure 9.5   *Correlations between DAT Subtest Scores and METRO Reading Score.*

DAT SCORE

	Verval Reasoning	Numerical Ability	Abstract Reasoning	Space Relations	Mechanical Reasoning	Clerical Speed and Accuracy	Spelling	Sentences
Reading Achievement Score (METRO)	.74	.58	.43	.26	.42	−.07	.39	.67

friendship for low scorers, the construct validity of the test can be determined.

Illustration

In the *Manual for the Differential Aptitude Tests* (*DAT*: Bennett et al., 1966), correlations are reported for 68 ninth grade boys between their scores on each subtest of the DAT and the Reading score derived from the Metropolitan Achievement Tests (METRO), as shown by Figure 9.5.

What do these correlations mean? Since all DAT subtests, except for Space Relations and Clerical Speed and Accuracy, represent the components or *constructs* on which the mastery of reading skills would seem to be based, with the exception of those two we would expect some relationship between each of the DAT subtests and the Reading achievement score. Note that the two correlations closest to zero are for Space Relations and Clerical Speed and Accuracy. Moreover, the DAT subtests that measure constructs which seemingly most clearly underlie the development of reading achievement are the Verbal Reasoning subtest (a verbal comprehension aptitude test) and Sentences (a grammar and punctuation aptitude test). Note that the two correlations closest to 1.00 are for these two tests (.74 and .67, respectively).[3] Consider the two scatter plots for the Verbal Reasoning and Space Relations Subtests each as related to the METRO Reading achievement score

---

[3] We would expect the test for clerical aptitude presumably measuring the construct of potential for learning clerical tasks (and we can only presume what construct a test measures) to be least related to reading achievement. (Reading would not seem to be a clerical task.) Indeed, the correlation of −.07 supports the construct validity of the clerical subtest.

shown in Figure 9.6. For Verbal Reasoning, the higher correlation is based on a smaller spread of scores around the 45° line that represents the perfect correlation of 1.00 (see Figure 9.2). For Space Relations, the lower correlation is based on a larger spread of scores around the 45° line, approaching the essentially random pattern of a correlation of 0.00 seen as a circle (see Figure 9.2).[4]

What do the above correlations between the DAT Subtest Scores of aptitudes and the METRO Reading achievement score tell about the construct validity of the DAT?[5] Although correlations to a single test score like the METRO Reading achievement score do not tell the whole story, the correlations do tell us that reading

Construct Validity and Correlations

Scatter Plots for the Relationship between DAT Verbal Reasoning and the METRO Reading Achievement Scores and between Space Relations Aptitude and the METRO Reading Achievement Scores.   **Figure 9.6**

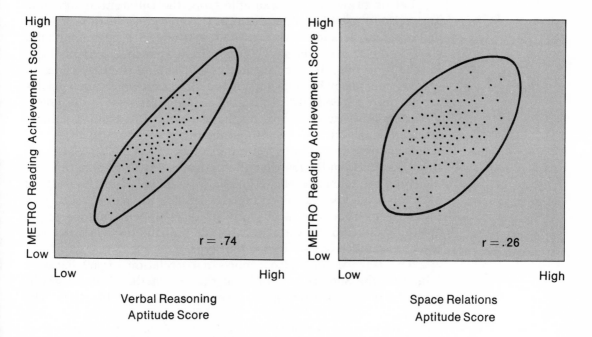

[4] For construct validity purposes, correlations of .40 and above are considered high. For concurrent validity purposes, correlations of .55 and above are considered high.
[5] Approximately one-third of the *DAT Manual* is concerned with validity.

achievement is a manifestation of constructs such as Verbal Reasoning aptitude and Language (i.e., Sentences) aptitude. Since these DAT subtests are intended to be measures of verbal and language aptitude, and since verbal and language aptitude constructs presumably underlie reading skill, the reasonably high correlations between Verbal Reasoning and Sentences subtests and the METRO Reading achievement score do tend to provide construct validity for these subtests of the DAT.

PREDICTIVE VALIDITY

Predictive validity indicates the degree of correspondence between scores on the test in question and future outcomes that are expected to be related to the characteristic measured by the test. As shown in Figure 9.1, predictive validity has a future time frame. The question is whether and to what degree a test taken in the present can predict outcomes in the future.

Let us draw another example from the Differential Aptitude Tests (DAT) used for illustration in the preceding section. If logic dictates that persons with a greater aptitude in a particular area should do better in courses related to that area than persons lacking that aptitude, then scores on the DAT should predict grades in various courses by identifying aptitude levels on which such grades are partially dependent.[6] In the *DAT Manual* (Bennett et al., 1966), a correlation between scores on the Mechanical Reasoning subtest attained at the end of eleventh grade and grades in a twelfth year science course for 107 boys is reported as r=.58. A correlation of this magnitude indicates that the aptitude test is reasonably predictive of the science grade. (Correlations above .45 are considered high for predictive validity purposes.) Since the test presumes to measure aptitude and accurately predicts a performance in an aptitude-related area, we may conclude that the test (i.e., the subtest) has predictive validity for that type of course.

The *DAT Manual* also reports a correlation of .69 between scores on the Sentences subtest at the end of the eleventh grade, and grades earned in English a semester later by 143 girls. The

---

[6] This reasoning is somewhat similar to the reasoning in the example given to illustrate construct validity where aptitude and reading achievement scores were related. The difference is that the aptitude and reading achievement levels were determined at the same time while in this illustration, aptitude scores were obtained prior to the students' taking the course.

"Your aptitude test shows you're very good at taking aptitude tests!"

magnitude of this correlation provides further evidence of the predictive validity of the DAT.[7] Finally, the *DAT Manual* also reports
a correlation of .69 between scores on the Space Relations subtest
taken at the time of admission into a watch repair training program and grades obtained by sixty boys at the end of the program.

Again, if we assume that specific aptitudes are predictive of
specific performances, and a test of an aptitude is correlated to the
appropriate performance, then we can conclude that the test has
some predictive validity and hence is a measure of the aptitude it
presumably intends to measure.

It is incorrect to say that because a test and a performance are   **Correlation**
correlated, the characteristic measured by the test has *caused* that   **Does Not Equal**
performance. It may well be that the performance has caused the   **Causation**
characteristic measured by the test, even though the test was taken
first. The fact that one measurement occurs before another does

---

[7] A correlation of this size indicates roughly fifty percent overlap between
test scores and grades (i.e., overlap equals the square of the correlation
times 100). Since aptitudes account for only half the influence on grades,
clearly other factors are also important.

not necessarily mean that the first caused the second. There is also the possibility that both the test score and the subsequent performance have had a third factor as their primary source of influence. For these reasons, we say that *correlation does not necessarily imply causation.* Correlation does imply relation but does not unequivocally identify causality.

Are we justified in saying that aptitude in space relations caused success in a job training program because the two are correlated? Perhaps motivation to succeed is more likely the cause for success on both measures. Although it is possible—perhaps probable—that aptitudes and performance are causally related, from a single correlation it is impossible to tell whether they are or not. We can, however, conclude from the correlation that a relationship exists.

Suppose, to take a fictitious example, that a correlation of .65 exists between the infant mortality rate in this country and the amount of money spent on road repairs. Are we to conclude that the death of babies causes roads to break up or that broken roads cause the death of babies? Neither seems likely. What seems more likely is that a third factor, extremes of temperature or level of industrialization or amount of pollutants in the air or poor driving, contributes to both outcomes: infant deaths and roads in disrepair, causing the two to correlate.

Let us draw a last example from the classroom. Suppose attendance and grades correlate .60. Are we to assume that presence in the classroom *alone* causes a student to learn? While it may be difficult to learn when not there, it is probably true to say that both attendance and grades reflect a third factor, motivation, that influences them both: to go to school and, once there, to do well.

CRITERION VALIDITY

Criterion validity indicates the extent to which students who have had training on the objectives being measured score higher on a test of those objectives than students who have not had training. Its time referent, as shown in Figure 9.1, is in the past since the effect of training already received is being used to evaluate the test. The distinction for this type of validity is based on the identification of a *criterion group,* that is, persons who we believe have already acquired proficiency in the trait or skill being measured.

Illustrations

Let us return to the *DAT Manual* for an example of criterion validity testing. The *DAT Manual* reports the scores on each of the subtests of the DAT for men and women in various educational and occupational groups. (The test scores were obtained *after* the groups experienced or became identified with the occupation or education.) The high scores of engineering and science majors in Numerical Ability, the low scores of liberal arts majors on Space Relations and Mechanical Reasoning, and the relatively greater performance on Mechanical Reasoning than on Verbal Reasoning by employed skilled tradesmen, support the criterion validity of the tests.[8]

A second illustration of criterion validity applies more directly to the classroom teacher. Before students have been given instruction on a particular set of objectives, they represent an untrained group. After such instruction has been completed, they constitute a trained group. If your test of proficiency on the given objectives has criterion validity, students should score lower on it when untrained (i.e., before instruction—when it is given as a pretest) than when trained (i.e., after instruction—when given as a posttest). In this case the same group serves as both the untrained and trained group with training or instruction intervening. The posttest's validity is evaluated with reference to the pretest.

Criterion validity can also be applied to a test with respect to its objectives or content. After a test has been developed, it can be submitted to a *panel of experts* or *jury* of presumed content specialists whose opinions serve as the *criterion* and validate the content coverage of the test. Their concurrence with the content of the test will provide support for the acceptance of its content validity or appropriateness.

Where do these experts come from? Colleagues can often serve this capacity—that is, members of your department or grade level team. Subject matter specialists such as a curriculum coordinator or subject-matter coordinating committee would also be suitable. If the purpose of the test is to measure objectives related to students' preparedness for college, then the panel of experts should be drawn from the college faculty ranks in the appropriate

---

[8] However, an indication of the inability of subtests to discriminate by field of training is that premedical students do better than and education students more poorly than other degree-seeking groups on all subtests, rather than each group having differential success on those subtests most closely related to their training, as might be expected.

subject matter. If the purpose of the test is to measure students' preparedness for jobs, then the panel of experts should be drawn from employers and employees in the specific occupational area. In a sense both of these latter types of groups (i.e., college professors and representatives from an occupational area) can attest to the validity of the content of a test as a measure of the kinds of skills and knowledge that is prerequisite to entry into the respective institution of each (i.e., college and the job). *The essence of criterion validity as described here, then, is not that the test fits a particular set of instruction but that the test fits the situation for which the instruction is presumably a prerequisite as judged by experts in that situation.*

One final example of criterion validity will be offered. This is the matter of whether members of the criterion group themselves obtained high scores on the test when they were students. This is quite similar to predictive validity; Cronbach (1970), in fact, uses the terms "predictive validity" and "criterion validity" synonymously. If those who were once high scorers on the test are now succeeding in higher education or on the job, then the test has criterion validity.

DETERMINING A TEST'S VALIDITY

Using the various types of validity (i.e., concurrent, construct, predictive, and criterion) a teacher can determine a test's validity. While the preceding discussion was intended to assist you in *understanding* test validity, this section is intended to assist you in *determining* test validity.

That portion of the test criterion checklist (pages 304–06) that applies to the determination of validity is shown below.

Is My Test VALID?
(1) Does It Discriminate between Performance Levels:
    a. Do students who are independently judged to perform better in the test area perform better on the test?
    b. Do different students with different degrees of experience perform differently on the various items?

(2) Does It Fit Any External Standard:
    a. Does success on the test predict subsequent success in areas for which the test topic is claimed to be a prerequisite?

   b. Do students who receive appropriate teaching perform better on the test than untaught students (or does a student perform better on the test after training than before)?

(3) How Do My Colleagues View the Coverage:
   a. Do my colleagues in the topic area or at the grade level agree that all necessary objectives and no unnecessary ones have been included?
   b. Do they agree that the items are valid for measuring the objectives?

(4) Does It Measure Something Other than Reading Level or Life Styles:
   a. Are the demands it makes on reading skill within students' capabilities?
   b. Is performance independent of group membership or any other socio-ethnic variable?

Ability of the Test to Discriminate

One approach to determining a test's validity is to ask yourself whether you have some other way of assessing the characteristic or skill presumably measured by the test. If your test is one way to assess performance and you have another way independent of the test, will the two produce similar results? While there might be some shortcomings in this independent source of judgment, if it represents a second way of finding out the same information as your test and the two sources agree, the external results would reinforce and provide validity for your test. The likelihood that both are invalid, while a possibility, would be small. (Remember that this approach is different from writing a list of objectives, constructing a test and comparing the two to see whether your test is measuring your objectives.) What one ordinarily does in using this approach to validity is to ask a judge, the student taking the test, the teacher, or someone else familiar with the student's abilities to evaluate the student on the characteristic or skill in question. *This judgment, made independently of the test, represents an attempt to determine the degree to which the student has the characteristic or the skill that the test is attempting to measure.* This is basically a procedure for determining *concurrent validity.*

For example, a test in electronics is being used to establish the level of a student's competency. Does it, in fact, measure or distinguish between more competent and less competent students in the target area? Does it discriminate between good and poor performance? Opinions of other teachers (or of yourself), of students, or others who see or have seen the student perform in electronics could be used as a means of *independently*[9] assessing the competence level of the student in the target area by using a simple scale that has at one end: *the student is very competent*, and at the other end: *the student is not very competent*. The numbers 1–10 are placed between the two ends. Results can be averaged across judges to provide a single concurrent judgment of the student's competency. These judgments for each student are then compared to his or her performance on the competency test.

A second basis for establishing a test's validity based on its ability to discriminate may be best classified as *criterion validity*. This procedure involves the comparison among individuals of different experience in the area of the test. If the test is valid, those individuals with greater relevant experience should perform better on the test than those with less relevant experience. Judgments of relevant experience, the criterion variable, can be obtained from the students themselves using a ten-point scale like that described above. For example, to validate the test of electronics you would ask each student to rate his or her own experience in electronics (based on being a ham radio operator or tinkering with other kinds of related equipment) on the scale shown below.

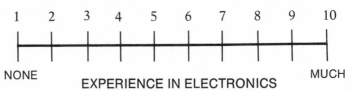

These self-ratings of experience can then be compared to each student's score on the test to determine their degree of correspondence.

The above procedures can be used to examine the validity of an instrument as a whole and of each of the individual items. The performance on any individual item can be recorded as a check or a no check (pass or fail) and can be correlated to the overall global ratings of the judges. Those items having the highest correlations can be retained and those having the lowest correlations rejected. Using this procedure you can build validity into your test instrument in terms of its ability to discriminate between performance

---

[9] "Independently" means without first seeing the scores on the test.

levels as judged by independent sources. You can also simply determine the validity of the total test rather than of the individual items by determining the correlation between students' scores on the total test and the global ratings of the judges, and continuing to use the test if its overall validity level is sufficient.[10]

Recall that *predictive validity* refers to the ability of a test to relate to or forecast a future outcome. If you can determine a future outcome that your test should relate to, you can compare test scores to this outcome to see if the expected relationship occurs. To continue with the electronics example, your competency test may be expected to predict ultimate success in the course, or success on next week's performance test, or getting an electronics job upon graduation, or performance on a licensing examination.

Ability of the Test to Relate to an External Standard

Construct validity refers to the relationship of two different tests whose conceptual bases seemed to be related. If the teacher's midterm or final examination in a specific subject-matter area is one of the two tests, a standardized achievement test in the same global area or of prerequisite skills and knowledge could be the second test or "external standard." Correlating scores on the two tests would tell you whether results on your test corresponded to those on the more general published test—a result that would help you decide on the validity of your test.

Another, and possibly easier, way to deal with the issue of validity in terms of an external standard (particularly for a classroom teacher who does not have access to other relevant sources of data) is to give a pretest and posttest to measure the effect of the intervening instruction. Determining whether posttest scores substantially exceed pretest scores of the test represents an assessment of the *criterion validity*.

The use of a pretest is much more common in research than in the classroom. Because an obvious way to find out if someone has changed is to know the point at which he or she started, researchers have come to view a pretest as a normal part of their procedures.

It is important to realize that a *pretest* is different from a *diagnostic test*. The latter is a way of finding out whether students

[10] For specific instructions on calculating different types of correlation coefficients, consult a statistics text. If you prefer to avoid statistical texts, you can examine the relationship between test scores and judges' ratings visually by plotting a scatter graph (see Figure 9.2 and 9.6, pages 233 and 237.

"If only 6 plus 2 equalled 9!"

have attained the prerequisites needed to master the particular
learning experience that confronts them. The purpose of a pretest
is to find out whether students have learned what a unit is attempting to teach before having had it. There is a difference. *A pretest is
a posttest or final exam given at the beginning of instruction
rather than the end.* While a diagnostic test may contribute to
instruction, it does not help you determine whether your achievement test is a good one.

If you (1) develop a measuring instrument before your students have a learning experience, (2) administer the instrument to
them first as a pretest, and (3) again (or in alternate form) after
they have had the experience, as long as the learning experience
has not been harmful or totally ineffective, if your test is valid it
will reflect higher scores for the class as a group on the posttest
than on the pretest. If we assume that you have taught what you
intended to teach and that through teaching, some reasonable

degree of learning has taken place, then the students will know more at the end (after teaching) than in the beginning (before teaching). If your pretest and posttest administrations do not render different scores, you may not necessarily conclude that the test is invalid because the absence of differences may be a function of the total ineffectiveness of instruction (unless you have some basis for considering the instruction effective). However, if posttest scores are substantially higher than pretest[11] scores, then you can conclude not only (1) that the instruction was reasonably effective, but also (2) that the test is sensitive enough to detect this effectiveness and hence is valid. To use this technique, however, you must be sure that you do not teach the answers to your specific test questions during instruction. You must cover your objectives but not your actual test items.

A third way to deal with test validity (and again a reasonably practical one for the classroom teacher) is to solicit the judgment of colleagues and others in determining whether (1) the right objectives have been chosen for instruction and (2) the right items chosen for testing. (This approach represents a way of using content validity or appropriateness as discussed in Chapter 8.) While the items on your test may reflect your objectives, the objectives themselves may not be suitable for the grade level and subject area. If the objectives used to evaluate test item appropriateness are themselves invalid, the test of these objectives will in turn lack validity.

Test Validity through Consensus by Colleagues

Although there is no absolute way of dealing with the validation of objectives, some group discussion among teachers should be useful. Researchers often send their instruments out to so-called juries or panels of experts. They present these expert colleagues with a list of items and ask: "Are these the right things to measure? Would you eliminate some? Would you include others? Would you measure this way?" The researchers then use these collective expert judgments to make decisions about what is or is not important or valid.

Teachers, too, can engage in this consensus process. They can meet and elicit each other's reactions through committees. They

---

[11] If pretest and posttest are to be given within four weeks or less of one another, alternate or parallel tests forms should be used to avoid a testing or memory effect. For longer intervals, the same form may be reused but must be taken out of circulation in the interim.

can ask each other: "Are these the right objectives and right test items for this age group? For these particular students? For this stage in the learning process? Do the test items adequately reflect the objectives or the domains within which the objectives fall?" It may be very difficult to answer these kinds of questions if you have teachers from only one grade level or from only a single discipline; you are bound to find conditions under which the same objective or same test item may be suitable for more than one grade level or for more than one discipline. A review of techniques for determining agreement among judges is provided by Light (1973).

Invalidity Based on Reading Level and Other Biases

One reason that many tests are invalid is that they measure a student's reading ability rather than what they are intended to measure. Too often tests are written at the reading level of the writer (e.g., teacher) rather than at the reading level of the user (e.g., student).

Obviously, if students cannot read the items they cannot demonstrate knowledge by providing the information called for even if they know it. Although there may be some relationship between students' reading levels and their ability to acquire the knowledge that is being tested for, a test written above their reading level should most properly be called a reading test and not a test of subject-matter achievement. To write a test at low reading level a good rule is to use small words and short sentences. In general the longer a word or a sentence, the more difficult it is to read and understand.[12]

We must also be concerned not to introduce other forms of bias such as *acquiescence response bias*—a student's checking the same answer on every item. There are various reasons why a student might adopt this response pattern: he or she is sleepy and not reading the item, or hostile and not inclined to cooperate, or likes the word "true" much better than "false," or does not know the answer. Often this kind of bias occurs because a test fails to engage a student's interest. One way to combat acquiescence response bias is to construct a test that is interesting and involves students, thus overcoming their tendency to choose answers without regard to the items themselves.

---

[12] Readability formulas such as that of Fry (1964) may be applied to tests to provide a rough approximation of their reading level.

Additional Information Sources

American Educational Research Association, American Psychological Association, National Council on Measurement in Education. *Standards for educational and psychological tests.* Wash., D.C.: American Psychological Association, 1974.

Cronbach, L. J. Validation of educational measures. *Proceedings of the 1969 Invitational Conference on Testing Problems.* Princeton, N.J.: Educational Testing Service, 1969, 35–52.

Cronbach, L. J. Test validation. In R. L. Thorndike (Ed.), *Educational measurement*, 2nd ed. Wash., D.C.: American Council on Education, 1971, Chap. 14.

Cureton, E. E. Measurement theory. In R. L. Ebel (Ed.), *Encyclopedia of educational research*, 4th ed. N.Y.: Macmillan, 1969, 785–804.

Dick, W. & Hagerty, N. *Topics in measurement: Reliability and validity.* N.Y.: McGraw-Hill, 1971.

Self-test of Proficiency

(1) Test validity is concerned with
   a. the accuracy of a test.
   b. the extent to which a test measures what it is intended to measure.
   c. improving a student's ability to score well on tests.
   d. the meaning of a test's scores.
   e. none of the above.

(2) To determine the validity of a test, it is necessary to apply _____ (internal, external, academic) standards.

(3) What could you say about the relationship between variables A and B based on the scatter plot below?

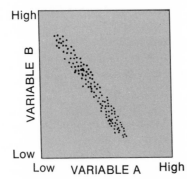

   a. their correlation is negative.
   b. their correlation is high.
   c. the predictability of one given the other is great.
   d. all of the above.
   e. none of the above.

(4) Below are three scatter plots. Which one illustrates a correlation coefficient that is closest to zero?

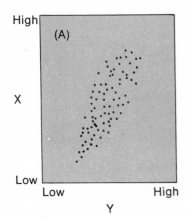

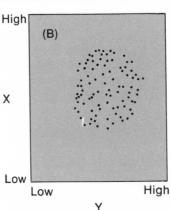

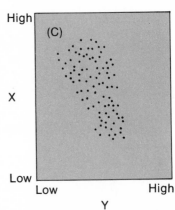

(5) Match the type of validity at left with its definition at right.

a. concurrent.
b. predictive.
c. construct.
d. criterion.

i. relation between scores on different tests of related variables.
ii. relation between scores on different tests of the same variable.
iii. extent of differentiation between scores of a trained group and scores of an untrained group.
iv. relation between scores on the same test taken twice.
v. relation between test scores and future outcomes.

(6) For each finding listed below, indicate if it is an instance of concurrent, construct, predictive, or criterion validity for the test underlined.

a. Students who were completing a chemical technology training program scored higher on the Chemical Technology Occupational Competency Examination than students who had not had such training.
b. Students who score high on the Sociability Scale are found to receive more friendship nominations than those who score low.
c. A positive correlation is found between scores on the Gates-McGinitie Reading Tests and the Iowa Silent Reading Tests.
d. Students who score high on the Cognitive Abilities Test taken at the start of eighth grade graduate from high school with a higher grade point average than those who score low.

(7) You have just constructed a test to measure aptitude for electronics. Describe in one sentence each how you would determine the a. predictive validity, and b. criterion validity of your test.

(8) You have just discovered a test to measure students' attitudes toward school. Describe in one sentence each how you would determine its a. concurrent validity and b. construct validity.

(9) You are an art teacher and have been asked by the head of the art department to construct a test of artistic ability. Describe two *practical* procedures you could use to judge its validity by determining its ability to discriminate or relate to an external standard.

(10) Describe two procedures for validating the self-tests of proficiency in this book.

chapter ten / Test Reliability

OBJECTIVES
1. Define reliability, a test criterion, as test accuracy or consistency over time and items.

2. Identify the standard error of measurement and its relationship to test reliability.

3. Identify and contrast five different types of test reliability, namely: *a.* Kuder-Richardson Formula 21, *b.* parallel item agreement, *c.* split-half (including the Spearman-Brown Formula) *d.* alternate forms, and *e.* test-retest.

4. Name overall sources of test variability and sources of error, and give examples of each.

5. Identify ways of building reliability into a test, namely: using a sufficient number of items, targeting, controlling conditions of test administration, controlling for general or specific skills, setting intermediate levels of difficulty, and following item writing rules.

6. Describe four checklist procedures that teachers can use to determine and improve the reliability of a test, namely: *a.* determining parallel item agreement, *b.* using item analysis, *c.* examining student response patterns, and *d.* improving reliability of scoring.

NO MEASUREMENT IS PERFECT

No measurement instrument or procedure is perfect. Neither a mechanical device such as a voltmeter nor a human device such as a test gives a result that is a perfect reflection of the property being measured. If you measured the same thing twice under the same conditions you would not get the *exact* same measurement each time. However, given an accurate measuring procedure, the values you would get if you measured twice would probably be so close that you could not tell them apart by eye. Measure the length of this page with a twelve-inch ruler. Now do it a second time; the result is probably the same as the first. Given a less accurate measuring procedure, the values you get if you measure twice will not be as close. Try measuring the page with a pencil instead of a ruler. Does the page measure the same number of pencil lengths each time?

When you measure some property of an object or person, you are attempting to discover the *true value* of that property. In measuring the length of the page, you were attempting to find out how long the page actually is, that is, its *true* length (sometimes referred to as *actual* length). When you read its length off the ruler, you were discovering its measured or *obtained* length. But are the two not the same? No, they are not because all measurement contains errors. If you were to measure the length of the page say 100 times, and then average all of the measurements, that average would be about as close to the true length as you are likely to get using a ruler. It might be possible to improve the accuracy of the measurement by using a more finely calibrated ruler, but, even so, the measured or obtained length and the true length would not be exactly the same.

Consider now a teacher-built test to measure achievement or learning. The teacher is really interested in how much the student has learned, that is, the learning score. To determine that score, the teacher must construct a measuring instrument—a test. However, because the test results reflect not only how much the student has learned but also how accurate a measuring instrument the test is, the score for each student is a less than perfect measure of how much he or she has learned.

Because teachers do not want to come to conclusions about student performance (or anything else for that matter) based on the scores of inaccurate tests, they want to build tests that are as accurate as possible. But since no test can be absolutely perfect, it is important to know how accurate a test is in order to know how much confidence to place in its results. To designate a test's accuracy, the term *reliability* is used. Reliability indicates the degree to which a test is consistent in measuring whatever it does measure—the degree to which the test measures the same thing time after time and item after item. *Consistency over time and items is basic to the concept of reliability.*

When a test is given to a group of students, or to the same student more than once, there is variability or variance in the scores (that is, the scores are not all the same; they differ). Part of this variability is a true variability in the property being measured; part reflects error in the test. The next section will consider the relationship of error in the test to its reliability.

The Standard Error of Measurement

If we follow Cronbach's (1970) lead and call the information we want out of a test its *signal* (that is, the true score), what we get when we use the test is a *signal-plus-noise*. Many factors contribute to this noise or inaccuracy. At the moment, let us restrict ourselves to only those noise factors that are likely to be present to some degree each time the test is given; that is, those noise or error factors that are within the test itself. We evaluate the magnitude of that error by determining the *standard error of measurement*. The standard error of measurement is the difference between a person's true score on the test and his or her obtained or measured score.

Consider the previous discussion of measuring a page length 100 times and averaging the 100 measurements. If a test were given 100 times, and if we averaged or obtained the mean score of the 100 (by adding the 100 scores and dividing by 100), we would have a pretty good approximation of the true score. The degree or amount to which the 100 scores varied around this mean or average would indicate the standard error of measurement of the test.

If we accept the mean score on the 100 tests as representative of the true score, then the standard error of measurement tells how close each measured score is to the true score and hence how accurate the test can be. Obviously the *larger* the standard error of measurement, the *less* accurate the test.

As we have said, though, all the variance in a set of scores cannot be considered error. Some of it is true variance based on the fact that students will actually vary on the property being measured. Though it is obviously important to have a measure of a test's accuracy, it is equally obvious that it would be impractical to give a test 100 times to obtain the standard error of measurement. Instead, test accuracy is typically expressed not as the standard error of measurement, but as a reliability coefficient. *The reliability coefficient is that portion of the variance in test scores that is not the result of errors of measurement.* It is, in fact, one minus the error variance (the square of the standard error of measurement) divided by the total test score variance.[1] As we increase error variance relative to total variance, we decrease reliability; as we decrease error, we increase reliability. The goal of the test builder, therefore, is to decrease the error in the test, that is, the standard error of measurement.

The questions we must now ask are: how can reliability be determined and how can it be improved?

FIVE PROCEDURES FOR ASSESSING RELIABILITY

It is not difficult to imagine a content outline (page 68) for which any of 100 tests would be appropriate, although few teachers would welcome the task of having to prepare that many. Most teachers simply prepare one test for a given situation. But if you had developed 100 tests rather than only the one you did develop, how do you know that scores of students on the one would be the same as their averaged scores on the 100? Moreover, even in the case of the single test, how do you know that students would obtain the same score each time if it were given 100 times? That is, how do you know that the test gives you a consistent measure of the property being measured? *The extent to which a particular test gives a consistent and accurate representation of the property being measured by that test is a function of the test's reliability.*

As we have said, reliability is an indication of the accuracy and consistency of a test based, at least in theory, on the degree

---

[1] This formula is not typically used for calculating reliability, only for representing the relationship between the standard error of measurement and test reliability. Reliability is usually determined using the procedures described in the next section.

of true variability in the total variability of test scores. In Cronbach's (1970) terms, reliability can thus be thought of as the ratio of the signal to the combination of signal-plus-noise. The more noise (or error variance) a test picks up, the less reliable it is.

The impracticality of giving 100 tests for the same content outline, or the same test 100 times, has led to the development of other procedures for assessing the reliability of a test. Each of these procedures represents a way of estimating the probability that the obtained test score is the same as the true score (or actual amount of the measured quality) possessed by the test taker. Five such procedures for estimating a test's reliability will be described, all but the second of which utilize the correlation coefficient as a statistical indicator of reliability.

Kuder-Richardson Formula 21

Instead of comparing scores on different administrations of a test to determine that test's reliability, it is far easier to estimate reliability by comparing scores on the test's items, in essence considering each item as a test in itself. If the test items show a high degree of agreement, then you can presume the test is an accurate or consistent measure. (You cannot say, however, what the test is a consistent measure of, based on this estimate; that is a question of validity. But whatever that test is measuring, if a high degree of agreement on students' item scores is obtained, you can only conclude that the test is *consistent*, hence, reliable.)

K-R 21 is a simple way of approximating the degree of agreement or correlations among items on a test. It is shown below.

$$\text{Reliability} = 1 - \frac{\overline{X}\,(n - \overline{X})}{ns^2}$$

$\overline{X}$ represents the mean or average score on the test by the class; s represents the standard error of measurement across scores (or standard deviation—a measure of the variability of a group of scores around a mean). The letter n stands for the number of items in the test.

The reliability of a test can vary between 0 and 1.00. A reliability of 0 indicates that a test has no reliability and hence is an inadequate test for making any judgments about students. (Such low reliabilities are quite rare since they indicate that a test measures nothing but error.) A reliability of 1.00 is a perfect reliability, indicating a perfect or error-free test (also an unlikely occurrence). Published tests usually require test reliabilities of .85 or above when based on the agreement among test items while teacher-built tests are usually considered adequate with reliabilities of .60 or above.

Imagine that you have just given your students a 12-item test on which each item is scored as either right or wrong (items must be scored in this manner if K-R Formula 21 is to be used). Your class of 10 students has obtained the following scores:

12	9
11	7
10	6
9	5
9	2

Since these scores add up to 80 and since there are 10 students, the mean score would be 8.0 (80/10). The square of the standard deviation (s^2), also called the *variance*, is obtained by subtracting each individual test score from the mean to get a deviation score, squaring each deviation score, adding the squares (which add to 82 in this example), and dividing by the number of scores to give a variance (of 8.2 in this example).

If we put these values into the K-R 21 formula we come out with a reliability of .67,[2] which would be considered adequate for a teacher-built test with as few as 12 items. You can see that as n, the number of items in the test increases, the reliability would increase also (assuming the other values stayed the same) since the fraction to be subtracted from 1 becomes smaller.

Let us try one more example in order to make a point. Consider the following 10 scores on the 12 item test.

12	11
12	11
12	10
11	10
11	10

These scores have a mean of 11.0 and a variance (s^2) of 0.6; putting these numbers into the K-R 21 formula yields a reliability value of less than 0. (Normally, the reliability value cannot go below zero but the K-R 21 formula is an approximate rather than an exact one—producing its greatest distortion on scores that appear in the above pattern.)

---

[2] $\text{Reliability} = 1 - \dfrac{8\,(12-8)}{12\,(8.2)} = 1 - \dfrac{32}{98.4} = 1 - .33 = .67$

Why does the first pattern (or as we say in technical terms, *distribution*) yield a much higher reliability than the second, at least in terms of the K-R 21 formula? The answer is important for our consideration of reliability. The K-R 21 formula is based on the assumption of what is called a *normal distribution* of test scores; that is, of the greatest frequency of scores occurring in the center of the distribution, about the mean, and a progressively decreasing frequency of scores as one moves to the extremes. This distribution is represented by what is commonly known as the bell-shaped curve.

Consider the distribution of scores as shown in Figure 10.1. Distribution *a* shows the scores in the first example, in which the K-R 21 reliability was .67. Distribution *b* comes from the second example, having essentially a zero reliability in terms of the K-R 21 formula. Distribution *c* is an ideal version of a normal distribution, representing the distribution of true scores in the total population. As the obtained distribution of scores approaches the normal or presumably true score distribution, the reliability approaches 1.00.

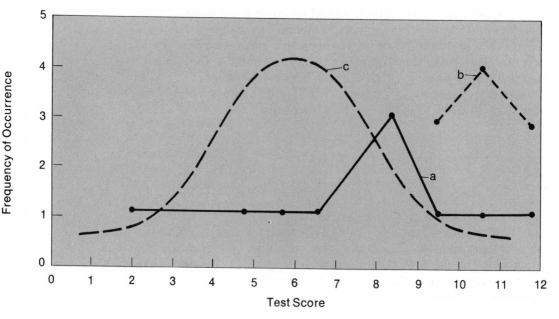

Figure 10.1   *Three Distributions of Test Scores. a. The first example b. The second example c. A normal distribution*

If, however, the instruction has been successful, it is not totally unlikely that a distribution such as *b* will result. Does this mean that tests on which most students succeed are unreliable and therefore unworthy for use? The answer may be *no*! For classroom tests of the type on which consistent success or the successful demonstration of *proficiency* by all students is the goal (what we will call criterion-referenced tests in the next chapter), another type of reliability determination than that provided by K-R 21 would be more suitable (described below). However, for tests whose scores are to be evaluated on a comparative or relative basis (and for which normal or bell-shaped distributions will be obtained) K-R Formula 21 provides a simple way to calculate test reliability.

Parallel-item reliability can be thought of as being suitable for tests on which proficiency by a large segment of the class is expected to be demonstrated (that is, criterion-referenced tests). *Parallel-item reliability is based on the determination of consistency of performance by students across items that are intended to measure the same objective.*

Parallel-item Reliability

Let us say, for example, that the 12-item test referred to earlier is an attempt to measure performance on 4 objectives and so 3 items have been written for each objective. In essence, then, each item in a 3-item set can be considered to be a measure of the same thing—the particular objective that that 3-item set has been written to measure. If students have acquired proficiency on that objective, they should get all 3 items right. If they have not acquired proficiency on that objective, they should get all 3 items wrong (assuming that all 3 items have been randomly sampled from the same domain and hence measure the same thing with approximately the same degree of difficulty). Where the characteristic pattern is for students to get 1 or 2 items right and 2 or 1 wrong, the mini-test of that objective can be considered to be low in parallel-item reliability.

Parallel-item reliability can be assessed by simply counting. Let us examine the performance of the 10 students on the 12 item test. The array of item scores has been laid out in Figure 10.2. You can see from the array that there is considerable consistency of performance across each 3-item set. The only exception to this is item 6 (in the set of items for objective 2). Six of the 10 students got item 6 wrong. However, all 10 students got items 4 and 5 right,

Figure 10.2   *An Array of Item Scores by 10 Students on a 12-item Test (X's indicate incorrect responses; blanks indicate correct responses).*

Students/ Items	Obj. 1			Obj. 2			Obj.3			Obj.4		
	1	2	3	4	5	6	7	8	9	10	11	12
1												
2						X						X
3								X				
4						X						
5												
6						X						
7						X				X		
8						X						
9												
10		X				X						

indicating that adequate proficiency on objective 2 had been attained. On this basis, we can conclude that item 6 is not parallel to items 4 and 5 and should be rewritten. Given this change, it would be safe to conclude that the 12–item test had high parallel-item reliability.

Split-half Reliability   Another form of reliability based on parallelism is split-half reliability. *Split-half reliability is based on the equivalence of performance by students on each half of a test.* However, it must be pointed out that split-half reliability is primarily applied to norm-referenced tests and so represents a variation on the use of the K-R 21 approach.

For purposes of calculating split-half reliability, a test is divided arbitrarily in half, one half containing the odd-numbered items, the other the even-numbered items. Now, instead of having one score for the total test, you have two scores—one for each half of the test. The two half-test scores can then be correlated with one another across the group of students who took the test, yielding a split-half reliability coefficient.

The correlation coefficient that results from comparing the two half-test scores, however, describes the reliability of only half of the test rather than the whole test. Since the test user will be using the whole test, it is that reliability which is important. To calculate the reliability of the whole test given the split-half reliability, the *Spearman-Brown Formula*, given below, can be used.

$$\frac{\text{reliability of}}{\text{total test}} = \frac{2 \times \text{reliability of half test}}{1 + \text{reliability of half test}}$$

In many cases, one of the reliabilities of published tests reported in test manuals is a split-half reliability that has been corrected by the Spearman-Brown Formula. Teachers, however, may find the parallel-item reliability procedure, described in the preceding section, more useful since their tests are often of the criterion-referenced type.

Another kind of reliability based on parallelism is alternate-forms reliability. *Alternate-forms reliability is based on the equivalence of scores on two tests that are intended to be substitutable measures of the same thing.* Sometimes test publishers publish two forms of a test—Form A and Form B, Form 1 and Form 2, or a long form and a short form. If a group of students takes both forms and their scores on each form closely correspond, the test can be said to have alternate-forms reliability. You can then use the forms interchangeably, a particularly important feature if you are going to use them to measure pupil growth (that is, to compare scores on the two tests with time or instruction intervening).

Alternate-forms Reliability

Test-retest reliability, as the name implies, is determined by giving students the same test twice. *It is based on the extent to which students' scores on each of two administrations of a test correspond.* Since consistency is the hallmark of reliability, a test that yields similar scores on each of two administrations with no significant events intervening is a highly reliable one.

There are, however, three shortcomings to the test-retest procedure. The first is that it is most difficult to minimize the significance of events intervening between the two test administrations; thus the two test administrations must occur close together in time. The second shortcoming is that many factors can affect the performance of students on a test each time it is taken and hence reduce its reliability. (These factors will be discussed in a later section.) When a test is given on two different occasions, these factors have two opportunities to influence the results (more-

Test-retest Reliability

over, different error sources may be operating each time), increasing the assessment of a test's unreliability and making test-retest reliability a severe estimate of reliability.

The third shortcoming to test-retest reliability is that its determination requires that students undergo two testings (a problem shared with the determination of alternate-forms reliability). Unlike split-half reliability or K-R 21 reliability which only require a single testing—and that would have been carried out anyway, test-retest reliability forces the test developer to use two parallel testing sessions within a short time span.

Because of the above three shortcomings, test-retest reliability determinations occur infrequently. That is unfortunate because this approach tells us about a test's consistency over time rather than its internal consistency as the other procedures do. Since consistency over time seems basic to the concept of reliability, more use of test-retest reliability would seem desirable. (When this approach is used, lower reliability coefficients must be expected because of the above-mentioned shortcomings.)

SOURCES OF TEST VARIABILITY

Recall that a test's reliability is that portion of the total variation in test scores that does not result from errors of measurement. Consequently, it is worthwhile examining variability in test scores to try to distinguish between true variability on the variable in question and variability that represents or contributes to test unreliability. Knowing the sources of errors of measurement may help us to reduce them and hence improve test reliability.

Overall Sources   Thorndike (1949) identified four general sources of test variability, shown in Figure 10.3. The first category, *lasting and general characteristics of the individual*, includes the general characteristics of the test taker that the test is attemping to measure along with other general characteristics he or she may have. IQ, aptitude, and reading tests, for example, each attempt to measure a general characteristic of the individual. However, on achievement tests, which attempt to measure specific characteristics, general characteristics constitute a source of measurement error or bias. When we are trying to measure how much a student has learned, variability based on a general ability, such as reading skill, serves only to confuse the issue. However, where the effect of general abilities on a test of specific skills is constant across the test, the reliability of that test will be unaffected. It is validity that will be lessened. Where reading skill affects performance on some items more than others, it will affect a test's reliability.

*Sources of Test Variability.**

Figure 10.3

I. Lasting and general characteristics of the individual
    (1) General skills (e.g., reading)
    (2) General ability to comprehend instructions, testwiseness, techniques of taking tests
    (3) Ability to solve problems of the general type presented in this test
    (4) Attitudes, emotional reactions, or habits generally operating in situation like the test situation (e.g., self-confidence)
II. Lasting and specific characteristics of the individual
    (1) Knowledge and skills required by particular problems in the test
    (2) Attitudes, emotional reactions, or habits related to particular test stimuli (e.g., fear of high places brought to mind by an inquiry about such fears on a personality test)
III. Temporary and general characteristics of the individual (systematically affecting performance on various tests at a particular time)
    (1) Health, fatigue, and emotional strain
    (2) Motivation, rapport with examiner
    (3) Effects of heat, light, ventilation, etc.
    (4) Level of practice on skills required by tests of this type
    (5) Present attitudes, emotional reactions, or strength of habits (insofar as these are departures from the person's average or lasting characteristics—e.g., political attitudes during an election campaign)
IV. Temporary and specific characteristics of the individual
    (1) Changes in fatigue or motivation developed by this particular test (e.g., discouragement resulting from failure on a particular item)
    (2) Fluctuations in attention, coordination, or standards of judgment
    (3) Fluctuations in memory for particular facts
    (4) Level of practice on skills or knowledge required by this particular test (e.g., effects of special coaching)
    (5) Temporary emotional states, strength of habits, etc., related to particular test stimuli (e.g., a question calls to mind a recent bad dream)
    (6) Luck in the selection of answers by guessing

* Reprinted from R. L. Thorndike, *Personnel Selection*, 1949, by permission of John Wiley & Sons, Inc.

We have all known people who were good test takers. This general characteristic, while not an objective of any specific test, has led these people to perform well on almost every test they took. Other people are test-anxious and characteristically perform poorly on tests even though they can demonstrate proficiency on the test content in a nontest situation. Thus, lasting and general characteristics include some that we want to measure and others that reduce the accuracy of the test for its intended purposes.

Then there are *lasting and specific characteristics of the individual* that often relate to specific items on a test. An item in which automobiles are used for purposes of illustration would be more closely attended to by car buffs while items relating to sports would favor the athletically inclined. On tests of general abilities, specific characteristics constitute undesirable sources of variability because they reduce reliability. However, on tests of specific characteristics such as achievement tests, specific characteristics represent the goal or objective of the measurement.

Temporary and general characteristics of the individual include those that are operating at the particular time when the test is taken. Everybody has a bad day and it is unfortunate to have to take a test on such a day. A recent death in the family, for example, or a failure in the heating system in the testing room will affect test performance. Such characteristics contribute to those portions of a test's variability that constitute errors of measurement since they do not relate to the true variability in the property being measured.

Finally, there are *temporary and specific characteristics of the individual* like good luck at guessing, pretest coaching, a look at last year's test, or problems in concentrating because of street noises or the murmuring of the student sitting at the next desk. These too reduce reliability.

Error Sources   We can trace many of the sources of variability in test performance to the test itself. The *number of test items* will affect test performance. Very short tests provide a very limited sample of performance on which to judge the lasting and general characteristics of an individual while very long tests produce fatigue, inattention, and other temporary and general characteristics. Longer tests do, however, minimize the effect of success based on guessing.

Then, too, *there is the quality of test items*. Bad items may be too easy, or too difficult, or too unrelated to the test's target area and hence quite susceptible to the various temporary, general, or

"You'd be surprised how many aptitude tests I had to take before
I found out what I was really fitted for!"

specific characteristics of the individual other than those that the
test is attempting to measure. Since a test is just a collection of
items, the test's characteristics will be based on the nature and
number of the items. These are the only two variables in the test
itself, both of which can be controlled by the test maker.

Conditions of test administration affect test performance and
hence test reliability by having differing effects on different test
takers. Temporary and general characteristics of the individual
are largely the result of the conditions of test administration. Performance on most any test given in a hot room will suffer, for
example, and confusion or noise will also affect test performance
and hence reliability of a test.

Conditions of scoring are also a source of variability and thus
error. Where scoring varies from test to test—as may be true for
essays—error variance is introduced which interferes with the
process of obtaining a true picture of the skills and competencies
or other characteristics of students.

These sources of test variability can be used as a basis for identifying ways and means of reducing that portion of the variability that is caused by errors of measurement (primarily the temporary ones) and thus increasing reliability.

STRATEGIES FOR BUILDING RELIABILITY INTO A TEST

If you can identify those factors that affect test performance over and above the single factors you are interested in measuring, you can construct reliable tests by controlling the extraneous factors to the greatest extent possible. Some recommended procedures for this purpose are discussed below.

Including Enough Test Items

A longer test is generally more reliable than a shorter one because it provides a larger and hence potentially more representative sample of a student's performance. Imagine a course with 10 objectives and a final exam with 10 items—one per objective. If a student were to make a careless error on one item, or if one item occurred in an unfamiliar context causing the student to miss it, you would conclude that the student had not learned one of the objectives. This conclusion would not reflect the student's failure; it would reflect the test's failure. Contrariwise, if a student had guessed correctly on an item, or glanced at his or her neighbor's paper, it would be inaccurately concluded that the student attained proficiency on that objective. If the test were doubled to 20 items —2 per objective—or tripled or quadrupled, the effect of these sorts of errors would be reduced. Careless errors and guessing would still occur but their effect on the conclusions drawn from the test would be lessened. It is recommended that no fewer than two items per objective be included and more where possible. If test length becomes a problem, tests should be constructed to measure fewer objectives.

Targeting Items

Items must be written for a goal or objective. Each item represents an attempt to measure some particular outcome or quality. To the extent that the overall objective of a test can be broken down into subobjectives, the more likely the test items can be made to correspond. Thus, the content outline approach presented in Chapter 3 not only contributes to test appropriateness but to test reliability as well. It is easier to write 10 pairs of items—two per objective—than it is to write 20 items for a single broad course objective. Subdividing helps the test writer to write targeted, hence specific items, increasing the likelihood that items within a cluster are measuring the same property. Since reliability is based on item correspondence or agreement, targeting helps insure reliability, particularly in the case of tests of specific skills such as achievement tests.

Box 10.1

ITEM VARIABILITY IN READING LEVEL AND INTEREST LEVEL

(1) The baseball "Most Valuable Player" awards were started in 1929.

                True   False

(2) Baseball honors its most outstanding player with an annual award known as the "Most Valuable Player" award, which was initiated in 1929.   True   False

(3) There are 5 states having farm income greater than $2,000,000.

                True   False

(4) Five states in the United States produce farm revenues in excess of $2,000,000.   True   False

The above four items, written by Anderson (1969), systematically vary in *reading level* (items 1 and 3 are easier to read—that is, are written at a lower reading level than items 2 and 4) and in interest level (items 1 and 2 were more interesting—at least to the boys in the Anderson Study—than items 3 and 4). Often, we unconsciously write items of varying reading and interest levels without realizing it. Reading level represents a lasting and general characteristic of individuals and interest level a lasting and specific characteristic. Keeping these characteristics *constant* on a test increases its *reliability* by increasing the likelihood that all items are measuring the same thing. Moreover, the overall level of reading ability required by a test and the nature of the interests or biases it involves will affect its validity. The best strategy may be to write items at the average reading level of the students and to avoid items that are likely to relate to strong, idiosyncratic (i.e., unshared) interests.

Controlling for General or Specific Skills

While the total or overall effect of reading level on an achievement test relates to a test's validity, the variability in the reading level of items within a test relates to its reliability. On tests of specific skills, such as achievement tests, reliability is likely to be higher if the effects of general skills such as reading level are kept constant. Thus, if the test is a measure of something other than reading skills, you should attempt to write all items at approximately the same reading level to avoid introducing variability across items based on an internal characteristic of the test itself.

In any test of specific skills, general skill requirements must be kept relatively constant across items. Reading is the most common of these skills but presumably test items must be consistent in relation to a person's attitudes or self-concept unless these are the qualities measured by the test. Constancy should also be applied to specific characteristics such as interests or particular competencies but this is particularly hard to do. Because all test items must have content, it is hard to control the extraneous variability in item performance that such content, when not intrinsic to the quality being measured, will introduce.

Setting Difficulty Level across Items at Intermediate Levels

Items that are too easy or too difficult do not adequately represent the domain of the objectives being measured. Moreover, where difficulty levels vary greatly from item to item, the internal consistency of a test is not likely to be high. According to Lord's (1952) findings, test reliabilities are highest when item difficulties fall into the 50–75% range (that is, when 50–75% of the test takers get an item right). While different groups of students may vary in their success on a test, overall difficulty levels between 50 and 60% would seem most suitable for reliability purposes.

However, very easy items may serve motivational purposes such as bolstering student confidence or making students feel comfortable with a test. Some easy items may be included, but the bulk of items should be of intermediate difficulty to give the test good reliability.

Controlling the Conditions of Test Administration

Wherever possible, test administrators should take care to control as many of the conditions of test administration as they can. It is wise to think of a test as more than just the written items. Tests include instructions and the conditions under which testing is to be conducted.

Testing conditions should be such as to avoid creating any extra and unnecessary stress for students beyond that normally experienced in a test situation. Distractions should be kept to a

INCENTIVES CAN AFFECT TEST PERFORMANCE

Farr, Tuinman, and Blanton (1972) discovered a way to get seventh and eighth grade students to improve their reading test performance. They randomly divided their group of 160 students into two groups and then pretested each group on the Nelson-Denny Reading Test. Four weeks later, with each group experiencing nothing beyond normal school instruction, they were posttested on the same test. However, *one of the two groups was offered prizes for raising their scores.* The six students who raised their scores the most from pretest to posttest (remember they knew nothing about the prizes at the time of the pretest or thereafter until coming in for the posttest session) would get transistor radios; the next nine, sweatshirts; and all the rest raising their scores at least one point would get a candy bar.

Can you guess what happened? All but one student in the incentive group gained at least one point. Students in the incentive group averaged over seven points higher on the posttest than students in the nonincentive group. Fifteen of the 81 students in the incentive group scored one year and five months or more higher on the posttest than on the pretest. Both the number of items correct and the number attempted on the posttest were significantly greater for the incentive group.

Needless to point out, the test-retest reliability of a test is severely affected by a change in the testing conditions from one test session to the other.

---

minimum and the teacher's direct intervention should be kept to a minimum. The physical environment should be made as comfortable as possible. If conditions vary widely from testing to testing, the results of the test will reflect these variations and hence will be less reliable than if conditions remain the same.

USING TEST RESULTS TO IMPROVE A TEST'S RELIABILITY

The preceding sections have dealt largely with the concepts of test reliability, the types of test reliability (e.g., Kuder-Richardson Formula 21, split-half, and so forth), sources of test unreliability, and procedures for constructing more reliable tests. Beyond following the recommendations for building their tests to be reliable, it is also possible for teachers to use test results to *improve* upon the reliability of their tests. These procedures for increasing reliability based on the results of testing are outlined in the test criterion checklist as follows.

Is My Test RELIABLE?

(1) Are There Paired or Parallel Items That Agree:
   a. Do students who get one item of a pair (per objective) right also get the other right and those who get one wrong get the other wrong?
   b. Have nonparallel items been rewritten?

(2) Is Item Performance Consistent with Test Performance:
   a. Is each item consistently passed by students who do well on the total test?
   b. Have inconsistent items been removed?

(3) Are All Items Clear and Understandable:
   a. Have student responses been used as a basis for evaluating item clarity?
   b. Have ambiguous items been removed or rewritten?

(4) Have Scoring Procedures Proved to Be Systematic and Unbiased:
   a. Have multiple scorings yielded consistent results?
   b. Are scoring criteria and procedures as detailed and as suitable as they can be?

Remember that reliability deals with the question of *accuracy*. A test is an instrument, a measuring device, a scale. If it does not measure some quality accurately and consistently, it is not a reliable instrument. The question is not what it measures, but *does it measure it consistently*. It will not be very consistent if it is sensitive to factors that go up and down from moment to moment, day to day, and item to item. If a test is not consistent within itself, that is from item to item, it holds little possibility of being consistent over time. Thus, for improving reliability we focus on first determining and then improving the consistency of a test from item to item.

Agreement between Parallel Items   Examining agreement between parallel items is a practical way for teachers to assess the reliability of their tests. After you have given a test, go back and look at the performance on the pairs of items per objective by each student and see how many students displayed the same performance on each of the two parallel items in each pair. If the items in each pair are consistent with one another, the majority of students should have gotten both of the items in any pair right or wrong. Those instances where students got one right and one wrong in a pair indicate that the two items are not consistent; they are, in fact, nonparallel items.

Therefore, as a two item mini-test, those pairs lacking agreement or consistency would detract from reliability. Item pairs in which up to a third or more of the students get one right and one wrong should be reexamined. These items should be rewritten as a pair or at least one member of such inconsistent pairs should be rewritten.[3]

After a test has been administered, an analysis of the relationship between item scores and total test scores, called *item analysis*, very often reveals items that are inconsistent with the total test or parts of it. The pattern of item scores shown in Figure 10.2 was used as a basis for determining the inadequacy of a specific item; that item was found not to relate to other items presumably measuring the same quality. The test writer would then rewrite or revise the bad item or items, thereby increasing the reliability of the total test. It is highly recommended that test writers, be they teachers or commercial test writers, reexamine the results of a test by means of an item analysis (or at least an examination of item results) in order to identify the bad items. *Item analysis is the procedure by which individual item performance by a group of test takers is compared to their performance on the total test.* It may be facilitated by preparing an array of responses by individual students to individual items as shown in Figure 10.2.

Item Analysis

The purpose of item analysis is to make each item consistent with the total test. To do item analysis, take the performance on an item by each individual and the performance on the total test by each individual and examine this relationship across a number of individuals.[4] You would then choose those items on which student performance corresponded most closely to total test performance. If you start with 100 items and want to end up with a test of 50 items, initially try all 100 and then keep the 50 items having the

---

[3] This procedure is based on the presumption that a test will be used more than once. If you go to the trouble to make better tests, it would be wasteful to use them once and throw them away. You may not want to use each test time after time after time, but you may want to build up a test item file from which you can select items for reuse.

[4] When this procedure is done statistically, the relationship between item scores and total test scores across individuals is expressed as a correlation coefficient.

closest correspondence to the total test score. That would give you the most reliable test.

Item analysis can be done most simply by separating test takers into high scorers and low scorers on the total test and then comparing the performance of each group on each item. You can then select those items that most differentiate between the two groups, that is, items that most of the high group get right and most of the low group get wrong.[5] These items, when revised, can be expected to yield the greatest degree of agreement.

You can also separate the students who have taken the test into high and low scorers and compute item discriminability and item difficulty using the following formulas.

$$\text{Item Discriminability} = \frac{\text{No. of high scorers}}{\text{who got it right}} - \frac{\text{No. of low scorers}}{\text{who got it right}}$$

$$\text{Item Difficulty} = \frac{\text{No. of high scorers}}{\text{who got it right}} + \frac{\text{No. of low scorers}}{\text{who got it right}}$$

Making Items Clearer and More Understandable

You can use student responses on a qualitative basis for making decisions about good items and bad items and for improving bad items. Just by looking at the answers students generate on completion items or the patterns of accepting and rejecting response choices on multiple choice items (i.e., which ones are chosen and which ones are not), you can learn a lot about which items are good and which items are poor and why the poor ones are poor.

Many teachers score tests very automatically, simply by grading the number of items right and items wrong and computing the total score. They do not look at responses and rarely count the number of times each distractor or wrong answer in a multiple choice situation is chosen by students and compare it to the number of students who chose the right answer. A single distractor that is chosen more often than the right answer, or a distractor or option that no one chooses may be interpreted by the students in a different way than you had intended it to be. Or you may have miskeyed an item, that is, included a distractor that is as good or

[5] If, simultaneously, you brought in judges and had them independently assess the same quality that you hoped your test was measuring, you could also run correlations between their judgments and the students' scores on the tests. You could use this piece of information on each item and its correlation with the total test score to attempt to maximize both reliability and validity. Given the resources, that is a reasonably effective strategy.

better an answer than the one keyed correct. That is the kind of item that has to be changed to improve test reliability. Particular distractors may require revision. If many such misinterpretations occur, consistency would be poor. It is also worthwhile to examine item difficulty based on overall student performance on an item in order to detect items that may be too easy or too difficult.

In addition to carefully and systematically examining student response patterns on items, it is helpful to discuss the items with students after they take the test. (Discussion of the items with colleagues is also helpful.) Such discussions may help point out sources of ambiguity and misunderstanding and suggest ways that problem items can be revised to overcome their shortcomings.

Reliability of Scoring Procedures

Often in education human beings are the measuring instruments. Other than in multiple choice or true–false or matching tests, which can be scored objectively and automatically, it is human judgment that determines the accuracy of answers.

On an essay test, for example, the teacher reads the responses and makes judgments about students' competency or proficiency. What would happen if the teacher were to read that essay a second time? Would the same judgments of performance be made? If the judgments the second time are different from the first, who is to say which is more accurate? Maybe some of the essays were read late at night when the teacher was tired, while the remainder were read in the morning when the teacher was more alert. Or perhaps the teacher read the name of the student before reading the response and because of the difficulty in making the judgments that the scoring of essay responses requires, was influenced by expectations based on the student's past performance and apparent ability. When your unconscious biases or expectations affect your scoring consistency, your reliability as a scorer suffers. (Relative to this point see Box 5.2 on page 135.

To determine the reliability of your scoring *you must do some rescoring.* If you can, score every essay item twice. If not, compromise; try to read some proportion of the essay questions twice and establish your own scoring reliability. The minimal number that is usually considered necessary for reliability is 1 out of 5. Try to read 1 out of every 5 essays twice to see how close you come the second time to the judgments you made the first time. If you set up scoring criteria (as described below), scoring can be done much more quickly. If you know exactly what you are looking for and how much you are going to weigh the different criteria, you can score all the essays and rescore 20% of them in the time it might have taken you to score them once without explicit criteria.

In performance testing or behavior measurement you are dealing with questions of judgment and should use reliability observers when possible. You need not necessarily use a second observer for every test or observation (that is, you need not collect two full sets of data), but you should include a second observer for one out of every five observations or make it yourself a second time. If you bring in another person to serve as a reliability observer, be sure that both of you are there at the same time so the two of you will be observing the same behavior, but be sure to make your judgments independently. The comparison between the two sets of judgments can then serve as an indication of the reliability of these judgments. You may also want to practice first with the other observer to increase the likelihood that you can get reasonably good reliability with respect to that person.

Here are some suggestions about how to improve your reliability as a scorer. First, cover the students' names before you score so that you cannot be influenced by your expectation of them. This is called *scoring blind*.

Second, structure your response key as much as you can in terms of what answer you are looking for, how many points you will give for organization, content, creativity, problem solution, and rationale. The more scoring specifications you can generate and write down (and hopefully communicate to students so they know what the criteria are), the more likely you will be able to make these judgments consistently, time after time, student after student.[6] Refer to pages 124–35 for a more thorough discussion of these points. (Also see Appendix B on test item specification.)

---

[6] Where multiple judges are used simultaneously, as in the judging of diving competition as described in Box 7.2 on page 187, the two most extreme judgments (that is, the highest and lowest) are discarded each time to increase scoring reliability. The performance score is obtained by averaging the judgments of the remaining judges.

Additional Information Sources

Dick, W. & Hagerty, N. *Topics in measurement: Reliability and validity.* N.Y.: McGraw-Hill, 1971.

Doppelt, J. E. How accurate is a test score? *Test Service Bulletin #50.* N.Y.: The Psychological Corporation, 1956.

Stanley, J. C. Reliability. In R. L. Thorndike (Ed.), *Educational measurement*, 2nd ed., Wash., D.C.: American Council on Education, 1971, Chap. 13.

Thorndike, R. L. Reliability. In *Proceedings of 1963 Invitational Conference on Testing Problems.* Princeton, N.J.: Educational Testing Service, 1964.

Self-test of Proficiency

(1) We use the term reliability to designate:
  - *a.* the fit between a test's objectives and its items.
  - *b.* the extent to which test scores predict future learning success.
  - *c.* the degree to which the test measures the same thing time after time.
  - *d.* the meaning of the scores on a test.
  - *e.* the absence of cultural bias.

(2) The reliability of a test can be used to express the extent to which it gives a consistent measurement across items.

TRUE   FALSE

(3) The standard error of measurement on a test is:
  - *a.* a measure that increases as the accuracy of a test increases.
  - *b.* the difference between predicted scores and obtained scores.
  - *c.* a measure of true variance of test scores.
  - *d.* the difference between true scores and obtained scores.

(4) The reliability coefficient is that portion of the variance in test scores that is the result of errors of measurement.

TRUE   FALSE

(5) Match the type of reliability at left with its definition at right.
  - *a.* Kuder-Richardson 21
  - *b.* Parallel item
  - *c.* Split-half
  - *d.* Alternate forms
  - *e.* Test-retest

  - *i.* consistency of performance across items that are intended to measure the same objective
  - *ii.* consistency of performance across different tests that are intended to measure the same objectives
  - *iii.* consistency of performance across different administrations of the same test
  - *iv.* consistency of performance across the odd-item and even-item segments of a test
  - *v.* approximation of the correlations among all the items on a test
  - *vi.* approximation of all the correlations among half the items on a test

(6) For each of the illustrations below and at the top of the next page, identify the type of reliability depicted.
  - *a.* After the students completed the test, it was divided into two parts and two separate scores were calculated for each student. Correlating the two scores yielded in a coefficient of .89.
  - *b.* The test had two items for each objective. On 90% of the objectives, students either got both the items measuring that objective right or both wrong.

c. When a formula was used to approximate the extent of variability in students' test scores not reflecting error, the resulting coefficient was .85.

d. The first period English class took the test on Monday and again on Friday. Scores on the two testings were correlated to provide a coefficient of .86.

e. The test came in Form A and Form B. Students were given both forms and their scores on each correlated to get a coefficient of .84.

(7) a. According to Thorndike, there are four categories of individual characteristics that serve as sources of test variability. Name and give an example of each of the four.

(8) You are administering a test to measure how much students have learned from a unit on primate biology. Below are factors that will affect how well students do on your test. Some of these factors contribute error variance, some true variance. Write *E* next to those that contribute error variance and *T* for true variance.

a. how well the student paid attention to what was taught
b. how much the student dislikes taking tests
c. how much of the information in the unit the student learned
d. whether the student can read all the words in each item
e. whether the student understands the test instructions

(9) Check those suggestions below that one should follow to build reliability into a test.

a. write items of intermediate difficulty levels
b. target items to the content outline
c. write all items at the same reading level
d. offer the poorer students rewards to heighten their attention
e. follow item writing rules when preparing items
f. write items in different areas of interest
g. avoid variations in testing conditions

(10) The _____ (shorter, longer) a test is, generally the more reliable it is.

(11) You have constructed and administered an achievement test on the events leading up to World War I. You plan to use this test again next year and so would like to improve its reliability.

a. Describe how you would conduct and use item analysis for this purpose.

b. Assume that the test was a multiple choice test. Describe how you could use student response patterns as the basis for revising to improve reliability.

c. Assume that the test was an essay test. Describe how you could improve the reliability of scoring.

(12) Describe how you would use parallel item agreement to improve the reliability of this self-test of proficiency.

chapter eleven/Interpretability and Usability of Test Results

OBJECTIVES

1. Define the test interpretability concept of *a.* norm-referencing, *b.* norms, and *c.* norming group.

2. Identify and contrast four kinds of normative scores, namely: *a.* standard score, *b.* stanine score, *c.* percentile rank, and *d.* grade-equivalent score.

3. Identify characteristics of norm-referenced tests, namely: *a.* item revisions, *b.* standard instructions, *c.* norms and interpretation based on them, and identify their strengths and shortcomings.

4. Identify characteristics of criterion-referenced tests, namely: *a.* based on objectives, *b.* designed to be appropriate, *c.* measuring performance, *d.* using predetermined cutoffs.

5. Describe the use of four criteria for determining the interpretability of a test, namely: *a.* relation of scores to performance, *b.* definition of accept-

able performance, *c.* diagnostic and evaluative value, *d.* useful relative information.

6. Distinguish between and apply four criteria for determining the usability of a test, namely: *a.* tedium, *b.* practicality, *c.* administrative procedures, and *d.* readability.

WHAT IS INTERPRETABILITY?

Interpretability has to do with what the scores on a test mean; that is, what they tell us about the test taker with respect to the characteristics being measured. While appropriateness and validity tell us whether the test measures what we want it to measure, interpretability provides us with a basis for understanding information conveyed by the test score. Not only should a test measure what we want it to measure, but it should provide the results in a form we can understand and use.

The result of a test is called a *raw score*. The question of interpretability is how can we interpret or understand what the raw score means? Is it high? Is it low? Is it good? Is it adequate? The raw score is only a number; its meaning is based on interpretation. For example, a student gets 30 items right on a 40 item chemistry test. What does this tell us? Would that performance be sufficient to pass the course? To go on to a more advanced course? To become a chemist? Unless a test provides us with a basis for interpreting—that is, unless a test provides us with a *point of reference* —it is not a useful test.

There are two types of reference points that can be applied to interpreting a test. The first is to relate a student's test score to the scores of other students on that test. We call this *norm-referencing*. The second is to establish an external standard and relate the student's test score to it. We call this *criterion-referencing*. These are different bases for interpretability. Each will be described.

NORM-REFERENCING

Teachers are often called upon to interpret the scores of tests that are norm-referenced—that is, *tests for which information about the relative performance of a specific group of people is available.* (We call this information *norms*.) In order to understand norm-referencing, it is necessary to know about norms—that is, the kinds of scores in which they are expressed (standard scores, including stanines, percentile ranks, and grade equivalents).[1]

Norms   Norms are sets of scores based on the test results of an external reference or standardization group; that is, persons who take the test for the express purpose of providing comparative data for interpretation. Norms, therefore, represent a set of test results obtained in order to help interpret the results of scores from future testings.

We may represent norms as (1) *standard scores*, which reflect the deviation of test scores from the mean score of the norm group; as (2) *percentile ranks*, which tell us what percent of the norming group scored at or below a particular score on the test; or as (3) *grade equivalents*, which tell us the school grade at which the given score is typical, or average, for members of the norming group. Each of these represents a way of expressing relative scores, that is, of transforming the raw or obtained scores based on the distribution of scores of the norming group. Let us first discuss the norming group and then consider the three types of normative scores.

Norming Groups.   Basically, there are two types of norms: *local norms* and *national norms*, each reflecting a different kind of norming group. National norms are the more common and provide for the widest generalizability. These norms are based on what is called a cross-national sample, or people sampled from all parts of the country—providing representation for all regions. Local norms, on the other hand, may represent a single state or community or school. Results based on local norms are limited in interpretation to just that locale from which the local norming group was drawn. However, in relating an individual's performance to the performance of other individuals with similar experiences, local norms may be more useful than national norms.

Norms are often separated by age or grade and, where appropriate, by sex. Achievement test norms, for example, are typically presented separately for students at each individual grade for which the test is appropriate. Stanines or percentile ranks pre-

---

[1] While teachers may do some norm-referencing of their own on a small scale, because of its computational aspects and data requirements, norm-referencing is primarily done by testing companies.

sented for an eighth grader will be based only on the scores of other eighth graders as a norm-reference group.[2]

Different norming groups (or breakdowns of norm by group) are relevant for different kinds of tests or uses of tests. Norms for different occupational groups or for groups with different educational majors are relevant in certain circumstances. The Graduate Record Examination and the Miller Analogies Test, for instance, provide norms for graduate students in the different disciplines so that chemistry majors, for example, can be compared to a national sample of chemistry majors; similarly for psychology majors, education majors, and so on. The use of specific norming groups allows for the comparison and evaluation of a student's score in terms of "like" people—that is, those who share some past experience in common or who have some developmental comparability. Information on many variables such as age, grade, sex, interests, region, IQ level, socio-economic status, school type and so forth aids test interpretation because it indicates how a person performed relative to a group into which he or she fits well. Given a person's raw score on a test and a full set of test norms, it is possible to interpret the score relative to any norming group available. However, where only individual normative test scores are presented, as is typically the case with achievement and aptitude test results, interpretations are restricted to the predesignated norming group.

Standard Score

A standard score is a score expressed in terms of its deviation from the mean score of the norming group. Rather than being absolute like a raw score, a standard score indicates the relative status of an individual within a group, that is, how his or her raw score compares to the mean raw score of the norming group. In one group of students a raw score of 50 may be high relative to the other scores while in another group it may be low. By converting the raw score to a standard score we can express and interpret the score relative to the other scores to judge its "highness" or "lowness." Standard scores are thus one form of norm-referencing.

Standard scores are based on the assumption of a normal curve as shown in Figure 11.1. (Recall that we encountered the normal curve or normal distribution in Figure 10.1 in the discussion of reliability.) The normal curve represents an idealized dis-

[2] Grade equivalent norms, however, are based on the average scores obtained by students across a number of grade levels.

tribution of test scores on a test, but one that fits the occurrence of most psychological and physical traits in the population. It is characterized by a predominance of scores in the middle range of the distribution with progressively fewer scores as we move toward either end of the distribution. In other words, many more people score at the average on a trait than at the extremes.

The mean of the normal distribution in Figure 11.1 has been designated as 0 standard deviations, and vertical lines have been drawn to indicate distances from the center in terms of standard deviation units. A standard deviation unit is one unit of variability in test scores, designated by the Greek letter sigma (σ) or by s.d. Recall that the standard deviation represents approximately the average of all differences between obtained scores and the mean.[3] The greater the differences between scores, the greater will be the standard deviation.

Note that 68.3% of all scores on the normal curve fall within one standard deviation of the mean ($\pm 1\sigma$). The percentage of scores falling within three standard deviations of the mean ($\pm 3\sigma$) is 99.9% or virtually all the scores. If a person obtained a score of 45 on a test, with the distribution of scores having a mean of 40 and a standard deviation of 5, that score would lie exactly one standard deviation unit above the mean ($+1\sigma$). A score of 35 ($40-1\sigma$) would fall at -1σ. A score of 30 ($40-2\sigma$) would lie two standard deviations below the mean (-2σ), and so on.

All standard scores are based on standard deviation units. In each case, the mean and the standard deviation unit for the distribution are set by the person norming the test at some predesignated number. When the mean is set at 0 and the standard deviation at 1, the resulting score is called a z-score; a predesignated mean of 50 and standard deviation of 10 yields a score called a T-score. The Wechsler IQ scores use a preset mean of 100 and standard deviation of 15 while the College Boards (CEEB) have a mean set at 500 and standard deviation of 100. These scores are all illustrated in Figure 11.1. Using the preset mean and standard deviation based on the distribution of test scores for the norming group, a given set of raw test scores can be converted to standard scores. A sample of the conversion of raw scores to standard scores is shown in Appendix C.

[3] The standard deviation is calculated by the following formula.

$$\text{s.d.} = \sqrt{\frac{\Sigma (X - \overline{X})^2}{N}}$$

where X is a score, $\overline{X}$ the mean score, and N the number of scores.

Again, the reason for converting raw scores to standard scores is to represent the scores on a relative basis within the test group itself. Neither the order of the scores nor the distribution of the scores is changed by this procedure, but the scores themselves are

The Normal Curve, Percentile Scores, and Types of Standard Scores.* **Figure 11.1**

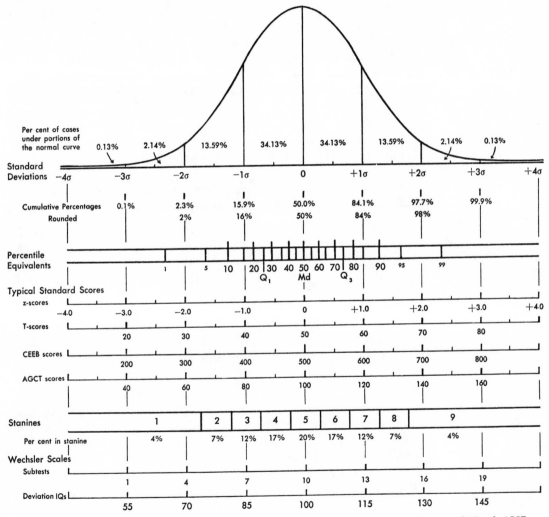

NOTE: *This chart cannot be used to equate scores on one test to scores on another test. For example, both 600 on the CEEB and 120 on the AGCT are one standard deviation above their respective means, but they do not represent "equal" standings because the scores were obtained from different groups.*

* From Test Service Bulletin No. 48, January, 1955, The Psychological Corporation, New York.

restated in terms of a standard, predesignated scale. Given standard scores, we can interpret them in terms of each test taker's relative standing. In other words, we state the score in such a way that we can tell its relative size.

Stanine Score   Another relevant type of standard score is the *stanine score*, based on dividing the normal curve into nine divisions.[4] (The term "stanine" was formed by combining the words "standard" and "nine".) The stanine score is a standard score with a mean of 5 and a standard deviation of two. As a result, each stanine, except for the first and ninth, is one-half a standard deviation unit in length (see Figure 11.1).

Stanine scores are easy to calculate using the conversion scale given in Figure 11.2.

Figure 11.2   *Stanine-raw Score-percentile Conversion Table.*

Stanine Score	Approximate Percent of Ranked Raw Scores	Percentile
9	Top 4%	96–99
8	7	89–95
7	12	77–88
6	17	60–76
5	20	40–59
4	17	23–39
3	12	11–22
2	7	4–10
1	Bottom 4	0–3

Scores can be normalized or standardized into approximate stanine scores by a counting procedure rather than by the computational procedure required for determining the other types of standard scores (like the z-score or T-score). Raw scores are converted to stanine scores by forcing them into a roughly normal distribution. Unlike the conversion to z-scores and T-scores, which

[4] Presumably nine divisions were originally chosen because nine is the largest number of one-digit categories possible and single-digit scores are easier for data processing. For example, in today's use of high-speed computers, stanine scores can be recorded in a single column of a punch card.

"If only he could think in abstract terms...."

leave the distribution of raw scores unchanged (only the score values themselves are changed), the conversion to stanine scores changes the original raw score distribution to an approximately normal distribution.

The stanine score has the great advantage of being easier to determine and easier to interpret (the latter being true because it is a single-digit score) than other types of standard scores. However, because each score represents a band on the continuum rather than a point, stanine scores are less precisely stated than other standard scores.

Percentile Rank

A percentile rank describes the relative standing of a raw score in a sequence of scores; it tells us what percent of the test takers scored lower and what percent scored higher. Again look at Figure 11.1. Note the part labeled "percentile equivalents" which represent percentile points on the distribution. The person who gets the

Figure 11.3 Student Profile Report on the Stanford Achievement Test.*

STUDENT PROFILE REPORT

STUDENT NAME

TYPE OF NORM OR OTHER INFORMATION

HARCOURT BRACE JOVANOVICH INC.

HBJ NEW YORK

TEST		BATTERY	FORM	GRADE	DATE TESTED	PROCESS NO.
STANFORD ACHIEVEMENT TEST		INT 1	Y	4	12/72	0642-005

TESTS	WD MNG	PAR MNG	SPELL	W ST SK	LANG	AR COMPAR	CON CAR	APPL SOC	STD SCIENCE
SCORES	989	928	999	847	999	666	505	234	746	666

HOW TO INTERPRET YOUR SCORES — The score on the right in each test box (in the shaded area) is your stanine score. This score makes it possible to compare yourself with other students of your grade level. In each column of numbers, below each test box, you will see a black letter over-printed on top of your score on the test. These letters are N for national norm stanine, or L for local norm stanine or B meaning both local and national norms are the same. Join similar letters with a straight line, which will show graphically your strengths and/or weaknesses in each test area compared to the respective norms.

The score on the left in each box is your percentile rank. A percentile rank of 42 means that you scored better than 42% of the pupils in your grade; a percentile rank of 73 means you scored better than 73%; etc.

* Reproduced from the Stanford Achievement Test, copyright © 1973, by Harcourt Brace Jovanovich, Inc. Reproduced by special permission of the publisher.

middle or *median* (Md)[5] score has done as well as or better than 50% of the test takers and hence is at the 50th percentile. Thus, the percentile rank is not based on the absolute size of a score but on its relative standing. Because the size of the interval between percentiles is not standard, that is, not uniform, the percentile rank is not considered a standard score. (An example of the calculation of percentiles appears in Appendix C.)

A student profile report on the Stanford Achievement Test appears in Figure 11.3. Note that both percentile ranks (PR) and stanines (S) are provided for scores based on both national and local norming groups, although only the former appear in this particular case. When compared to a national sample of fourth graders who took this test at the time of its standardization (the norming group), the student whose achievement is reported in Figure 11.3 scored particularly high in the language arts area and at about an average level in the other areas. This is shown graphically in the charting of stanines.

Since norms are provided for an entire grade level, and achievement occurs continuously throughout the grade level, normed scores will be partly dependent on when the test is taken. The student reported on in Figure 11.3 took the Stanford Achievement Test part way through the grade (specifically, in December). Further experiences in the grade may not produce any measurable effect on the particular form of language arts subtests used when scores are already so high relative to the norm group. Such is a limitation of percentile ranks where you are typically limited to a single grade level within which to make comparisons even though (1) test taking may occur at different times throughout the grade for different school districts, and (2) some students are performing at levels closer to students in other grade levels than in their own.[6]

Figure 11.4 shows a table of norms for a portion of a specific grade level as taken from the Stanford Achievement Test. With this table it is possible to convert an individual raw score into a percentile rank thereby providing test score interpretability without recourse to standard score calculations. Tests such as these provide test takers with both their standard score and their percentile rank, each of which relates their test score to the scores

---

[5] The median score is the middle score in the sequential ranking of scores; the mean score is the mathematical average of scores. They are seldom the same except in the perfect or ideal normal distribution.
[6] Those deficiencies may be somewhat overcome by using grade equivalents in addition to percentile ranks.

Stanines and Selected Percentile Ranks Corresponding to Raw Scores by Test End of Grade 2

NUMBER RIGHT

Sta-nine	%ile Rank	Vocab-ulary	Reading Part A	Reading Part B	Part A + Part B	Word Study Skills	Math. Concepts	Math. Computa-tion	Math. Applica-tions	Spelling	Social Science	Science	Listening Compre-hension	%ile Rank
9 99		36-37	45	47-48	92-93	65	34-35	36-37	28	43	26-27	26-27	47-50	99
98		35			91	64	33	35	27	42	25	25	46	98
96		34		46	90			34	26	41			45	96
8 94					89	63	32	33	25	40	24	24	44	94
92		33	44	45	88		31						43	92
90						62		32		39	23			90
89		32		44	87				24					89
7 88							30					23	42	88
86			43		86	61		31		38				86
84		31		43	85		29		23		22		41	84
82					84	60		30		37		22		82
80		30	42	42					22					80
78					83	59	28	29					40	78
77														77
6 76		29		41	82					36	21			76
74			41		81	58	27	28	21			21	39	74
72				40	80	57				35				72
70		28			79				20					70
68			40	39	78	56	26	27					38	68
66					77	55				34	20			66
64		27	39	38	76	54	25	26	19			20		64
62				37	75	53							37	62
60			38	36	74	52	24			33				60
5 58		26			72-73	51		25	18				36	58
56			37	35	71						19			56
54		25		34	70	50	23			32		19		54
52			36	33	68-69	49		24	17				35	52
50			35	32	67	48								50
48		24		31	65-66	47	22	23		31			34	48
46			34	30	63-64	46			16		18	18		46
44			33	29	61-62	45	21							44
42		23		28	60	44		22		30			33	42
40			32	27	58-59	43	20		15					40
4 38		22	31	26	56-57			21		29		17	32	38
36			30	25	54-55	42			14		17			36
34			29	24	53	41	19						31	34
32		21	28	23	52	40		20		28				32
30				22	50-51	39	18		13			16	30	30
28		20	27	21	48-49			19		27	16			28
26			26	20	46-47	38	17						29	26
24		19	25		45	37		18	12	26		15		24
23				19	44								28	23
3 22			24		43	36	16							22
20		18	23	18	41-42	35		17	11	25	15		27	20
18			22	17	40		15	16		24		14	26	18
16		17	21	16	38-39	34		15	10	23			25	16
14			20	15	36-37	33	14			22	14	13	24	14
12		16	19		35	32		14	9	21				12
11				14	34	31				20			23	11
2 10		15	18		33	30	13	13		19	13	12	22	10
8		14	17	13	31-32	29	12	12	8	18			21	8
6		13	16	12	29-30	28	11	10-11	7	17	12	11	20	6
4		12	14-15	11	26-28	26-27	10	9	6	14-16	11	10	17-19	4
1 2		11	12-13	9-10	24-25	23-25	8-9	7-8	5	12-13	10	9	14-16	2
1		9-10	10-11	7-8	21-23	21-22	7	6	4	10-11	9	8	13	1

Figure 11.4 *A Sample Norms Table Taken from the Stanford Achievement Tests.**

of a norming group. The percentile rank gives the test score a high degree of interpretability on a relative basis since without it, it is hard to determine the quality of a student's performance.

Norm-referenced scores on achievement tests can be expressed in a form other than percentile ranks or stanine scores, which as we have seen, are based on the comparison of present scores to those already obtained on the test by a norm group of the same age and grade level. An alternative approach is to compare a student's score to scores across a number of grade levels and identify the grade level at which the given score is most similar to that of the norming group average. Such a procedure results in *grade-equivalent scores*.

Grade-equivalent Score

To obtain a score that represents an average or typical performance take the standard scores or raw scores of norming groups at each grade level and compute the average or mean. Any student getting one of these average scores on a test (that is, average for the norming group at that grade level) would be assigned the grade-equivalent score of that grade level. If the score corresponded to the average of the beginning fourth grade norming group, the grade-equivalent score would be 4.1; if it corresponded to the average for the beginning fifth grade norming group, the grade-equivalent score would be 5.1; and so on. The greater likelihood is that actual scores will fall between these norming group averages rather than directly on one. To deal with this, the score range between the average standard or raw score for each grade level norming group and that of the succeeding one has been arbitrarily divided into ten equal parts based on a 10-month school year and the necessary but possibly false assumption of uniform growth over time. Thus, if a student gets a score halfway between the average for the fourth grade norming group and the fifth grade norming group, the grade-equivalent of that score would be 4.6. If the score is at the upper limit of fourth grade average performance, the grade-equivalent score would be 4.9. (Most achievement tests are normed at .1, .6, or .9 within grade levels.)

Figure 11.5 shows the grade-equivalent scores for the Word Knowledge subtest, Metropolitan Achievement Test (1970 edition), each in terms of its corresponding standard score. Grade-equivalent scores are provided by the publisher based on administrations of the test given only once, at the end of the first school month (usually in early October) for each elementary grade level; these scores appear in bold face type in the figure. (All grade-equivalent

Figure 11.5 *Standard Scores and Corresponding Grade-equivalents on the Word Knowledge Subtest of the Metropolitan Achievement Test.*

Grade Equivalent	Standard Score	Grade Equivalent	Standard Score
2.0	45	5.6	77
2.1	**46**	5.7	77
2.2	47	5.8	78
2.3	49	5.9	78
2.4	50	6.0	79
2.5	52	**6.1**	**80**
2.6	53	6.2	80
2.7	54	6.3	81
2.8	55	6.4	81
2.9	56	6.5	82
3.0	57	6.6	82
3.1	**58**	6.7	83
3.2	59	6.8	83
3.3	60	6.9	84
3.4	61	7.0	84
3.5	62	**7.1**	**85**
3.6	63	7.2	86
3.7	64	7.3	87
3.8	65	7.4	87
3.9	66	7.5	88
4.0	66	7.6	88
4.1	**67**	7.7	89
4.2	68	7.8	89
4.3	68	7.9	90
4.4	69	8.0	90
4.5	70	**8.1**	**91**
4.6	70	8.2	91
4.7	71	8.3	91
4.8	72	8.4	92
4.9	72	8.5	92
5.0	73	8.6	93
5.1	**73**	8.7	93
5.2	74	8.8	94
5.3	75	8.9	94
5.4	76	9.0	94
5.5	76	**9.1**	**95**

* Adapted from the Metropolitan Achievement Test Teacher's Handbook, copyright © 1971, by Harcourt Brace Jovanovich. Adapted by special permission of the publisher. (Boldface grade-equivalents are empirically determined; others are determined by interpolation.)

scores are based on this single administration.) If the middle standard score among students at grade level 2.1 is 47 on the Word Knowledge subtest, as Figure 11.5 shows it to be, then any students who obtain a standard score of 47 can be assigned a grade-equivalent score of 2.1. They are performing at the same level as the middle child at this grade level. They may, in fact, be fourth graders or first graders, but their score of 47 matches that of the middle scorer in the 2.1 grade level. Thus, they would be assigned a grade-equivalent score of 2.1 meaning that they are scoring on the test at the middle level for beginning second graders.

Since students are not tested and retested every month of school, but are typically tested once (or at most, twice), actual empirical data for use in assigning grade equivalents are available for only one or two months within each grade level. To get the grade-equivalent scores for the other eight or nine months in the school year, interpolation is used to prepare conversion tables as shown in Figure 11.5. Keep in mind that these interpolated grade equivalency figures are determined by dividing the interval between empirically-determined scores by 10, a process that automatically assumes that equal learning occurs each month—a dubious assumption indeed.

When students take an achievement test such as the Metropolitan Achievement Test, their raw scores (the actual numerical scores they obtain—usually the number of right answers) are transformed into standard scores based on the scores of the norming group. The standard scores can then be "transformed" into grade-equivalent scores for purposes of interpretability. If a child has just begun the fourth grade and obtains a grade-equivalent score of 3.5, this indicates that the child is scoring on this one test at the average level of students halfway through the third grade rather than at the average level of his or her grade-mates (beginning fourth graders).

Grade equivalents are not comparable across subtests of a battery for students who are well above or below average for their grade. A student whose percentile rank position within his or her grade is the same in all subtests may have grade equivalent scores in the different subtests varying by five or six months of score. Furthermore, grade equivalents (like percentile ranks) are not of equal size across the scale. At the extremes, a single point of raw score may make several months of difference in grade equivalents, whereas at the middle, an increase of one raw score point may make only one month of difference. Finally, grade equivalents cannot be interpreted literally. If a second grade student obtains a math computation score of 4.8, that does not mean he or she can be moved immediately into the fourth grade.

Thus, each type of normed score has its advantages and limitations. Each serves a different purpose, and most publishers of standardized tests provide all the different kinds. In general, stanines and percentile ranks are most appropriate for comparing scores across different subtests; standard scores are used most often to compare scores across levels and forms of the same subtest; grade equivalents are best used to report group averages. Interpreting the same raw score in various ways increases perspective.

Standardized Tests   The last Part of this book will discuss standardized tests (which are also called published tests). These tests whose interpretability is based on norm-referencing, are known by three general characteristics.

First, *the items on a standardized test have been analyzed and refined.* In other words, the items on a standardized test are not necessarily the originals. They have been tried out and the results of the tryout analyzed. Based on the analysis, poorer items have been deleted or revised so that the items that remain are reasonably effective (in separating high scorers from low scorers, or in other ways). Similarly, scoring keys and answer choices have been revised to eliminate ambiguity.

Second, *the instructions for administering a standardized test have themselves been standardized or formalized.* Standardized tests are accompanied by manuals that include a specific set of instructions for test administration, thus increasing the likelihood that whenever the test is administered, it will be administered in the same manner. In other words, for the test results to be comparable from time to time and from place to place, the instructions given the test takers have to be the same, the amount of time allowed the same, and so on.

Finally, *standardized tests are accompanied by norms that permit interpretation of test performances relative to a national population of test takers.* It is this last feature—that standardized tests are norm-referenced—that is the most critical. It is this feature that provides a standardized test with its interpretability, for it is the norms that enable a test performance to be evaluated by comparing it with a large number of preexisting test performances, those of the norming group.

The basic value of norms is to indicate how high or low a student's score is, independent of the difficulty of a test, by comparing it to scores of others on the same test over a period of years. Standard scores, stanine scores, percentile ranks, and grade-equivalent scores are normative or relative versions of raw scores. They tell about performances and characteristics of test takers relative to the performances and characteristics of other test takers in a reference testing group. If a test was hard—it was hard for all; if easy —easy for all. Norm-referenced scores thus help us to (1) interpret individual scores by comparison to group data, and (2) make conclusions based on test scores, therefore, somewhat independent of the failings or weaknesses of the test. This latter point is worth amplifying. We may not be sure whether a particular test is too easy or too hard; to compensate for the test's possible inexactness we use it not as an absolute measure of capability but as a way of determining the relative capabilities of students one to the other.

In Summary

Two shortcomings of norms must be kept in mind. First, people, cultures, and societies change over time and norms can become dated and no longer reflect the types of performances of which people are capable based on the pattern of their experiences. As educational practices change, old norms can pose a serious problem and lead to misinterpretation. Second, an emphasis on the relative interpretation of tests tends to obscure the relation between the content of those tests and any bearing on the past or future reality of the test takers. If the test results are to have any bearing on evaluating the educational past or determining the educational future of a student, norms should not be seen as a substitute for appropriateness.

Moreover, there are times when we are interested in the absolute value of a score rather than the relative one. For this purpose we now turn to criterion-referenced tests.

CRITERION-REFERENCING

Thus far in this chapter on test interpretability, only norm-referencing has been considered—that is, only the interpretation of test scores on a relative basis. Standardized or published tests are usually norm-referenced although, as we shall see in Chapter 13, published criterion-referenced tests are beginning to appear. Most published tests are norm-referenced because they are typically designed by someone other than their user and are constructed in such a way as to have their primary meaning in terms of how different groups perform on them. It is possible, though, to interpret scores on some tests in terms of how many items students get right regardless of how this number compares to group performance. In such cases we say that the test represents a performance criterion and that students who get every item right or some predetermined number of items right are capable of the total performance demanded by the test. We call such an approach *criterion-referencing*.

It is important to note that a test cannot be automatically called criterion-referenced simply because it is not norm-referenced. Criterion-referenced means that test performance is linked or related to behavioral referents (Glaser, 1963) and that the test has been designed and constructed on such a basis (Jackson, 1970). In other words, the test, by design, must furnish information about a student's ability to carry out certain performances in absolute terms. If the test is one of adding and subtracting fractions, we must have some basis for saying that a student knows how to add and subtract fractions if he or she can correctly complete all the items on the test. If no student can pass the test, and if it truly has a behavioral or performance criterion, then we must conclude that no student has met the proficiency criterion for the skill being tested.

Where do the criteria come from by which a test is referenced? Cox and Vargas (1966) suggest that a major criterion for referencing be that training has resulted in an increase in proficiency. If a test is given to a group both before and after training and the group scores noticeably better on the test after training than before, then the test can be considered to be sensitive to the outcomes of training. Put another way, the test results can be interpreted as an indication of acquisition of the skills and knowledge which the training has aimed at producing.[7] Such a test is criterion-referenced.

Unfortunately, few of the tests that teachers build are actually rigorously criterion-referenced. In order to talk about a test being criterion-referenced, it is necessary to attempt to determine the relation between performance on that test and criterion behavior. To be justified in considering a test to be criterion-referenced, we might go through steps such as the following in its construction and referencing.

[7] Such a procedure, you will recall, was recommended on page 245 for establishing the validity of a test.

(1) Prepare a content outline listing the skills and knowledge that the test is an attempt to measure (this is the content outline prepared as a basis for appropriateness—see pages 67–70).

(2) Identify the performances (i.e., measurable objectives) of which the test taker should be capable assuming that he or she has acquired proficiency in the skills and knowledge measured by the test.

(3) Identify the domain that each objective defines; write items according to the specifications of that domain, and randomly select at least two per objective to make up the test (refer to *domain-referencing* on pages 217–19 and to Appendix B).

(4) Validate the fact that the skills and knowledge measured by the test are in fact prerequisite to the performance objectives identified in step 2; this is perhaps the most variable aspect of the process since the validation begins with the application of one's own judgment (that is, establishing face validity) and extends to include the judgment of a group of experts or actual data obtained by giving the test to a group that has demonstrated proficient performance to see whether they possess the skills and knowledge on the test.

(5) Decide upon or determine a criterion or cutoff score showing the test performance a person must obtain to indicate sufficient proficiency in the skills and knowledge to be able to perform the criterion behaviors.

The important features of criterion-referenced tests, therefore, are:

(1) that they are based on a set of behavioral or *performance* objectives which they are an attempt to measure;

(2) that they are designed to have a high degree of appropriateness by virtue of being based on objectives;

(3) that they represent samples of actual behavior or performance;

(4) that performance on them can be interpreted in terms of predetermined cutoff scores.

It is important to point out that there is not a clear dichotomy between norm-referenced and criterion-referenced tests. They can be thought of as complementary; in fact, it is possible to interpret the same test in either or both ways provided that objectives or discrete content categories are used as the basis for writing items. The essential difference between criterion-referenced and norm-referenced interpretation is that the former is based on predetermined cutoff scores (presumably intrinsic to the required performance itself) while the latter is based on the performance of a norm group (an extrinsic basis for interpretation).

Criterion-referencing is most applicable in the area of skill testing and most difficult to apply, as Ebel (1970) has pointed out, to the measurement of complex behavior such as thinking and problem-solving. Nevertheless, there is an interest in making greater use of criterion-referencing in school achievement testing, both in teacher-built tests and published ones. Criterion-referencing is used by (1) generating or selecting a set of objectives representing the desirable performance outcomes of instruction, (2) designing or finding items to adequately measure each objective (that is, representing its domain), (3) presetting acceptable performance levels,[8] (4) administering the test to students and evaluating their performance in terms of the number of objectives whose performance requirements they can adequately meet.

Criterion-referencing involves the task of writing or finding objectives and items to measure those objectives. While this can be readily done by teachers in their own classrooms, writing the objectives and items required for a district-wide criterion-referenced achievement test is a major undertaking, perhaps more suitable for testing companies than for local school personnel. But even a testing company will find it difficult to prepare a criterion-referenced test on a national or even regional basis since such an approach would sacrifice the targeting of a test to the needs of a particular school system. The fact that local inputs are most necessary for local use but that few local personnel have the time or skill to build district-wide achievement tests limits the availability or practicality of systematically built criterion-referenced achievement tests. However, the increasing availability of *banks* or repositories of performance objectives and test items, the increasing inclination by school administrations to have teachers develop lists of performance objectives for their districts, and the developments by testing companies in this area, have increased the likelihood that criterion-referenced tests will be available and used for measuring school achievement.

---

[8] It is perhaps somewhat ironic that these levels are mainly set in a kind of normative way, i.e., 80% of pupils getting 80% of the items correct, rather than in a way truly intrinsic to the objective. This may be due to the work required to collect necessary data for an empirical determination and/or to the fact that so little in our world is absolute. Box 7.1 (*Pass/Fail!*) bears directly on this point.

Such criterion-referenced tests, as they appear, will have the advantage of allowing each school district to target its testing program to its own goals and to monitor goal attainment in an absolute rather than a relative sense. It will not suffice to say that Blair has learned more than Bret. We will have to know the number of goals that each has met in order to certify advancement to new and more complex ones. Considerable help will be afforded by test publishers who offer schools test items matched to objectives so that each school can shape and form its own achievement test, geared to the needs of its own students.

DETERMINING A TEST'S INTERPRETABILITY

By applying the concepts of interpretability described on the previous pages a teacher can determine a test's interpretability. To assist the teacher the checklist questions below are offered.

Is My Test INTERPRETABLE?

(1) Do I Know How the Scores Relate to Relevant Performance:
   a. Is my test referenced in terms of some criterion (e.g., my objectives)?
   b. Can I tell what a high score and a low score mean? Or, can I report the specific objectives on which proficiency has been demonstrated?
   c. Can the results for an individual student be used as a specific indication of level or degree of proficiency?

(2) Do I Know What Defines Acceptable Performance:
   a. Have I preestablished cutoff scores (e.g. passing grade) and if so, on what basis?
   b. Do I have some concrete and verifiable way to say whether a particular performance suffices in terms of objective specifications of acceptability?

(3) Does the Test Provide Diagnostic and Evaluative Information:
   a. Does it tell me the areas in which a student needs help?
   b. Does it tell me the areas in which the class needs help?
   c. Does it tell me the areas in which instruction needs improvement?

(4) Does It Provide Useful Relative Information:
   a. Does it provide the kind of data that I can compare meaningfully with results of past and future testings?
   b. Can the results be interpreted on a norm-referenced basis if that is desired?

The question of interpretability boils down to how do you tell what a score on a test means? After all, it is only a number. Usually it is the number of items right. What does that information convey? Has the student demonstrated proficiency on the objectives being measured? Does the student have the ability to move to the next level of performance? Does he or she have the capability to perform skills at a level required for beginning employment in some occupation? In itself, a test score tells you very little; to be useful, test scores must be interpreted.

If a test is based on a set of objectives and if the objectives themselves have some validity, then the score on a test should tell us something about a student's ability to perform in the test area A *criterion-referenced test* should provide information about students' degree of proficiency in the objectives of which the test is a measure. A high score on the test should be indicative of achievement of objectives and a low score of lack of achievement. You may think, perhaps, that the test items are too easy or too hard and hence not a fair measure of achievement. If your test has already met the criteria of appropriateness, validity, and reliability, it is likely that the items are adequate for assessing achievement and thus you can conclude that test success reflects achievement of objectives.

    To adequately interpret achievement, it may be helpful not to restrict yourself to the total test score. Since a criterion-referenced test is like a collection of mini-tests, each measuring a single, but related objective (and each containing a minimum of two, and often many more, items), achievement can be described by reporting the specific objectives that each student has demonstrated proficiency on by virtue of passing the appropriate mini-test. Thus, instead of having to decide how high a score must be to be considered "high," you would simply list for each student the name of each objective on which he or she has demonstrated proficiency along with (if desired) an indication of the level of proficiency attained. Interpretability of such a test is primarily based, therefore, not on the total test score but on indications of degree of proficiency attained for each objective of which the test is a measure. Since the objectives represent our real interest, and criterion-referenced tests measure achievement of objectives, we can focus our test results and interpretations on the very learning we are interested in enhancing.

Relation of Test Scores to Relevant Performance

Must a student pass every item that measures a given objective to be judged as competent on that objective? That is, how are we to interpret performance on each mini-test? Because of variability on item difficulty and the appearance of various types of unsystematic errors, it is not unreasonable to allow some room for error Each teacher must decide for each objective what the acceptable margin of error shall be. Often, test performance can first be examined in order to facilitate this judgment. However, if items that seem to be too difficult are replaced or revised during the

Defining Acceptable Performance

establishment of reliability, the remaining margin or error can be made as small as 10 to 20 percent to allow for unsystematic errors.

The amount of error that can be tolerated is proportionate to the number of items used to measure a particular objective. Where a single item, or even two items, are used, proficiency will require 100% success. In order to allow for 20% error, a minimum of five items would be required to measure an objective. In that case, it would be necessary to answer only four out of five (80%) correctly to indicate proficiency. Where fewer items are used, the 80% criterion could be used for evaluating total test performance (across related objectives) but not performance on individual objectives.

Diagnostic and Evaluative Information

Test results provide a basis for drawing conclusions about learning and teaching. A useful test not only tells you about student achievement but tells you about instructional effectiveness as well. If you examine individual performance, you should be able to determine each student's degree of proficiency on each objective. Where proficiency is sufficient, progress can continue to new learning areas. Where proficiency has not been demonstrated, remedial instruction aimed directly at those objectives can be instituted. In this way, a test can have diagnostic value. Test performance not only serves to certify success but to provide the kind of information that will make it possible to overcome failure.[9]

Where instruction is of a group nature, test results must be applicable to judgments of group progress. If group success has largely been attained, then instruction on new material can begin. If group gains have been minimal, then remedial instruction should be provided before instruction can progress to new areas.

Finally, the interpretable test gives you information on the adequacy of instruction. If proficiency on a particular objective has not been demonstrated by many students, it is probably because instruction in this area has been less than successful. Frequency breakdowns of student performance using a table such as the one opposite may be helpful. When the number of students who do not show proficiency reaches or exceeds the number who do show proficiency you can probably conclude that instructional

---

[9] As the number of items per objective increases, so too does the reliability with which these objectives are measured. In order to use test results for individual diagnostic purposes, reliabilities must be high; hence, such tests should probably have at least four or five items per objective. This can usually be accomplished by keeping the number of objectives measured by a test to a maximum of five.

OBJECTIVE 1

Number of students showing proficiency	Number of students not showing proficiency

experiences were insufficient for achievement of this objective. Changes in lesson plans or learning materials for teaching this objective should be seriously considered for subsequent instruction to augment or replace those currently in use.

Useful Relative Information

Test results also represent a source of relative information about student performance. That is, we can evaluate a student's performance by comparing it to the performance of other students. In the largest sense, this is called *norm-referencing*. To use the concept of norm-referencing in your own classroom, place the total scores on the test of all your students who are taking (or who have taken) the test in rank order going from the highest score to the lowest, and then assign each score a rank starting with 1 for the highest. You can then assign each score a percentile rank or convert it to a stanine score (using the procedures described earlier in this chapter and in Appendix C), or simply separate scores into the top fifth, second fifth, middle fifth, fourth fifth, and lowest fifth with approximately one-fifth of the scores in each category.

You must now decide whether this kind of information is useful in interpreting test scores in addition to or in place of the criterion-referenced concept of proficiency on objectives relative to some intrinsic standard. (On attitude tests, for example, relative information is considerably easier to interpret than absolute information because specific objectives or subtopical content areas do not have quite as much independence and meaning as they do in cognitive or performance areas.) However, a comparative look at test scores does represent a way to provide them with some meaning at least in relative terms. Where you are less sure about the properties of your test, the normative or comparative approach is recommended. Where you have more confidence in the meaning of your objectives and the appropriateness with which your test measures them, criterion-referenced interpretation is the more informative of the two approaches for evaluating students.

DETERMINING A TEST'S USABILITY

Listed below are checklist criteria for checking on the usability of a test.

Is My Test USABLE?

(1) Is It Short Enough to Avoid Being Tedious:
   a. Does it stop short of creating fatigue? stress? boredom?
   b. Have I tried to make it as short as possible within the limits of reliability?

(2) Is It Practical for Classroom Use:
   a. Can it be used conveniently in a classroom?
   b. Is it within the limit of available teacher time?
   c. Can it be used to test all students?
   d. Is it realistic about the kinds of equipment and physical set-up it requires?

(3) Are There Standard Procedures for Administration:
   a. Are there clear, written instructions?
   b. Can it be administered by someone other than me?
   c. Can it be given in a nonthreatening, nondiscriminatory way?

(4) Can Students Comprehend It and Relate to It:
   a. Is it written at a level students can understand?
   b. Is it interesting, clever, or provocative?
   c. Is it written to engage students?

Our consideration would not be complete were we to overlook the criterion of usability. Tests must be taken by people, often children, and to be at all meaningful they must attain a minimum level of practicality. We must consider, briefly, at least the minimal criteria of usability.

Tedium   Many tests suffer from the obvious failing of being too long. Such tests provoke hostility or at least produce boredom and fatigue—often resulting in invalid test responses. There is no absolute rule as to how long a test should be. Typically, the more items therefore, the more reliability; however, tedium can cause unreliability. What is this point of diminishing returns? It can best be determined by initially building your test to fill the amount of time allowed for its completion and then observing students in the process of taking it. You can generally tell from their reactions (or from an item analysis) whether your test is too long. If it provokes restlessness, visible fatigue, and complaints, shorten it for subsequent use. Occasionally, it may be necessary to divide a test into two tests and administer it in two sittings in order to cover all necessary test material. Keep in mind that at least two items per objective (and if possible more) must be included for reliability purposes on a criterion-referenced test.

Practicality

Some tests are highly inconvenient for classroom use; for example, they require movement or the use of equipment or perhaps oral responses. If these features are critical to the appropriateness of the test then you may choose to sacrifice some practicality for appropriateness (which is not at all unreasonable). However, be sure that you are gaining something in return for the demands in practicality. Your goal in testing should be to try to maximize practicality and appropriateness simultaneously. Often, if you think about it you can conduct a test in a more practical way than you might have originally thought. Take-home tests, for example, might be one way to overcome certain forms of impracticality. Also, testing rooms may be set up for individualized testing (or self-testing) without requiring that all students take a test at the same time.

Administrative Procedures

The written procedures and instructions for administering a test are part of the test. They should be clear and nonthreatening. Often, it is helpful if you read them aloud. Opportunities for questions should be provided. However, if your instructions are clear and understandable, few questions should be asked. Questions can serve as a source of information to tell you how your instructions might be improved.

Instructions should cover such things as (1) what the test is about, (2) why it is being given, (3) what response format will be used and how it is to be used, (4) how much time will be allowed, (5) whether questions will be answered, and (6) how it will be scored. Proper instructions at the outset may save you having to give them over and over again on an individual basis.

Readability

As has been said before, a test is useless if students cannot read it. It must be written at their reading level and not yours. It is also helpful from the point of usability if students find the test interesting or even fun to take. Occasionally, humor can be introduced;

sometimes novelty of format helps keep interest. Readability does not only mean that students *can* read it; it also means that they *want to* read it. Try to be sensitive to their interests and orientations and to their language. Just as you relate to students through instruction, you should also try to relate to them through tests. To test you must communicate; without communication no testing occurs. Test construction can be creative.

SELECTING A TEST: A SUMMARY

In evaluating, selecting, or building a test, you should ask yourself five questions:

(1) Is the test *appropriate*; that is, does the test measure my objectives?

(2) Is the test *valid*; that is, does it measure the things it says it measures?

(3) Is the test *reliable*; that is, is it a consistent and accurate measuring instrument?

(4) Is the test *interpretable*; that is, can I tell you what different performances on the test mean?

(5) Is the test *usable*; that is, can it be conveniently employed in the circumstances which present themselves?

The overall test criterion checklist appears in total in Figure 11.6, for summary purposes.

Figure 11.6   *A Checklist for Criterion-referenced Tests.*

YES   NO   I. *Is My Test APPROPRIATE?*
(1) Does It Fit My Objectives:
a. Are there 2 items or more for each and every objective and 0 items that fit no objectives?
b. Do the number of items per objective accurately reflect the relative importance of each objective?
(2) Does It Reflect the Action Verbs:
a. Does each item for a given objective measure the action called for by the verb in that objective?
b. Have I used the item format most appropriate for each action?
(3) Does It Utilize the Conditions:
a. Does each item for a given objective employ the statement of givens or conditions set forth in that objective?

(4) Does It Employ the Criteria: YES   NO
   a. Is the scoring of each item for a given objective based on the criteria
   stated in that objective?

II. *Is My Test VALID?*
   (1) Does It Discriminate between Performance Levels:
      a. Do students who are independently judged to perform better in the test
      area perform better on the test?
      b. Do different students with different degrees of experience perform dif-
      ferently on the various items?
   (2) Does It Fit Any External Standard:
      a. Does success on the test predict subsequent success in areas for
      which the test topic is claimed to be a prerequisite?
      b. Do students who receive appropriate teaching perform better on the
      test than untaught students (or does a student perform better on the
      test after teaching than before)?
   (3) How Do My Colleagues View the Coverage:
      a. Do my colleagues in the topic area or at the grade level agree that all
      necessary objectives and no unnecessary ones have been included?
      b. Do they agree that the items are valid for measuring the objectives?
   (4) Does It Measure Something Other than Reading Level or Life Styles:
      a. Are the demands it makes on reading skill within the capabilities of
      the students?
      b. Is performance independent of group membership or any other socio-
      ethnic variable?

III. *Is My Test RELIABLE?*
   (1) Are There Paired Items That Agree:
      a. Do students who get one item of a pair (per objective) right also get
      the other right and those who get one wrong get the other wrong?
      b. Have nonparallel items been rewritten?
   (2) Is Item Performance Consistent with Test Performance:
      a. Is each item consistently passed by students who do well on the total
      test?
      b. Have inconsistent items been removed?
   (3) Are All Items Clear and Understandable:
      a. Have the student responses been used as a basis for evaluating item
      clarity?
      b. Have ambiguous items been removed or rewritten?
   (4) Have Scoring Procedures Proved to Be Systematic and Unbiased:
      a. Have multiple scorings yielded consistent results?
      b. Are scoring criteria and procedures as detailed and as suitable as they
      can be?

YES   NO   IV. *Is My Test INTERPRETABLE?*
- (1) Do I know How the Scores Relate to Relevant Performance:
  - *a.* Is my test referenced in terms of some criterion (e.g., my objectives)?
  - *b.* Can I tell what a high score and a low score mean? Or, can I report the specific objectives on which proficiency has been demonstrated?
  - *c.* Can the results for an individual student be used as a specific indication of level or degree of proficiency?
- (2) Do I Know What Defines Acceptable Performance:
  - *a.* Have I preestablished cutoff scores (e.g. passing grade) and if so, on what basis?
  - *b.* Do I have some concrete and verifiable way to say whether a particular performance suffices in terms of objective specifications of acceptability?
- (3) Does the Test Provide Diagnostic and Evaluative Information:
  - *a.* Does it tell me the areas in which a student needs help?
  - *b.* Does it tell me the areas in which the class needs help?
  - *c.* Does it tell me the areas in which instruction needs improvement?
- (4) Does It Provide Useful Relative Information:
  - *a.* Does it provide the kind of data that I can compare meaningfully with results of past and future testings?
  - *b.* Can the results be interpreted on a norm-referenced basis if that is desired?

V. *Is My Test USABLE?*
- (1) Is It Short Enough to Avoid Being Tedious:
  - *a.* Does it stop short of creating fatigue? stress? boredom?
  - *b.* Have I tried to make it as short as possible within the limits of reliability?
- (2) Is It Practical for Classroom Use:
  - *a.* Can it be used conveniently in a classroom?
  - *b.* Is it within the limit of available teacher time?
  - *c.* Can it be used to test all students?
  - *d.* Is it realistic about the kinds of equipment and physical set-up it requires?
- (3) Are There Standard Procedures for Administration:
  - *a.* Are there clear, written instructions?
  - *b.* Can it be administered by someone other than me?
  - *c.* Can it be given in a nonthreatening, nondiscriminatory way?
- (4) Can Students Comprehend It and Relate to It:
  - *a.* Is it written at a level students can understand?
  - *b.* Is it interesting, clever, or provocative?
  - *c.* Is it written to engage students?

On a published test, answers to the criterion questions can usually be gleaned from the manual of the test coupled with an examination of the test itself. In the last section of this book, dealing with published tests, these questions will be applied to some published tests for purposes of illustration.

The five criteria have been termed *appropriateness, validity, reliability, interpretability, and usability.* If a test is not appropriate for your objectives, it should not be selected, regardless of the adequacy of its other properties. If it is appropriate, then it must also fit its own label or title, and hence be valid, to be useful. If both appropriate and valid, it must then be an accurate or reliable instrument. It must also be one whose results are interpretable, since results that cannot be interpreted are meaningless. Finally, it must be usable if it is to work at all under the prevailing classroom conditions.

The same five criteria can be applied to teacher-built tests as well. Teachers must state their purposes or objectives and their tests must meet them in an appropriate and valid way. Their tests must also possess accuracy as measuring instruments and their results must be interpretable. In addition, the criterion of usability must be considered. Usability refers to the practical characteristics of a test, such as its cost to purchase or develop, the degree of sensitivity it is likely to arouse, the amount of time it takes to administer, and the ease in scoring the test and reporting the results.

The final section of this book deals with using published tests. Throughout that discussion, the terms and concepts described in this section will be applied to assist teachers in the selection, use, and interpretation of these tests.

Additional Information Sources

Anghoff, W. H. Scales, norms, & equivalent scores. In R. L. Thorndike (Ed.). *Educational measurement*, 2nd ed., Wash. D.C.: American Council on Education, 1971, Chap. 15.

Gardener, E. F. Interpreting achievement profiles—uses and warnings. *NCME Measurement in Education: A Series of Special Reports of the National Council on Measurement in Education, 1,* (2), 1970.

Lennon, R. T. Scores and norms. In R. E. Ebel (Ed.). *Encyclopedia of educational research*, 4th ed., N.Y.: Macmillan, 1969.

Lyman, H. B. *Test scores and what they mean*. Englewood Cliffs, N.J.: Prentice-Hall, 1963.

Womer, F. B. Test norms: Their use and interpretation. Wash. D.C.: National Association of Secondary School Principals, 1965.

Self-test of Proficiency

(1) Norm-referenced interpretation relates a person's test score to _____ on that test by other people.

(2) Define, in one sentence each, a. *norms*, and b. *norming group*.

(3) For each of the illustrations below, identify the type of score depicted, that is, standard score, stanine score, percentile rank, or grade-equivalent score.
   a. Bobbie's score on the test was higher than 82% of the students in the norming group at the same grade level.
   b. Although Bobbie is in the fourth grade, her test score was as high as the average fifth grader on the fourth grade test.
   c. Bobbie's test score was two standard deviation units above the norming group average score for her grade level.
   d. Bobbie's test score fell into a band of scores of the norming group that was represented by the score of 7.

(4) Refer to the sample norms table in Figure 11.4 on page 288 to answer the questions listed below.
   • Jeff got 48 items right on the Word Study Skills test.
   a. What was Jeff's stanine score?
   b. What was Jeff's percentile rank?
   c. Which of the following words would you use to describe Jeff's performance? *Poor   Average   Exceptional*

(5) Check all of the statements below that are characteristic of standardized tests.
   a. items are purposely written to include ambiguity
   b. formal instructions for administration are provided
   c. scores are best interpreted in terms of the number of correct responses.
   d. items have been analyzed and refined
   e. norms are available for score interpretation

(6) Name one strength or advantage and one shortcoming or disadvantage of norm-referencing a test.

(7) a. Criterion-referenced test interpretation is most applicable in the area of _____ (creativity, skill-testing, problem-solving).
   b. Criterion-referenced tests are interpreted on an _____ (intrinsic, intuitive, extrinsic) basis.

(8) Check all of the statements below that are characteristic of criterion-referenced tests.
   a. measure samples of actual performance
   b. scores do not relate to absolute proficiency
   c. based on objectives
   d. interpreted in terms of predetermined cutoffs
   e. reflect preformance relative to other students

(9) You have just administered a math test to your sixth grade class. Describe how you might interpret individual scores in terms of a. relevant performance, and b. acceptable performance.

(10) How would you use the test results obtained in item 9 a. to identify ineffective instruction, and b. to provide useful relative information about student performance?

(11) Which usability criterion does each example below violate?
   a. The test required that each student individually view pictures that were unavailable in original form and which, had they been available, would have been too costly to reproduce in sufficient numbers.
   b. A test was written at the vocabulary level of the teacher, not that of the students.
   c. The test went on and on and everyone started to fall asleep.
   d. The teacher was absent on the day of the testing and the substitute had trouble figuring out how to explain to the students how to take the test.

(12) How might each of the problems illustrated in item 12 be solved to make the test usable?

part four/Using Published Tests

chapter twelve / Measuring Intelligence or Mental Ability

OBJECTIVES

1. Identify and explain definitions of intelligence or mental ability as *a.* a general intellectual capacity, *b.* groups of traits, *c.* adaptability, *d.* whatever an IQ test measures, *e.* a structural configuration of discrete factors, *f.* learning ability, *g.* school performance, *h.* a two-level process, *i.* a composite of mental abilities, *j.* a distinct characteristic (in relation to aptitude and achievement).

2. Classify verbal and figural types of intelligence test items.

3. Distinguish among and determine three types of intelligence test scores, namely: mental age, intelligence quotient (ratio IQ), and deviation IQ.

4. Categorize the scores on intelligence tests in terms of their *a.* reliability, *b.* stability, and *c.* validity.

5. Describe some commonly used intelligence or mental ability tests and distinguish among their characteristics.

6. Describe tests to measure creativity.

7. Explain the meaning and educational value of intelligence test scores.

THE CONCEPT OF INTELLIGENCE OR MENTAL ABILITY

Intelligence is a concept surrounded with considerable controversy. To be able to place that controversy in perspective and to evaluate the use of intelligence tests, teachers must understand what this type of test measures. Before moving on to the more recent, and more widely used, types of published tests, intelligence testing will be discussed. Because of the general and amorphous nature of the intelligence concept, test publishers have begun to replace it with the perhaps more delimited concept of *mental ability*. In this chapter, we will use both terms as they seem appropriate but the reader is urged to keep in mind that mental ability may be a less charged and more apt term in our times.

Because of the many uses of the term *intelligence* and the fact that intelligence tests are often used to predict human potential, it is important to be as specific as possible about what the term *intelligence* (and its companion term, *mental ability*) means. Let us consider some specific definitions of these terms.

Binet (1916; see also Varon, 1935) was interested in measuring intelligence in order to identify children who required special educational treatment. He took the position that intelligence was a general intellectual capacity made up of the following abilities: (1) to reason and judge well, (2) to comprehend well, (3) to take and maintain a definite direction of thought, (4) to adapt thinking to the attainment of a desirable end, and (5) to be autocritical. Although Binet defined intelligence operationally in terms of discrete abilities, he viewed intelligence as a single but complex mental process. He believed it could be measured by using diverse materials designed to evaluate integrated mental processes rather

Intelligence as a General Intellectual Capacity

than be measured as separate elements.[1] Binet operationalized his belief by the use of a single score to represent a child's performance across all of the 30 different tests (or tasks) that made up his scale.

Box 12.1

THE 1908 BINET-SIMON SCALE

The grouping of items at the appropriate age levels is shown below. Items are included that about 75% of the children of that age group could pass. Many of the items still appear in current intelligence tests.

Age 3

(1) Points to nose, eyes, mouth
(2) Repeats sentences of six syllables
(3) Repeats two digits
(4) Enumerates objects in a picture
(5) Gives family name

Age 4

(1) Knows own sex
(2) Names certain familiar objects shown to him (key, knife, penny)
(3) Repeats three digits
(4) Perceives which is the longer of two lines 5 and 6 cm. in length

Age 5

(1) Indicates the heavier of two cubes (3 and 12 grams; 6 and 15 grams)
(2) Copies a square
(3) Constructs a rectangle from two triangular pieces of cardboard, having a model to look at
(4) Counts four coins
(5) Repeats a sentence of ten syllables

Age 6

(1) Knows right and left; indicated by showing right hand and left ear
(2) Repeats sentence of sixteen syllables

---

[1] In other words, he defined intelligence as a capacity and then attempted to build a test to estimate the degree to which that capacity was present in individual children.

(3) Chooses the prettier in each of three pairs of faces (aesthetic comparison)
(4) Defines familiar objects in terms of use
(5) Executes three commissions
(6) Knows own age
(7) Knows morning and afternoon

Age 7

(1) Perceives what is missing in unfinished pictures
(2) Knows number of fingers on each hand an on both hands without counting.
(3) Copies a written model ("The little Paul")
(4) Copies a diamond
(5) Describes presented pictures
(6) Repeats five digits
(7) Counts thirteen coins
(8) Identifies by name four common coins

Age 8

(1) Reads a passage and remembers two items
(2) Adds up the value of five coins
(3) Names four colors; red, yellow, blue, green
(4) Counts backwards from 20 to 0
(5) Writes short sentence from dictation
(6) Gives differences between two objects

Age 9

(1) Knows the date: day of week, day of month, month of year
(2) Recites days of week
(3) Makes change: four cents out of twenty in playstore transaction
(4) Gives definitions which are superior to use; familiar objects are employed
(5) Reads a passage and remembers six items
(6) Arranges five equal-appearing cubes in order of weight

Age 10

(1) Names the months of the year in correct order
(2) Recognizes and names nine coins
(3) Constructs a sentence in which three given words are used (Paris, fortune, gutter)
(4) Comprehends and answers easy questions
(5) Comprehends and answers difficult questions (Binet considered item 5 to be a transitional question between ages 10 and 11. Only about one-half of the ten-year-olds got the majority of these correct.)

Age 11

(1) Points out absurdities in statements
(2) Constructs a sentence, including three given words (same as number 3 in age 10)
(3) States any sixty words in three minutes
(4) Defines abstract words (charity, justice, kindness)
(5) Arranges scrambled words into a meaningful sentence

Age 12

(1) Repeats seven digits
(2) Gives three rhymes to a word (in one minute)
(3) Repeats a sentence of twenty-six syllables
(4) Answers problem questions
(5) Interprets pictures (as contrasted with simple description)

Age 13

(1) Draws the design made by cutting a triangular piece from the once-folded edge of a quarto-folded piece of paper
(2) Rearranges in imagination the relationship of two reversed triangles and draws results
(3) Gives differences between pair of abstract terms: pride and pretension

(It is interesting to speculate on how many of these age-graded tasks from 1908 could be passed by 75% of today's children of those respective ages. More than likely today's 4-year-olds could name objects like a key, knife, or penny but how many 13-year-olds today could distinguish between the terms "pride" and "pretension?" Have we become less bright or is it simply a matter of changing cultures? Such differences in standards certainly point up the importance of constantly updating tests.)

From Binet, A. and Simon, T. "Le Développement de l'intelligence chez les enfants." *L'Année Psychologique*, 1908, *14*, 1–94.

The position that intelligence is largely a general intellectual capacity was championed by Charles Spearman, who believed that all mental activity is dependent primarily upon and is an expression of a common or shared *general factor* (Spearman, 1927). He called this factor g and characterized it as mental energy that is possessed by all individuals, but in varying degrees, and that operates in all mental tasks as a function of the demand they place

*Intercorrelations among Intelligence Test Subtest Scores**   **Figure 12.1**

	1	2	3	4	5	6	7
(1) Analogies	—						
(2) Completion	.50	—					
(3) Understanding							
Paragraphs	.49	.54	—				
(4) Opposites	.55	.47	.49	—			
(5) Instructions	.49	.50	.39	.41	—		
(6) Resemblances	.45	.38	.44	.32	.32	—	
(7) Inferences	.45	.34	.35	.35	.40	.35	—

* From Spearman, C. *The Ability of Man.* N.Y.: Macmillan, 1927, p. 149.

upon intelligence. He based the existence of *g* on the interrelatedness of performance on each of an intelligence test's subtests. (Interrelatedness is traditionally expressed in terms of a correlation coefficient that can range from −1.00 to 1.00 with zero indicating no relationship.) Spearman (1927) obtained the pattern of intercorrelations shown in Figure 12.1, which indicates that all the subtests have something in common in terms of performance.

While the intercorrelations between subtest scores are high but not perfect, Spearman postulated the existence of *specific factors*, called *s*, specific to particular types of activity. Thus, all mental activities were seen as having a general component, reflecting general intellectual capacity, and a specific component, somewhat unique to the activity itself, with the general one being the more important. It is this belief that justifies the practice of adding the items correctly passed in the various types of test activities to provide a single score that is then used to represent an individual's general intelligence level.

Given the kinds of interrelationships among subtests illustrated in Figure 12.1, one can either be impressed with the degree of overlap or the degree of nonoverlap. The latter emphasis gave rise to a more trait-oriented view of intelligence.

Intelligence has also been viewed as a combination of groups of traits or factors. Each of the traits within a group has more in common with other traits within that group than with traits outside the group. Thurstone (1938, 1943) called this *group-factor*   **Intelligence as Groups of Traits** *theory* and identified the following "primary" mental abilities as group-factors.

(1) The Number factor (N): "ability to do numerical calculations rapidly and accurately."
(2) The Verbal factor (V): "found in tests involving verbal comprehension."
(3) The Space factor (S): "involved in any tasks in which the subject manipulates an object imaginally in space."
(4) The Word Fluency factor (W): "involved whenever the subject is asked to think of isolated words at a rapid rate."
(5) The Reasoning factor (R): "found in tasks that require the subject to discover a rule or principle involved in series or groups of letters."
(6) The Rote Memory factor (M): "involving the ability to memorize quickly."

It must be noted that performance on each of Thurstone's six primary factors is related to performance on each of the others, suggesting that there is some generality to the concept of abstract intelligence as hypothesized by Spearman. It seems reasonable to conclude that to some extent intelligence is best defined as a collection of different factors and to some extent as a general, unifying factor. In other words, both points of view seem to have some validity.

Some intelligence tests have been based on the primary factors approach and others on the general factor approach. However, most current intelligence (or mental ability) measures provide a single overall score usually called the IQ, which suggests an endorsement, at least operationally, of the general factor approach.

Intelligence as Adaptability   Wechsler (1944, p. 3) defined intelligence as "the aggregate or global capacity of the individual to act purposefully, to think rationally and to deal effectively with his environment." Stoddard (1943, p. 4) defined intelligence as "the ability to undertake activities that are characterized by (1) difficulty, (2) complexity, (3) abstractness, (4) economy, (5) adaptiveness to a goal, (6) social value, and (7) the emergence of originals, and to maintain such activities under conditions that demand a concentration of energy and a resistance to emotional forces."

One must question whether definitions such as these have much utility for the measurement of intelligence. Surely, one would be hard-pressed to argue whether the elements in either definition are measured, or can be measured, in an intelligence test. While it may be useful to think of intelligent people as being adaptable (although notable exceptions can be found), the evidence for such adaptability would have to come from a reasonably long-term examination of a person's behavior and not from a test. If a concept is reasonable but not measurable, its usefulness in education is limited.

Boring (1923) suggested that the best definition of intelligence is *whatever the test measures.* Certainly, this definition is operational, although it has some notable failings. First of all, many different tests are available for measuring intelligence (as we shall see). Which of these will constitute the standard for measuring intelligence? To use this definition we must settle on one test since different tests may yield different results. But how is that one test to be developed itself without a definition to guide its development? In addition, current concern over cultural biases in

Intelligence as Whatever an Intelligence Test Measures

"I don't care if he does have an I.Q. of 169—I still think he's faking."

the measurement of intelligence suggests that such an arbitrary definition as this would put a considerable number of people at a distinct disadvantage.

Boring's definition helps us see that the intelligence test we use represents an operational statement of what we consider intelligence to be. In other words, when we test for intelligence we implicitly accept as intelligence whatever the "intelligence" test measures.

Intelligence as a Structural Consideration of Discrete Factors

Guilford (1967) has proposed a three-dimensional model of intelligence that is shown in Figure 12.2. His dimensions are (1) content, (2) operation, and (3) products. *Content* refers to what a test is about, that is, the realm or area in which the items are found. When drawings are the content, for example, the content is labeled F (Figural). *Operations* refers to the kind of performance required of the test taker. When the task to be performed

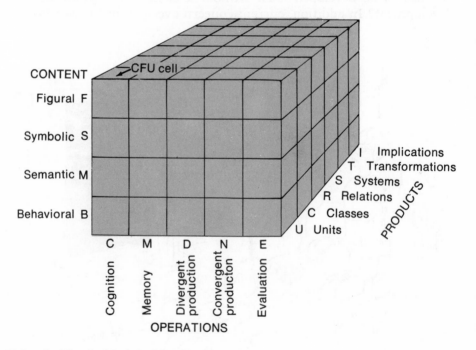

Figure 12.2 *Guilford's Model of Intellect**

* From *The Nature of Human Intelligence* by Guilford. Copyright 1967 McGraw-Hill. Used with permission of McGraw-Hill Book Company.

is to detect a relation and apply it, for example, the operation would be C (Cognition). *Products* refers to the kind of outcomes to be produced. In the model, for example, *units* refers to discrete outcomes such as synonyms.

Guilford's model produces 120 cells (4×5×6) of possible discrete intelligence factors.[2] It suggests types of tests that have hitherto never been invented. It also portrays intelligence, a highly complex phenomenon, as a combination of small pieces that conceivably fit together to make a whole. Not only is the approach quite helpful in understanding intelligence, it is also helpful in suggesting types of measurement procedures educators need.

Intelligence tests have been criticized on the grounds that they measure what a person *has* learned, not what he or she *can* learn, and (it is argued) the two are distinctly different. If the purpose of intelligence testing is to make decisions about future learning experiences, the value of the tests may be greatest if they can tell us how likely a person is to learn given the proper circumstances. Piaget (1950, 1952), for example, defines intelligence in terms of assimilation and accommodation. *Assimilation* refers to changes that are made in what is taken into the mind in order to fit it into one's scheme of things while *accommodation* refers to changes that occur in one's own internal structures as a result of new experiences. These two processes occur together to enable a person to learn and grow.

If intelligence were to be defined as learning ability, it might be measured in terms of one's ability to improve as a result of instruction. Feuerstein (1968) has developed a procedure wherein he first attempts to teach a child something and then measures how well he or she has learned it. If that which is to be learned is unfamiliar, then the ease with which a child learns it would be indicative of his or her learning ability. (Courses or review books designed to prepare students for such tests as the College Boards, suggest the application of this definition of intelligence.) To utilize this definition of intelligence would require a dramatic change

Intelligence as Learning Ability

---

[2] After hearing the model described by its author, one psychologist proclaimed: "If I were the Almighty, I wouldn't have made so many little boxes." Whereupon another quipped: "And if I'd used that many boxes, I wouldn't have stacked them that neatly." These comments suggest the difficulty of thinking about something in terms of such a systematic organization of elements rather than as a totality or as a collection of less organized parts.

in current major approaches to intelligence testing. Rather than attempting to find out what a child knows or can do, we would first have to teach it to him or her so that we could determine how easily it was learned.

Intelligence as School Performance

Many people consider school performance to be the application of intelligence and hence define intelligence in terms of school success. The high correlations that have been obtained between intelligence test scores and school performance reinforce such a view by suggesting that school performance is a manifestation of intelligence. However, we know that *correlation does not necessarily imply causation*; that is, the fact that intelligence and school achievement are correlated does not necessarily mean that high intelligence causes good school performance.[3]

There are instances when, in fact, we might conclude the reverse to be true. Rosenthal and Jacobson (1968) showed that teachers' expectations could affect students' scores on intelligence tests presumably by improving their performance in school. (They demonstrate this in a way that did suggest causation.) Students who perform in school as they are expected to may come to regard themselves as bright (since others view them that way) and subsequently perform brightly—in class as well as on IQ tests. For this reason and because of the other factors that affect school performance (such as hunger, fatigue, dissinterest), it is wise not to regard intelligence and school performance as synoymous. Both probably reflect the kinds of prior experiences a person has had, others' expectations for him or her, and to a high degree, a person's self-expectations; this overlap in causality accounts in part for the high intercorrelation.

Intelligence as a Two-level Process

Jensen (1968) hypothesizes that intelligence is a two-level process with Level I being *associative intelligence* and Level II being *abstract intelligence*. The first level refers to those kinds of tests that rely on memory and the building of simple associations. Gagné (1965) separates the association process into (1) signal learning, (2) stimulus–response learning, (3) chaining, and (4) verbal association. The second level refers to thinking and prob-

---

[3] When intelligence test scores predict school achievement, they do acquire a degree of predictive validity. However, when intelligence test scores and school achievement become indistinguishable, the tests should more legitimately be considered achievement tests.

lem-solving skills, which Gagné subdivides into (5) multiple discrimination, (6) concept learning, (7) principle learning, and (8) problem solving.

Most intelligence tests would seem to be mixtures of these two processes with some tasks relying principally on association (e.g., identifying and recalling things that go together) and some relying on abstraction (e.g., finding common elements). For the most part, however, the more common emphasis is on abstraction, thereby penalizing those with associative but not abstract intelligence.

Considering all of these definitions of intelligence an attempt will be made here to create some reasonable composite for educational purposes. It would seem *intelligence might be defined as a composite of intellectual skills or mental abilities that can be specified in detail based on the tests themselves and that are influenced by and related to a learning environment designed to reinforce or require these skills.*

The above definition has two parts. The first part specifies the kinds of performances that are measured by intelligence or mental ability tests, these being areas such as:

Intelligence as a Composite of Mental Abilities

inductive reasoning
verbal comprehension and fluency
spatial relations
numerical skills
figure comprehension

Note the wide range of these skill categories in covering the range of intellectual performance or mental ability.

The second part of the definition relates in part to where intelligence comes from and in part to where it leads. According to the definition intelligence is "more than a blessing and less than a blessing." It is derived in part by experiencing an environment—both home and school—that reinforces it (i.e., its use or manifestation is rewarded), and it can be successfully applied in an environment that requires its application for success (of which school is the prime instance).

The composite definition gives us a way of thinking of intelligence in terms of many of the properties that have already been discussed under the preceding definitions. For the remainder of the chapter it will be helpful to think of intelligence as a limited cluster of mental abilities with both a source and a function.

Intelligence as a Form of Ability, Aptitude, and Achievement

There is an understandable confusion among many people about the terms *intelligence, aptitude, mental ability*, and *achievement*. Some attempt to clarify their differences in meaning at this point would seem in order.

Intelligence, as we have seen from the preceding pages, is not easily defined nor is a single definition readily accepted by all. Using a composite of the definitions, we would have to say that intelligence describes a somewhat general set of mental traits that are commonly referred to as *mental abilities*. In fact, the terms intelligence and mental ability are often used interchangeably (with more current usage tending toward the latter).

Freeman (1955) offers the following as the definition of an *aptitude*.

> An *aptitude* is a condition or combination of characteristics indicative of an individual's ability to acquire with training some specific knowledge, skill, or set of responses, such as the ability to speak a language, to become a musician, to do mechanical work, etc. An aptitude test, therefore, is a device designed to indicate a person's *potential ability for performance of a certain type of activity of a specialized kind and within a restricted range.* (p. 306.)

When such aptitude tests measure perceptual, mechanical, or clerical skills such as hearing, manual dexterity, or motor speed, they can be easily differentiated from intelligence tests. When they measure such single things as verbal reasoning, numerical ability, abstract reasoning, space relations, mechanical reasoning, and clerical speed and accuracy, they are considered aptitude tests. However, since the verbal reasoning and numerical ability subtests often correlate highly with intelligence test scores, these subtests have been used in combination to create an "intelligence" score.

Hence, intelligence, mental ability, and general academic aptitude are indeed often different terms for the same quality and thus difficult to differentiate. The student of measurement can only be confused by the use of multiple terms to mean essentially the same thing.

Tests of achievement will be examined in detail in the next chapter. Let it suffice at this point to say that tests of achievement are intended to measure what an individual has already learned while tests of intelligence, mental ability, and academic aptitude attempt to measure potential for learning. However, even the measurement of learning potential is dependent to a large extent on the detection of prior learning. Thus, at the level of definition, achievement may be no easier to separate from intelligence than were aptitude and ability. In the final analysis we will have to examine the tests themselves and the uses to which they are put to determine the nature of the differences.

It is important to reinforce the point that intelligence tests and achievement tests have different purposes. Achievement tests are used to assess what a student *has* learned while intelligence or mental ability tests are used to predict what a student *can* learn. That is to say that achievement tests are *edumetric* and intelligence tests *psychometric*—as delineated in Box 8.1 on page 210. Consequently, in intelligence testing, the content of the items is not as important as their predictive validity, that is, their value for educational decision making. However, the success of this distinction as an operational fact is limited in the eye of some. An examination of test items and test properties may help clarify this point.

TEST ITEMS TO MEASURE INTELLIGENCE OR MENTAL ABILITY

What intelligence or mental ability tests measure may be better understood by examining some of the kinds of test items (that is, the kinds of performances) utilized in them. The items used in a test serve as the best operational definition of intelligence as used within that test. After examining a test's items, you can determine for yourself what the test seems to be measuring.

The kinds of items used for illustrations on the next page are ones that one might find primarily on group-administered intelligence tests. No attempt has been made to illustrate every variation—just the main types. Both verbal and figural item types are shown. They are based on Guilford (1967).[4]

---

[4] These items are not taken directly from published intelligence or mental ability tests and are not written at a level intended for children. They are intended to illustrate some of the processes tested by both individual and group tests. Only verbal and figural items are covered. Other types of items, such as memory items, have not been illustrated. In memory items, for instance, the test taker is given a list—usually of words or numbers—and asked thereafter to *recall* as many of them as he or she can. Or else, he or she will be given a list of words, numbers, or pictures to examine and then given a second list containing some of those on the original list and asked to *recognize* or *identify* all of the stimuli on the second list that also appeared on the first list.

Verbal Items: Examples

Word Substitution

- Which of the words below is the best substitute for the italicized word in the following sentence?

  He was a good doctor, but alcohol was his *ruin*.

a. plague	*c.* fate
b. undoing	*d.* destiny

Synonyms

- Which word means the same as the given?

  TEMPERAMENT

a. angriness	*c.* hostility
b. popularity	*d.* disposition

Word Classification

- Which word does not belong?

a. horse	*c.* mosquito
b. flower	*d.* snake

Verbal Analysis

- Which word should go in the blank space to fulfill relationships that call for it?

  COLD:HOT   UP:————

a. down	*c.* low
b. high	*d.* under

Word Class

- Into which one of the four classes does the given word best fit?

  PALM

a. plant	*c.* tree
b. flower	*d.* leaf

Verbal Relations

- Which alternative pair comes nearest to expressing the relation of the given pair?

  BIRD:SONG

a. fish:water	*c.* pianist:piano
b. person:speech	*d.* horse:ranch

Figural Items: Examples

Recognition of Objects

- What is the object?

Figure Matching

- Which alternative (at the right) is most nearly like the test object (at the left)?

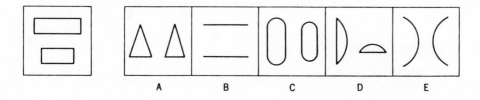

Figural Relations

- What kind of figure should appear in the cell with the question mark?

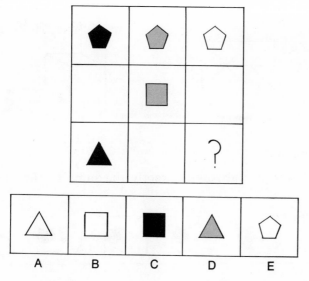

Spatial Visualization

- Diagrams I and II show two steps in folding a square piece of paper and cutting a notch in a certain location. Which alternative shows how the paper would look when unfolded?

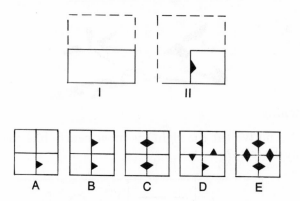

Hidden Figures

- Which of the five simple figures at the top is concealed in each of the item figures?

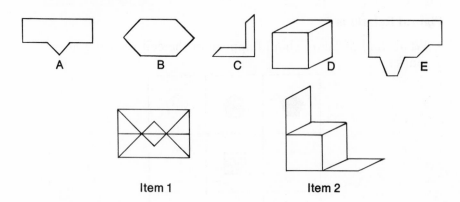

Identical Figures

- Which figure in the row is exactly the same as the one at the left?

Recognition of Figural Classes

• Which figure does not belong to the class determined by the other three figures?

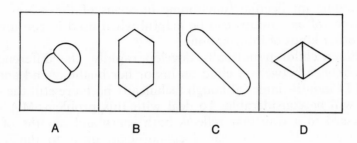

A	B	C	D

TYPES OF SCORES

In this section we will consider how intelligence tests are used in terms of the types of test scores: mental age, intelligence quotient, and deviation IQ.

Mental Age

Mental age is a score that is determined by comparing a child's score with the average score of his or her age-mates and with the scores obtained by younger and older children in the norming group.[5] A score equaling a mental age of 5-0, for example, would indicate that the score was exactly the same as the average score obtained by a sample group of five year olds, although the child obtaining the score might be older or younger than five.

Describing performance on intelligence or mental ability tests in terms of mental age or M.A. may be helpful in interpretation. However, like grade equivalents, mental ages should not be interpreted literally because they are based on *average* performances for given chronological ages. Since we often relate educational decisions to a child's age though, the idea of being able to express

---

[5] While this term may be commonly referred to, it is not the most commonly reported or interpreted one on group intelligence or mental ability tests. Its major use is in individual intelligence tests.

Answers

b, d, b, a, c, b; airplane, *c, a, c,* 1—*a,* 2—*d, d, c.*

intelligence in terms of mental age, that is, *the age of children obtaining that same score on the average*, provides the kinds of numbers we are accustomed to using and interpreting. In other words, age groups are meaningful reference groups for educators and so referencing intellectual functioning in terms of the average performance of age groups can be helpful when used in conjunction with other kinds of information.

Since children normally develop rapidly, the difference in performance between a child on his or her birthday and another child 11 months later (although technically both are still the same age) will be considerable. To deal with this problem, M.A.'s are expressed in a way that reflects both years and months of age. Because the 12-month year does not lend itself to the use of decimals, M.A.'s are expressed as shown below.[6]

5 years, 0 months	5 - 0
5 years, 2 months	5 - 2
5 years, 4 months	5 - 4
5 years, 6 months	5 - 6
5 years, 8 months	5 - 8
5 years, 10 months	5-10

Normally, the test publisher identifies the test score and age of each child in the norming group or standardization sample. The average score for each age group in the norming sample is determined. The mental age for a particular score, then, is the chronological age of children in the norming group for whom that score was the average score. These mental age "equivalents" are shown in a norms table in the test manual.

Such a table is shown in Figure 12.3 as taken from the manual of the Peabody Picture Vocabulary Test (Dunn, 1965). Once a child's score is determined, the scorer looks up that score in the table to discover the age of children for whom that score was the average. That score, expressed in years and months, represents the tested child's mental age: for example, a child who obtained a raw score of 91 on Form A of the PPVT (as shown in Figure 12.3) would have performed as a 13-year, 2-month old person, that being the average age of people in the norming group who earned a score of 91.

[6] Mental ages are derived by test publishers in a similar way to grade equivalent scores although for the latter a 10-month school year is used (bringing in decimals) rather than a 12-month chronological year (reported in terms of years and months).

Raw Scores	Mental Ages Form A	Mental Ages Form B	Raw Scores	Mental Ages Form A	Mental Ages Form B
111	-	18-0	57	6-3	6-4
110	-	17-10	56	6-1	6-2
109	18-0	17-7	55	5-11	5-11
108	17-9	17-3	54	5-9	5-10
107	17-6	17-1	53	5-7	5-8
106	17-2	16-10	52	5-5	5-6
105	16-11	16-7	51	5-2	5-4
104	16-7	16-5	50	5-1	5-3
103	16-3	16-1	49	4-11	5-1
102	15-11	15-9	48	4-10	4-11
101	15-9	15-6	47	4-8	4-9
100	15-7	15-3	46	4-7	4-7
99	15-5	14-11	45	4-5	4-6
98	15-3	14-8	44	4-3	4-4
97	15-1	14-5	43	4-1	4-2
96	14-10	14-2	42	4-0	4-0
95	14-6	13-11	41	3-11	3-11
94	14-3	13-8	40	3-10	3-10
93	13-11	13-4	39	3-9	3-9
92	13-7	13-0	38	3-8	3-8
91	13-2	12-10	37	3-7	3-8
90	12-11	12-8	36	3-6	3-7
89	12-9	12-6	35	3-5	3-6
88	12-7	12-4	34	3-4	3-5
87	12-5	12-2	33	3-3	3-4
86	12-3	11-11	32	3-3	3-2
85	12-1	11-7	31	3-2	3-1
84	11-9	11-3	30	3-1	3-0
83	11-4	11-0	29	3-0	3-0
82	11-0	10-10	28	2-11	2-11
81	10-10	10-9	27	2-11	2-10
80	10-8	10-7	26	2-10	2-10
79	10-7	10-5	25	2-9	2-9
78	10-5	10-4	24	2-8	2-8
77	10-4	10-2	23	2-8	2-8
76	10-2	10-1	22	2-7	2-7
75	10-0	9-10	21	2-6	2-6
74	9-8	9-6	20	2-6	2-6
73	9-5	9-4	19	2-5	2-5
72	9-2	9-1	18	2-5	2-5
71	8-11	8-11	17	2-4	2-4
70	8-9	8-9	16	2-4	2-4
69	8-7	8-6	15	2-3	2-3
68	8-5	8-4	14	2-3	2-3
67	8-3	8-2	13	2-2	2-2
66	8-1	8-0	12	2-2	2-2
65	7-10	7-10	11	2-1	2-1
64	7-8	7-7	10	2-1	2-1
63	7-6	7-5	9	2-0	2-0
62	7-3	7-3	8	1-11	1-11
61	7-1	7-0	7	1-11	1-11
60	6-10	6-10	6	1-10	1-10
59	6-8	6-8	5	1-9	1-9
58	6-6	6-6			

*Norms Table for Converting Raw Scores on the Peabody Picture Vocabulary Test to Mental Ages: Forms A and B.** **Figure 12.3**

* Reproduced with permission of the author, Lloyd M. Dunn, Ph.D.

Intelligence
Quotient
(Ratio IQ)

Although the initials "IQ" have come to be synonymous with intelligence, they originally stood very specifically for *a quotient or ratio representing intelligence computed by dividing mental age* (M.A. as described above) *by chronological age* (C.A.) *and multiplying by 100.*[7]

$$IQ = MA/CA \times 100$$

If a child who is exactly 5 years of age (C.A. = 5-0) gets a score equivalent to a mental age of 5 (M.A. = 5-0), the resulting IQ would be 100, which would be considered average. It is average in the sense that the child's mental age and chronological age exactly correspond. When a child is able to perform intellectually in a way that is comparable to children older than he or she, then the IQ would exceed 100. If his or her mental performance is equivalent to the average of younger children, the IQ would be under 100 or "below average." Naturally, if enough children of a given age began performing above or below "average," the average itself would move up or down since the average represents the exact arithmetic midpoint of the distribution of scores. A child, therefore, can be above or below average only with respect to other

Box 12.2

SUGGESTED CLASSIFICATION OF IQ'S:
STANFORD-BINET SCALE, 1916

IQ	Classification
Above 140	"Near" genius or genius
120–140	Very superior intelligence
110–119	Superior intelligence
90–109	Normal, or average, intelligence
80–89	Dullness
70–79	Borderline deficiency
Below 70	Definite feeblemindedness

From Terman, L. M. *The Measurement of Intelligence*, 1916 (reproduced by permission of Houghton Mifflin Company).

---

[7] Again, this is primarily an individual intelligence test score, and one, moreover, that is not currently in great use although it does represent an important step in the development of intelligence testing.

children of the same age who have taken the test. Above average simply means better than one's age-mates. (A classification of different ratio IQ scores that was used in the early days of intelligence testing appears in Box 12.2.)

Although it was used for many years as a mental ability score (and to some extent is being used today) the intelligence quotient poses certain problems. The primary problem occurs in the measurement of intelligence among adolescents and adults. As a person approaches the performance limit of the test, his or her mental age tends to stabilize. Naturally, as the person's chronological age increases, the IQ ratio will decrease (the numerator, M.A., stays the same while the denominator, C.A., increases). Thus, a person will *seem* to get less intelligent as he or she grows older while his or her intelligence is probably staying the same. To compensate for this, the maximum C.A. of 16 was established for the Stanford-Binet, a limitation in using this ratio in measuring adults.[8]

To compensate for shortcomings in the intelligence quotient score, the so-called deviation IQ was developed.

The deviation IQ (DIQ) is *a standard score having a mean of 100 and a constant value* (usually 15 or 16) *for the standard deviation* (that is, variability) *of scores.*[9] This fixed mean and standard deviation would be constant across age groups and across levels of a single test. Briefly, the mean or average score for each age group is determined. Any student who scores at the average level for his or her age group automatically receives the score of 100 even though the raw score will obviously vary from age group to age group. The degree of variability, expressed as the standard deviation (a measure of the amount tends to depart form the average), is also determined for each age group.

Deviation IQ

---

[8] A second limitation in the intelligence quotient as a mental ability score is the fact that the variability of such ratio scores from test to test is not the same. In other words, on a test with less variability a person would have to earn a higher score to be as far above average as on a test with more variability. This fact makes it difficult to compare ratio scores from different intelligence tests since the relative size of a score depends on the degree of variability in scores. Also, the variability in scores is not constant for different age groups on the same test. This means that a person's intelligence quotient might vary as he or she grew older even though his or her position relative to age-mates stayed the same.

[9] Refer to the discussion of the standard score on pages 281–84 in the preceding chapter. The term *IQ* has been retained even though its common determination as a standard score does not yield a *quotient.*

If a student receives a score that is exactly one standard deviation (the "average" amount of variability) above the mean, the deviation IQ score would be 115 or 116. If his or her score is one-half a standard deviation above the mean, the DIQ would be 108; two standard deviations above, 130 or 132, and so on. A score of 84 or 85 would mean that the person's DIQ fell below the average of his or her age-mates by an amount equal to about the average amount of variability in scores.[10]

Before you interpret an IQ score, it is important to know whether it is a ratio IQ score or a deviation IQ score because the two do not parallel one another. *The commonly used intelligence or mental ability tests* (described in a subsequent section) *all use the DIQ score.* Intelligence test scores may also be expressed as percentile ranks.[11] (Percentile ranks were discussed on pages 285–89.)

A form for reporting scores on the Short-form Test of Academic Aptitude is shown in Figure 12.4. Raw scores are presented for each subtest and raw scores, mental ages, deviation IQ scores, percentiles, and standard scores (called reference scale scores), are presented for language, nonlanguage, and total. A table for converting raw scores to deviation IQ scores on the Short-form Test of Academic Aptitude is shown for illustrative purposes in Figure 12.5 and a table for converting raw scores on this test to mental age scores is shown in Figure 12.6. If you look up the total raw score reported on the form in Figure 12.4 (67) in the table shown in Figure 12.5 you will see how the total DIQ score was obtained (all relevant values from Figure 12.4 are circled in Figure 12.5). Similarly Figure 12.6 was used to convert the raw scores on the form to their mental age equivalents.

PROPERTIES OF TESTS

In this section we will discuss three properties of tests: reliability, stability, and validity, as they apply to intelligence or mental ability tests.

---

[10] To interpret a person's relative position in his or her age group as a function of the number of standard deviations he or she falls above or below the mean, it will be useful to refer to Figure 11.1 on page 283.

[11] There is also the question of whether the score is age-based or grade-based. As was stated above, DIQ scores are ordinarily age-based. However, when scores on mental ability tests are presented as percentile ranks, they may be either age-based or grade-based, or both. Those shown in Figure 12.4, for example, are grade-based.

Figure 12.4 *A Sample Student Record Form for the Short-form Test of Academic Aptitude.* *

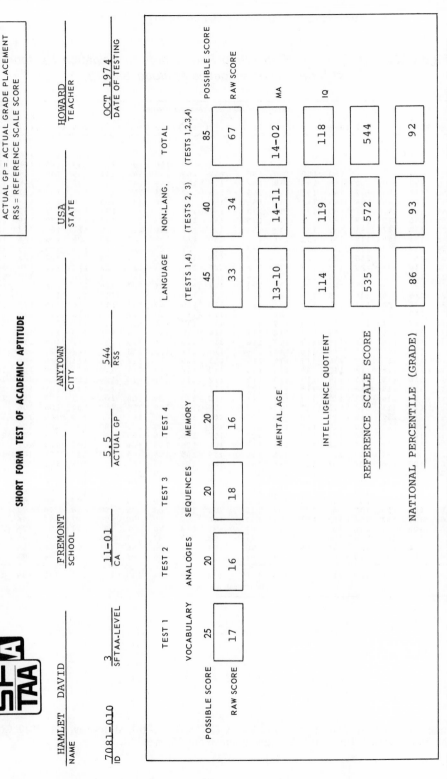

* Reproduced by permission of the publisher, CTB/McGraw-Hill, Monterey, CA 93940. Copyright © 1970 by McGraw-Hill, Inc. The Reference Scale Score is a score standardized at grade 10-6 with a mean of 600 and an sd of 100, which has equal size units across all levels of this test and hence can be used to chart an individual's mental growth.

Figure 12.5   *A Table for Converting Raw Scores to Deviation IQ Scores on the Short-form Test of Academic Aptitude, Level 3.**

RAW SCORE TOTAL	CHRONOLOGICAL AGE (IN YEARS AND MONTHS)																	RAW SCORE TOTAL
	10-4	10-5	10-6	10-7	10-8	10-9	10-10	10-11	11-0	11-1	11-2	11-3	11-4	11-5	11-6	11-7	11-8	
85																		85
84														150	150	150	150	84
83										150	150	150	150	149	149	148	147	83
82				150	150	150	150		150	149	148	147	146	145	145	144	143	82
81		150	150	150	149	149	148	147	146	145	144	143	143	142	141	140	139	81
80	150	149	148	147	146	145	144	143	143	142	141	140	139	139	138	137	136	80
79	147	146	145	144	143	142	141	140	140	139	138	137	136	136	135	134	134	79
78	144	143	142	141	140	139	138	138	137	136	135	135	134	133	132	132	131	78
77	141	140	139	138	137	137	136	135	134	134	133	132	131	131	130	129	129	77
76	138	138	137	136	135	134	133	133	132	131	130	130	129	128	128	127	126	76
75	136	135	135	134	133	132	131	131	130	129	129	128	127	126	126	125	125	75
74	134	133	133	132	131	130	129	129	128	127	127	126	125	125	124	123	123	74
73	133	132	131	130	129	129	128	127	126	126	125	124	124	123	122	122	121	73
72	131	130	129	129	128	127	126	126	125	124	124	123	122	122	121	120	120	72
71	129	128	128	127	126	125	125	124	123	123	122	121	121	120	119	119	118	71
70	128	127	126	125	125	124	123	123	122	121	121	120	119	119	118	118	117	70
69	126	126	125	124	123	123	122	121	121	120	119	119	118	118	117	116	116	69
68	125	124	124	123	122	122	121	120	120	119	118	118	117	116	116	115	115	68
67	124	123	122	122	121	120	120	119	118	118	117	117	116	115	115	114	113	67
66	123	122	121	121	120	119	119	118	117	117	116	115	115	114	114	113	112	66
65	122	121	120	120	119	118	118	117	116	116	115	114	114	113	113	112	112	65
64	121	120	119	118	118	117	117	116	115	115	114	113	113	112	112	111	111	64
63	120	119	118	118	117	116	116	115	114	114	113	113	112	112	111	110	110	63
62	119	118	117	117	116	115	115	114	113	113	112	112	111	111	110	109	109	62
61	118	117	116	116	115	115	114	113	113	112	112	111	110	110	109	109	108	61
60	117	116	115	115	114	114	113	112	112	111	111	110	109	109	108	108	107	60
59	116	115	115	114	113	113	112	112	111	110	110	109	109	108	108	107	107	59
58	115	114	114	113	113	112	111	111	110	110	109	108	108	107	107	106	106	58
57	114	114	113	112	112	111	111	110	109	109	108	108	107	107	106	106	105	57
56	113	113	112	111	111	110	110	109	108	108	107	107	106	106	105	105	104	56
55	112	112	111	110	110	109	109	108	108	107	106	106	105	105	104	104	103	55
54	112	111	110	110	109	108	108	107	107	106	106	105	105	104	104	103	103	54
53	111	110	109	109	108	108	107	107	106	105	105	104	104	103	103	102	102	53
52	110	109	109	108	107	107	106	106	105	105	104	104	103	103	102	102	101	52
51	109	108	108	107	107	106	106	105	104	104	103	103	102	102	101	101	100	51
50	108	108	107	106	106	105	105	104	104	103	103	102	102	101	101	100	100	50
49	107	107	106	106	105	104	104	103	103	102	102	101	101	100	100	99	99	49
48	107	106	105	105	104	104	103	103	102	102	101	101	100	100	99	99	98	48
47	106	105	105	104	103	103	102	102	101	101	100	100	99	99	98	98	97	47
46	105	104	104	103	102	102	101	100	100	100	100	99	99	98	98	97	97	46
45	104	103	103	102	102	101	101	100	100	99	99	98	98	97	97	96	96	45
44	103	103	102	101	101	100	100	99	99	98	98	97	97	97	96	96	95	44
43	102	102	101	100	100	99	99	98	98	97	97	97	96	96	95	95	94	43
42	101	101	100	100	99	99	98	98	97	97	96	96	95	95	94	94	94	42
41	100	100	99	99	98	98	97	97	96	96	95	95	94	94	94	93	93	41
RAW SCORE	124	125	126	127	128	129	130	131	132	133	134	135	136	137	138	139	140	RAW SCORE

CHRONOLOGICAL AGE (IN MONTHS)

A Table for Converting Raw Scores to Mental Age Scores on the   **Figure 12.6**
Short-form Test of Academic Aptitude, Level 3. *

RAW SCORE	MENTAL AGE			RAW SCORE	MENTAL AGE
	LANG	NON-LANG	TOTAL		TOTAL
0				46	11-01
1				47	11-03
2				48	11-04
3	5-06			49	11-06
4	5-06			50	11-08
5	5-11	5-06		51	11-09
6	6-05	5-06		52	11-11
7	6-10	5-09		53	12-00
8	7-03	6-00		54	12-02
9	7-07	6-04		55	12-04
10	8-00	6-07		56	12-05
11	8-04	6-11	5-06	57	12-07
12	8-08	7-02	5-06	58	12-09
13	8-11	7-06	5-07	59	12-10
14	9-03	7-09	5-10	60	13-00
15	9-06	8-01	6-00	61	13-02
16	9-09	8-04	6-02	62	13-04
17	10-00	8-08	6-04	63	13-06
18	10-02	9-00	6-07	64	13-08
19	10-05	9-03	6-09	65	13-10
20	10-08	9-07	6-11	66	14-00
21	10-10	9-11	7-01	(67)	(14-02)
22	11-01	10-03	7-04	68	14-05
23	11-03	10-07	7-06	69	14-07
24	11-06	10-11	7-08	70	14-10
25	11-09	11-03	7-10	71	15-01
26	12-00	11-08	8-00	72	15-04
27	12-02	12-00	8-02	73	15-08
28	12-05	12-04	8-04	74	16-00
29	12-08	12-09	8-06	75	16-05
30	13-00	13-01	8-08	76	16-10
31	13-03	13-06	8-10	77	17-05
32	13-06	13-11	9-00	78	18-00
(33)	(13-10)	14-05	9-02	79	18-00
(34)	14-02	(14-11)	9-04	80	
35	14-06	15-07	9-06	81	
36	14-10	16-06	9-08	82	
37	15-03	18-00	9-10	83	
38	15-09	18-00	9-11	84	
39	16-03		10-01	85	
40	16-11		10-03		
41	17-09		10-05		
42	18-00		10-06		
43	18-00		10-08		
44			10-10		
45			10-11		

Reliability   All the major publishers' intelligence or mental ability tests currently in common use shown a high degree of reliability whether computed as the relationship among items of a test (internal consistency) or between alternate forms of a test. Correlations representing internal consistency (that is, the relationship among items) generally average about .90. Except for younger children, correlations between alternate forms run at about .80. (See discussion if stability below.) While both correlations are high, neither is perfect. This tells us that performance on an IQ test is influenced by factors other than the test taker's actual level of intelligence. Chance is one such factor. However, in terms of typical test criteria, intelligence tests clearly attain a level of reliability that is satisfactory.

Stability   As a measure of potential, a person's intelligence or mental ability can be expected to remain at about the same level throughout most of his or her life. Consequently, the scores on intelligence or mental ability tests should not only be reliable, that is, consistent over short time spans, but stable, that is, consistent over longer time spans. When you are 20, for example, will you test out at the same level as you did when you were 10? If intelligence tests measure a basic characteristic of people, we would expect a reasonably high degree of stability of IQ test scores.

How are we to determine whether IQ test scores are stable or not? The most obvious way would be to get a sample group of children, retest them at periodic intervals, and correlate the scores from one testing to the next. Bloom (1964) did just this and obtained a correlation of 0.80 between Stanford-Binet deviation IQ scores of students at grade 3 and again at grade 12. Such a high correlation suggests a high degree of stability. However, the following must be considered. A high correlation indicates a high predictive relationship but does not necessarily suggest constancy. Average IQ's from grade 3 to 12 could have increased 30 points but if everyone's increase was proportional, a high correlation would result. More specifically, the world changes in nine years. A general increase in the availability and quality of education over this period might enhance the IQ's of most, if not all, students dramatically and thereby reduce the constancy but not the correlation. If, however, educational improvement was vastly uneven causing only some IQ's to improve, the correlation would have been substantially lower.

Hopkins and Bracht (1971) started with first graders and followed them through high school. They gave them the California Test of Mental Maturity in grades 1, 2, and 4 and the Lorge-Thorndike Intelligence Tests in grades 7, 9, and 11. They found that first grade IQ's were not that highly predictive of subsequent IQ's, even of those in the second grade. However, fourth grade verbal IQ's (that is, those scores based only on language portions of the test) correlated .77 with eleventh grade verbal IQ's, indicating a high degree of stability starting from grade 4.

In interpreting scores on intelligence or mental ability tests, we must keep certain points in mind. First, it is not appropriate to generalize from one IQ test to another. Second, IQ data on young children have reasonably little stability. Third, that part of the IQ based on language portions of the test is considerably more stable than that part based on nonlanguage portions. Fourth, while studies of IQ stability have been based primarily on individually-administered IQ tests, the tests more frequently used in education are group-administered tests for which less information about stability of scores is available.

We will return to this issue at the conclusion of this chapter in the discussion of IQ tests in relation to educational theory and practice.

Validity

Estimates of the predictive validity of intelligence tests are based largely on the relationship between test scores and (1) success in school, and (2) level of occupation entered. The issue of biases in the tests that affect their validity will be discussed in the last section of this chapter.

Success in School. There is considerable evidence that scores on IQ tests are related to school performance. This does not mean that a student's measured IQ determines how well he or she will do in school; it does indicate that the skills needed to do well in school are very much like the skills needed to do well on IQ tests. The relationship between a particular IQ test and school achievement is usually presented in the manual of that test. Some samples of these results will be presented. The Cognitive Abilities Test includes verbal, nonverbal,[12] and quantitative batteries of cognitive

---

[12] Note that in various IQ and mental ability tests the part of the test that does not rely on reading of words is alternatively referred to as non-language or figural.

or mental ability. The Iowa Tests of Basic Skills (ITBS) are commonly used achievement tests for the elementary grades. They include tests for vocabulary, reading, language, study skills, and arithmetic, each with its own subtests. The Test of Academic Progress (TAP) are standardized achievement tests used at the high school level and include tests of social studies, composition, science, reading, mathematics, and literature. The correlations between Cognitive Abilities Test scores and composite scores on those school achievement tests are illustrated in Figure 12.7. For the verbal scores, the correlations range from a high of .80 in third grade to a low of .72 in ninth grade. For nonverbal scores, the correlations remain at about .60 throughout the grade levels. For quantitative scores, correlations stay at approximately .70. The correlations are substantial, particularly for verbal and quantitative ability. This seems to say that mental ability or intelligence tests and school achievement tests are tapping common or related skills and that students of high intelligence (as measured by this test) tend toward better school achievement (as measured by these tests). This conclusion is least accurate in the nonverbal area, an area of less emphasis in the school curriculum.

Figure 12.7   *Average Correlations between Verbal, Nonverbal, and Quantitative Scores on the Cognitive Abilities Test and Composite Scores on the Iowa Tests of Basic Skils and Tests of Academic Progress.**

COGNITIVE ABILITIES TEST

	Grade Level	Verbal	Nonverbal	Quantitative
	3	.80	.59	.68
	4	.75	.57	.68
	5	.79	.60	.70
ITBS	6	.78	.58	.70
	7	.76	.60	.73
	8	.78	.61	.71
	9	.72	.59	.71
TAP	10	.73	.59	.70
	11	.73	.58	.69
	12	.73	.61	.68

* Thorndike and Hagen, 1971. Reproduced by permission of the Houghton Mifflin Company.

Findings also show that students who score higher on IQ tests are more likely to earn higher grades in school (as schools currently operate) and attain a higher graduating class standing than students who score lower on IQ tests. Again, the relationship does not suggest that one is the cause of the other; only that the two performances require essentially the same or similar skills.

Level of Occupation.   Studies have demonstrated differences in the mean intelligence tests scores of persons in different occupations. A sample of accountants, for example, was found to have a mean IQ of about 122 while a sample of lumberjacks was found to have a mean IQ of about 90 (Stewart, 1947). There were, however, a few lumberjacks who scored higher than did some accountants. For the most part, though, accountants were among the highest IQ test scorers, lumberjacks among the lowest. Overall, people in the professions tend to score higher than people in the trades.[13]

What does the relationship between intelligence test score and level of occupation tell us? It tells us that the kinds of skills measured by the intelligence test (e.g., language, reasoning, arithmetic) tend to be the same ones that are needed to gain entry to and stay in the professional occupations; this is less so in the trades. Since tested intelligence relates to school performance (high test scorers perform better in school) and since the professions generally require considerably more schooling than do the trades, it is not surprising to find the higher IQ test scorers in the professions followed by skilled and then unskilled workers.

SOME SPECIFIC TESTS OF INTELLIGENCE OR MENTAL ABILITY

Considerable information about published tests in current use can be gotten from a reference book entitled the *Mental Measurements Yearbook*, compiled by Oscar Krisen Buros every five or so years and available in the reference section of most libraries. The *MMY* entry for each test includes descriptive information, the name and

[13] Of course, if IQ test scores are used to select people to study for the professions, then these data reflect that bias rather than an inherently higher IQ among professionals than tradespeople. Moreover, test scores and school performance are also susceptible to the influence of expectations, both of student and teacher. This influence may in part account for the relationship between IQ and occupation.

address of the test publisher, the test's costs, and often one or two critical reviews. (Test publisher's catalogs are also a useful source of up-to-date information on test availability and costs.)

Individual Intelligence Tests   Individual intelligence tests are administered to children on a one-to-one basis by persons trained in test administration. Such tests are often given to children with presumed learning disabilities who have been referred to the school psychologist or learning disabilities specialist and for whom group testing would be difficult, perhaps untimely, and probably not sensitive enough. Al-

"I'm studying for my I.Q. test."

though teachers do not have to know how to administer such tests, upon occasion they have to interpret the scores. Scores may be available for classes of students or for those having difficulties or considered gifted. Testing may be done to make decisions about school entrance, grade placement, rapid advancement, or to detect various forms of impairment or maladjustments. Scores on such tests are usually reported as deviation IQ's and mental ages (see pages 329–35).

Three widely used individual intelligence tests are the Stanford-Binet Intelligence Test, Wechsler Intelligence Scale for Children (WISC), and Peabody Picture Vocabulary Test (PPVT).

Stanford-Binet. This intelligence scale measures the general mental ability of individuals from age 2 to adult, although it tends to be used primarily with children from ages 2 to 8. It is a scale based on age standards of performance and attempts to measure how high up the scale a child can go before the tasks become too difficult. A single revised form (L-M) is available with norms based on data as recent as 1972. It is published by Houghton Mifflin Co.

The test measures skills in seven content categories. Sattler (1965) has labeled them as follows.

- *language*: Naming objects in pictures, defining words, naming rhyming words.
- *reasoning*: Drawing an orientation, pointing out why a verbal statement is absurd.
- *memory*: Remembering sentences, remembering digits.
- *conceptual*: Explaining a proverb, indicating a basis of similarity.
- *social intelligence*: Understanding social identities and relationships, finding absurdities in pictures.
- *numercal reasoning*: Making change, ingenuity in solving a math problem.
- *visual-motor*: Making a form on a form board, copying a square.

Stimuli used include words, objects, and pictures. Responses are speaking, drawing, calculating, writing, or other motor acts.

The scale covers a wide number of levels with six subtests at each age. The examiner starts the child on tasks below his or her chronological age and then moves the child upward until he or she reaches a level at which he or she fails all the subtests. About an hour is required for a typical administration. Intelligence is expressed as a single overall DIQ score.

Wechsler (WISC-R). This intelligence scale developed by David Wechsler (1974 revision) has five subtests forming a Verbal score and five other forming a Performance (or nonverbal) score with both together giving the Full Scale score. (Each group also includes a supplementary or alternate sixth subtest.) These subtests are all intended to measure general mental ability.

Verbal subtests: examples
- *information* (recall of knowledge)   Given a question, provide the particular fact that is called for.
- *comprehension* (understanding of knowledge)   Given a particular object or event, explain one or more of its particular properties or causes.
- *arithmetic* (numerical ability)   Given a verbal problem involving numbers, compute a solution.
- *similarities* (reasoning)   Given *A* and *B*, determine the relationship.
- *vocabulary* (verbal ability)   Given a word, tell its meaning.
- *digit span* (memory; optional)   Given three numbers, repeat them in order.

Performance subtests: examples
- *block design* (analysis of a complex whole)   Given a picture of a design, arrange four blocks with different markings to form that design.
- *picture completion* (analysis of the parts from the whole)   Given a picture, name the part that is missing.
- *picture arrangement* (identification of the whole from the parts)   Arrange three pictures in the sequence that correctly tells the story.
- *object assembly* (synthesis of the whole from the parts)   Put the pieces together to make an object.
- *coding* (digit-symbol substitution)   Match the numbers with their given symbol codes.
- *mazes* (optional)   Find the route through the maze.

This scale usually takes an hour to administer. Subtests are administered one after the other with the child being given subtest items in graded order of difficulty until he or she can proceed no further. The next subtest is then begun. Children from ages 6 to 16 can be tested. (The Wechsler Preschool and Primary Scale of Intelligence is available for younger children and the Wechsler Adult Intelligence Scale for adults.) Scores on each

An Item Illustrative of Those on the Peabody Picture Vocabulary   **Figure 12.8**
*Test.**

Point to "chair".

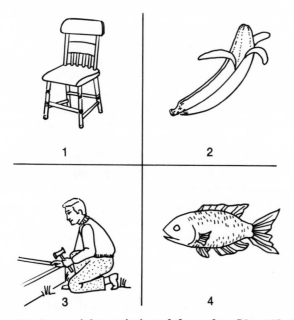

* Reproduced with the special permission of the author, Lloyd M. Dunn.

subtest are reported as are DIQ's representing the Verbal score, Performance score, and Full Scale score. It is published by The Psychological Corporation.

Peabody Picture Vocabulary Test. The PPVT (Dunn, 1965) is an individually-administered intelligence test that uses no words as stimuli. Each item of the scale is made up of four pictures (see Figure 12.8 for a sample). The test administrator reads the name of the object or scene in one of the pictures and the child must point to the appropriate picture. Paradoxically, although the test requires no reading, it measures intelligence strictly in terms of vocabulary—that is a child's verbal ability or whether he or she knows what different words mean. For this reason, the test must be considered one that is highly subject to cultural influences.[14]

[14] Since the same cultural influences may affect school achievement, this influence may actually enhance the predictive validity of the test (a plus for the test, perhaps, but a minus for school).

The manual suggests a convenient starting point as that at which the child can get eight consecutive items correct. This constitutes the child's basal level. He or she continues through the items, sequenced in order of increasing difficulty, until he or she makes 6 errors in 8 consecutive responses. The item number of the last correct item less the items missed constitutes the raw score. The test contains a total of 150 items.

Tables are provided for converting raw scores into mental ages, deviation IQ's, and percentiles by age. Moreover, the same pictures provide the basis for two forms, A and B, which differ in terms of which of the four pictures is correct. The test has a reported median alternative forms reliability of 0.77 over 19 age levels. Correlations between the PPVT and the '60 Stanford-Binet have a median of 0.71; between the PPVT and the Wechsler Intelligence Scale for Children-Verbal a median of 0.67; between the PPVT and adult Wechsler full scale a median of 0.79. These values suggest reasonable (concurrent) validity. The test is recommended for use with nonreaders within the restriction of its cultural susceptibility. It is published by American Guidance Service.

Group Tests of Mental Ability

There are a number of group-administered intelligence or mental ability tests currently in use in the classrooms of elementary and secondary schools. We will describe here only the more well-known among them, particularly those that are given on a district-wide basis at one or more grade levels—since these are the tests teachers are more likely to come in contact with.

Short-form Test of Academic Aptitude (SFTAA, 1970). The SFTAA was developed from the California Test of Mental Maturity series. It comes in five levels as follows: Level 1—grades 1.5 to 3.4; Level 2—grades 3.5 to 4; Level 3—grades 5 to 6; Level 4—grades 7 to 9; Level 5—grades 9 to 12. Levels 2 to 5 each take 38 minutes to administer; Level 1 takes 31 minutes.

SFTAA contains the following subtests: Vocabulary (which measures verbal comprehension, knowledge of word meanings, and the ability to relate words that are not exact synonyms), Analogies (requiring recognition of pictorial relationships), Sequences (the student must identify the missing or incorrect element in a series of numbers, letters, or geometric figures), and

Memory (recalling facts or ideas, making inferences, and recalling the logical flow of a story).

Subtest raw scores are provided along with language and nonlanguage subtotals and an overall total score in the form of deviation IQ's, percentile ranks, or stanines (see Figures 12.4, 12.5, and 12.6). In addition a reference scale score (another standard score) is also available. The SFTAA is published by California Test Bureau/McGraw-Hill and may be coordinated with either of their standardized achievement testing programs or used independently.

Otis-Lennon Mental Ability Test (OLMAT, 1967). The OLMAT has six levels as follows: Primary I (grades K.5–K.9), Primary II (grades 1.0–1.5), Elementary I (grades 1.5–3.9), Elementary II (grades 4.0–6.9), Intermediate (grades 7.0–9.9), and Advanced (grades 10.0–12.9). Administration time varies from 30 minutes for the primary levels to 50 minutes for the other levels. Although only a total score is reported (consistent with the definition of intelligence as a general capacity described on pages 313–17), it is reported six ways: as a raw score, as a deviation IQ score, percentile rank and stanine by age, and as a percentile rank and stanine by grade. The test is constructed to measure verbal, numerical, and abstract reasoning abilities.

OLMAT is a widely used test, particularly in conjunction with the Metropolitan Achievement Tests (1970) or the Stanford Achievement Tests (1973). Correlations between it and a wide variety of aptitude, intelligence, and achievement tests (as well as school grades) as reported in the *Technical Handbook* are quite high. It is published by Harcourt Brace Jovanovich.

The OLMAT evolved from the various Otis intelligence and mental ability tests, which were among the first large-scale group tests used for measuring individual characteristics. Otis originally designed these tests more than 50 years ago to cast Binet-type items into paper-and-pencil format.

Cognitive Abilities Test (1968–71). This test, published by Houghton Mifflin, was developed from the Lorge-Thorndike Intelligence Tests. It comes in a Multi-level Edition suitable for grades 3–12 and a Primary Edition for K–3. The Multi-level Edition contains three separate batteries (each of which takes 35 minutes to complete plus about 15 minutes to administer), which are Verbal (vocabulary, sentence completion, verbal classification, and verbal analogies), Quantitative (number series, quantitative relations and equation building), and Nonverbal (figure classification, figure analogies, and figure synthesis). Eight different but overlapping levels cover the third to twelfth grade range. This test may be coordinated with the Iowa Tests of Basic Skills and/or Tests of Academic Progress, both achievement test batteries. The major feature of these tests is that separate scores (DIQ's, Percentile ranks, and Stanines) are reported for each battery thus providing an indication of verbal, quantitative, and nonverbal ability.

The Primary Battery (I and II) uses pictorial materials and oral instructions and includes subtests of oral vocabulary, relational concepts, multimental (identifying the one that doesn't belong) concepts, and quantitative concepts. Administration procedures feature item-by-item pacing to assure that the test is not one of speed. A shortened version of Primary I is also available.

Cooperative School and College Ability (SCAT Series II, 1966). These tests, representing a complete revision of SCAT I, are available at four levels: grades 4–6, 7–9, 10–12, and 12–14, with two forms (A and B) available at each level. Published by Educational Testing Service, these "academic aptitude tests" are "intended primarily as a measure of a student's ability to succeed in future academic work" (as described in the *Handbook for SCAT Series II* along with a raft of psychometric information about the tests). SCAT II is a good predictor of academic performance as well as of scores on the College Boards; like other tests of mental ability, it has high reliability.

Testing time on SCAT II is 40 minutes with an additional 10 minutes for test administration. There are two subtests, a verbal one in which all items involve verbal analogies, and a mathematical one in which quantitative comparison items appear. Verbal, mathematical, and total scores are reported as percentile ranks and percentile bands (a score range going from one standard error of measurement below to one standard error of measurement above the actual score). IQ scores are not reported.

Henmon-Nelson Tests of Mental Ability (1973 Revision). These tests are published by Houghton Mifflin and available as Form 1 for grades 3–6, 6–9, and 9–12 and in a Primary Battery for grades K–2. Areas covered by the 90 items in Form 1 are vocabulary, sentence completion, opposites, general information, verbal analogies, verbal classification, verbal inference, number series, arithmetic reasoning and figure analogies. The Primary Battery includes a Listening Test, Picture Vocabulary Test, and Size and Number Test. Each form takes 30 minutes and for each, DIQ's (by age), stanines, and percentile ranks (by age and grade) are reported.

Primary Mental Abilities Tests (PMA, Revised 1962). These tests, developed originally by L. L. Thurstone and published by Science Research Associates, are based on the definition of intelligence as a group of traits originally proposed and operationalized by Thurstone himself (see pages 317–18). Batteries are available for grades K–1, 2–4, 4–6, 6–9, and 9–12 and measure (1) verbal meaning (ability to work with words), (2) number facility (ability to work with numbers), (3) spatial relations (ability to conceptualize), (4) perceptual speed (ability to distinguish size and shapes; grades K–6 only), and (5) reasoning (ability to think logically; grades 4–12 only). These represent a variation on Thurstone's original six factors listed on page 318. Testing time is listed as approximately 1½ hours and scores are reported for subtests and for the total battery as DIQ's (called "deviation ability quotients" for these tests) and percentile ranks. Ratio IQ, mental age, and stanine scores are also available for some of the batteries.

Like many of the other mental abilities tests, this test has strong historical roots. Unlike most of the others, it reports discrete factor or subtests scores reflecting its basis in the definition of intelligence as a group of traits rather than as a single, general one.

Culture Fair Intelligence Test (IPAT, 1961–63). This test was developed by R. B. Cattell and is published by the Institute for Personality and Ability Testing, hence the designation IPAT. It can be administered to both children and adults, and, in each case, has three scales. The scales take from 30 minutes to an hour to complete and claim to be relatively independent of school achievement, social advantages, and environmental influences. They attempt to measure fluid ability (the general intelligence factor as defined on pages 313–17), which presumably manifests itself through adaptive mental behavior in situations so unfamiliar that previously learned skills can be of no help in guiding such behavior. To accomplish this, the test includes nonsense (meaningless) material, universally unfamiliar material, and commonplace material. The evidence on whether this test is free of cultural bias is mixed. Some sample items appear in Figure 12.9.

Figure 12.9   *Sample Items from the Culture Fair Intelligence Test.**

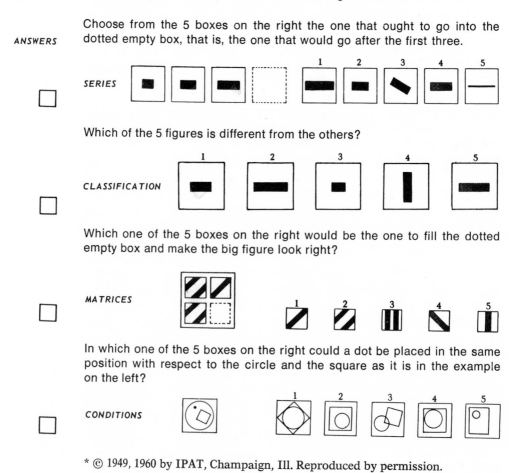

ANSWERS

Choose from the 5 boxes on the right the one that ought to go into the dotted empty box, that is, the one that would go after the first three.

SERIES

Which of the 5 figures is different from the others?

CLASSIFICATION

Which one of the 5 boxes on the right would be the one to fill the dotted empty box and make the big figure look right?

MATRICES

In which one of the 5 boxes on the right could a dot be placed in the same position with respect to the circle and the square as it is in the example on the left?

CONDITIONS

* © 1949, 1960 by IPAT, Champaign, Ill. Reproduced by permission.

Answers

1, 4, 1, 3

Differential Aptitude Tests (DAT; Fifth Edition, 1973).   These tests, developed by G. K. Bennett, H. G. Seashore, and A. G. Wesman and published by The Psychological Corporation, are designed to measure specific aptitudes. Their subtests include verbal reasoning, numerical ability, abstract reasoning, clerical speed and accuracy, mechanical reasoning, space relations, spelling, and language usage. However, if one follows the trait-factor conception of intelligence described by Thurstone (see pages 317–18), the subtests of the DAT can be thought of as including within them the measurement of mental ability. In fact, the tests provide a measure of general scholastic aptitude (which can be interpreted as mental ability) by combining scores on verbal reasoning and numerical ability subtests.

Scores on each subtest of the DAT and on verbal and numerical combined are presented as percentile ranks and percentile bands in a profile such as that shown in Figure 12.10 on the next page. This information can be used to help students decide which courses to take in school and the kinds of occupations to explore as career possibilities as part of a Career Planning Program. (Career relevant tests such as interest tests are described in Chapter 14.)

Two forms, S and T, are available for use with students in grades 8–12. The complete battery takes about three hours to complete.

The choice of a classroom-administered IQ test is not ordinarily made by the teacher. Often it is part of the total district-wide testing program and is based on the achievement battery chosen for use; that is, the companion IQ test to the achievement battery chosen is used. Moreover, choosing among the various group intelligence tests is a difficult task. The clearest form of variability is on the verbal–nonverbal distinction. Beyond that, most available and commonly used group tests, like those described, utilize the same general types of items (except perhaps for a nonlanguage test like the IPAT), report the same types of scores, feature the same strengths in terms of quality of standardization, have approximately the same degree of predictive validity (that is, predict school success; again except perhaps for the nonverbal tests), and fall heir to the same shortcomings. Perhaps the major difference is in an orientation toward intelligence as a single general factor or as a group of traits, a difference reflected in the number of specific subtest scores reported.

Figure 12.10 *A Sample Profile of a Student's Differential Aptitude Test Scores.**

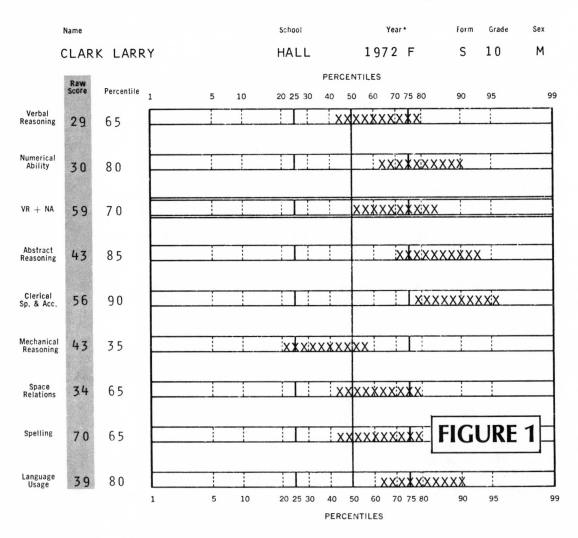

TESTS OF CREATIVITY

Although not as widely used as mental ability tests, tests of creativity measure a different aspect of the mental process. Guilford (1967) has emphasized the point that creativity requires *divergent thinking* rather than the *convergent thinking* measured by mental ability tests. In convergent thinking, one seeks to reduce much information to the one correct answer. In divergent thinking, one attempts to expand from a small amount of information to many correct answers. Consistent with this definition, tests of creativity require students to construct novel but appropriate responses to given situations. Such multiple and imaginative responses cannot be scored by computer because their individual acceptability must be judged. For this reason and also perhaps because of a lack of acceptance of creativity as a legitimate educational goal, tests of creativity have not enjoyed widespread use in the schools. Two tests of creativity will be briefly described below.

The Torrance Tests of Creativity (1966). These tests have both a Verbal and Figural section. The Verbal section includes (1) ask-and-guess: the student is given a picture and asked *a.* to guess what might have led to the scene pictured and *b.* to guess what might happen next (as in all the Torrance tests, the student is asked to produce as many answers as he or she can); (2) product improvement: a picture of a toy is shown and the student is asked to suggest changes that would make the toy more fun to play with; (3) unusual uses: the student is asked to list as many unusual uses as he or she can think of for a commonplace object such as a tin can. The Figural tests ask the student to make drawings, to represent an object, or to tell a story with a picture. Each Figural subtest gives the student something to start with, such as a page of circles, and asks him or her to make as many different pictures as possible, with the circle a key part of each picture. Working time for each half is 45 minutes and the test can be used at most any elementary grade level (K–8).

Scoring requires some degree of training. Three scores are given: *fluency* (total number of acceptable responses), *flexibility* (number of categories in the manual used by the student), and *originality* (number of responses not on the list of frequent responses). Norms are not provided; each student's responses are evaluated against a set of common criteria; hence these tests may be considered criterion-referenced.

The validity of the Torrance tests as measures of creativity has not been clearly established. The evidence is mixed. Yamamoto's (1963) results suggest acceptable validity (i.e., a 0.50 correlation between Torrance score and evaluation of imaginative stories for 40 fifth graders) while Wodtke's (1964) attempted replication holding IQ constant suggested otherwise (r=0.24). The work on creativity and intelligence by Getzels and Jackson (1962) and Wallach and Kogan (1965) suggests that the concepts of IQ and creativity can be measured separately. The Torrance tests are published by Personnel Press.

Remote Associates Test (1971). In the 40-item RAT, a high school student is presented with three words (e.g., *base, snow, dance*) and asked to supply a fourth somehow related to each of the three (e.g., *ball*). The three words are considered to be from "remote associative clusters" and the fourth word to provide a "mediating link."

This test, authored by S. A. Mednick and M. T. Mednick and published by Houghton Mifflin, is untimed but takes about 40 minutes. Its norms are somewhat limited but its reliability (split-half) is high. However, its major weakness may be in the area of validity where no data on high school students are cited (Backman and Tuckman, 1972). IQ and RAT correlations tend to be about .40. Worthen and Clark (1971) contend that the RAT is primarily a measure of sensitivity to language structure rather than a measure of creativity. Backman and Tuckman (1972) recommend that this test be restricted primarily to research uses rather than used for individual placement decisions until more validity data are available.

ISSUES IN INTELLIGENCE TESTING

There is a great and continuing debate going on in intelligence testing that questions its very basis and utility. The critics of intelligence testing claim that it adds nothing to the educational process and may subtract quite a bit. Their claim is based on their contention that intelligence tests discriminate not between the more mentally able and the less mentally able (and in more extreme form the bright and dull) as is intended, but between groups having different cultural experiences. They contend that intelligence tests serve only to keep those who are "down" (by virtue of income status, race, or other personal characteristics) from sharing in full educational opportunity. The questions seem to be: What do scores on the test mean? Do the tests measure intellectual capacity, do they measure relevant experience, or both? And of what educational use are the scores? Since it is important in the study of measurement to consider both "how to" and also "should we," these questions deserve attention.

Do scores on an IQ test reflect how bright a person is or the kinds of experiences he or she has had? Jensen (1968, 1969) cites evidence to show that identical twins regardless of whether they are raised in the same home or in different homes have intelligence test scores that are closely related, much more closely related than are the scores of children who have no biological relation to one another but are raised in the same home. In the study Jensen shows that people low in socio-economic status score lower than people at middle and high socio-economic levels. He also cites evidence to show that blacks score lower than whites on IQ tests, such as Progressive Matrices, that would not seem to relate to specific cultural experience.

The Meaning of the Scores

In truth it must be said that we do not know how much a person's genes contribute to his or her scores on an intelligence test and how much his or her life experiences contribute. We can only conclude that an intelligence test score reflects in part a person's born capacity and in part the kind of experiences he or she has had and been conditioned by. Moreover, such experiential effects may be considerably more subtle and more pervasive than we have heretofore thought. The more meaningful question for education may not be what the scores mean but what their educational value is regardless of what they mean. However, the tendency to define performance in terms of a composite of mental abilities may help to overcome some of the indeterminancies of the intelligence concept.

The purpose of education is to enable children to learn and grow. Any educational practice that contributes to this purpose presumably should continue; conversely, any practice that adds nothing to or detracts from this purpose should be terminated. Regardless of what IQ or mental ability tests measure, it is possible to question the general education value of the scores when used on a wide scale. Although it is true that the scores are often related to subsequent school achievement, it is possible that the

The Educational Value of the Scores

scores influence the very outcomes they are intended to predict, making them a form of self-fulfilling prophecy.

It may be reasonable to view intelligence tests as achievement tests for which all children have not been equally well-prepared—

Box 12.3

PUTTING INTELLIGENCE TESTING IN MODERN PERSPECTIVE

We are not so certain of what intelligence is, how to measure it, what its properties are, or what it should be a prerequisite for that we can use it as a basis for making major life decisions for children in perhaps other than extreme cases. Controversy is currently raging over whether intelligence as it is presently used is a universal or culturally-bound concept. Anne Anastasi, a former president of the American Psychological Association and expert in differential psychology, offers the following five points on the way that intelligence may best be viewed.

1) First, intelligence should be regarded as a descriptive rather than an explanatory concept. An IQ is an expression of an individual's ability at a given point in time, in relation to his age norms. No intelligence test can indicate the reasons for his performance.

2) Second, the IQ is not fixed and unchanging; and it is amenable to modification by environmental interventions.

3) An individual's intelligence at any one point in time is the end product of a vast and complex sequence of interactions between hereditary and environmental factors.

4) Intelligence is not a single, unitary ability, but a composite of several functions. The term is commonly used to cover that combination of abilities required for survival and advancement within a particular culture, and finally,

5) An individual's relative ability will tend to increase with age in those functions whose *value* is emphasized by his culture or subculture; and his relative ability will tend to *decrease* in those functions whose value is deemphasized.

in which case, the scores can be used to provide supplementary instruction in the areas measured by the tests to students whose performance is lower than that of their age-mates. There is reason to suspect that such instruction, if done well, will cause such students to perform better on intelligence tests. If this is to be done simply for the sake of scoring high on a test, it should not be done at all. If, however, it is to be done in order to improve a child's chances of subsequent academic success, it should be done systematically and with vigor. The far wiser course may be to focus on achievement testing as the more profitable and meaningful form of educational testing for the majority of school children and thereby focus intelligence or mental ability testing on the identification of exceptionality for purposes of enhancement or remediation.

Additional Information Sources

Barron, F. The measurement of creativity. In D. K. Whitla (Ed.). *Handbook of measurement and assessment in behavioral sciences.* Reading, Mass.: Addison-Wesley, pp. 348–66.

Bloom, B. S. *Stability and change in human characteristics.* N.Y.; Wiley, 1964.

Freeman, F. S. *Theory and practice of psychological testing*, 3rd ed. N.Y.: Holt, Rinehart, and Winston, 1962.

Hawes, G. R. *Educational testing for the millions: What tests really mean for your child.* N.Y.: McGraw-Hill, 1964.

Hoepfner, R. & Klein, S. *CSE elementary school test evaluation.* Los Angeles: Center for the Study of Evaluation, UCLA Graduate School of Education, 1970.

MeClelland, D. Testing for competence rather than for "intelligence." *American Psychologist*, 1973, *28*, 1–14.

McNemar, Q. Lost: Our intelligence. Why? *American Psychologist*, 1964, *19*, pp. 871–82.

Nelson, M. J. Intelligence and special aptitude tests. In R. L. Ebel (Ed.). *Encyclopedia of educational research*, 4th ed. N.Y.: Macmillan, 1969, pp. 667–77.

Tarczan, C. *An educator's guide to psychological tests: Descriptions and classroom implications.* Springfield, Ill.: Chas. C Thomas, 1972.

Tuddenham, R. D. Intelligence. In R. L. Ebel (Ed.). *Encyclopedia of educational research*, 4th ed. N.Y.: Macmillan, 1969, pp. 654–64.

Self-test of Proficiency

(1) For each of the definitions or descriptions of intelligence on the left, match up the appropriate illustration on the right.

a. general intellectual capacity

b. group of traits

c. adaptability

d. what the test measures

e. structural configuration of discrete factors

f. learning ability

g. school performance

h. two-level process

i. improvement as the result of instruction

ii. abstract ability built on the ability to identify and recall

iii. the by-product of heredity

iv. ability to do well in an intellectual situation

v. a single persuasive ability that operates on different mental tests

vi. ability to deal effectively with the environment

vii. the score on the measuring instrument itself

viii. the combination of an operation on a content that yields a product

ix. composed of a number of discrete mental abilities

(2) The terms *intelligence, mental ability*, and *aptitude* are used to describe clearly differentiable qualities.

TRUE   FALSE

(3) Which of the following should not be considered for inclusion when preparing a composite definition of intelligence?

a. verbal comprehension

b. figural comprehension

c. drawing skill

d. inductive reasoning

e. spatial relations

f. musical ability

g. two-hand coordination

h. numerical skill

i. two-point threshold

j. visual acuity

(4) Intelligence was defined as a composite of skills that are *influenced by and related to a learning environment designed to reinforce or*

require these skills. To what does the italicized portion of this definition refer and what does it mean?

(5) Consider the following item:
Which word does not belong? chair table pencil bed
This item is illustrative of the item category
a. word substitution.
b. synonyms.
c. word classification.
d. verbal analysis.
e. recognition of objects.

(6) Consider the following item:
Which alternative at the right is most nearly like the illustration shown at the left?

 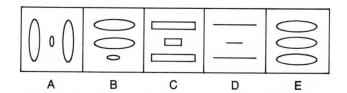

A   B   C   D   E

This item is illustrative of the item category
a. figure matching.
b. spatial visualization.
c. recognition of objects.
d. identical figures.
e. figural relations.

(7) a. Ted's performance on an intelligence test was the same as that of the average 7 year old child. Seven is Ted's _____ (chronological, mental) age.
b. Ted has just celebrated his 7th birthday. Seven is Ted's _____ (chronological, mental) age.
c. Based on the above information, we can say that Ted's _____ (ratio, deviation) IQ is 100.

(8) Miranda, who has just turned 11, took the Short-form Test of Academic Aptitude and obtained a total raw score of 47.
a. What is Miranda's deviation IQ?
b. What is Miranda's mental age (in years and months)? (Use Figures 12.5 and 12.6 on pages 336 and 337.)

(9) Reliability coefficients (based on internal consistency) for the major intelligence or mental ability tests tend to average about

a. .99   c. .79   e. .55

b. .88   d. .68

(10) Which one of the following statements about the stability of IQ scores is accurate?

a. IQ scores are unpredictable at all ages.

b. Third grade IQ scores cannot be used to predict scores at grade 12.

c. First grade IQ scores are an accurate indication of adult IQ.

d. Fourth grade IQ scores can be used to predict scores at grade 11.

e. None of the above.

(11) Check all of the statements below that are true, thereby contributing to the validity of IQ tests.

a. Students who score higher on IQ tests tend to get lower scores on school achievement tests than students who score lower on IQ tests.

b. Students who score higher on IQ tests tend to get better grades in school than students who score lower on IQ tests.

c. Persons in the professions tend to score higher on IQ tests than persons in the trades.

d. Messengers score higher on IQ tests than accountants.

e. IQ test scores and scores on tests reflecting amount of school learning are negatively correlated.

(12) The questions below are based on the following list of mental ability or intelligence tests:

i. Peabody Picture Vocabulary Test

ii. SCAT

III. Differential Aptitude Tests

iv. Cognitive Abilities Test

v. Stanford-Binet

vi. SFTAA

vii. IPAT Culture Fair Test

viii. WISC

ix. Otis-Lennon Mental Ability Test

x. Henmon-Nelson

a. Which ones are group-administered?

b. Which ones are individually-administered?

c. Which ones use only pictures as stimuli?

d. Which one yields no IQ score?

e. Which one of the group tests has evolved from a test designed over 50 years ago?

f. Which group test provides separate verbal, nonverbal, and quantitative scores?

(13) Which one statement below correctly distinguishes between the Stanford-Binet and Wechsler intelligence scales?
   a. S-B has been recently revised; WISC has not.
   b. S-B can be used with children; WISC only with adults.
   c. S-B comes in a single form; WISC comes in 2 forms.
   d. S-B is individually administered; WISC is group administered.
   e. S-B provides only a single score; WISC provides 3 scores.

(14) The Torrance Tests of Creativity require students to _____.

(15) The Remote Associates Test requires students to _____.

(16) The scores a person gets on an intelligence test is a function of his or her
   a. genetic make-up.
   b. environmental experiences.
   c. both of the above.
   d. neither of the above.
   e. nobody knows.

(17) Among the following, which is the best educational use to which IQ scores can be put?
   a. to help rid the schools of children that get into trouble
   b. to identify children who need enhancement or remediation
   c. to separate children into ability groups or tracks
   d. to help teachers to know what school performance to expect from each child
   e. to help children become aware of their own deficiency

(18) Among the following, which is the least desirable way to increase a person's intelligence test score?
   a. increase the value of intelligence in his or her culture
   b. provide training in the areas covered by the test
   c. relate the test more closely to his or her culture and vice versa
   d. use tests that place less reliance on verbal ability
   e. make the person and his or her teachers aware of the low score

chapter thirteen / Measuring Achievement with Published Test Batteries

OBJECTIVES

1. Identify and describe the types of skills and competencies measured by survey achievement batteries (i.e., general achievement in language arts, reading, mathematics, social studies, science, and study skills).

2. State similarities and differences between standardized and teacher-built achievement tests on appropriateness, validity, reliability, interpretability, and usability.

3. Distinguish between achievement and mental ability tests and and their degree of specificity on the "continuum of ability testing."

4. List and explain rules to follow in administering published achievement test batteries.

5. Distinguish among the following standardized achievement test scores: *a.* raw score, *b.* percen-

tile rank, *c.* stanine, *d.* grade equivalent, *e.* stand-ard achievement score, *f.* anticipated achievement score; use item performance to interpret results.

6. Distinguish between criterion-referenced tests and norm-referenced tests.

7. Identify the characteristics of tests for the measurement of reading skills.

WHAT DO STANDARDIZED ACHIEVEMENT TESTS MEASURE?

Standardized achievement tests enjoy a widespread use in the public schools of this country. Many school systems administer these tests once a year to all students or at least to all elementary school students. The first question that must be dealt with in understanding standardized achievement tests and their role in the schools is what they measure.[1]

Reading skill is generally measured in terms of vocabulary, word analysis, and reading comprehension.

General Achievement in Reading

Vocabulary. In vocabulary tests, respondents are given a definition or synonym and asked to *identify the word that is a synonym or that fits or completes the definition.*[2]

- If you tear a piece of paper, you

  rip it   cry about it   stain it
   o   o   o

---

[1] The description of achievement tests in this chapter is based largely on an analysis of the major achievement batteries: Stanford Achievement Test (1973 edition), California Achievement Tests (1970 edition), Comprehensive Tests of Basic Skills (1973 edition), the Iowa Tests of Basic Skills (1972 edition), Tests of Academic Progress (1964 edition), and Metropolitan Achievement Tests (1970 edition).

[2] All examples are patterned after actual achievement test items. Unless otherwise specified, the first sample item in a pair is an early elementary item (i.e., grades 1–3) and the second item, a middle school or junior high item (i.e., grades 7–9). At the lower levels, test items and answer choices are read aloud by the teacher while students have answer choices before them at the same time. Answers to sample items appear at the bottom of page 372.

- You could best describe an *extrovert* as being
  - *a.* pensive
  - *b.* exuberant
  - *c.* outgoing
  - *d.* self-conscious

Word Analysis.   This type of test at early grade levels re-quires a student to correctly identify a word that he or she hears—more specifically, to *distinguish a word given orally from poten-tially confusable forms*. Items often require both listening and reading ability, together with the ability to distinguish from among the confusable forms. For example:

- SAID (read aloud by teacher)
  seed   sod   sad   said   (seen by student)
   o   o   o   o

At the later elementary grades, this test may also deal with the similarities between sounds in words, asking the respondent to *select a word that has the same sound as the underlined part of a given word*. For example:

- rhyme   happy   rich   pile
             (A)   (B)   (C)

For older students word analysis items also often require stu-dents to *select the sound that is the same as a designated part of a given word*:

- The underlined sound in *particular* (pẽr-tik' yoo-lẽr)
  17 rhymes with the *a* in *fan*
  18 is pronounced like the *a* in *play*
  19 has the *e* in *penny* sound
  20 has the *u* sound in *curtail*

As you can see from the various illustrations, word analysis focuses on the sounds and structure of words.

Reading Comprehension.   Reading is sometimes measured in part by determining whether the student can *identify the word that fits a given picture*. A first grade item might look like this:

-
  o bat
  o mat
  o but

At higher grade levels, a story is provided, which the student reads. He or she must then *identify the correct answer to a question based on the content of the given story.* A fifth grade item might be as follows.

- The sea otter who lives in the Pacific Ocean is covered with a coat of beautiful and valuable fur. Between 1700 and 1910, hunters and trappers tried to kill the otters. They would then skin them and sell their fur. In order to protect the otters from being wiped out, a law was passed in 1910 that said that people couldn't kill otters.

People killed sea otters
1 because it was fun to do.
2 to get their fur.
3 to keep them from eating up all the fish.
4 to keep them from spreading.

From the story we can tell that
5 all the settlers were so greedy for fur that they would do anything to get it.
6 you can't buy an otter fur coat today.
7 by 1910 there was a danger that no otters would be left.
8 between 1700 and 1910, more otters were caught than any other furry animal.

A considerable number of the items in achievement batteries are devoted to the measurement of language skills—for example, spelling, mechanics (or grammar), and usage.

General Achievement in Language

Spelling. In the multiple choice, machine scorable format of published test batteries, respondents cannot be tested for spelling by having them actually construct the spelling of a word. Hence, a form or forms of the word must be given (often in a sentence that the person administering the test reads aloud), and then the respondent is asked to *choose the correct spelling of a given word or indicate whether a given spelling is correct or incorrect.* For example:

- Don't you *believe* me? believe (read aloud by teacher)
  believe   RIGHT   WRONG   (seen by student)
  o   o

Another format is to give all but one correctly spelled word and ask the respondent to *distinguish the incorrectly spelled word from the correct ones* (as illustrated below).

- Which word is spelled incorrectly?
  5 temperature   7 athletic
  6 sophmore   8 religion

Mechanics. Language mechanics focuses on aspects such as punctuation, capitalization, and sentence structure. For example, the respondent is given an unpunctuated or uncapitalized sentence and asked to *identify the correct punctuation or correct capitalization for each part of the given sentence.*

- Did you find the book I left at your house
  .   ,   ?   "
  o   o   o   o

Which word in the sentence should start with a capital letter?

- The boys all laughed at jimmy.
    •   •   •   •   •

Students may also be asked to *distinguish between complete and incomplete sentences.*

- No matter how much he tried.
  complete sentence   incomplete sentence
        A   B

Usage. Language usage or expression deals with *selecting the right form of a word or phrase to complete or rewrite a sentence in standard, written English,* or *distinguishing between proper and improper usage of words.*

- Which of the following is a correct standard sentence?
  o My friend she get hurt.
  o She were at the doctor's.
  o I felt sorry for her.

- Yesterday, we ——————— a president for our club.
  1 choosed
  2 choose
  3 chose
  4 will choose

"Look, Tom, look. It is good. Yes. Good. The end. Published by Kaleidoscope Enterprises, 432 Schermerhorn Boulevard."

In addition to language skills and reading, mathematics is a common component of standardized achievement batteries. Most batteries subdivide mathematics into two or three components with a variety of labels. For our purposes we will use the terms computation, concepts, and applications to describe achievement in mathematics.

General Achievement in Mathematics

Mathematics Computation.   This type of test deals with the respondent's ability to *add, subtract, multiply, divide, determine equals and unequals, take square roots,* and perform basic mathematical or arithmetic operations in general. For example:

- $12 - 4 =$ _____   16   9   8   7
  o   o   o   o

- The lowest common denominator of ⅓, ¼,.and ⅙ is

6	12	13	24
A	B	C	D

Mathematics Concepts.   Math concepts are more difficult to define than computation because they cover a wide area of mathematical understanding. In essence, these items require the respondent to *demonstrate his or her understanding of the basic rules, laws, or definitions of math by making identifications that involve these rules, laws, or definitions.* (Moreover, the computation level in concept problems is kept low so as not to confound the measurement.) For example:

- What number is· three hundred seventy-two?

327	372	30027	30072
o	o	o	o

- What is the reciprocal of the integer y?

y^2	$1-y$	$1/y$	$y-1$
o	o	o	o

Mathematics Applications.   In math applications respondents must *demonstrate their understanding of math principles and operations by solving problems involving these principles and operations.*

- You can buy 3 jelly beans for a nickel and 6 pieces of gum for a dime. What is the cost of 12 jelly beans and 12 pieces of gum?

15¢	20¢	40¢	70¢
o	o	o	o

- Rosa drove her car at a speed of 40 miles per hour. At this rate, how far could Rosa drive in a half an hour?

20 miles	25 miles	40 miles	80 miles
E	F	G	H

General Achievement in Social Studies   Social studies, or social science as it is alternatively called, is an area often measured in standardized achievement batteries (but not so commonly as reading, language, or mathematics). Test items measure (1) the acquisition and retention of factual information, (2) the application or interpretation of either given or retained information, and (3) the use of specific skills such as map and graph reading. Respondents are called upon to identify the correct piece of factual information regarding history, geography, or culture as illustrated in the following item for third graders.

- The largest of the 50 United States in terms of area is
  - (A) Texas.
  - (B) New York.
  - (C) California.
  - (D) Alaska.

Seventh graders might be asked:

- Which of the following people was *not* an inventor?
  - 5 Thomas Edison
  - 6 John D. Rockefeller
  - 7 Alexander Bell
  - 8 Robert Fulton

In another kind of item, respondents are called upon to *identify the choice that represents the correct interpretation of a social science problem or situation.* Fifth graders, for example, might be asked:

- Which of the following could be considered a political slogan?

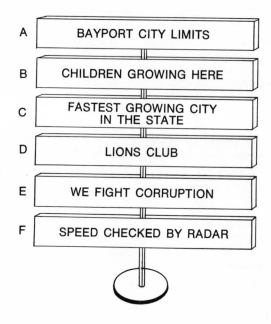

A   BAYPORT CITY LIMITS

B   CHILDREN GROWING HERE

C   FASTEST GROWING CITY IN THE STATE

D   LIONS CLUB

E   WE FIGHT CORRUPTION

F   SPEED CHECKED BY RADAR

Finally, students are asked to *demonstrate the application of specific skills in areas such as map reading and figure interpretation* as the following second grade item illustrates.

- The first picture shows a symbol for a factory. Which one of these three maps shows a place where factory products are made?

General Achievement in Science

Science items, like social studies items, require respondents to (1) *identify the correct fact, label, or phenomenon*, (2) *identify the correct explanation or application of a principle to the solution of a problem or description of a phenomenon*, and (3) *demonstrate the application of specific skills such as graph reading*. These are respectively illustrated by the following three examples for the fourth, eighth, and sixth grades, in that order.

- Which planet is farthest from the sun?
  - (A) Pluto
  - (C) Mars
  - (B) Uranus
  - (D) Saturn
- Two balls, *A* and *B*, are dropped from the roof of a building at the same time. Both balls are made of solid steel. Which of the following three pictures accurately shows them reaching the ground?

- The class members each wrote their height on the blackboard and the graph at the top of the next page was made of their heights.

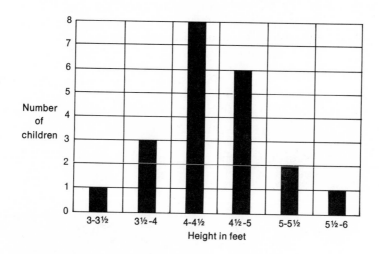

The height common to the greatest number of class members is

A 3½–4 feet   B 4–4½ feet   C 4½–5 feet   D 5–5½ feet

General Achievement in Study Skills

Some achievement tests provide separate subtests to measure what is called *study skills*. Others include this area in subtests like science or social science, some may not include it at all. *Study skills* refers to a student's ability to *identify the correct information from printed and graphic materials.* Presumably if a student has learned how to use a library and reference sources contained in it, such as a dictionary, encyclopedia, atlas, and so forth, he or she will be able to correctly identify information taken from these sources. The last examples for both social studies and science illustrate measurement of study skills within a subject area test. Some additional examples of study skills items from the fifth grade level appear below. (The first two illustrate library skills, the third is a map reading item.)

- Which of the following books would you look in to find a history of commercial fishing?
  atlas   encyclopedia   dictionary   almanac
  A   B   C   D

- im·me·di·ate (i-mē′di-it), *adj.* 1. occurring or accomplished without delay; instant: an *immediate reply.* 2. pertaining to the present time or moment: *our immediate plans.* 3. having no time intervening: *the immediate future.* 4. having no object or space intervening; nearest or next: *in the immediate vicinity.*

- Which of the above definitions fits the use of the word *immediate* in this sentence?
  Because I am in a hurry, I must have an *immediate* answer.

  1   2   3   4

- According to the map shown below, in what direction must you go to get from the airport to the lake?

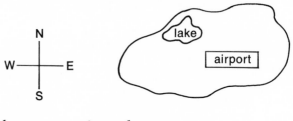

  1 northeast   3 northwest
  2 southeast   4 southwest

General Achievement in Listening   Some current achievement test batteries include the measurement of listening comprehension—the ability to *identify the correct response to a question based on information presented orally.* While the question or story itself is only given orally, the answer choices may be given in pictorial or written form or they may only be given orally as well. The example below (sixth grade level) illustrates one of these formats.

(Read by teacher and not seen by student)
- Blair and Jackie are in the second grade. They often work together. They are working on a project together now. This project is for their teacher.

Answers

rip it, *c.* outgoing, said, Ⓒ pile, 20 as the *u* sound in *curtail*, bat, 2 to get their fur, 7 by 1910 there was a danger that no otters would be left, right, sophmore, ?, jimmy, B incomplete sentence, I felt sorry for her., 3 chose, 8, 12, 372, 1/y, 40¢, E 20 miles, Ⓓ Alaska, 6 John D. Rockefeller, 3 E, 3, Ⓐ pluto, 2, B 4–4½ feet, B encyclopedia, 1, 3 northwest, C. some second grade students do projects for their teachers.

Which statement is based on the story? (The statements are read by the student.)
- A. Blair is doing most of the work on the project.
- B. Jackie keeps bothering Blair when she is trying to work.
- C. Some second grade students do projects for their teachers.
- D. The library is a good place to work on a project.

It is useful to examine the procedures that a standardized achievement test battery goes through to earn the label "standardized." In the next section, using the five test criteria described in Part III, we will compare standardized achievement tests with teacher-built tests.

Why These Tests Are Called Standardized

Tryout, Item Analysis, and Revision. The first two steps in the construction of a standardized achievement test are the same as those in the construction of a teacher-built test, that is, the developing of a content outline and the writing of items. In the case of the standardized test, more than one person may write the items. Here the selection of content or objectives is based on an examination of existing curriculums and textbooks used throughout the nation.

As part of its development, the standardized test is tried out on a sample of students, not to measure their achievement but to determine the properties of the items themselves. The results of the tryout are then used to eliminate items that are too easy, too hard, ambiguous, poorly worded, or inconsistent with the majority of like items. Some decisions are based on statistical results while others are based on comments by teachers and students. After the item writers see the results of the tryout and subsequent analysis, they can tell which items are poor. The poor items are eliminated since more items are used in the tryout then would be needed in the final instrument.

For example, the following item was contained in the original version of a social studies test.

- Ponce de Leon was
  - *a.* a governor of precolonial Florida.
  - *b.* the discoverer of the fountain of youth.
  - *c.* a conqueror of Mexico.
  - *d.* a famous pirate.

The tryout results showed that choice *b* was the most frequent choice but the correlation between getting this item right and total score on the test was below chance level. A close examination of choice *b* revealed that it inadvertently contained a trick. While Ponce de Leon is most well-known for his search for the fountain of youth (and hence his name is closely associated with it), he never succeeded in *discovering* it and hence cannot be called its *discoverer*. He was, however, a governor of precolonial Florida—a fact that most people do not know. The item would have been better if choice *a* had been "discoverer of Puerto Rico" (which is wrong) and *b* "seeker of the fountain of youth" (which is right).

Similarly, tryout and item analysis makes it possible to construct a test that is internally consistent, reasonably free of ambiguity, and graded in terms of item difficulty (if that is the goal).

Uniform and Widespread Use and Reuse.   As the test items are being developed, a set of standard instructions for their administration is also being developed to insure that time limits and other procedural requirements remain constant from use to use; thus administrative procedures as a differential source of influence on students' test scores are eliminated.

All of this "standardization" is predicated on a major characteristic that differentiates the published achievement test from the one the teacher builds, that is, the matter of reuse. Often teacher-built achievement tests are used only once and, on those rare occasions of reuse, are used again by the same teacher or perhaps the same school, while standardized achievement tests are constructed for multiple use in varied schools across the country. Clearly, if an achievement test were to be used but once, there would be little value to its improvement or standardization, but multiple and repeated use gives these processes value.

The Existence of Norms.   The feature of standardized achievement tests that probably has gone furthest to earn them the label of "standardized" is the availability of comparison data in the form of norms.[3] When teachers administer their own achievement tests, they usually discard the results after they have used them to evaluate the students who took the test, but standardized achievement test data are collected and used to provide a relative basis for the interpretation of test scores. Hence, when you give a standardized achievement test, it is possible to compare or refer-

[3] Norms and their use were described in Chapter 11 on pages 279-93.

ence the performance of students in terms of members of a specific norming group who have taken it before them. It is also possible to compare their performance to all those in their own district who have taken the test in the past or who have taken it at the same time. Widespread test use contributes to the availability of concurrent data, both nationally and locally. (The interpretation of norm-referenced, standardized achievement test scores will be discussed on pages 385–91.)

After a standardized achievement test is constructed and edited, its developers administer it to a national sample of students who will serve as the norming group. This presumably representative group will serve as the basis for the establishment of national norms on the test, clearly marking the test as a "standardized" one. The same process will also be gone through for each test revision.

COMPARING STANDARDIZED AND TEACHER-BUILT ACHIEVEMENT TESTS

School achievement can be measured by either a teacher-built test or a standardized test. Teachers use their own tests to measure the achievement of their own students on their own objectives. School districts typically use standardized tests to get a broader view of student attainment throughout the district. While teacher-built tests may be given as often as daily or weekly, a standardized achievement test battery will probably only be given once, or at most, twice a year. It should be useful to compare the two types of tests on the five test criteria of appropriateness, validity, reliability, interpretability, and usability.

Appropriateness

Appropriateness, as you recall, refers to the fit of a test's items to a set of given objectives. The better the fit between what a test measures and what a teacher wants it to measure, the greater the appropriateness of that test.

We can assume that teacher-built achievement tests have a high degree of appropriateness since teachers build them themselves. Standardized achievement tests on the other hand are more general; since they are intended for wider use, their coverage must be broad enough to cover the objectives of many teachers. The appropriateness of standardized achievement tests depends on what extent a field of study has uniform and commonly agreed upon objectives. In a field like high school industrial arts where local curriculums may vary widely, standardized achievement tests will be low in appropriateness (Tuckman and Corman, 1971). In first grade reading, on the other hand, where objectives from school to school are similar, appropriateness will be higher.

When teachers give their own tests, they know that the material or objectives to be tested have been covered in class. However, a standardized achievement test may be given *before* some of the objectives it measures are taught. In other words, these objectives may be in the curriculum but not yet taught. This happens because most standardized test levels cover more than one year of work while teacher-built tests cover much smaller segments. Hence, standardized tests will be appropriate only in a general sense.

Standardized achievement tests are based largely on the content in standard textbooks in the subject area for each grade level. Where teachers follow the content of the standard textbook—as is frequently the case, especially at the elementary level—standardized achievement tests will be higher in appropriateness. Test manuals for each of the major standardized achievement batteries report item content categories by level for each item on each test. This tells you the topics measured in each subtest and the numbers of the specific items that measure each topic. (One page of such a table of item content categories for the California Achievement Tests has been reproduced in Figure 13.1 to illustrate the nature of achievement test coverage.)

The appropriateness of standardized achievement tests as used will be increased when either (1) teachers are given a list of the content categories for each subtest at the beginning of each school year, or (2) teachers are to go through the content coverage table before the test is given and indicate those areas or categories that have been covered in class. For instance, if "modifiers" had not been taught, responses to items 35, 36, and 38 on Level 3 of the CAT can be expected to be wrong, thus reducing the appropriateness of the instrument for measuring this objective.

For a curriculum such as Individually Prescribed Instruction (IPI) in math, the curriculum teaches what the IPI math test measures. If these tests were to be used on a district-wide basis, teachers could begin the year with a list of the test's objectives to guide their instruction. In fact, the prescriptive tests (to be described later in this chapter) represent an attempt to increase the appropriateness of commercially available achievement tests. Rather than using *norms* as the basis for interpretation, these tests are referenced in terms of the *specific objectives* they measure.

Language Item Content Category by Level for the California Achievement Tests. **Figure 13.1**

The CAT Usage and Structure section is designed to test the student's ability to differentiate between standard and non-standard English usage; to recognize possible sentence transformations, and to identify sentence elements and their functions as well as total sentence structure and type.

USAGE and STRUCTURE

The CAT Spelling section is designed to show the student's ability to discriminate between those words which are spelled correctly and those which are misspelled.

SPELLING

Categories	LEVEL 1	LEVEL 2	LEVEL 3	LEVEL 4	LEVEL 5
Standard English*					
Case					
Nominative	6, 13, 16	9, 17, 19	3, 12, 23	1, 26	5, 8
Objective	10, 15	1, 3	7	3, 14, 18	6, 13, 14, 17, 18, 20, 23
Possessive	2	6, 13	10		
Tense					
Simple	3, 8, 12, 19	2, 12, 22	8, 19, 22	6, 24	10
With Auxiliary	1, 17	14, 18, 25	13, 15, 16, 18, 20, 21	12, 21	11, 16, 21, 27
Number	4, 7, 20	5, 7, 10, 21	2, 6	4, 13, 15, 22, 25, 27	1, 2, 9, 19, 24, 28
Usage	5, 9, 11, 14, 18	4, 8, 11, 15, 16, 20, 23, 24	1, 4, 5, 8, 9, 10, 11, 14, 17, 24	2, 5, 7, 8, 9, 10, 11, 16, 17, 19, 20, 23, 28	3, 4, 7, 12, 15, 22, 25, 26, 29
Sentence Structure					
Complete			26, 27		
Simple				37	35, 37
Complex				38, 39	40
Compound				40	38
Incomplete			25, 28, 29	35, 36	36, 39
Sentence Parts & Functions					
Nouns, Pronouns, & Phrases			39	42, 48, 50	42, 43, 45, 50
Verbs, Verbals, Phrases			37	43, 47, 49	41, 47, 49, 51, 52, 53
Modifiers			35, 36, 38	41, 45, 46	44, 46, 48
Connectors, Prepositions			40, 41	44	54
Inflectional Morphemes			37	43, 50	50, 52
Transformation					
Negative			32, 33	32	
Question			30, 31, 34	29, 30, 31, 34	32
Exclamation			33	33	
Single Base					32, 30, 31
Double Base					33, 34
Silent Letter	3, 4, 7, 11, 15, 18, 20	3, 7, 8, 10, 15, 17, 18, 19, 23	1, 8, 9, 13, 15, 18, 20, 23, 24, 28, 29	6, 9, 10, 13, 14, 15, 16, 17, 19, 21, 28, 30, 32	3, 7, 13, 19, 23, 26, 28, 30, 31, 32
Double Consonant	1, 6, 15	1, 3, 18, 19	14, 15, 24, 28	3, 6, 14, 16, 28, 32	3, 7, 19, 27
Multi-Sound Consonant		10, 20, 24	5, 7, 16, 22, 27	5, 7, 10, 15, 20, 24	1, 12, 14, 16, 3
Internal Vowel	7, 10, 11, 13, 16, 19, 20	4, 6, 10, 11, 12, 13, 17, 21, 22, 23	1, 10, 13, 18, 26, 29, 32	9, 11, 12, 18, 19, 23, 26, 27, 31	9, 10, 13, 15, 18, 21, 23, 24, 25, 28, 29, 31
Vowel plus "r"	8, 12, 17	16, 25	3, 31	29	11
Letter Reversal & ei-ie			10, 12, 21, 30	1, 22, 25	5, 18, 22, 28
Suffix			11, 17, 19	26	14, 17, 29, 30
Two Words			14	3	
Mispronunciations			25	22	
No Error	2, 5, 9, 14	2, 5, 9, 14	2, 4, 6	2, 4, 8	2, 4, 6, 8, 20

* From *Test Coordinator's Handbook*, Tiegs & Clark, reproduced by permission of the publisher, CTB/McGraw-Hill, Monterey, CA 93940. Copyright © 1970 by McGraw-Hill, Inc.

In summary, then, it would seem that standardized achievement test batteries are appropriate for the general purposes for which they are used but should not be considered measures of the attainment of each teacher's own objectives. (We will return to this issue of specificity–generality of coverage in the discussion of achievement and intelligence tests on page 382.)

Validity The concept of validity has been applied to achievement testing primarily in terms of college entrance testing and subsequent college success. With regard to the kinds of achievement tests discussed in this chapter, only concurrent validity has been established by demonstrating the correlations between different ones, since the kinds of standardized achievement tests given in elementary, middle, and secondary schools are not intended to predict future performance but to reflect upon the results of past learning experiences. It is difficult to establish validity for teacher-built tests; they must be evaluated based on content coverage which is, in fact, a question of appropriateness.

Ebel (1961) suggests that the facts that (1) standardized tests go beyond purely local objectives and (2) their content is reviewed by experts tend to be strong points in their favor. The use of expert judgment in deciding on broad content coverage does provide standardized achievement tests with validity as measures of *general* learning.

Reliability Reliability is one of the greatest strengths of standardized achievement test batteries. Because item analysis and revision based on that item analysis are steps in the development of these tests, it is possible to eliminate or improve inconsistent items to achieve a high degree of internal reliability.

Figure 13.2 presents reliability for the different levels of the 1970 Edition of the California Achievement Tests (Tiegs and Clark, 1970b). Reliabilities reported for other achievement batteries such as the Stanford or Iowa are in the same, equally high range.

While the reliabilities of teachers' tests typically are neither calculated nor reported, the fact that their tests are not usually analyzed or revised suggests that reliabilities much in excess of .65 would not be expected. However, it must be pointed out that high reliabilities do not overcome other deficiencies. It is often easier to improve a test's reliability than to improve its status on the other test criteria.

Reliabilities (Kuder-Richardson Formula 20) for the 1970 Edition of **Figure 13.2**
the California Achievement Tests.*

	Grade 1.6	Grade 2.6		
Level 1	.979	.982		

	Grade 2.6	Grade 3.6	Grade 4.6	
Level 2	.982	.982	.986	

	Grade 4.6	Grade 5.6	Grade 6.6	
Level 3	.978	.982	.983	

	Grade 6.6	Grade 7.6	Grade 8.9	Grade 9.6
Level 4	.977	.981	.980	.982

	Grade 9.6	Grade 10.6	Grade 11.6	Grade 12.6
Level 5	.979	.977	.978	.981

* From California Achievement Tests, Test Manual, Tiegs and Clark, reproduced by permission of the publisher, CTB/McGraw-Hill, Monterey, CA
93940. Copyright © 1970 by McGraw-Hill, Inc.

There are two basic vehicles for the interpretation of achievement **Interpretability**
data: norms and criteria for the evaluation of proficiency. Teacher-
built tests utilize criteria for the evaluation of proficiency while
standardized tests use norms. For illustrative purposes, Figure 13.3
shows a norms table for one level of one standardized achievement
battery, the Iowa Tests of Basic Skills (such norms tables are to
be found in the Test Manuals of all major achievement batteries).
Both types of interpretations are valuable and both have been
described in Chapter 11. Specific interpretation of standardized
achievement test results based on norms will be described in detail
later in this chapter, and the relative role of each kind of interpretation will be described in the last chapter.

Since teachers give tests mainly to evaluate student progress,
their interpretations are usually based on proficiency criteria.
Hence, teachers' needs for test data are likely to be met directly
by their own tests. The kind of information that administrators
find useful is most readily obtained from standardized tests, which
enable them to compare classes within a school, schools within a
district, and districts within the nation.

Since each typically uses a different basis for interpretation,
teacher-built tests and published tests cannot be directly compared
in terms of interpretability. Moreover, each type should be seen

Figure 13.3   *Sample Percentile Norms Table for Level 7 (Grades 1.7–2.5) of the Iowa Test of Basic Skills Given at End of Year.**

%ile Rank	Test Li	Test V	Test WA	Test R	Test L: Language L-1	L-2	L-3	L-4	Total L	Test W: Work-Study W1&2	W-3	Total W	Test M: Mathematics M-1	M-2	Total M	St'd. C	Basic C	%ile Rank	Stanine
99	38	38	37	45	42	42	47	46	43	38	39	39	35	37	35	38	38	99	
98	36	36	36	43	41	40	45	44	41	37	37	37	33	35	33	36	36	98	9
97	35	35	35	41	—	39	43	43	39	36	35	35	—	33	32	35	35	97	
96	34	34	34	40	40	38	42	42	38	35	33	33	32	32	31	33	34	96	
95	33	33	33	38	39	37	41	—	37	34	32	32	—	31	—	32	33	95	
94	32	32	32	37	38	36	40	41	36	33	31	31	31	30	30	31	32	94	
93	—	—	31	36	—	—	39	40	35	32	—	—	—	29	—	—	—	93	
92	31	31	30	—	37	35	—	39	34	—	30	30	30	—	29	30	31	92	8
91	—	30	—	35	—	34	38	—	33	31	29	—	—	28	—	—	—	91	
90	30	—	29	34	36	33	37	38	—	—	—	29	29	—	28	29	30	90	
89	—	29	—	—	35	—	36	37	32	30	28	—	—	—	—	—	—	89	
88	29	—	28	33	—	32	35	—	31	—	—	28	—	27	27	28	29	88	
87	—	—	—	—	34	—	34	36	—	29	—	—	28	—	—	—	—	87	
86	—	28	—	32	—	31	—	—	30	—	27	27	—	—	—	—	—	86	
85	28	—	27	—	33	—	33	35	—	—	—	—	—	26	26	27	28	85	
84	—	—	—	31	32	30	32	—	29	28	—	—	—	—	—	—	—	84	7
83	—	27	—	—	—	—	—	34	—	—	26	26	27	—	—	—	—	83	
82	27	—	—	30	31	29	31	33	28	—	—	—	—	—	—	26	27	82	
81	—	—	26	—	—	—	—	—	—	27	—	—	—	25	25	—	—	81	
80	—	—	—	—	30	28	30	32	—	—	—	—	26	—	—	—	—	80	
79	26	26	—	29	—	—	—	—	27	—	25	25	—	—	—	—	26	79	
78	—	—	—	—	—	27	29	31	—	26	—	—	—	—	—	25	—	78	
77	—	—	25	28	29	—	—	—	26	—	—	—	25	—	24	—	—	77	
76	25	—	—	—	—	—	28	30	—	—	—	24	—	24	—	—	25	76	
75	—	25	—	—	28	26	—	—	—	25	24	—	—	—	—	24	—	75	6
74	—	—	—	27	27	—	27	29	25	—	—	—	24	—	—	—	—	74	
73	—	—	24	—	—	—	—	—	—	—	—	23	24	—	—	—	—	73	
72	24	—	—	26	—	25	—	28	—	—	—	—	—	—	23	—	24	72	
71	—	24	—	—	26	—	26	—	24	24	—	—	—	23	—	23	—	71	
70	—	—	—	—	—	—	—	27	—	—	23	—	—	—	—	—	—	70	
69	—	—	23	25	25	24	25	—	—	—	—	—	23	—	—	—	23	69	
68	—	—	—	—	—	—	—	26	—	—	—	22	—	—	—	—	—	68	6
67	23	23	—	—	—	—	24	—	23	—	22	—	—	—	—	22	—	67	
66	—	—	—	24	24	23	—	25	—	23	22	22	—	—	22	—	22	66	
65	—	—	22	—	23	—	23	—	—	—	—	—	22	22	—	—	—	65	
64	—	—	—	—	—	—	—	—	—	—	—	—	—	—	—	—	22	64	
63	22	22	—	23	—	—	—	24	22	22	—	21	—	—	—	—	—	63	
62	—	—	—	—	—	22	—	—	—	—	—	—	—	—	21	21	—	62	
61	—	—	—	22	22	—	22	23	—	—	21	—	21	—	21	—	—	61	
60	—	—	—	—	—	—	—	—	—	—	—	—	—	21	—	—	21	60	
59	21	21	21	—	—	—	—	—	21	—	—	—	—	—	—	—	—	59	
58	—	—	—	21	21	21	21	22	—	21	—	20	—	—	—	20	—	58	
57	—	—	—	—	—	—	—	21	—	—	20	—	20	—	—	—	—	57	
56	—	—	—	—	—	—	—	21	—	—	—	20	20	—	20	—	20	56	
55	—	20	20	—	—	—	—	—	—	—	—	—	20	—	—	—	20	55	
54	20	—	—	—	20	20	20	—	20	20	—	—	—	—	—	—	—	54	
53	—	—	—	20	—	—	—	20	—	—	—	19	—	—	—	—	—	53	
52	—	—	—	—	—	—	—	—	—	—	—	—	—	—	—	19	—	52	
51	—	—	—	—	—	—	—	—	—	—	19	—	—	—	—	—	—	51	
50	19	19	19	19	19	19	19	19	—	19	—	19	19	19	19	—	19	50	5
49	—	—	—	—	—	—	—	—	19	—	—	18	—	—	—	—	—	49	
48	18	—	—	—	—	—	—	18	—	—	—	—	—	—	—	—	—	48	
47	—	—	—	—	—	—	—	—	—	—	18	—	—	—	—	—	—	47	
46	—	18	18	18	—	18	—	—	—	18	—	—	18	18	18	18	18	46	
45	—	—	—	—	18	—	18	—	—	—	—	—	—	—	—	—	—	45	
44	—	—	—	—	—	—	—	—	—	—	—	—	—	—	—	—	—	44	
43	17	—	—	—	—	—	17	18	—	—	—	—	—	—	—	—	—	43	
42	—	17	17	—	—	17	—	—	—	17	—	17	—	—	—	—	—	42	
41	—	—	—	17	—	—	—	—	—	—	17	—	—	17	—	—	—	41	
40	16	—	—	—	17	—	—	—	—	—	—	—	—	—	—	—	17	40	
39	—	16	—	—	—	—	17	16	—	16	—	—	17	—	17	17	—	39	
38	—	—	16	—	—	—	16	—	17	—	—	16	—	16	—	—	—	38	
37	—	—	—	—	—	—	—	17	—	—	16	16	—	—	—	—	—	37	
36	15	—	—	16	16	—	—	—	—	—	—	—	16	—	—	16	—	36	
35	—	15	—	—	—	—	—	15	—	15	—	—	—	15	16	—	16	35	
34	—	—	15	—	—	—	16	—	—	15	—	—	15	—	—	16	—	34	4
33	—	—	—	—	—	15	—	—	—	—	—	—	16	—	—	—	—	33	
32	—	—	—	15	—	—	—	—	—	—	15	15	—	—	—	—	—	32	
31	14	14	—	—	15	—	—	14	16	14	—	—	—	14	—	—	—	31	
30	—	—	14	—	—	—	—	—	—	—	—	—	11	—	—	—	—	30	
29	—	—	—	—	—	—	15	—	—	—	—	—	—	—	15	—	—	29	
28	13	13	13	—	—	14	—	—	—	13	14	14	—	13	—	15	—	28	
27	—	—	—	—	—	—	—	13	—	—	—	—	15	—	15	—	—	27	
26	—	—	—	14	14	—	—	13	—	13	14	14	15	—	—	—	—	26	
25	12	12	12	—	—	13	14	—	—	—	—	—	—	12	—	—	—	25	
24	—	—	—	—	—	—	—	—	15	12	—	—	—	—	14	14	—	24	
23	—	—	—	—	13	—	—	12	—	—	13	13	14	—	13	—	—	23	
22	—	—	—	—	—	13	14	—	15	12	—	—	—	—	—	—	14	22	
21	—	—	—	—	—	—	—	12	—	—	13	13	14	—	—	—	—	21	
20	11	11	11	—	13	—	—	—	—	—	—	—	—	11	13	14	—	20	
19	—	—	—	—	—	12	—	—	—	11	—	—	13	—	—	—	—	19	3
18	—	—	—	—	—	—	13	—	—	—	—	—	—	10	—	—	13	18	
17	—	—	—	—	—	—	—	11	—	—	12	12	—	—	12	13	—	17	
16	10	10	10	—	12	11	—	14	—	10	—	—	12	9	11	—	—	16	
15	—	—	—	12	—	—	—	—	14	—	—	—	—	—	—	—	12	15	
14	—	—	—	—	—	—	12	—	—	—	11	—	12	—	—	—	—	14	
13	—	9	—	11	—	10	—	10	13	9	—	—	—	—	—	—	—	13	
12	9	—	9	—	11	—	—	—	—	—	—	11	11	8	11	12	—	12	
11	—	—	—	—	—	—	11	—	—	9	—	—	—	—	10	—	—	11	
10	—	—	—	10	10	9	—	9	—	—	—	10	10	7	10	12	—	10	2
9	8	8	—	9	—	—	10	—	9	8	9	—	—	6	—	11	—	9	
8	—	7	8	—	10	8	9	8	12	—	—	10	10	—	9	—	11	8	
7	—	—	7	8	9	7	8	7	—	7	8	—	9	6	8	—	—	7	
6	—	6	—	7	8	6	6	6	11	6	7	9	8	5	7	10	10	6	
5	—	—	—	8	9	—	7	8	—	—	8	—	—	—	6	—	—	5	
4	—	—	—	—	—	—	—	7	—	—	—	—	9	—	8	11	—	4	
3	—	—	—	7	8	7	6	—	11	9	—	9	8	5	7	10	10	3	
2	6	5	6	—	7	6	6	6	10	6	7	8	8	4	7	10	9	2	1
1	5	4	5	5	6	5	5	5	9	5	6	7	7	3	6	9	9	1	

as serving a different function—one that is consistent with its basis for interpretation. Testing in the schools is improved not only by making better use of standardized tests but by helping teachers to be better designers and developers of their own tests. Standardized tests are not substitutes for teacher-built tests; rather they are supplements. Nonetheless, because results of standardized tests often become part of a student's permanent record, teachers should treat these tests with utmost seriousness.

Although test publishers provide highly specific instructions for the administration of standardized achievement tests, they are inevitably more difficult to administer than teacher-built tests. Teacher-built tests, except perhaps for mid-terms or finals, are confined to a single class period and hence do not disrupt the schedule. Standardized achievement tests take three or more hours to complete—usually in multiple sittings—and so usually necessitate an alteration in the schedule for an entire school or school district. Moreover, the infrequent use of standardized tests makes their administration special to both teachers and students. With understanding and a high degree of cooperation, standardized test administration can be minimally disruptive. When teachers and students alike fail to understand the value of these tests, the level of disturbance increases accordingly.

Usability

COMPARING STANDARDIZED ACHIEVEMENT AND INTELLIGENCE TESTS

Is there really a difference between a standardized achievement test battery and an intelligence or mental ability test or is the difference more definitional than real? In this regard, Anastasi (1968) makes the following observation.

> It should now be apparent that all ability tests fall along a continuum with regard to their dependence upon specified prior experience. In this respect, traditional achievement tests, broad achievement tests, and intelligence tests differ only in degree.   (p. 485.)

Anastasi (1968) thus offers the concept of a continuum defined by the degree to which the skills measured by a test are based on a specific experience (that has usually been created to meet a set of objectives). A version of this continuum is shown in Figure 13.4.

Figure 13.4   *A Continuum of Ability Tests.*

Objective-based Achievement Tests	General Achievement Batteries	Group Verbal-type Mental Ability Tests	Individual Intelligence Tests	Nonlanguage and Performance Tests
TEACHER-BUILT TESTS	CALIFORNIA ACHIEVEMENT TESTS STANFORD ACHIEVEMENT TEST IOWA TESTS OF BASIC SKILLS	OTIS-LENNON MENTAL ABILITY TEST SHORT-FORM TEST OF ACADEMIC APTITUDE	STANFORD-BINET WECHSLER INTELLIGENCE SCALE FOR CHILDREN-REVISED (VERBAL)	WECHSLER INTELLIGENCE SCALE FOR CHILDREN-REVISED (PERFORMANCE) CULTURE FAIR TEST

As we move from the left end of the continuum characterized by teacher-built achievement tests to the right end characterized by the so-called culture-free intelligence tests, the experiences that the tests measure the effect of become less and less specific and identifiable (in which case the concept of appropriateness becomes less and less applicable and we move from edumetric tests to psychometric ones).

Coleman and Cureton (1954) have presented data to show that ". . . a group intelligence test and selected subtests from a school achievement battery measure substantially identical functions." (They argue that the terms "intelligence" and "achievement" are an instance of the "jangle fallacy," using two different words to make two situations that are the same seem different.) They found that the Otis Quick-Scoring Intelligence Test and Word Meaning, Paragraph Meaning, and Arithmetic Computation subtests of the Stanford Achievement Test (1954 edition) when given to sixth graders showed as high an interrelationship with one another as each did within itself (i.e., the reliability of each). Their calculations indicated a better than 80% overlap between scores on the two tests, suggesting that each may be a reflection of native capacity, school motivation, and effectiveness of instruction.

Levine (1958) describes a situation in which the Navy was trying to predict which recruits would be able to pass the electronics training program. By using both an electronics achievement test and the Navy General Classification Test (an aptitude or intelligence test) rather than just the latter alone it was possible to predict success more accurately. This suggests that the more specific achievement test measures something somewhat beyond what the more general aptitude or intelligence test measures.

However, Educational Testing Service (1960) reports a greater interrelationship between the aptitude tests of the Graduate Record Examination and the GRE achievement tests than between the different aptitude tests themselves. For example, the Verbal Aptitude score and scores on the Social Science or Humanities Achievement tests correlate above .70 while the scores on Verbal and Quantitative aptitudes have correlations under .50. This suggests that the verbal-mathematic distinction may be more pointed than the mental ability–achievement distinction.

Cronbach (1970) has also examined the relation between intelligence or aptitude and achievement tests and posits a "spectrum of ability tests" similar to Anastasi's. His continuum ranges from tests that reflect the most adaptation or transfer of learning, such as the nonverbal IQ tests, to tests that measure "crystallized achievements" resulting from direct training—achievement tests.

Cronbach (1970) also shows an analysis of the Lorge-Thorndike Verbal (LT-V) and Nonverbal (LT-NV) Intelligence Tests in terms of their overlap with achievement tests. He sees the LT-V as having 76% overlap with achievement tests and 15% distinctiveness while the LT-NV has 59% overlap and 29% distinctiveness.[4]

From all points of view it must be concluded that the difference between standardized achievement tests and intelligence tests is one of degree of specificity or reliance on specific prior learning. We must be careful in interpreting intelligence tests apart from considering past learning experience and we must be careful in interpreting standardized achievement tests apart from considering native capacity. Each test has similarities to and differences from the other.

ADMINISTERING A STANDARDIZED ACHIEVEMENT TEST

For very young children standardized achievement tests are given orally. Thereafter, except for the instructions, they are usually read by the student himself or herself. For all standardized tests, certain general rules can be established for administration.

    (1) *Familiarize yourself before the testing date with all instructions for administration.* This means reading the Teacher's

---

[4] The remaining 9% and 12% respectively are measurement errors.

Directions for Administering carefully and completely so that you know exactly what to do. For example, some standardized achievement test batteries come with practice tests that are to be given a few days before the actual testing. Had you not read the directions thoroughly you might not have known about this and hence might have overlooked it.

(2) *Make sure all students have everything they need to take the test and no more.* Students must have number 2 lead pencils, test booklets, and answer sheets. They should not have books or papers out other than scratch paper when allowed.

(3) *All information called for in the Pupil Information Box must be filled in by the student.* This information typically includes name, date of birth, grade level, sex, teacher, school. For younger students, the teacher is usually requested to fill in this information.

(4) *All test instructions, both general and specific, must be clearly given by the teacher to the students exactly as called for in the directions.* For example, students are told to mark only one answer for each item and to erase an answer completely if they decide to change it. Giving more or fewer instructions may cause variability in student performance and render the norms unusable for that testing.

(5) *Time limits must be adhered to exactly.* Standardized achievement tests are almost always timed tests. The test Directions tell you precisely how much time is allowed per test. Use a watch with a second hand to be sure that students start and stop each test exactly on time. If students complete a test ahead of time, they may not go on to the next test. If time runs out before they are finished, they must stop nevertheless.

(6) *Make sure that all students know how to take the test.* Answer any questions by reading again appropriate instructions. Make sure, particularly, that all students know how to mark their answer sheets.

(7) *Monitor the test taking from various points in the room.* Check that all students are following directions. Be available for questions about procedures.

(8) *Make sure the students take the testing seriously.* The students should not be frightened by testing but they must take it seriously. Teachers should prepare but not scare students by explaining its purposes to them in advance. They will be more likely to take it seriously if you take it seriously but calmly and positively. Give it the same importance as you would your own

final exam. Show that you feel the results will help students; do not show annoyance with the administration for wasting your time. The students will sense your feelings and will behave accordingly.

INTERPRETING STANDARDIZED ACHIEVEMENT TEST RESULTS

Standardized achievement test batteries may be scored by hand but they are usually scored by machine to save time and effort. Testing companies have available a wide variety of reporting forms or formats of which two are primarily used by the teacher: the individual test record and the class list. (Other forms and other applications of these forms are described in Chapter 15. Most of the concepts of measurement that will be used in this chapter have already been described in Chapter 11. The reader is urged to use this section in conjunction with Chapters 11 and 15.) A sample individual test record appears in Figure 13.5 (see also Figure 16.3) and a sample class list appears in Figure 13.6. Our discussion will focus on each of the kinds of scores reported and their interpretation.[5]

Raw Score. The raw score (RS) refers to the number of items the student got right on a particular test or subtest (No RT). This is sometimes reported along with the total number of items on that subtest (No POS). (Obviously if different subtests have different numbers of items, raw scores cannot be compared from subtest to subtest.) The raw score is a relatively meaningless piece of information for describing performance on a standardized achievement test.

Percentile Rank. A student's percentile rank (%ile or PR) is the percentage of students in the norm group (either national or local) that scored lower than he or she. It is usually computed as the percent with a lower raw score plus one half of those with the same raw score. If a student's raw score converts to a percentile rank of 70, this means that approximately 70% of the students in the norm group performed less well than he or she did. Thus, the

[5] The kinds of scores reported for the various standardized achievement test batteries tend to be about the same and the reporting forms tend to be similar. Additional reporting forms can be found in Chapter 15.

Figure 13.5 Sample Individual Test Record for the Comprehensive Tests of Basic Skills.*

⬡ CTBS

NAME ▶ THOMAS, BETTY TEACHER ▶ KELLY, L BATCH ▶ 1200
SCHOOL ▶ JEFFERSON GRADE ▶ 04.8 GROUP ▶ 004
CITY ▶ ASH GROVE DATE OF TESTING ▶ 05/74 RUN DATE ▶ 09/23/74

TEST	RS	OGE	AGE	DIFF	NP
READING VOCABULARY	35	8.3	8.3		96
READING COMPREHENSION	33	7.3	9.3		78
TOTAL READING	68	7.7	8.6		88
SPELLING	38	5.5	7.9		65
LANGUAGE MECHANICS	12	4.2	9.1	-4.9	43
LANGUAGE EXPRESSION	27	8.7	9.8		85
TOTAL LANGUAGE	77	6.3	9.0		70
MATHEMATICS COMPUTATION	39	7.0	6.4		93
MATHEMATICS CONCEPTS	19	7.7	8.1		87
MATHEMATICS APPLICATIONS	24	10.8	8.1	+2.7	99
TOTAL MATHEMATICS	82	7.8	7.2		96
TOTAL BATTERY	227	7.5	7.2	+3.1	90
REFERENCE SKILLS	19	11.7	8.6		99
SCIENCE	25	9.5	9.3		91
SOCIAL STUDIES	30	10.6	9.9		97

NATIONAL PERCENTILE: 1 2 5 10 20 30 40 50 60 70 80 90 95 98 99

READING VOCABULARY
RECOGNITION/TRANSLATION
RECALL OF SYNONYM

READING COMPREHENSION
RECOGNITION/APPLICATION — TRANSLATION (REWORDING, CONTEXT CLUES) — INTERPRETATION (LITERAL RECALL, DESCRIPTIVE WORDS, MAIN IDEA, CONCLUSIONS) — ANALYSIS (STRUCTURE/STYLE)

MATHEMATICS COMPUTATION
APPLICATION — ADDITION — SUBTRACTION — MULTIPLICATION — DIVISION

REFERENCE SKILLS
RECOGNITION/APPLICATION (PARTS OF A BOOK, DICTIONARY SKILLS, LIBRARY USE)

SCIENCE
RECOGNITION — CLASSIFICATION — QUANTIFICATION — INTERPRETATION OF DATA — PREDICTION FROM DATA — HYP. EVAL. & DESIGN ANA.

LANGUAGE MECHANICS
RECOGNITION/APPLICATION — PUNCTUATION — CAPITALIZATION

LANGUAGE EXPRESSION
RECOGNITION/APPLICATION — USAGE — TRANSLATION (DICTION) — INTERPRETATION (SYNTACTIC RELATION) — ANALYSIS (ORGANIZATION)

SPELLING
RECOGNITION/APPLICATION — RECALL OF RULE — TRANSLATION (CONTEXT CLUES)

MATHEMATICS CONCEPTS
RECOGNITION (GEOMETRY) — INTERPRETATION/ANALYSIS (NUMBER SYSTEMS, MEASUREMENT, PROBLEM SOLVING)

MATHEMATICS APPLICATIONS
INTERPRETATION (NUMBER SYSTEMS, MEASUREMENT) — PROBLEM SOLVING — ANALYSIS (PROBLEM SOLVING)

SOCIAL STUDIES
RECOGNITION — TRANSLATION — INTERPRETATION — APPLICATION — ANALYSIS

LEGEND
RS RAW SCORE
GE GRADE EQUIVALENT
SS SCALE SCORE
NP NATIONAL PERCENTILE RANK
AGE ANTICIPATED ACHIEVEMENT GRADE EQUIVALENT
AASS ANTICIPATED ACHIEVEMENT SCALE SCORE
DIFF DIFFERENCE BETWEEN OBTAINED AND ANTICIPATED SCORE WHEN SIGNIFICANT
LP LOCAL PERCENTILE RANK

Figure 13.6 Sample Class Analysis for the Stanford Achievement Test.*

STANFORD ACHIEVEMENT TEST — CLASS ANALYSIS for MISS L JONES

School SOUTH ELEMENTARY   System WESTERNER
Grade 3   Date of Testing 10/73
Level: PRIMARY 2   Form A   SAT: O-LMAT: ELEMENT 1 J
Page 1 of 2   Norms Used GRADE 3.2   GR 3 BEG
PART 1 OF 2   Process No. 000-0000-000

VOCABULARY

STANINE 9: Crew, Carrie; Nunez, Lupe; Thompson, Tom T; Wysong, Will U
STANINE 8: Alexis, Sue; House, Hannah H
STANINE 7: Early, James S; Franco, Carl L
STANINE 6: Day, Max; Stell, Dora
STANINE 5: Brown, Charli; Mann, Mary; Schlitz, Dot D; Yeates, Perciv P
STANINE 4: Green, Susan; Opton, Carol; Varney, Vic
STANINE 3: Luck, Tsung; Looney, Tom L; McKenna, Lou A

READING PART A

STANINE 9: Alexis, Sue; Crew, Carrie; Thompson, Tom T; Wysong, Will U
STANINE 8: Green, Susan; House, Hanna H; Nunez, Lupe
STANINE 7: Brown, Charli; Mann, Mary
STANINE 6: Day, Max; Early, James S; Franco, Carl L; Opton, Carol; Stell, Dora
STANINE 5: Luck, Tsung; Schlitz, Dot D; Yeates, Perciv P
STANINE 4: Klick, Tim E; McKenna, Lou A; Varney, Vic; Zak, Ivan

READING PART B

STANINE 9: Crew, Carrie; Nunez, Lupe; Wysong, Will U
STANINE 8: Day, Max; Early, James S; House, Hannah H; Mann, Mary; Thompson, Tom T
STANINE 7: NONE
STANINE 6: Alexis, Sue; Franco, Carl L; Green, Susan; McKenna, Lou A; Opton, Carol; Stell, Dora; Schlitz, Dot D; Varney, Vic
STANINE 5: Zak, Ivan; Luck, Tsung
STANINE 4: Tipton, Ted

READING COMP

STANINE 9: Crew, Carrie; Nunez, Lupe; Thompson, Tom T; Wysong, Will U
STANINE 8: House, Hannah H
STANINE 7: Alexis, Sue; Brown, Charli; Day, Max; Early, James S; Mann, Mary; Stell, Dora
STANINE 6: Franco, Carl L; Green, Susan; Opton, Carol; Varney, Vic; Yeates, Perciv P
STANINE 5: Luck, Tsung; McKenna, Lou A; Schlitz, Dot D
STANINE 4: Klick, Tim E; Tipton, Ted

WORD STUDY SKILLS

STANINE 9: Crew, Carrie; Thompson, Tom T; Wysong, Will U
STANINE 8: Alexis, Sue; Early, James S; House, Hannah
STANINE 7: Franco, Carl L; Nunez, Lupe
STANINE 6: Green, Susan; Mann, Mary; Opton, Carol; Schlitz, Dot D
STANINE 5: Brown, Charli; Day, Max; Luck, Tsung; Stell, Dora; Varney, Vic; Yeates, Perciv P
STANINE 4: McKenna, Lou A
STANINE 3: Klick, Tim E

LISTENING COMP

STANINE 9: Alexis, Sue; House, Hannah; Mann, Mary; Nunez, Lupe; Wysong, Will U
STANINE 8: Brown, Charli; Crew, Carrie; Thompson, Tom T
STANINE 7: Stell, Dora; Varney, Vic
STANINE 6: Opton, Carol; Parsons, Floyd; Yeates, Perciv P
STANINE 5: Day, Max; Early, James S; Franco, Carl L; Green, Susan
STANINE 4: Luck, Tsung; Schlitz, Dot D
STANINE 3: Looney, Tom L

* From *HBJ Service Reports* for: Stanford '73/Task '73, by Harcourt Brace Jovanovich, Inc. Reproduced by special permissi[on] the publisher.

percentile rank measures the student's standing on a particular subtest relative to a group of other students who have taken the test, the norm or comparison group. (Raw scores can be converted to percentile ranks using conversion tables that the test publishers provide. This is done for you if you use the computer scoring service.) It is useful to compare the percentile ranks that each student scores on a subtest relative to his or her scores on the other subtests to get a picture of the individual's strengths and weaknesses. (This comparison can be made even more directly among stanine scores.)

It is important to emphasize that the percentile rank reported by the test publisher represents *percentage of students with lower scores* and *not percentage of items answered correctly.* A percentile rank is a way of telling how well or poorly a student did relative to students in the norming group.[6]

Some test publishers also report a student's percentile rank for each subtest within a *percentile band*. The percentile band represents the *range* within which a student's true percentile rank is likely to be found. This range is computed by adding and subtracting one standard error of measurement (an indication of the variability in the test itself) to the actual percentile rank the student obtained. The individual test record shown in Figure 13.5 has a section labeled *National Percentile* where each subtest performance is represented by a series of X's. These X's stretch across the percentile band surrounding that student's percentile rank on each subtest. Where bands overlap from subtest to subtest, it is possible that the student's performances on those two subtests are not really different even though percentile ranks may differ by as many as 30 points. The less the bands overlap, the greater the likelihood that the differences between subtest performances are real differences as opposed to chance differences.

Stanine.   The stanine(s) is a STAndard score (i.e., a score based on the deviation of scores of the norming group from the mean and hence reflecting performance relative to that group) on a scale of NINE units. The scores may be interpreted on the following scale.[7]

---

[6] Test publishers provide supplementary technical information that describes their norming group membership. When achievement tests are revised (every 10–12 years), they are also renormed.

[7] See Figure 11.2 on page 284 for a stanine-percentile rank conversion table.

9—highest level	4—slightly below average
8—high level	3—well below average
7—well above average	2—low level
6—slightly above average	1—lowest level
5—average	

Grade Equivalents. Scores on standardized achievement test batteries are often given as grade equivalents (GE). The grade equivalent that corresponds to a particular raw score represents the year (i.e., grade level) and month of school of students who obtained that raw score as their median score (score obtained by the student in the middle of the distribution). If one of your fourth grade students, for example, got a grade equivalent of 5.4 on a sub-test, that would mean that among all the students in the norming group who were in the fourth month[8] of the fifth grade of school, the median score on the given subtest was the same as that obtained by your fourth grade student. We could say that in that particular area, your student was performing like an "average" student in the fourth month of the fifth grade. (Please refer to Chapter 11 for a more complete description of grade equivalent scores.)

It is important to note that a GE of 5.4 does not place your fourth grader at the same level as the fifth graders in your school on that subtest. It only tells you that he or she is performing at the same level as the fifth graders in the norming group or sample. In your school many students in all grades including fifth may be performing above grade level since grade equivalents are computed in terms of the entire norming group. Thus, your fourth graders may be performing above grade level and still be a year behind your fifth graders who are also performing above grade level.

It must be pointed out that norming groups are large, highly representative groups of students from schools throughout the country. Obviously, their representativeness is important since they represent the benchmark against which all test takers are compared. A weakness occurs when such norms get badly out-of-date, but renorming can solve that problem. The scores in your

[8] Recall that grade equivalents are computed on a 10-month (school) year while mental ages (see Chapter 12) are computed on a 12-month year. Also, grade equivalent scores, like mental ages, may be based on a single test administered during the year with the other nine points in that year being determined by interpolation or extrapolation.

school will not become part of the norm. The norm group is a distinct group chosen representatively for standardization purposes.[9]

Standard Score.   A standard score is one based on a given mean and standard deviation. Such standard scores, reported by some publishers, are useful for charting an individual student's growth or development on a given test or subtest over the course of his or her education. For purposes of comparing scores between subtests, however, stanines (normalized standard scores) are recommended.

Anticipated Achievement Score.   Some standardized achievement test batteries, when they are administered together with a mental ability or intelligence test, report an anticipated achievement grade equivalent.[10] The purpose of this score is to determine if a student is performing "up to ability." This grade equivalent score represents the mean grade equivalent of students in the norming group of the same age, sex, and intelligence (i.e., performance on the mental ability or intelligence test) as the student in question. It is an indication of how well a student is performing relative to others of the same intelligence. It can be used as a basis for interpreting grade equivalents by suggesting whether they might have been expected to be higher or lower based on the performance of students of like intelligence.[11]

Item Performance.   In addition to or instead of reporting scores (such as those described above), test results can be reported in terms of student performance on each individual item (as shown in Figure 13.5) along with the percentage (p) of students in the norming group and/or local sample getting each item right (as shown in Figure 13.9). This kind of reporting represents a transition between norm-referencing and criterion-referencing.

---

[9] The publishers of standardized achievement test batteries do not recommend contrasting a student's GE in one subtest with his or her GE in another (some, in fact, do not place much emphasis on GE's at all) for reasons given in Chapter 11. Percentile rank or stanine scores are better for this purpose as is another form of the standard score such as that described above.

[10] When the California Achievement Test or Comprehensive Tests of Basic Skills are given in conjunction with the Short Form Test of Academic Aptitude, for example, these scores are available.

[11] Caution must be exercised in using these scores because they may bias you to expect too much or too little from students. However, these scores do illustrate the use of intelligence tests results for predictive purposes.

Items responded to correctly are marked with a plus, those responded to incorrectly with a minus or the option number of the wrong choice. Given a content outline of the tests so that he or she knows the topic measured by each item, the teacher may attempt to use the results of the tests to determine individual and collective weaknesses. Teachers are cautioned not to attempt to make important educational decisions on the basis of single item results. Results from groups of items measuring the same or related objectives should be examined. (The question of uses of test results is discussed further in Chapter 15.)

CRITERION-REFERENCED ACHIEVEMENT TESTS

Most of the preceding discussion has focused on the interpretation of achievement test scores by comparing them to the scores already obtained by other students who constitute the *norming group*. We determine whether a score is low or high by contrasting it with scores obtained by students of the same grade level in the norming group. *Norm-referencing* is one of the essential ingredients of standardized tests (see pages 374–5).

   We have said that, at least *potentially*, teacher-built achievement tests are *criterion-referenced* because they are designed to measure the degree of proficiency attained on a given set of objectives. (Ironically, many teachers do not build their tests around specified objectives. Many even score their tests as if they were norm-referenced by basing their scoring on the relative performance of the test takers.) It is possible to score and interpret a test in terms of performance on objectives or items, which we will now consider.

Features of Criterion-referenced Tests

In norm-referenced tests the major concern is: How does the individual or group compare with others? Answers to this question are most useful in insuring a minimum level of relative performance in a class, school, or school district. Criterion-referenced tests, on the other hand, ask: In what way does the individual or group behave? What does he or she know? What does the group know? Thus, norm-referencing gives *summative* results, that is, it tells you where the individual or group is, while criterion-referencing gives you *formative* results, that is, it tells you in what areas to prescribe instruction in order to facilitate the achievement of proficiency. Criterion-referenced tests help the teacher to monitor student progress, diagnose strengths and weaknesses, and pre-scribe instruction.

While teachers can construct their own criterion-referenced tests, published versions give them a higher degree of quality control of the test instrument and potentially good reporting features. Teachers can then interpret the results in the light of their own instructional objectives.

It is possible to build a "standardized" achievement test that is criterion-referenced by altering only one of the three criteria described earlier in the chapter. You may recall that standardized achievement tests were said to possess three properties: (1) items that have been tried out, analyzed, and revised, (2) widspread and standard use and reuse, and (3) the availability and use of norms for interpretation. If we alter (3) to read: "the availability and use of objectives including criteria for evaluating proficiency for interpretation," we will have created the basis, at least definitionally, for a "standardized" achievement test that is criterion-referenced. (This also suggests a basis—altering the third property—for converting a norm-referenced test to a criterion-referenced one as illustrated in Box 13.1.)

Some Published Criterion-referenced Achievement Tests

The Prescriptive Mathematics Inventory (PMI) is built around a set of 345 behaviorally-stated objectives covering 36 topics in mathematics. The Inventory is available from the California Test Bureau/McGraw-Hill in three levels. The scoring report indicates those objectives on which proficiency has been attained. Rather than describing performance in an area by a single score, as is true of the achievement batteries previously described, this inventory describes performance on each objective, giving the teacher a profile of the student's mathematics achievement. Moreover, this test offers students a response format that does not limit them to four or five response alternatives. Unfortunately, proficiency on an objective on the PMI is based only on the performance of one item.

Another example is Houghton Mifflin's Individual Pupil Monitoring System in Reading (including study skills) and in Mathematics. Like the PMI, IPMS provides a lengthy, detailed set of measurably-stated objectives and a key indicating which item(s) measures which objective. Available in two forms for grades 1–6, IPMS comes with hand scoring procedures, and forms and instructions for monitoring and recording pupil achievement on each objective measured by the test. This provides the basis for a continuous system for monitoring the performance of individual students (and, as we shall see later, the performance of the class as a group). Testing systems such as IPMS combine the best features of standardized tests (e.g., high quality items, hence high reliability) with the best features of teacher-built tests (e.g., high appro-

---

Box 13.1

GETTING CRITERION-REFERENCED INFORMATION

The functional difference between a criterion-referenced (CR) and standardized or norm-referenced (NR) test is threefold:

(1) CR scores are specifically targeted to objectives while NR scores are more global; hence you get more scores from a CR test (because there is one score per objective) but there are fewer items per score;
(2) NR scores can be interpreted via norms that the publisher supplies while CR scores require you to set your own cutoff for "adequate proficiency";
(3) NR test items are written to produce maximal variability in performance across students while CR test items are written to represent the domain of the objective as the item writer sees it.

After examining these differences and knowing that NR test items are written using a content outline or skills classification (see Figure 13.1), it does not seem unreasonable to consider using a NR test as if it were a CR test provided that the publisher reports results by skill or content area. The large publishers will do this for many heretofore NR (or standardized) tests such as the Metropolitan Achievement Tests or Iowa Tests of Basic Skills.

CR interpretations of test results are likely to be more helpful to teachers than NR interpretations (see Chapter 15) but two points must be kept in mind. First, it is important that the skills and contents measured are specifically the ones you need information about and that there are a sufficient number of items per skill for reliability purposes. Second, since the items are written for maximum differentiation between high and low scorers, you may have to examine the scores of your students on the test to decide what cutoffs to use for adequate proficiency on each skill (rather than using a fixed cutoff). In a sense, this is still a form of norm-referencing because the choice of cutoff points would be based on the relative performance of students—for example, the number of items answered correctly by 70% of the students.

---

priateness). Teachers can use IPMS to create, in effect, their "own" tests, that is, tests that are appropriate to measure their own objectives and monitor student progress on them. A sample list of objectives on the IPMS Reading Test appears in Figure 13.7.

Another prescriptive, criterion-referenced achievement test currently available for grades 3–5 is the Harcourt Brace Jovanovich Skills Monitoring System (SMS) in Reading. Like the others, this system is designed to provide a basis for diagnosing the needs of individuals or, groups and to provide teacher support materials for prescriptive action to meet those needs. SMS is organized into "Skill Minis," each consisting of a single page and measuring a single objective in reading. Each is untimed and is both self-administered and self-scored. The self-scoring feature was included primarily to provide students with immediate feedback. Systems like SMS more readily help teachers to monitor achievement on their own objectives than do the norm-referenced batteries because of the presence of clearly stated objectives, multiple numbers of items per objective, and procedures for reporting results that focus on proficiency per objective. Such a modularized testing system can be adapted by teachers to fit their own needs.

Reporting Criterion-referenced Results   The print-out (Figure 13.8) of results from the PMI is called the Individual Diagnostic Matrix. The objectives are listed with abbreviated names in the left-hand boxes. The numbers alongside each box represent the numbers of the items that measure each objective. In an actual print-out, a plus is printed alongside the item number if the student answered correctly and a minus if he or she answered incorrectly.

Performance on standardized or norm-referenced tests can also be reported on a criterion-referenced basis by examining performance on specific items linked to (that is, appropriate for measuring) an objective or content category (see also Box 13.1).

A form for reporting criterion-referenced results on an otherwise norm-referenced test (the Stanford Achievement Test) appears in Figure 13.9. Not only does this form report individual performance on each objective (by pupil-reference number), it also reports class and school system performance and the proportion of students getting the item right in the national sample. This record enables the teacher to identify individual and class performance on each objective and to evaluate these results relative to school, system, and nation.

Some Sample Behavioral Objectives from the Individual Pupil Monitoring System for Reading, Word Attack Booklet, Level 5.*   **Figure 13.7**

PHONICS

CONSONANT IDENTIFICATION

501. Consonants, Beginning, Middle, & Ending — Blends & Digraphs: Identify a consonant blend (e.g. *str, mp*) or digraph (e.g. *ch, ng, tch*) that will complete an incomplete word in a sentence.

CONSONANT SUBSTITUTION

502. Consonants, Beginning, Middle, & Ending — Single, Blends, & Digraphs: Substitute a single consonant, blend (e.g. *str, mp*), or digraph (e.g. *ch, ng, tch*) for specified letters of a printed word, forming a different real word.

VOWELS

503. Vowel Combinations — Digraphs: Identify the correct phonetic pronunciation of a vowel combination in a word in which the two vowels have the long sound of the first vowel (e.g. *ea, ai, oa*).

504. Vowel Combinations — Diphthongs: Identify the vowel combination (*au, ou, oi, oy, aw, ow,* or *oo*) that will complete an incomplete word in a sentence.

505. *r*-, *w*-, and *l*- Controlled Vowels: Match a word that has an *r*-, *w*-, or *l*- controlled vowel to a word that has the same vowel sound.

506. Vowels, Short vs. Long: Identify the vowel sound as short or long in a printed word (vowel + final *e*, closed syllable, open syllable).

VARIANTS

507. Variant Consonant Sounds: Choose the correct stable consonant symbol that represents the sound made by a specified consonant in a word (*c* as *k* or *s*, *g* as *g* or *j* or *zh*, *ph* as *f*, *s* as *s* or *z* or *sh*, *ch* as *ch* or *k*, *ed* as *d* or *t*).

508. Silent Consonants: Identify the unsounded consonant in a word with the pattern *kn*, *st*, *mb*, *wr*, or *gn*.

509. Consonants + Vowels (Word-Blending): Identify the group of letters that will complete an incomplete word (e.g. *scr* + *eam* = *scream*).

* Reproduced by permission of Houghton Mifflin Company.

NAME ▶	STATE ▶	GRADE ▶
SCHOOL ▶	TEACHER ▶	
CITY ▶	DATE OF TESTING ▶	

OPERATIONS AND THEIR PROPERTIES		CONCEPT QUESTION	WHOLE NUMBERS				POSITIVE FRACTIONS				DECIMAL NUMBERS			
			+	−	×	÷	+	−	×	÷	+	−	×	÷
ADDITION — NO REGROUPING	NUMBER LINE	1	2	3	4	5								
	BASIC FACTS		14				PICTORIAL FRACTIONS			47				
							LIKE			51				
ADDITION — REGROUPING	2 DIGIT		15											
	3 DIGIT		16											
	4 DIGIT		17											
	5 DIGIT		18											
	COLUMN		19											

SUBTRACTION		WHOLE NUMBERS	POSITIVE FRACTIONS			
NO REGROUPING	BASIC FACTS	20	LIKE			57
REGROUPING	2 DIGIT	21				
	3 DIGIT	22				
	4 DIGIT	23				
	5 DIGIT	24				

MULTIPLICATION		WHOLE NUMBERS ×	WHOLE NUMBERS ÷	POSITIVE FRACTIONS
	MULT. AS REPEATED ADDITION	25		GCF 63
	MULT. IN ROWS AND COLUMNS	26		
	BASIC FACTS	27		
	1 DIGIT X 2 DIGIT	28		
	1 DIGIT X 3 DIGIT	29		
	1 DIGIT X 4 DIGIT	30		
	2 DIGIT X 2 DIGIT	31		
	2 DIGIT X 3 DIGIT	32		
	3 DIGIT X 3 DIGIT	33		
	3 DIGIT X 4 DIGIT	34		
	MULTIPLES OF TENS AND HUNDREDS	35	46	

DIVISION		WHOLE NUMBERS ×	WHOLE NUMBERS ÷
NO REMAINDERS	BASIC FACTS		37
REMAINDERS	3 DIGIT ÷ 1 DIGIT		38
	2 DIGIT ÷ 1 DIGIT		39
	3 DIGIT ÷ 1 DIGIT		40
	2 DIGIT ÷ 2 DIGIT		41
	3 DIGIT ÷ 2 DIGIT		42
	4 DIGIT ÷ 1 DIGIT		43
	4 DIGIT ÷ 2 DIGIT		44
MEAN (AVERAGE)		332	◄────► 332
ROUNDED NUMBERS (ESTIMATED)	129	130	131

PROPERTIES	Concept		
COMMUTATIVE	134		135
ASSOCIATIVE	143		144
DISTRIBUTIVE	152	◄──►	152
IDENTITY ELEMENT	157		158
INVERSE RELATION	166		167

Figure 13.8 *Individual Diagnostic Matrix, Level A for the Prescriptive Mathematics Inventory.**

	MATHEMATICAL SENTENCES	CONCEPT QUESTION	WHOLE NUMBER				POSITIVE FRACTIONS				DECIMAL NUMBERS			
			+	–	×	÷	+	–	×	÷	+	–	×	÷
MATHEMATICAL SENTENCES	NUMBER SEQUENCES	176	177	178	179	180	181	182						
	MISSING ADDENDS AND FACTORS		189	190	191									
	MULTIPLES, EVENS AND ODDS	207												
	INEQUALITIES	213												

MEASUREMENT	**METRIC GEOMETRY**	ESTIMATION	214												
		NON STANDARD UNITS	215												
		INCH, FOOT, YARD	223	224	225										
		TEMPERATURE	226												
		AREA	229												
		VOLUME	231												
		METRIC SYSTEM	219												
		GRAPHS	235												
	DENOMINATE NUMBERS	MONEY	236	237	238	239	240								
		LIQUID	241	242	243										
		WEIGHT	244												
		CLOCK	247												
		CALENDAR	250												

NON-METRIC GEOMETRY	POINTS	280												
	LINE, LINE SEGMENT	281												
	REGIONS	282												
	CIRCLES	283												
	SYMMETRY	284												
	PRISMS AND PYRAMIDS	286												
	RAY AND ANGLE	287												
	INTERSECTION	291												
	PARALLELS, PERPENDICULARS	292												
	POLYGON CLASSIFICATION	299												
	CARTESIAN COORDINATES	300												

SETS	PICTORIAL SETS	312												
	LISTING ELEMENTS	313												

NUMERATION SYSTEMS	**PLACE VALUE**	0 - 999	252												
		1,000 - 99,999	253												
		100,000 - 999,999,999	254												
	EXPANDED NOTATION	THREE DIGIT	257												
		FOUR DIGIT	258												
	ROMAN NUMERALS	I, V, X	260												
		L, C	261												
		D, M	262												

Miss Smythe
Hootville Elem
Hootville Sch Dist   Grade 3

National *p* Values - Grade 3.8

PUPIL REFERENCE NUMBERS FOR THIS REPORT		
01 Alexis	T J	05 Gustovson P H
02 Bastian	K B	06 Halverson B I
03 Bowles	C C	07 Merden C N
04 Browning	E C	08 Quarles T S

ITEM GROUPING: Instructional Objective	ITEM NO.	EXP. % COR.	RIGHTS DATA			
			CLASS Number	CLASS %	SCHOOL %	SYSTEM %
Number: The pupil						
chooses number which belongs in a given number series.	5	12	40*		49	51
ditto	7	5	17*		54*	52*
identifies number which is at a particular point on a number line.	18	10	33		38	35
represents whole number in terms of a specified fraction	20	14	47*		59	45*
identifies set consisting only of even numbers.	25	18	60		63	58
indicates position of a number relative to three given numbers.	27	8	27		37	35
determines point at which given number is located on number line.	31	20	67¤		53	68¤
adds in finite system of a clock module.	32	5	17*		62¤	47
ITEM GROUP MEAN P-VALUES			39		52	49
Notation: The pupil						
selects numeral for which digit in thousands place has greatest value.	1	24	95¤		83	87

Figure 13.9 *Report of Individual and Class Performance on the Stanford Achievement Tests Using Criterion-referenced Scoring and Interpretation.**

STANFORD Achievement Test or TEST OF ACADEMIC SKILLS

Scoring
Service

ITEM ANALYSIS

| Test | Math. Concepts | No. of Items | 32 | Item Format | All dictated |

Page 1 of 2 for this Class report.

NAT'L. p VALUE	OMITS DATA				CORRESP	PUPIL REFERENCE NUMBER 0000000001 1 1 1 1 / 1 2 3 4 5 6 7 8 9 0 1 2 3 4
	CLASS Number	%	SCHOOL %	SYSTEM %		
59	0	0	3	5		2 + + + 3 + 1
75	0	0	2	4		4 + 3 3 3 3 + 1
40	0	0	5	6		3 + 1 + 1 1 + 1
69	0	0	4	4		2 + + + 3 + + 1
56	0	0	3	5		2 3 4 + + + + 1
37	1	3	6	8		3 + 4 4 + 4 + 1
52	2	6	10	12		2 + 3 + + + + 1
38	20	67	6	8		3 0 0 0 0 0 + 1
53						
84	0	0	0	0		3 + 1 + 2 + + + 1

MEASURING ACHIEVEMENT IN A SELECTED AREA: READING

All published achievement testing is not restricted to the kinds of multiple achievement test batteries described throughout most of this chapter, although such batteries do represent the most prevalent form of achievement testing.

Consulting the table of contents in the *Mental Measurements Yearbook* (*MMY*) reveals that there are achievement tests in business education, English, fine arts, foreign languages, mathematics, agriculture, driver education, education, etiquette, handwriting, health and physical education, home economics, industrial arts, philosophy, psychology, religious education, reading, science, social studies, and specific vocations (e.g., engineering, nursing). Of all of the specific area achievement tests, perhaps the most widely used are tests of reading. In addition to published achievement tests, some reading textbooks are accompanied by their own tests.

Tests of Reading Achievement   Apart from the sections of the standardized achievement test batteries and prescriptive tests that measure reading achievement, there are standardized achievement tests that have been designed exclusively for the measurement of reading achievement and that often enable teacher and reading specialists to detect and characterize reading deficiencies. A few of the better known ones will be described.

Davis Reading Test (1960, 1961).   This reading test, available in two levels, grades 8–11 and grades 11–13, takes about one hour to administer. It serves the need for measuring reading skills among high school and junior and community college students. It yields two scores—level of comprehension and speed of comprehension. This test is easy to administer and easy to hand score. It is well standardized, has high levels of reliability, and shows high correlations with English grades. Reviewers are high in its praise (see the *MMY*). It is published by The Psychological Corporation.

Gates–MacGinitie Reading Tests (1965).   There is a series of three Gates-MacGinitie Reading Tests: the Primary Test (A, grade 1; B, grade 2; C, grade 3), Survey Tests (D, grades 4–6; E, grades 7–9; F, grades 10–11, and the Readiness Skills Test (grades K–1). The Primary contains two subtests, vocabulary and comprehension and takes 40 minutes to administer. (Form CS for grades 2–3 meas-

"I just learned to spell February—and now it's gone!"

ures speed and accuracy and takes only seven minutes to administer.) The Survey Tests have three subtests, vocabulary, comprehension, and speed and accuracy and take 45 minutes to administer. The Readiness Skills Test has eight subtests which are administered in four half-hour sessions. Primary and Survey Tests are available in machine scoring and hand scoring editions; the Readiness Skills Test is available in a hand scoring edition only. The primary value of these tests seems to be for the identification of specific reading deficiencies. Unlike many of the other reading tests, these include coverage for very young children including measuring readiness in kindergarteners and first graders. They are published by Teachers College Press and distributed by The Psychological Corporation.

Iowa Silent Reading Tests (1973). These are available at three levels: 1, grades 6–9; 2, grades 9–14; 3, grades 11 and up for accelerated students. Each provides scores for vocabulary, reading comprehension, and reading efficiency (this latter uniquely reflects on both speed and accuracy). Level 1 and 2 tests also provide a score for directed reading. Working time for Levels 1 and 2 is an hour and a half and for Level 3, an hour. These tests should work well for sixth graders on up with the reading efficiency score feature being an appealing one. Scoring reports include pupil profiles. The tests are published by Harcourt Brace Jovanovich.

Nelson-Denny Reading Test (1973).   This test is available at one level (in three forms) designed for grades 9–16 and adults. It is enjoying somewhat widespread use at the junior or community college level. It requires only 30 minutes of working time and measures vocabulary, reading comprehension, total reading score, and reading rate. This seems to be a good test with a clear applica-

Box 13.2

NEW DIRECTIONS IN SCHOOL ACHIEVEMENT TESTING

There are two new trends in school achievement testing. The first of these is called Statewide Assessment (a National Assessment program is also in operation) and is characterized by the administration of a common achievement battery on a statewide basis to chart the strengths and deficiencies of individual school districts. Students at various grade levels in the public schools of a state are tested on criterion-referenced achievement tests that have been developed specifically for this purpose. This program makes achievement testing part of a school district's overall self-evaluation and may ultimately provide part of the basis for allocating state aid to education.

The second new direction is an orientation toward the measurement of more varied, goal-related achievement beyond the general language, reading, math, social studies, science, and study skills measured by the commonly used batteries (e.g., Stanford Achievement Tests, California Achievement Tests). Many school districts are now engaged in setting their own district-wide goals and measuring their own students' achievement of these goals. These goals often include the acquisition of knowledge in such areas as health, ecology, fine and performing arts, occupations, and future trends. (See Figure 15.8 for an example of 18 differentiated district goals.)

---

tion for screening purposes. (There is now available a revised edition of the Nelson Reading Test suitable for grades 3–9 which can also be completed in a half an hour.) It is published by Houghton Mifflin.

Stanford Diagnostic Reading Test (1973). This test comes in two levels: Level 1 for grades 2-5–4-5, and Level 2 for grades 4-5–8-5. Both Levels have subtests in reading comprehension, vocabulary, syllabication, sound discrimination, and blending. Level 1 also has subtests in auditory discrimination and beginning and ending sounds while Level 2 has a rate of reading subtest. Most noteworthy about this test is that it utilizes the diagnostic-prescriptive approach. Diagnostic testing is concerned with in-depth coverage in a single curricular area—in this case, reading. The subtests are specific enough (seven for Level 1, six for Level 2) to enable teachers or reading specialists to identify individual student weaknesses in reading skills. Rather than trying to discover what a group of students know, this test helps uncover the specific skills on which each pupil needs help so that remediation can be prescribed. Testing time (not including administration time) for Level 1 is two hours and 17 minutes, for Level 2 and hour and a half, but neither need be taken in a single sitting. It is published by Harcourt Brace Jovanovich.

Additional Information Sources

Blanton, W., Farr, R., & Tuinman, J. J. *Reading tests for the secondary grades: A review and evaluation.* Newark, Del.: International Reading Assoc., 1972.

Buros, O. K. (Ed.). *Reading tests and reviews.* Highland Park, N.J.: Gryphon Press, 1968.

Coffman, W. E. Achievement tests. In R. L. Ebel (Ed.). *Encyclopedia of educational research,* 4th ed. N.Y.: Macmillan, 1969, pp. 7–17.

Educational Testing Service. *Anchor test study. Equivalence and norms tables for selected reading achievement tests (grades 4, 5, 6).* Wash. D.C.: U.S. Government Printing Office (stock #1780-01312), 1974.

Farr, R. & Anastasiow, N. *Tests of reading readiness and achievement: A review and evaluation.* Newark, Del.: International Reading Assoc., 1969.

Katz, M. *Selecting an achievement test: Principles and procedures,* 2nd ed. Princeton, N.J.: Educational Testing Service (Evaluation and Advisory Service Series, No. 3), 1961.

Myers, S. S. & Delon, F. G. *Mathematics tests available in the United States.* Wash. D.C.: National Council of Teachers of Mathematics, 1968.

Seibel, D. W. Measurement of aptitude and achievement. In D. K. Whitla (Ed.). *Handbook of measurement and assessment in behavioral sciences.* Reading, Mass.: Addison-Wesley, 1968, Chap. 8.

Self-test of Proficiency

(1) A statement or brief story is read aloud by the teacher. A question based on the story is then read aloud along with four answer choices. The student must identify the correct answer choice. This procedure is used on an achievement test to measure
   a. reading comprehension.
   b. word skills.
   c. language mechanics.
   d. listening comprehension.
   e. vocabulary.

(2) Many standardized tests measure three aspects of achievement in mathematics: computation, concepts, and applications. Below are three sample items. Which of the three aspects does each measure?
   a. You place $50 in a savings account that earns simple interest at the rate of 4½% per year. At the end of one year, your bank balance would be
      $52.50 $52.00 $52.75 $52.25
   b. $\sqrt{14} =$ 4.0   3.8   3.5   3.0
   c. 10^4 is   1,000   10,000   100,000   1,000,000

(3) Consider the comparison between a teacher-built achievement test, such as a mid-term, and a standardized achievement test. Which one of the five test criteria (i.e., appropriateness, validity, reliability, interpretability, usability) do you think most favors the teach-built test (at least ideally) and why?

(4) Continuing with the consideration in item 3, which of the five test criteria most favors the standardized achievement test and why?

(5) There is a clear and distinct separation between what an intelligence test measures and what an achievement test measures.
                    TRUE   FALSE

(6) Below are five categories of tests. Number them from 1 to 5 to indicate their place in a continuum with regard to dependence upon specified prior knowledge, with number 1 being the most dependent.
   a. group verbal-type mental ability tests
   b. individual intelligence tests
   c. general achievement batteries
   d. nonlanguage and performance tests
   e. objective-based achievement tests

(7) Cite two reasons why it is important to familiarize yourself with *all* instructions before administering a standardized test.

(8) In addition to familiarizing yourself with all instructions before administering a standardized test, list four other important rules to follow in test administration.

(9) Match the description on the right with the type of score on the left.

a. raw score

b. percentile rank

c. stanine

d. grade equivalent

e. standard achievement score

f. anticipated achievement score

g. item performance

i. one of nine-scale scores reflecting performance relative to a norming group.

ii. the number of items the student got right

iii. report of scores on each individual test item

iv. a score in standard deviation units that reflects the distance from the norming group mean

v. the percentage of students scoring lower

vi. the number of students who took the test

vii. a score based on the performance of students of the same age and IQ

viii. a score expressed as grade level of median norm group student who achieved it

(10) At the beginning of second grade, Deedie took a standardized achievement test in reading.

a. Each of the following represents a different type of score, that is, a different way of reporting Deedie's performance on the reading test. Label the type of score that each represents.

i. 2.7

ii. 85

iii. 61 right

iv. 1.5 S.D.

v. 7

b. Which word(s) below would you use to describe Deedie's performance?

i. highest level

ii. well above average

iii. lowest level

iv. average

v. slightly below average

(11) If you know that a student scored at the 90th percentile in mathematics, state one conclusion you could draw about the student's performance in mathematics and one conclusion you could not draw.

(12) Percentage figures are used in both criterion-referenced tests and in norm-referenced tsts. Describe the defference between performances reported as 85% on a criterion-referenced test and 85th percentile on a norm-referenced test.

(13) List three characteristics on which reading tests can differ.

(14) Using this book as a test reference source, identify
    a. a reading test that can be used at the junior college level.
    b. a reading test that can be used in kindergarten.
    c. a reading test that can be used for sixth graders.

chapter fourteen / Measuring Interests, Attitudes, and Personality Orientation

OBJECTIVES

1. Distinguish among the following tests of interests and career-related orientations in terms of what each measures and how it measures it: *a*. Strong Vocational Interest Blank, *b*. Kuder General Interest Survey, *c*. Ohio Vocational Interest Survey, *d*. Self-directed Search, and *e*. Career Maturity Inventory.

2. Distinguish between attitudes toward self and school, and their measurements, by the *a*. Tennessee Self-concept Scale, *b*. Self-appraisal Inventory, and *c*. School Sentiment Index.

3. Identify measurement for the concepts of personality, adjustment, needs, and values by means of tests, namely: *a*. California Psychological Inventory, *b*. California Test of Personality, *c*. Edwards Personal Preference Schedule, *d*. Scale of Values, and *e*. Embedded Figures Test.

4. State potential uses for affective measures.

MEASURING INTERESTS AND CAREER ORIENTATION

It is not uncommon for guidance counselors to administer measures of interests and career orientation to students. Such information is useful for students in making educational and career decisions and for counselors, teachers, and parents in assisting the decision-making process. It is important in interpreting these tests that we know what they measure and how they measure it. This section will describe the more commonly used tests.

The tests described in this section should also be viewed from the perspective of career education and its many efforts across the country to assist students in choosing and preparing for careers. Certainly, interest testing can be considered an important component of the process of gaining self- and ultimately career-awareness.

The Strong Vocational Interest Blank (SVIB)[1]

In the area of interest testing the Strong has been as much a landmark as the Stanford-Binet in intelligence testing (Cronbach, 1970). Considered one of the most thoroughly studied and understood test instruments in existence, it was first published in 1927; its current revision (1974) is called the Strong-Campbell Interest Inventory. Although originally designed for use with college students and adults employed in professions and in business, studies (Carter, 1940; Strong, 1943) have shown that the test can be used with persons as young as 14 or 15 years of age and that Strong scores are rather well fixed between the ages of 18 to 20. Originally, separate forms, similarly structured, were used for men and women but in the new Strong-Campbell edition, these forms have been merged into a single one.

Content. The new SVIB Form contains 325 items grouped by the type of content. The seven content areas are:

occupations (131 items)
school subjects (36 items)
activities (51 items)
amusements (e.g., games, sports; 39 items)
types of people (i.e., personal traits; 24 items)
preference between two activities (30 items)
your characteristics (14 items)

[1] The Strong-Campbell Form (SCII) of the SVIB, the Manual for the SVIB-SCII, and The Handbook for the SVIB are all published by Stanford University Press.

The student marks each item according to whether he or she would like doing it, would dislike doing it, or is indifferent to it. The test is untimed but about an hour should be allowed for its administration. An example of one item for each content area patterned after those on the SVIB appear below.

	Like	Indifferent	Dislike
Jazz musician			
History			
Giving a lecture			
Playing backgammon			
People who travel			
Going to a basketball game vs. going to a museum	*Prefer*	*Neutral*	*Prefer*
(I) can put other people at ease	*Yes*	*?*	*No*

Scoring. The essence of understanding the Strong is understanding the manner in which it is scored. The scoring procedure is called *criterion keying* and compares the student's response pattern to the response pattern of people in a variety of occupations to see which one he or she is closest to. *The answer the student gives to each item is assigned a weight based on the degree to which the answers of men, women, or people in a given occupation differ from those of men-, women-, or people-in-general.* Scoring for the first item ("Actor, Actress") on the Strong Blank for the "engineer" key using male norms appears in Figure 14.1.

Figure 14.1   *Determination of Weights in Strong Vocational Interest Blank Item #1 "Actor/Actress" on Male Norms.**

GROUP	% LIKE	% INDIFFERENT	% DISLIKE
Engineers	9	31	60
Men (Gen'l)	21	32	47
Difference	−12	−1	13
Weight	−1	0	1

* Edward K. Strong. Reprinted by permission of Stanford University Press.

You can see from Figure 14.1 that male engineers like the occupation "actor, actress" less and dislike it more than men-in-general. In scoring the SVIB of a young man who thinks he wants to be an engineer, but who indicates on item 1 that he would *like* to be an actor, one point would be deducted from his engineering score (based on a weight of −1). He has shown on this item that he is more like other men than like male engineers. If he said he was *indifferent* to the acting profession on item 1, he would neither gain nor lose a point on his engineering score (weight=0). If he said he *disliked* "actor or actress" (which agrees with 60% of the engineers), his engineering score would gain a point (weight=1). Note that engineers' dislike for the acting profession exceeds that of men-in-general by 13%.[2]

A student's total score for a given occupation such as engineer is computed by adding the weights based on the correspondence between the student's responses and the responses of same sex engineers on each of the 325 items. The results tell the student how closely his or her likes and dislikes resemble those of a sample of professional engineers of the same sex as the student. The procedure would be repeated, that is, each of the 325 items would be scored again in order to get the total score for another occupation or for another reference group (e.g., women). Each occupation score is based on a different occupational sample and hence each scoring key has its own weights. (Since the SVIB can be scored for 124 occupations, the necessity for machine scoring is obvious.)

The SVIB makes no assumptions about men or women in the different occupations. *It relies entirely on responses to the test items to define the likes and dislikes of satisfied people in each occupation.* The weights are *not* based on expectations and preconceptions but on actual responses of people, and a student's inclination toward a particular job based on how similarly he or she responds to people of the same sex in that job. Naturally, much depends on how representative the criterion sample group is, and some question has been raised about whether the chosen sample of people is truly like the majority of successful people in their respective fields (Super and Crites, 1962). However, scoring keys for occupations not included in previous forms have been added, and old ones updated on the 1974 revision.

Correlations between scores on the SVIB and intelligence test scores vary from one occupational-SVIB score to another. Correlations between intelligence and scores on the SVIB "psychologist"

[2] We could obtain a score on our hypothetical young man by comparing his responses to those of a general reference group. For a young woman, both a general reference group and women as specific reference group would be used as a normative source. While both sexes use the same test form and profile report form, separate norms by sex as well as combined norms are used to interpret scores on the SVIB-SCII. Separate norms are used to reflect male–female differences in reported interests.

key, for example, are as high positive as .43 while intelligence test correlations with scores on the SVIB "vacuum cleaner salesperson" key are as high negative as $-.40$ (Strong, 1943). The manual reports split-half reliability coefficients averaging .88 for college seniors while D. P. Campbell (1966a,b) reports a 22-year retest correlation of .67 for college seniors. Considerable fluctuations in interest profiles are found for students below age 17 or 18 on the SVIB (and on the Kuder General Interest Survey, described next; Crites, 1969).

Application.   A sample profile form for reporting results on the 124 occupational scales appears in Figure 14.2. The 1974 Strong-Campbell also reports results on John Holland's six personality types (called "general occupational themes" here) as described on page 420 in conjunction with the self-directed search. In addition, scores on 23 "basic interest scales" are reported (also in conjunction with Holland's typology), enabling students to link their interests with more general occupational areas (e.g., "medical science").

In using the SVIB-SCII, the counselor would be wise to heed the advice of Darley and Haganah (1955) to base interpretations on patterns (as would be reported in Figure 14.2 and the other profile form on occupational themes and areas) rather than on particular occupational keys.

Kuder General Interest Survey-Form E   First published in 1939 as the Kuder Preference Record-Vocational and revised in 1964 as the Kuder Form E General Interest Survey, the Kuder is used with high school students, college students, and adults, of both sexes.[3] It is published by Science Research Associates. Stefflre (1947) determined the vocabulary level of the old Kuder to be two years lower than the Strong, suggesting that it can be used with the more able eighth graders and certainly with ninth and tenth graders. Malcolm (1950), in comparing earlier forms of the tests, found that the Kuder was preferred to the Strong for both sexes at the high school level because it seemed to lead to a greater understanding of interests.

One shortcoming of the Kuder is its susceptibility to faking, that is, consciously and knowingly distorting responses. This is

---

[3] The Kuder Form DD Occupational Interest Survey was first published in 1956 and revised in 1970. This test is more like the SVIB in scoring (it also uses criterion-keying) than like the Kuder Form E General Interest Survey. The Kuder Form DD is less widely used than is the Kuder Form E; Form DD will not be described in this book.

Occupational Scales

Code	Scale	Sex Norm	Std Score	Very Dissimilar	Dissimilar	Ave	Similar	Very Similar
RC	FARMER	m						
RC	INSTRUM. ASSEMBL.	f						
RCE	VOC. AGRIC. TCHR.	m						
REC	DIETITIAN	m						
RES	POLICE OFFICER	m						
RSE	HWY. PATROL OFF.	m						
RE	ARMY OFFICER	f						
RS	PHYS. ED. TEACHER	f						
R	SKILLED CRAFTS	m						
RI	FORESTER	m						
RI	RAD. TECH. (X-RAY)	f						
RI	MERCH. MAR. OFF.	m						
RI	NAVY OFFICER	m						
RI	NURSE, REGISTERED	m						
RI	VETERINARIAN	m		15	25	45	55	
RIC	CARTOGRAPHER	m						
RIC	ARMY OFFICER	m						
RIE	AIR FORCE OFFICER	m						
RIA	OCCUP. THERAPIST	f						
IR	ENGINEER	f						
IR	ENGINEER	m						
IR	CHEMIST	f						
IR	PHYSICAL SCIENTIST	m						
IR	MEDICAL TECH.	f						
IR	PHARMACIST	f						
IR	DENTIST	f						
IR	DENTIST	m		15	25	45	55	
IR	DENTAL HYGIENIST	f						
IRS	PHYS. THERAPIST	f						
IRS	PHYSICIAN	m						
IRS	MATH-SCI. TEACHER	m						
ICR	MATH-SCI. TEACHER	f						
IC	DIETITIAN	f						
IRC	MEDICAL TECH.	m						
IRC	OPTOMETRIST	m						
IRC	COMPUTER PROGR.	f						
IRC	COMPUTER PROGR.	m						
I	MATHEMATICIAN	f						
I	MATHEMATICIAN	m		15	25	45	55	
I	PHYSICIST	f						
I	BIOLOGIST	m						
I	VETERINARIAN	f						
I	OPTOMETRIST	f						
I	PHYSICIAN	f						
I	SOCIAL SCIENTIST	m						
IA	COLLEGE PROFESSOR	f						
IA	COLLEGE PROFESSOR	m						
IS	SPEECH PATHOL.	f						
IS	SPEECH PATHOL.	m						
IAS	PSYCHOLOGIST	f						
IAS	PSYCHOLOGIST	m		15	25	45	55	
IA	LANGUAGE INTERPR.	f						
ARI	ARCHITECT	m						
A	ADVERTISING EXEC.	f						
A	ARTIST	f						
A	ARTIST	m						
A	ART TEACHER	f						
A	PHOTOGRAPHER	m						
A	MUSICIAN	f						
A	MUSICIAN	m						
A	ENTERTAINER	f						
AE	INT. DECORATOR	f						

Code	Scale	Sex Norm	Std Score	Very Dissimilar	Dissimilar	Ave	Similar	Very Similar
AE	INT. DECORATOR	m						
AE	ADVERTISING EXEC.	m						
A	LANGUAGE TEACHER	f						
A	LIBRARIAN	f						
A	LIBRARIAN	m						
A	REPORTER	f						
A	REPORTER	m						
AS	ENGLISH TEACHER	f						
AS	ENGLISH TEACHER	m						
SI	NURSE, REGISTERED	f						
SIR	PHYS. THERAPIST	m						
SRC	NURSE, LIC. PRACT.	m						
S	SOCIAL WORKER	f						
S	SOCIAL WORKER	m						
S	PRIEST	m		15	25	45	55	
S	DIR., CHRISTIAN ED.	m						
SE	YWCA STAFF	f						
SIE	MINISTER	m						
SEA	ELEM. TEACHER	m						
SC	ELEM. TEACHER	f						
SCE	SCH. SUPERINTEND.	m						
SCE	PUBLIC ADMINISTR.	m						
SCE	GUIDANCE COUNS.	m						
SER	RECREATION LEADER	f						
SEC	RECREATION LEADER	m						
SEC	GUIDANCE COUNS.	f						
SEC	SOC. SCI. TEACHER	f		15	25	45	55	
SEC	SOC. SCI. TEACHER	m						
SEC	PERSONNEL DIR.	m						
ESC	DEPT. STORE MGR.	m						
ESC	HOME ECON. TCHR.	f						
ESA	FLIGHT ATTENDANT	f						
ES	CH. OF COMM. EXEC.	m						
ES	SALES MANAGER	m						
ES	LIFE INS. AGENT	m						
E	LIFE INS. AGENT	f						
E	LAWYER	f						
E	LAWYER	m						
EI	COMPUTER SALES	m		15	25	45	55	
EI	INVESTM. FUND MGR.	m						
EIC	PHARMACIST	m						
EC	BUYER	f						
ECS	BUYER	m						
ECS	CREDIT MANAGER	m						
ECS	FUNERAL DIRECTOR	m						
ECR	REALTOR	m						
ERC	AGRIBUSINESS MGR.	m						
ERC	PURCHASING AGENT	m						
ESR	CHIROPRACTOR	m						
CE	ACCOUNTANT	m						
CE	BANKER	f		15	25	45	55	
CE	BANKER	m						
CE	CREDIT MANAGER	f						
CE	DEPT. STORE SALES	f						
CE	BUSINESS ED. TCHR.	f						
CES	BUSINESS ED. TCHR.	m						
CSE	EXEC. HOUSEKEEPER	f						
C	ACCOUNTANT	f						
C	SECRETARY	f						
CR	DENTAL ASSISTANT	f						
CRI	NURSE, LIC. PRACT.	f						
CRE	BEAUTICIAN	f						

Sample Profile Form for Reporting Occupational Scale Results on the Strong Vocational Interest Inventory.*   **Figure 14.2**

* Reprinted with permission of the publisher from the Profile for the *Strong-Campbell Interest Inventory*, Form T325 of the Strong Vocational Interest Blank, by Edward K. Strong, Jr. and David P. Campbell (Stanford: Stanford University Press, 1974).

particularly true when the scale is used in conjunction with job screening (Heron, 1956). However, when used with high school students for their own counseling benefit, faking is much less likely to occur. Mallinson and Crumrine (1952) report data from high school students tested in the ninth grade and retested in the twelfth grade that suggests that Kuder interests are stable enough to afford a basis for prediction in counseling, yet changeable enough to allow for suitable modification through counseling.[4]

Content.   The Kuder-E contains 168 items that assess interest in a total of 10 different interest areas. Each item consists of three choices of activities of which the student must indicate the one he or she *likes best* (which he or she marks as his or her first choice) and the one he or she *likes least* (which he or she marks as his or her third choice). The activities in each item are written to tap three different types of interest. Consider the illustrative item below.

Build bird houses
Write articles about birds
Draw sketches of birds

The first choice taps mechanical interest, the second *literary* interest, and the third *artistic* interest. The other interest areas are *outdoor, computational, scientific, persuasive, musical, social service*, and *clerical*.

There is no time limit on the test; it takes students from 45 minutes to one hour. Answers are indicated by punching holes in the designated spot with a pin. Machine scoring forms are also available.

Scoring.   Students can score their own tests, convert the scores to percentiles, and plot the results graphically. With the Kuder, one examines the relative strength of each of 10 different interests within an individual, while in the Strong comparisons are all with groups of individuals classified by occupations. Unlike the Strong, Kuder scores are not generated by matching responses directly with occupations nor are profiles evaluated in contrast to those from occupational groups. Item choices in the Kuder are grouped to form ten interest-type scales based on a combination of face validity considerations (which of the 10 types each choice

---

[4] It must be pointed out that all self-report measures have a high susceptibility to faking. The Kuder-E includes a Verification (V) scale to determine whether the respondent has answered sincerely.

"Now, the trick is to pick a profession that won't be obsolete when you're ready to enter it."

seems to fit) and item analysis of the responses of sample students (a correlational procedure that helps to identify item choice combinations that are internally consistent with one another and distinct from other clusters). Thus, each item choice can be predesignated to fit a single interest-type that students choose within the forced-choice format. Numbers of choices per interest-type are then counted to provide 10 raw scores that can be converted to percentiles based on large samples of high school students. While the Strong scoring was referred to as criterion-keying (comparing a choice to a criterion group), Kuder scoring is best described as *item cluster tallying*—wherein the number of choices per cluster is counted and compared.

Application.   A sample Kuder profile appears in Figure 14.3. It is used as a basis for interpreting the pattern of a student's interests and recommending career directions that are consistent with that interest pattern. To aid the interpretation process, recent editions of the manual have provided occupational profiles, supplemented by curricular norms in a number of different fields, obtained by administering the Kuder to sample groups employed in different occupations and determining the collective or group profile of each. These profiles illustrate how different occupational and curricular groups respond to the Kuder items and the patterns on the 10 interest clusters that they generate. This represents

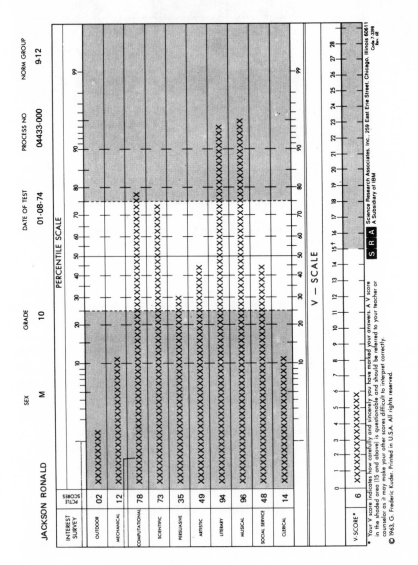

Figure 14.3   *A Sample Kuder Profile.**

* From the Profile Form of Kuder General Interest Profile-Form E. Copyright 1963 by G. Frederic Kuder. Reprinted with permission of the publisher, Science Research Associates, Inc.

movement in the direction of occupational keying—but on scores for entire scales rather than on individual items as is true for the Strong.

In terms of internal reliabilities, the Kuder has been found to be as reliable as the Strong. Test-retest reliabilities on the Kuder-E range from the low .70s to low .90s. Correlations between specific occupationally keyed scores on the Strong and interest cluster scores on the Kuder (earlier versions of both tests) range from .25 to .73 (Triggs, 1944). For example, office worker and computational interest scores correlate .25 while chemist and scientific interest scores correlate .73.

The OVIS was designed specifically for use by high school coun- **Ohio Vocational** selors and their students in making career decisions. It first ap- **Interest Survey** peared in 1966 and was standardized in 1969. It is published by **(OVIS)** Harcourt Brace Jovanovich. In some ways, as we shall see, it is similar to the Strong and in some ways similar to the Kuder and in some ways different from each. It is based conceptually on a system used in the *Dictionary of Occupational Titles* (*DOT*) for classifying occupations in terms of the extent to which an occupation involves data, people, or things. Its authors (D'Costa and Winefordner, 1969) call this the cubistic model.

Content. The *DOT* has classified 21,741 jobs according to their Data-People-Things involvement and grouped them into 114 homogeneous areas or "worker trait groups." From these groups, the authors of the OVIS developed 24 interest scales, each of which is assigned a three-digit designation. The first digit reflects involvement of the occupational group measured by the scale with data, the second with people, the third with things. Degree of involvement can range from a low of 0 to a high of 2.[5]

Some of these occupational interest categories and the model they fit into are illustrated in Figure 14.4.

---

[5] The 24 OVIS scales and their three-digit numbers are as follows: manual work (001), machine work (002), personal services (010), caring for people or animals (011), clerical work (100), inspecting and testing (101), crafts and precise operations (102), customer services (110), nursing and related technical services (111), skilled personal services (112), training (120), literary (200), numerical (200), appraisal (201), agriculture (202), applied technology (202), promotion and communication (210), management and supervision (210), artistic (212), sales representative (212), music (220), entertainment and performing arts (220), teaching, counseling, and social work (220), and medical (222).

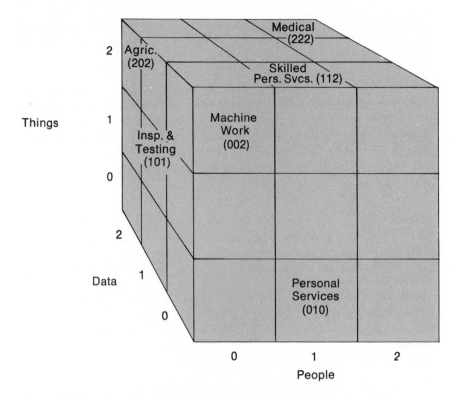

Figure 14.4   *The Cubistic Model of Vocational Interests and the Location of Some Sample OVIS Scales.**

* Adapted from the OVIS Manual for Interpreting, copyright © 1969, Harcourt Brace Jovanovich, Inc. Adapted by permission of the publisher.

Each of the 24 scales on the OVIS contains 11 items. Like the Kuder, the items represent activities for the student to respond to but, unlike the Kuder, the items appear singly rather than in groups of three. Students use the five-point scale, *like very much—like—neutral—dislike—dislike very much*, to react to each item. (This response scale is similar to that used on the Strong with the addition of the two extreme categories.) Some items like those on the OVIS are offered below for illustrative purposes.

- Repair tables and chairs
- Write programs for a computer
- Read books and magazines to sick people
- Make drawings for children's readers
- Raise vegetables

Scoring.   In most respects scoring the OVIS is similar to scoring the Kuder. The items on the OVIS are grouped into scales as they are on the Kuder. The determination of which items belong to which scale was based originally on *DOT* Descriptions (that is, of traits that seemed to fit each scale). Item analysis was then done to assure that items on the same scale were internally consistent with one another and different from items on other scales. Based on the student's responses, he or she gets one score for each of the 24 scales (on the Kuder it is one score for each of 10 scales) reflecting liking and disliking of activities that fit on that scale. These scores are presented as raw scores and as percentiles, the latter based on a large standardization sample. The five response alternatives are scored 1 to 5 with 5 being the most positive. Agreement with all 11 items on a scale yields a raw score of 55, agreement with none yields a raw score of 11.

While the OVIS is scored like the Kuder, it differs from the Kuder in that its scores, like the Strong, relate *directly* to occupations rather than to orientations like the Kuder. Moreover, by relating to occupational clusters taken from the *DOT*, OVIS scores tell a student something about his or her orientation to an entire group of occupations that share a common relationship to data, people, and things.

Application.   Results on the OVIS reflect an individual's relative interests in different occupations; they also reflect his or her interest in each occupation relative to the interest in that occupation by members of the norming group. This information can be used to lead into a program of career awareness. By "following" scores into the *DOT* with its detailed listing of occupational information and orientations, the student can explore his or her tested interests and relate them to the specifics of occupations. The OVIS can be used with students at grade levels as low as the eighth with adequate reliability. Moreover, the OVIS clearly attempts to span the entire occupational spectrum rather than restricting itself to those occupations usually associated with a college education.

This self-assessment kit was developed by John L. Holland of the Johns Hopkins University Center for Social Organization of Schools. It is published by Consulting Psychologists Press. It is intended to help students discover occupations that they are best suited for by providing them with a description of their own personality orientation and with a handbook of classified careers.   **Self-directed Search (SDS)**

Content.   The student first fills out the *assessment booklet*, which contains sections dealing with Occupational Daydreams, Activities, Competencies, Occupations, and Self-estimates. In these sections he or she must rate activities, competencies, occupations, and self-estimates.

Scoring.   Scoring is done in terms of Holland's six personality types—Realistic, Investigative, Artistic, Social, Enterprising, and Conventional—which form the basis for his theory of vocational choice. Based on the self-scoring procedure, each student who takes the "test" gets a three letter summary score indicating his or her personality tendencies and their relative strength. For example, a student might be scored **SEC**: social-enterprising-conventional.

Once students have completed their self-assessments, they are ready to match themselves to jobs. The SDS comes with an Occupation Finder—a listing of 431 occupational titles representing 95% of the labor force. Moreover, each of these occupations has been classified in terms of the personality it seems to require using the same classification system as that used in the assessment booklet for the students to describe themselves. In addition, the Occupations Finder gives other pertinent information about the jobs it classifies.

Application.   Students seem to enjoy taking the SDS and are not typically frightened by it as they are by other "tests" because they give it to themselves, score it themselves, and usually interpret it themselves.

Career Maturity Inventory (CMI)   The CMI was developed by John Crites to measure the maturity of attitudes and competencies that are critical in career decision making. It is published by the California Test Bureau/McGraw-Hill. Presumably, a person's readiness to make a career decision increases as he or she grows older, particularly if life experiences are provided to enhance this readiness. As schools introduce relevant programs like career education, the measurement of career maturity becomes important.

Content.   The CMI Attitude Scale contains 50 true–false response attitude statements that fit the following five attitudinal clusters: (1) the involvement of the student in the career choice process (e.g., "I'm not going to worry about choosing an occupation until I'm out of school"),[6] (2) the student's orientation toward work (meaningful or drudgery; e.g., "Work is dull and unpleasant"), (3) the student's independence in decision making (e.g., "I plan to follow the line of work my parents suggest), (4) the student's preference for career choice factors (e.g., "You should choose a job that allows you to do what you believe in"), and (5) the student's conceptions of the career choice process (e.g., "You get into an occupation mostly by chance").

The CMI Competence Test measures cognitive variables involved in choosing an occupation. These are: (1) how well the student can appraise his or her job-related strengths and weaknesses (*Self-Appraisal—Part 1: Knowing Yourself*), (2) how much he or she knows about the world of work (*Occupational Information—Part 2: Knowing about Jobs*), (3) how adept he or she is in matching personal characteristics with occupational requirements (*Goal Selection—Part 3: Choosing a Job*), (4) how foresightful he or she is in planning for a career (*Planning—Part 4: Looking Ahead*), and (5) how effectively he or she can cope with the problems that arise in the course of career development (*Problem Solving—Part 5: What Should They Do?*) A sample from the 100 competence items appears below[7] (from **Part 1**).

> Ollie has enjoyed drawing pictures at home. He hangs them in his room and shows them to his friends. His parents have praised his work, but he was disappointed that none of his drawings from the art class at school were chosen for an exhibit. His art teacher told him they were not as good as those of the other students.

What do you think?
>   *a.* His art teacher is the best judge.
>   *b.* He should get somebody else's opinion.
>   *c.* His parents know him better than his art teacher.
>   *d.* He likes to draw, so he's probably good at it too.
>   *e.* Don't know.

The Attitude Scale is estimated to take 30 minutes and the Competence Test 20 minutes per part.

---

[6] These and other illustrations are actual items from the CMI. Reproduced by permission of the publisher, CTB/McGraw-Hill, Monterey, CA 93940. Copyright © 1973 by McGraw-Hill, Inc.
[7] Items were designed to be readable by sixth graders.

Answer

b.

Scoring.   Scores on the CMI are presented on a *career matur-ity profile* which provides *a*. raw score, *b*. percentile score, and *c*. right response record for the Attitude Scale and for each of the five parts of the Competence Test. (Other types of summary reports are also available.) Percentile scores are based on a lim-ited, somewhat localized norming group or standardization sample (particularly in the case of the Competence Test) but additional norms are promised for the future.

Application.   The CMI is still in its early and experimental form, and there is much to be learned about its properties. Work on its validity and reliability is still pending.

Its author, John Crites, has done considerable research on vocational development and career maturity. Based on the Career Pattern Study (Super, Crites et al., 1957), a model of career maturity in adolescence was formulated (Crites, 1971). This model identified career competence and attitudes as two of four factors contributing to career development (the others being consistency and realism of career choices).

Used in conjunction with the school guidance program or a teacher-involved program of career education, the CMI can provide useful information for diagnosing individual developmental needs. Until its validity and reliability have been established, results must be interpreted cautiously. Users in particular must gain a "feel" for the concepts of career maturity embodied in the test.

USING EXISTING SCALES TO MEASURE ATTITUDES

There are many different types of attitudes and many different tests available for measuring them. Although many of the attitude scales are taken by teachers and administrators rather than admin-istered by them, we shall focus here on attitude scales that teach-ers administer to students.

Specifically, we will examine tests of two types of attitudes: (1) attitudes toward self and (2) attitudes toward school. Tests of self-attitude will be described first.

Attitudes toward Self   Attitudes toward self are referred to by a variety of terms includ-ing self-appraisal, self-concept, self-esteem, self-image, and self-worth. It is likely that the way a student performs in school affects how he or she feels about himself or herself, and that how he or she feels about himself or herself affects the way he or she performs in school (Tuckman and Bierman, 1971). Moreover, many school systems, programs, and teachers consider the enhancement of a student's self-image to be one of the general goals of education. There are some students whose self-image tends to be particularly negative—the "disadvantaged" or "deprived" (Tuckman, 1969)—in their case, the improvement of self-image becomes a particularly important objective of the educational process.

Attitudes like self-image fall into the *affective domain* (discussed in Chapter 6) and measurement in this area is not as well-developed nor as widespread in use as measurement in cognitive areas. This is partly because of measurement difficulties (such as tendencies to fake or respond on the basis of social desirability, as described in Chapter 8 and partly because of a limited acceptance of objectives in the affective domain as part of the mission of the schools. (However, acceptance of affective objectives is showing a tendency to increase.) Some appropriate measures are described below.

Tennessee Self-concept Scale.   This measure of how students view themselves, developed by William H. Fitts in 1965, comes in two forms, a Counseling Form and a Clinical and Research Form. Both forms contain the same items but the latter yields more scores. Only the former will be described here.

Content.   The scale contains 100 items (which appear in scrambled order in the test booklet). Each item presents the student with a self-descriptive statement, some of which are illustrated below (by permission).

- I sometimes do very bad things.
- I try to play fair with my friends.
- I am neither too tall nor too short.
- I despise myself.
- I am satisfied with my moral behavior.

Some of the items are written in a positive direction reflecting a positive self-concept and some in a negative direction indicating a negative self-concept. The student uses the following five-point scale to respond to each item.

completely false	mostly false	partly false and partly true	mostly true	completely true
1	2	3	4	5

The classification of the 100 items into subgroups makes possible the many types of scores described below.

Scoring. The scale provides five types of scores, most important of which are the *Positive Scores* (P). The *Total P Score* is basically the self-concept score, that is, it reflects a student's overall level of self-esteem. It is based on the number of positive self-descriptive items the student agrees with and the number of negative ones he or she disagrees with. It is based on items that describe "what I am," "how I feel about myself," and "what I do." It distinguishes between people who like themselves ("I am a decent sort of person"), feel that they are persons of value and worth ("I have a lot of self-control"), have confidence in themselves ("I am popular"), and act accordingly ("I am satisfied with my family relationships"), and people who doubt their own worth ("I am a nobody"), see themselves as undesirable ("I wish I could be more trustworthy"), often feel anxious, depressed, and unhappy ("I am losing my mind"), and have little faith or confidence in themselves ("I am no good at all from a social standpoint").

In addition to the Total P Score, separate P Scores are provided for (1) *Identity* ("I am a hateful person"), (2) *Self-satisfaction* ("I feel good most of the time"), (3) *Behavior* ("I do poorly in sports and games"), (4) *Physical Self* ("I have a healthy body"), (5) *Moral–Ethical Self* ("I am a moral failure"), (6) *Personal Self* ("I am as smart as I want to be"), (7) *Family Self* ("I treat my parents as well as I should"), and (8) *Social Self* ("I ought to get along better with other people").

In addition to P Scores, other types of scores obtained are (1) a *self-criticism* score (a "lie" scale) indicating the student's willingness to give honest self-criticism, (2) *variability* scores indicating the extent to which the student is inconsistent, (3) a *distribution* score which is a measure of certainty, and (4) a *time* score indicating how long the student took to complete the test (it is without time limits).

The Tennessee Self-concept Scale can be scored by the person who gives it (a teacher, counselor, or school psychologist) and the results plotted on a profile sheet reflecting T scores (i.e., standard scores) and percentiles. A test–retest reliability for the Total Score of .92 is reported in the Manual.

Application. The Scale is a way to determine not only whether a person likes himself or herself but the nature of his or her self-likes and dislikes. Students usually take less than 20 minutes to complete the test and the counselor less than 10 minutes to score it. Its results can help teachers and counselors reach out to individual students to help them overcome negative feelings toward themselves. The Tennessee Self-concept Scale is published by Counselor Recording and Tests. This publisher also offers the Piers-Harris Children's Self-concept Scale (1969 edition), an 80-item inventory for use with students from grades 3 to 12. This scale is somewhat less clinical than the Tennessee and simpler in both scoring and interpretation (but, at the same time, provides less detailed information). Items (responded to as "yes" or "no") deal with the way children feel about their (1) behavior, (2) intellectual and school status, (3) physical appearance and attributes, (4) anxiety, (5) popularity, and (6) happiness and satisfaction. Interpretations may be made of a single total score for which norms from a group of over 1,000 fourth through twelfth graders are provided. This scale is recommended for research use but use as a classroom screening device is also possible.

Self-appraisal Inventory.   The Self-appraisal Inventory appears in a collection of test instruments entitled Measures of Self-concept K–12 (Revised Edition). It appears in three versions, a Primary Level version for grades K–3, an Intermediate Level Version for grades 4–6, and an Advanced Level version for grades 7 and over. All three are group administered but the Primary Level version is administered orally so that it may be taken by non-readers. (The answer sheet for this version is picture coded.) Unlike the Tennessee Self-concept Scale, which provides for the reporting and interpretation of individual scores for individual students, the Self-appraisal Inventory is typically used only for the reporting of group data (such as for a class although individual reporting may be done) making it useful for evaluating instructional experiences rather than for evaluating individuals. The Self-appraisal Inventory can be obtained from the Instructional Objectives Exchange.

Content.   The Self-appraisal Inventory is written to fit the following four objectives.

(1) students will display positive self-concepts in the *peer* dimension by indicating agreement (disagreement) with statements that describe positive (negative) perceptions of the self in

social situations (e.g., "Other children are interested in me," "Other children are often mean to me");

(2) students will display positive self-concepts in the *school* dimension by indicating agreement with statements that describe scholastic success or esteem of self in school and disagreement with statements that describe school failure or lack of achievement (e.g., "School work is fairly easy for me," "I forget most of what I learn");

(3) students will display positive self-concepts in the *family* dimension by indicating agreement (disagreement) with statements describing positive (negative) perceptions of self in terms of family relationships or situations (e.g., "I do my share of work at home," "I often get in trouble at home," "My family understands me," "I feel that my family doesn't usually trust me");

(4) students will display positive self-concepts in *general* by indicating agreement (disagreement) with statements that describe a person with positive (negative) self-esteem (e.g., "I am satisfied to be just what I am," "I'm not very smart," "I'm not a very happy person").

The Primary Level version has 36 items written in the form of questions to which children respond "yes" or "no." The Intermediate Level version has 77 items and the Advanced Level version 62 items, each of which is in statement form and responded to as "true" or "untrue." All three versions are written to measure the four objectives (namely, peer, school, family, and general) and each may be subscored or item sets removed as necessary.

Scoring. Scoring is accomplished by simply counting the number of positive items responded to as "true" (or "yes") and adding to it the number of negative items responded to as "untrue" (or "no"). The test–retest reliabilities range from .73 to .87 for the three forms.

Application. The Self-appraisal Inventory gives the teacher a way of monitoring the level of self-esteem of the students in his or her class. For greater specificity, the teacher can use only those self-appraisal items that relate to the school dimension and school success.[8]

---

[8] These scales are not copyrighted. Teachers may buy the source book and then reproduce the scales themselves.

A second area of important attitudes is attitudes toward school, in terms of giving the teacher feedback about the positiveness of educational experiences for his or her students. An instrument designed for this purpose is the School Sentiment Index which, like the Self-appraisal Inventory, comes in versions for primary, intermediate, and secondary levels. It is distributed in uncopyrighted form by the Instructional Objectives Exchange.

Attitudes toward School—The School Sentiment Index

Content.   The SSI was developed to measure the following objectives.

(1) students will indicate positive attitudes toward *teachers* by responding "yes" ("no") to statements reflecting positive (negative) aspects of teacher behavior in terms of
   a. adequacy and fairness of instruction and grading (e.g., "I usually get the grade I deserve in a class," "Most of my teachers give assignments that are too difficult";
   b. fairness in authority and effectiveness of control (e.g., "My teacher treats me fairly," "My teacher bosses the children around");
   c. consideration, friendliness, and concern in interpersonal relationships with students (e.g., "My teachers are interested in what I have to say," "Many of my teachers have 'pets' ");
(2) students will indicate positive attitudes toward *learning* by expressing agreement (disagreement) with statements describing interest and/or involvement (or lack of them) in learning-related activities of the following types:
   a. new or difficult activities and assignments (e.g., "I like trying to work difficult puzzles"),
   b. independent pursuits of learning activities (e.g., "I don't do very much reading on my own"), and
   c. extra school work (e.g., "I hate having to do homework");
(3) students will indicate positive attitudes toward the *school social structure and climate* by expressing agreement (disagreement) with statements relating positive (negative) student perceptions of the
   a. bureaucracy (e.g., "My school has too many rules"),
   b. school organization (e.g., "Students have a voice in determining how this school is run"),
   c. traditions (e.g., "In order to win an office in this school you've got to be in the right crowd"), and
   d. activities (e.g., "Lunch time at school is not fun");

(4) students will indicate positive attitudes toward their *peers in school* by expressing agreement (disagreement) with statements describing positive (negative) aspects of
  a. the openness and fairness of friendship patterns (e.g., "School is a good place for making friends"),
  b. friendliness (e.g., "The other children in my class are not friendly toward me"),
  c. social distance (e.g., "Other children bother me when I'm trying to do my school work"), and
  d. stratification (e.g., "Older children often boss my friends and me around at my school");
(5) students will indicate positive attitudes toward *school in general* by expressing agreement (disagreement) with statements describing the positive (negative) aspects of
  a. holding power of the school (e.g., "It is clear to me why I shouldn't drop out of school"),
  b. being in school vs. remaining home from school (e.g., "I enjoy learning in school more than learning on my own"), and
  c. going to school (e.g., "Each morning I look forward to coming to school").

The primary level version has 37 items in question form that are presented orally and responded to by either "yes" or "no." The intermediate and secondary level versions have 81 and 82 items respectively in statement form that are self-administering and responded to respectively as "true" or "untrue" and "strongly agree," "agree," "disagree," and "strongly disagree."

Scoring.   The SSI is easily hand scored. Usually a single, total score is sufficient; however, if desired, separate scores may be computed for each objective since the book containing the tests lists the item numbers that fit each objective for each form. Test–retest reliability coefficients are reported for the Primary, Intermediate, and Advanced Level versions as .87, .83, and .49 respectively (the last being quite low).

Application.   Webb et al. (1966) suggest the use of a *morale ballot* at least once a year to monitor attitudes toward school (in much the same way we monitor achievement). The SSI can serve this purpose. It can also serve for program evaluation. Tuckman Cochran, and Travers (1974), for example, showed that students in "open" classrooms liked school more than students in "conventional" classrooms.

MEASURING PERSONALITY ORIENTATION

In this section *orientation* can be taken to mean any disposition or predisposition a person has vis-à-vis his or her needs, values, likes, or dislikes. When these orientations form a cluster, the word *personality* will be used to label or describe it; hence "personality orientation."

With the increasing concern for the education of the whole person, teachers need to be aware of individual differences and the development of character and values. Some types of measurement in the area of personality orientation are described below. (However, since personality is a core part of the person, teachers must exercise caution in measuring it.)[9]

California Psychological Inventory (CPI)

The CPI is a measure of a broad spectrum of personality characteristics (18 in all) associated with favorable and positive aspects of human behavior rather than the pathological. It is primarily intended for persons 16 years of age and older. It is published by Consulting Psychologists Press.

Content.   The CPI contains 480 items which fall into the following 18 scales.

Class I. Measures of Poise, Ascendancy, and Self-assurance
 (1) *Dominance (Do)*—distinguishes those who are aggressive, persuasive, independent and have leadership potential from those who are inhibited, avoid decisions, and lack self-confidence.
 (2) *Capacity for Status (Cs)*—distinguishes those who are ambitious, resourceful, self-seeking, effective, and broad in interests from those who are shy, slow, stereotyped in thinking, restricted in outlook, and awkward in unfamiliar situations.
 (3) *Sociability (Sy)*—distinguishes those who are outgoing, competitive, enterprising and original from those who are awkward, submissive, unassuming, passive, and overly influenced by others.
 (4) *Social Presence (Sp)*—distinguishes those who are clever, quick, spontaneous, talkative, active, and ebullient from those who are deliberate, self-restrained, vacillating, and unoriginal.
 (5) *Self-acceptance (Sa)*—distinguishes those who are sharp-

---

[9] Teachers may want to discuss their interests in and use of personality measurement with a school psychologist and/or school administrator.

witted, self-centered, and self-confident from those who are conservative, conventional, narrow, and self-abasing.

(6) *Sense of Well-being (Wb)*—distinguishes those who are energetic, versatile, productive, and who value work from those who are unambitious, cautious, self-defensive and constricted.

Class II. Measures of Socialization, Maturity, and Responsibility

(7) *Responsibility (Re)*—distinguishes those who are planful, independent, dependable, efficient, and moral from those who are lazy, spiteful, impulsive, and moody.

(8) *Socialization* (So)—distinguishes those who are honest, industrious, steady, conscientious, and conforming from those who are defensive, resentful, stubborn, deceitful, and given to excess.

(9) *Self-Control (Sc)*—distinguishes those who are calm, patient, self-denying, deliberate, thorough, and honest from those who are impulsive, irritable, uninhibited, and hedonistic.

(10) *Tolerance (To)*—distinguishes those who are permissive, accepting, and nonjudgmental from those who are narrow, distrustful, and overly judgmental.

(11) *Good Impression (Gi)*—distinguishes those who are con-

cerned with and capable of creating a favorable impression from those who are cool, distant, and little concerned with others.

(12) *Communality (Cm)*—distinguishes those who are dependable, moderate, steady, and "normal" from those who are changeable, nervous, and have problems.

Class III. Measures of Achievement Potential & Intellectual Efficiency

(13) *Achievement via Conformance (Ac)*—distinguishes those who are cooperative, organized, sincere, persistent, and who value achievement from those who are stubborn, opinionated, disorganized, and pessimistic.

(14) *Achievement via Independence (Ai)*—distinguishes those who are mature, self-reliant, and have superior judgment and ability from those who are submissive, compliant, wary, and lacking in self-insight.

(15) *Intellectual Efficiency (Ie)*—distinguishes those who are planful, alert, thorough, and value intellectual matters from those who are confused, unambitious, and lack self-discipline.

Class IV. Measures of Intellectual and Interest Modes

(16) *Psychological-Mindedness (Py)*—distinguishes those who are interested in and responsive to the inner states of others from those who are slow, deliberate, and overly conforming.

(17) *Flexibility (Fx)*—distinguishes those who are informal, adaptable, rebellious, sarcastic, and fun-loving from those who are methodical, rigid, pedantic, and deferential.

(18) *Femininity*[10] *(Fe)*—distinguishes those who are appreciative, patient, gentle, sincere, and sympathetic from those who are hard-headed, ambitious, opportunistic, and blunt.

The CPI items are self-descriptive statements (e.g., "When I get bored I like to stir up some excitement" and "I am afraid of deep water")[11] that are answered by either "true" or "false."

Scoring.   A profile of standard scores on the 18 scales is available. Reliabilities per scale for high school students are not as high as for achievement tests but still reasonably high.

---

[10] Since this test was originally published, the idea of separating traits by sex has become less socially acceptable.

[11] Reproduced by special permission from Manual for the *California Psychological Inventory* by Harrison G. Gough, Ph.D., copyright 1956. Published by Consulting Psychologists Press Inc.

Application.   The CPI has been fairly widely used and substantial literature on it is available. In those cases where a broad picture of students' personality is needed, it will easily suffice. It is usually beyond the scope of typical classroom use but might be a valuable counseling aid or a vehicle for promoting self-awareness in conjunction with a program such as career education. (More specific uses are suggested in the last section of this chapter.)

California Test of Personality   The California Test of Personality should not be confused with the CPI. The California is an older test (originally published in 1942 and revised in 1953) and serves primarily the same purposes as the CPI. Perhaps its most important distinction from the CPI is that it includes a form for use with children in the primary grades. It is published by the California Test Bureau/McGraw-Hill.

Content.   The California Test of Personality has 13 scales which fall into the categories of (1) personal adjustment and (2) social adjustment. The *personal adjustment* scales are as follows: *a. self-reliance* (independent, self-directing, emotionally stable, responsible); *b. sense of personal worth* (sense of being well-regarded, of being capable, attractive, and of having faith in one's future success); *c. sense of personal freedom* (self-determination, control over one's fate); *d. feeling of belonging* (experiencing love, friendship, and cordiality; getting along well with people); *e. withdrawing tendencies* (fantasizing, being lonely, being self-concerned); and *f. nervous symptoms* (loss of appetite, eye strain, chronic fatigue, and so forth, indicative of emotional conflicts).

The *social adjustment* scales are as follows: *a. social standards* (understanding the rights of others, knowing right from wrong, and subordinating certain individual desires); *b. social skills* (liking people, assisting them, practicing diplomacy, subordinating self for others); *c. anti-social tendencies* (bullying, being disobedient, destroying, being unfair to others); *d. family relations* (feeling loved at home, having a sense of security at home, good parental control); *e. school relations* (feeling liked by teachers and students, liking school, feeling important); and *f. community relations* (relating well to neighbors, taking pride in community, being tolerant, respecting laws and regulations). Test items are self-descriptive questions that are answered either "yes" or "no."

Scoring.   The test can be hand scored. Results are reported for each of the 13 scales as well as separate scores for *a. personal* adjustment, *b.* social adjustment, and *c.* total adjustment in the form of standard scores and percentile ranks. The test takes about 45 minutes to administer

Application.   The focus of the California Test of Personality is on adjustment. It has different forms that may be used with students from kindergarten through college and gives an indication of their level of adjustment, both personal and social. By asking students questions about their life and perceptions (e.g., "Do children at school ask you to play games with them"[12]) those with adjustment problems can be identified.

The EPPS is designed primarily for college students and adults but may be used as early as age 15. It is published by The Psychological Corporation. It measures orientation to each of 15 personality variables that may be considered predominant *needs* that a person has to fulfill.

Edwards Personal Reference Schedule (EPPS)

To avoid the tendency toward faking (common among "yes–no" type personality inventories, such as those described above), the Edwards uses a forced-choice format. Item choices are presented in equally desirable pairs from which the respondent must choose one. By equating the desirability of each choice in the pair, the tendency to distort can be minimized. (See the sample item on page 434.)

Content.   The 15 EPPS scales are as follows: (1) *achievement* (*ach*)—to do one's best, to succeed, to gain recognition, to solve difficult problems, to do things better than others; (2) *deference* (*def*)—to follow instructions, to conform, to let others make decisions, to do what is expected; (3) *order* (*ord*)—to be neat and organized, to plan beforehand, to arrange; (4) *exhibition* (*exh*)— to be witty and clever, to be noticed, to be the center of attention, to talk; (5) *autonomy* (*aut*)—to do and say what you want when you want, to criticize, to nonconform, to be unconventional; (6) *affiliation* (*aff*)—to be loyal, to have friends, and share and participate with them, to avoid being alone, to form strong attachments; (7) *intraception* (*int*)—to analyze yourself, to observe, judge, and understand others, to predict what others will do; (8) *succorance* (*suc*)—to be helped, encouraged, and understood by others, to

---

[12] Reproduced by permission of the publisher, CTB/McGraw-Hill, Monterey, CA 93940. Copyright © 1953 by McGraw-Hill, Inc.

receive help and affection; (9) *dominance (dom)*—to be the leader, to make decisions, to influence, supervise and direct others; (10) *abasement (aba)*—to feel guilty, to accept blame, to need to be punished, to feel timid and inferior, to need to confess; (11) *nurturance (nur)*—to help others, to be kind and sympathetic, to forgive, to be generous, to show affection; (12) *change (chg)*—to experience novelty, experiment, do new and different things; (13) *endurance (end)*—to keep at a job until it is finished, to work long hours, to avoid interruption; "sticktoitiveness"; (14) *heterosexuality (het)*—to go out with, interact with, be seen as attractive by, and love members of the opposite sex; (15) *aggression (agg)*—to attack contrary points of view, to criticize, poke fun, tell off, disagree with, blame, and get even with others.

The EPPS contains 225 pairs of items. One such pair is illustrated below.[13]

> *a.* I like to forgive my friends who may sometimes hurt me.
> *b.* I like my friends to encourage me when I meet with failure.

The *a* choice fits the *nurturance* scale (i.e., wanting to take care of others) while the *b* choice fits the *succorance* scale (i.e., wanting to be taken care of by others). The respondent must choose either *a* or *b*.

Scoring.   Respondents each receive 15 scores, one for each of the needs or orientations. Each raw score is then converted to a percentile rank using tables provided in the manual and the results plotted on a profile chart. The results show the relative predominance of each need with respect to the others.[14]

Application.   Like the other personality measures, the EPPS provides a personality profile of an individual. Because the needs measured by the EPPS are measured one against the other, using the forced-choice format, the results give a clearer relative picture of the different orientations than do other personality measures. To the extent that educational experiences are undertaken with the objective to strengthen certain needs relative to others (e.g., increase affiliation relative to aggression), the EPPS can be used to monitor the effectiveness of the effort.

---

[13] Reproduced by permission. Copyright 1953 by The Psychological Corporation, New York, N.Y. All rights reserved.
[14] Like the Kuder-E, the EPPS is a forced-choice, or ipsative, measure.

The Scale of Values, which first appeared in 1931, attempts to categorize a student's preferred value orientation as a basis for increasing self-awareness, providing guidance, or individualizing experiences. It is published by Houghton Mifflin.

Content. Like the EPPS the Scale of Values uses the forced-choice format, asking the student to indicate the number of a group of choices he or she prefers. Moreover, in Part I (30 items), he or she can weight preferences: a "3" versus a "0" for a marked preference, or a "2" versus a "1" for a slight preference. In Part II (15 items), there are four choices in the group and the student must rank preference for each, from 4 (most preferred) to 1 (least preferred). In this case, ranking serves as a form of weighting.

The items bring together choices reflecting the following six value orientations.

(1) *theoretical* orientation toward the scientific and the abstract;
(2) *economic* orientation toward business and finance;
(3) *aesthetic* orientation toward beauty and the arts;
(4) *social* orientation toward other people, group situations, and helping;
(5) *political* orientation toward government and decision making;
(6) *religious* orientation toward the moral and spiritual.

Examples of an item from Part I (for which there are 2 answer choices) and one from Part II (which has 4 answer choices) appear below.

- When witnessing a gorgeous ceremony (ecclesiastical or academic, induction into office, etc.), are you more impressed
  a. by the color and pageantry of the occasion itself;
  b. by the influence and strength of the group?
  [choice *a* is *aesthetic*; choice *b* is *political*]
- If you lived in a small town and had more than enough income for your needs, would you prefer to
  a. apply it productively to assist commercial and industrial development;
  b. contribute to the advancement of the activities of local religious groups;

---

[15] Sample items from the Scale of Values, Allport, Vernon, Lindzey, are reproduced by permission of The Houghton Mifflin Company.

    c. give it for the development of scientific research in your locality;

    d. give it to the Family Welfare Society.

    [Choice *a* is *economic*; *b* is *religious*; *c* is *theoretical*; *d* is *social.*]

Scoring.   The Scale of Values is designed so that in 5 to 10 minutes, the student can compute his or her numerical score for each value orientation. "Correction figures" are then used to reflect the relation of the scores to normative choices; the final scores are plotted on a "Profile of Values."

Application.   The greatest value of the Scale is probably in enhancing self-awareness and increasing a student's sensitivity to values. In addition, it is possible that the Scale of Values contributes to the process of affective instruction itself.

Embedded Figures Test (EFT)   The EFT, developed by Herman Witkin (1950), is a very different kind of personality orientation test from those described previously. It utilizes complex perceptual figures with simpler perceptual figures embedded within them.

Content.   The EFT consists of 24 complex figures and 10 simple figures (such as the ones shown in Figure 14.5; the complex figures are in color, the simple figures appear as shown).

COMPLEX FIGURE   SIMPLE FIGURE

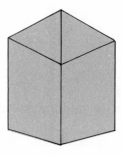

Figure 14.5   *Sample Figures from the Embedded Figures Test.**

* Reproduced by permission of Herman A. Witkin.

Box 14.1

A COMPENDIUM OF TEST EVALUATIONS

Tests in the affective and interpersonal areas can be difficult to locate since many are highly experimental and therefore scattered throughout the literature. To make their location and subsequent evaluation easier, the Center for the Study of Evaluation in collaboration with Research for Better Schools, Inc., has published a compendium (1972), which includes tests in affective and interpersonal areas.* In addition to listing a large number of tests along with their classification, age level, and source, the compendium provides a comprehensive evaluation of each. This evaluation provides information about and a rating (good–fair–poor) of each test's (1) validity, (2) examinee appropriateness, (3) normed excellence, (4) teaching feedback, (5) usability, (6) retest potential, and (7) ethical propriety.

An example is the Personal Orientation Inventory whose self-acceptance and self-regard scales are both listed and reviewed under category 3A3 *Self-esteem: Self-judgment.* Both are appropriate for ages of 13 and over and both are supplied by Educational and Industrial Testing Services. The self-acceptance scale is judged to have fair validity and the self-regard scale poor validity. In the other categories both scales receive equal ratings, namely: *good* examinee appropriateness, *fair* normed excellence, *poor* teaching feedback, *good* usability, and *poor* retest potential. No comments about the ethical propriety of either have been raised. These ratings seem to be about the par for these kinds of measures.

* Copies of the *CSE-RBS Test Evaluations* edited by Hoepfner and others may be obtained from the Dissemination Office, Center for the Study of Evaluation, Graduate School of Education, University of California.

Scoring. The student (tested individually) is shown the complex figure alone for 15 seconds, and then the simple figure alone for 10 seconds. The simple figure is then removed and he or she must locate it within the complex figure. The score is the number of minutes it takes the student to correctly trace the outline of the simple figure on the complex figure, with an upper limit of 5 minutes.

Application. What has this seeming perceptual task to do with personality? Witkin et al. (1954, 1962) have shown that people can be roughly categorized into *field-independent* and *field-dependent* on the basis of it. Field-independent types can separate figure from ground while field-dependent types cannot break apart a figure from its background. Each of these two types also shows a striking array of characteristics that are consistent with their ability or inability to separate figure from ground. On a companion perceptual test, the Rod-and-Frame Test (RFT) for instance, field-independents can more accurately judge the verticalness of the rod even when the frame is tilted than can field-dependents.

More interesting perhaps is the relation between scores on the EFT and various personality characteristics. Field-independent types can differentiate or keep things apart in experience; they show relatively greater individuality and a more personal orientation even in the face of pressure. Field-dependent types display a global, ill-articulated way of perceiving their social world. They are likely to change their views to agree with authority. Field-independents are more self-centered and more nonconformist (Pemberton, 1952) with a tendency to be more achievement oriented than are field-dependents.

According to Witkin et al. (1954, 1962) there is some advantage to being more field-independent, as it tends to be associated with flexibility and a greater ability to operate on one's own.

USING PUBLISHED AFFECTIVE MEASURES

Making students aware of their interests, values, and personality orientations may aid them significantly in their growth and development. By heightening students' own self-awareness these tests can play an "instructional" role in the sense of providing the kind of feedback required for self-enhancement and career decision making. The kinds of tests described in this chapter can be used by classroom teachers at the high school level as part of their classroom activities possibly in conjunction with a program of affective education or career education. (It is most helpful to have some training in this area or to seek the assistance of a person trained in the use of these tests.)

The kinds of tests described in this chapter can be used by counselors to help students make important decisions: choice of high school curriculum, choice of college, or choice of career.

Finally, the effectiveness of classroom learning experiences can be partially judged by measuring students' attitudes toward school and toward themselves.

The personal and interpersonal growth of students is an area of growing importance in school. In this chapter we have identified and described tests that can be useful in stimulating and evaluating outcomes in that emerging area.

Additional Information Sources

Beatty, W. H. (Ed.) *Improving educational assessment and an inventory of measures of affective behavior.* Wash. D.C.: Association for Supervision and Curriculum Development, NEA, 1969.

Bonjean, C. M., Hill, R. J., & McLemore, S. D. *Sociological measurement: An inventory of scales and indices.* San Francisco: Chandler Publishing Co., 1967.

Buros, O. K. (Ed.) *Personality tests and reviews.* Highland Park, N.J.: The Gryphon Press, 1970.

Cattell, R. B. & Warburton, F. W. *Objective personality and motivation tests: A theoretical introduction and practical compendium.* Urbana, Ill.: University of Illinois Press, 1967.

Comrey, A. L., Backer, T. E., & Glaser, E. M. *A sourcebook for mental health measures.* Los Angeles: Human Interaction Research Institute, 1973.

Edwards, A. L. *The measurement of personality traits.* N.Y.: Holt, Rinehart, & Winston, 1970.

Hoepfner, R. et al. (Eds.) *CSE–RBS test evaluations: Tests of higher order cognitive, affective, and interpersonal skills.* Los Angeles: Center for the Study of Evaluation, 1972. (See Box 14.1)

Instructional Objectives Exchange. *Attitude toward school K–12* (revised ed.). Los Angeles: Instructional Objectives Exchange (Box 24095), 1972.

Instructional Objectives Exchange. *Measures of self-concept K–12* (revised ed.) Los Angeles: Instructional Objectives Exchange (Box 24095), 1972.

Johnson, O. G. & Bommarito, J. W. *Tests and measurements in child development: A handbook.* San Francisco: Jossey-Bass, Inc., 1971.

Rosen, P. (Ed.) *Test collection bulletin.* Princeton, N.J.: Educational Testing Service, 1967 to present.

Super, D. E. & Crites, J. O. *Appraising vocational fitness* (revised ed.) New York: Harper & Row, 1962.

Walker, D. K. *Socioemotional measures for preschool and kindergarten children: A handbook.* San Francisco: Jossey-Bass, Inc., 1973.

Wylie, R. C. *The self-concept: A critical survey of pertinent research literature.* Lincoln, Neb.: University of Nebraska Press, 1961.

Self-test of Proficiency

On items requiring recall of specific test information, you may refer to the text.

(1) The following questions refer to the five career-related tests, namely: Strong Vocational Interest Blank, Kuder General Interest Survey, Ohio Vocational Interest Survey (OVIS), Self-directed Search (SDS), and Career Maturity Inventory (CMI). Indicate which test you would use in each instance.

a. To help students relate their personality orientation to occupations for which they are best suited.

b. To help students identify the pattern or profile of their interests in areas such as mechanical, literary, artistic, scientific, and so on.

c. To help students determine the category of occupations within the *Dictionary of Occupational Titles* toward which their interests dispose them.

d. To help students discover the occupational group with which the pattern of their preferences is most similar.

e. To help students become aware of their attitudes toward and competence for making a career decision.

(2) The Strong, Kuder, and OVIS represent different ways of measuring a student's interests. As such, they differ on a number of characteristics, properties, or dimensions on which most tests generally differ (such as number of items) as well as on properties that differentiate specifically between interest inventories. Most important among these differences are those in *scoring* and *interpretation*. Describe how the three tests differ on these two important properties.

(3) The following questions refer to tests of attitudes and self-concept, namely: the Tennessee Self-concept Scale, Self-appraisal Inventory, and School Sentiment Index. Indicate which one of the three you would use in each instance.

a. To discover if the students in your class share positive feelings about their school experience.

b. To determine whether an individual student likes himself or herself *and* the nature of these feelings.

c. To find out whether a class or group of students has a positive or negative image of themselves.

(4) It is important to be able to distinguish between attitudes toward self and toward school. Below is a list of labels, items, descriptions, and content categories. Mark *self* next to those which refer to attitudes

toward self and *school* next to those that refer to attitudes toward school.

a. "People like me."

b. "My classmates are smarter than I."

c. "Homework should be abolished."

d. "My family understands me."

e. "My teacher is kind."

f. "I am good looking."

g. "It's hard to get to school on time."

h. "I like to read."

(5) The following items refer to the California Psychological Inventory (CPI), California Test of Personality (CTP), Edwards Personal Preference Schedule (EPPS), Scale of Values, and Embedded Figures Test (EFT). Indicate for each purpose below which one of the above five tests you would use.

a. To help students discover their own preferences and dispositions toward orientations such as the religious, economic, aesthetic, and so on.

b. To classify students on a broad spectrum of personality characteristics associated with positive aspects of human behavior such as sociability, self-control, and flexibility.

c. To determine whether students use a more global, poorly articulated way to perceive their world or a more differentiated, individualized way.

d. To help students uncover their own patterns of needs for such important things as achievement, affiliation, and dominance.

e. To find out the extent to which students of all ages are experiencing personal and social adjustment.

(6) Below are a list of items. If you think an item measures *personality*, put a *P* next to it: if *adjustment*, an *A*; if *needs*, an *N*; if *values*, a *V*.

a. I have a good sense of security at home.

b. I am organized in activities and projects I undertake.

c. I like to read magazines that deal with science.

d. I consider myself to be a gentle and patient person.

e. I often find it necessary to be helped by others.

f. I find that I have lost my appetite.

(7) List three uses for affective measurement in the classroom.

(8) Select any one of the tests described in this chapter and indicate how it might be used in the classroom.

chapter fifteen / Getting the Most from the School Testing Program

A TEACHER-BUILT TESTING PROGRAM: THE TEST ITEM FILE

Since teacher-built tests constitute a major portion of the school testing program, obviously strategies for improving teacher testing would be desirable; one major strategy is the development of a test item file. A test item file is a collection of test items each of which has been shown to possess the qualities of appropriateness, validity, reliability, interpretability, and usability and can be reused. A curriculum or a textbook is not used once and then discarded. Why, then, should a test be used once and discarded? (To some extent, in reusing a test security may be a problem, but a problem that can be solved. See below.)

If we consider the typical teacher-built test as being highly appropriate and reasonably interpretable with, however, limited reliability and validity and the standardized test as being somewhat the reverse, then the best strategy would be to seek a middle ground: teacher tests with increased reliability and validity and standardized tests with greater appropriateness and interpretability. Testing companies are moving to the prescriptive or criterion-referenced achievement test (as described in Chapter 13), which has greater appropriateness and clearer interpretability than its precursors, but little move has been made to improve teacher testing. The reason for this is that teacher tests are typically used once and then discarded, and test improvement demands test reuse.

A test item file works as follows. Teachers prepare test items to fit their instructional objectives (as illustrated in Chapter 3) and use these items in their classroom tests.[1] Test results are then used to evaluate the items themselves in terms of the five criteria as set forth in Chapters 8–11. Poor items are discarded; good items are retained. (It may be useful to put item along with the objective it measures on an index card and keep it in an index card file.) Each time the teacher wants to test for proficiency on a particular set of objectives, he or she can construct a test largely by taking items from the file. The date that an item is used should appear on the back of the card. By mixing up items, adding new ones every testing period, and not reusing items in successive testings, the security problem could be minimized.

When you consider the curriculum resources available to teachers and the amount of training teachers receive in utilizing

---

[1] Testing or evaluation companies or other school districts may also serve as a source of items.

these resources, and then consider how few resources, if any, are made available to assist teachers in testing, the difference is considerable. Teachers are encouraged to develop their own resources by developing individual test item files and by pooling their test item files on a school, grade level, or even district basis.

Teachers' committees should also be formed to examine and review published achievement tests and identify those that are most appropriate for a particular school, grade level, or district.

OVERALL FUNCTIONS OF TESTING

It is possible for a school district to be involved to some degree in each of the following types of testing.

(1) teacher testing for the achievement of knowledge and compresion (Chapter 4)

(2) teacher testing for the development of problem-solving skills (Chapter 5)

(3) teacher assessment of students' attitudes (Chapter 6)

(4) teacher assessment of students' performance competencies and behavior (Chapter 7)

(5) standardized testing of intelligence or mental abilities (Chapter 12)

(6) standardized testing of achievement in reading, language arts, mathematics, science, social studies, and study skills (Chapter 13)

(7) standardized testing of personality orientation and of students' interests and attitudes toward school and self (Chapter 14).

The purposes for which these types of tests can be applied are also numerous but consist basically of the following three types: (1) *individual applications*, (2) *classroom applications*, and (3) *system applications*. Individual applications have traditionally received the most attention and classroom applications have been largely ignored; in an era of increasing demands for accountability, system applications are coming to the fore. All three rely on individual data but in classroom applications these data are pooled to provide information about classroom effects and in system applications these data are pooled to provide information about school effects, grade level effects, and district effects. All three types of applications emphasize the instructional improvement value of test data as illustrated in Figure 15.1.

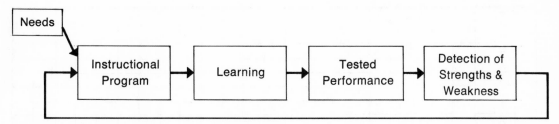

The Role of Testing in Program Improvement.   **Figure 15.1**

The purpose of the rest of this chapter will be to describe the many aspects of individual, classroom, and system applications of test data in the school testing program to the educational needs of the students. Since individual applications are the more traditional, and are more the role of the teacher, they will be described first.

INDIVIDUAL APPLICATIONS OF TEST DATA

There are basically four broad areas in which test data can be applied to individual student needs. These are: (1) monitoring and certifying student progress, (2) diagnosing individual strengths and weaknesses, (3) prescribing instruction, and (4) providing student feedback. Each will be described.

Teachers have the responsibility to maintain a knowledge of a student's continuing progress to certify growth and to prescribe instruction. The most common measures of student learning are teacher-built tests and standardized achievement tests.[2]

Monitoring and Certifying Student Progress

Teacher-built Tests. The success with which teachers' tests evaluate student progress depends on the extent to which these tests meet the five criteria outlined in Chapters 8–11. Since these criteria have been thoroughly described, they will not be covered again. However, it cannot be overemphasized that the quality of decisions about individual student progress will vary as a function of the quality of the tests on which these decisions are based.

[2] Of course, teachers also use such nontest evidence as homework and observation of classroom performance to assist them in judging individual student learning.

Figure 15.2 *Sample Roster for Recording Students' Performance by Objective.*

OBJECTIVE

	1	2	3	4	5	6	7	8	9	10	11	12	13	14	15	16	17	18	19	20	21	22	23	24	25	26	27	28	29	30	31	32	33	34	35	36	37	38	39	40	Total
Student no. 1																																									
Student no. 2																																									
Student no. 3																																									
Student no. 4																																									
Student no. 5																																									
Student no. 6																																									
Student no. 7																																									
Student no. 8																																									
Student no. 9																																									
Student no. 10																																									
Student no. 11																																									
Student no. 12																																									
Student no. 13																																									
Student no. 14																																									
Student no. 15																																									
Student no. 16																																									
Student no. 17																																									
Student no. 18																																									
Student no. 19																																									
Student no. 20																																									
Student no. 21																																									
Student no. 22																																									
Total																																									

It is recommended that teachers do their recordkeeping of test performance in terms of objectives and that testing be undertaken for the degree of proficiency on each objective. Figure 15.2 shows a sample recordkeeping system for a class of 22. Names of the students are listed down the side of the chart and the objectives across the top. There is, then, one box for each student's performance on each objective. The entry in this box could be the date on which adequate proficiency on that objective was demonstrated or a number indicating *degree* of proficiency attained.[3] Where adequate proficiency was not attained, the box would be left blank.

This recordkeeping procedure is based on the objective as the unit of analysis rather than on content area, test, book chapter or the like. Since the teacher's tests are designed to measure degree of proficiency on specific objectives (at least if the position laid out in this book is followed), it makes sense to utilize the objective as the unit of analysis for recordkeeping and evaluating as well. All of the objectives listed do not have to be cognitive in nature. Objectives describing attitudes and behavior (the affective domain) can be included as well. Moreover, among cognitive objectives, all do not have to deal with the acquisition of knowledge. Objectives dealing with cognitive skills such as analysis and synthesis are also quite appropriate. (Refer to Chapter 3 for a description of the relationship between objectives and tests designed to measure them.)

This procedure for certifying student proficiency presents three possible ways for dealing with individual differences in performance. One is to allow students to proceed through instruction at their own rate so that individual capability will be reflected in terms of the number of objectives on which a student has acquired proficiency. A second is to measure degree of proficiency based on the percentage of items measuring the objective that the student answers correctly. A third is to distinguish between objectives in terms of their complexity or difficulty with more capable students concentrating on the more difficult objectives.

Published Tests.   Norm-referenced standardized tests are typically of less use in evaluating student progress than teacher tests because they do not conform as closely to a teacher's objectives as

---

[3] For example, degree of proficiency may be recorded as the number of items used to measure that objective that were passed divided by the number used, such as 6/8 meaning 6 out of 8 were passed.

Figure 15.3 *Student Profile Chart.*[*]

Individual Cumulative Record
of performance on the
Tests of Academic Progress

Record of Testings

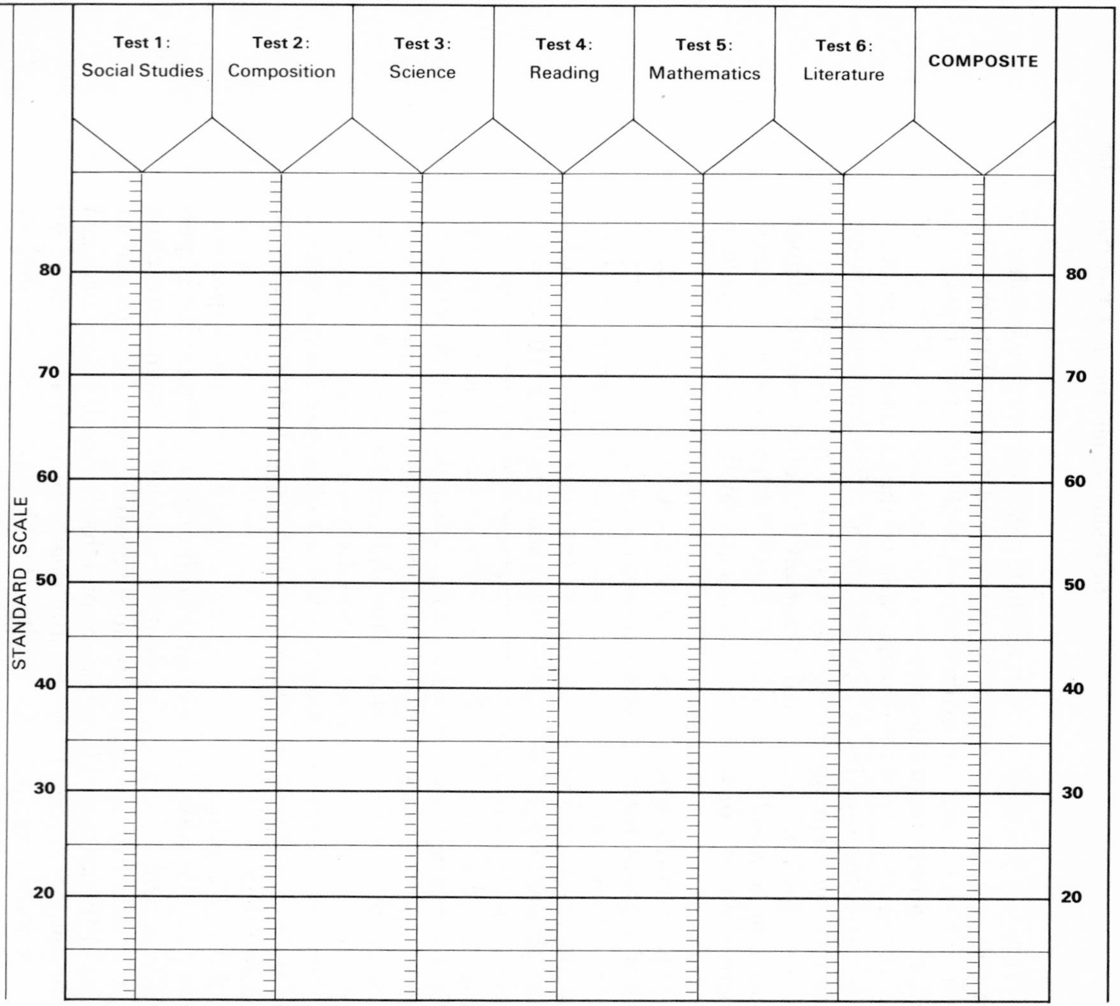

STANDARD SCALE

do his or her own tests. (However, they can be used to some extent in this capacity by comparing a student's standard scores over time, using a form like that shown in Figure 15.3.) Published criterion-referenced achievement tests are written in terms of specific objectives and hence may be more useful than their norm-referenced counterparts for evaluating or certifying progress made by the student.

To increase the appropriateness of a standardized achievement test, a teacher would have to go through it and select only those items that relate to his or her specific objectives of instruction; this procedure, however, would negate the norm-referencing and hence make the scores difficult to interpret. Since standardized achievement tests are written for national use, they must be based on a set of objectives that is generally appropriate and hence not specifically appropriate for an individual class. While standardized tests have applicability as part of the school testing program, this applicability is only minimal in the area of monitoring and evaluating individual student progress with respect to the objectives of instruction. However, item screening in terms of objectives can be done on published criterion-referenced tests since these are interpreted in terms of objectives rather than norms.[4] Thus, these tests have potential for evaluating in-class learning progress using the kind of recordkeeping scheme shown in Figure 15.2. (Refer also to the report forms shown in Figures 13.8 and 13.9 for criterion-referenced reporting.)

When your interest is in evaluating a student's progress relative to the performance of other students rather than relative to objectives, then use a standardized achievement test. A report form such as appears in Figure 15.4 provides grade equivalence scores which can be used to compare a student's performance to that of his or her grade-mates.

The purpose of diagnostic testing is not to identify students' levels of proficiency on specific instructional objectives but to identify more general levels of learning, performance, and abilities. This kind of testing is concerned with the skills and competencies that students need to have acquired to advance in the learning sequence. Because prerequisites are often hard to identify, diagnostic

Diagnosing Individual Strengths and Weaknesses

---

[4] Some test publishers have made certain standardized tests interpretable on a criterion-referenced basis (see Box 13.1).

tests must either *a.* survey a wide range of such skills and competencies (thereby having the likelihood of covering all prerequisites) or else *b.* measure specific objectives on which proficiency is required before the student can move on to subsequent objectives in the sequence.

At lower levels of instruction, reading and arithmetic are the basic general areas on which much learning is built. Testing students in these areas can provide information about general strengths and weaknesses in individual students. By looking at the performance of each student in the class on a standardized achievement test (as shown in Figure 15.4; see also Figures 11.3 and 13.5) the teacher can detect potential problem areas before their influence over a child's performance becomes serious. A student, for example, like Charlie Brown in Figure 15.4, is performing at or above grade level in all test areas except two: word study skills and social science. If this pattern continues, Charlie's reading ability may begin to become limited by his difficulty in acquiring word meanings. Certainly, in social science he is in need of assistance. Without this test information, Miss Jones, Charlie's teacher, would perhaps not have known of these two areas of difficulties. Had she already perceived them, the test scores would serve to increase her confidence in her judgment.

Teachers do not, for the most part, build diagnostic tests but depend, instead, upon published ones. Achievement test results in particular can be helpful to teachers in detecting patterns of accomplishment relative to ability. Perhaps the most potentially useful tests for diagnostic purposes are the published criterion-referenced tests. Designed to cover a lengthy instructional sequence (which may span two or three school years) they are highly specific about performance on earlier objectives in the sequence. Where earlier failures are blocking current learning, these tests will enable the teacher to detect (that is, diagnose) such deficiencies. Diagnosis of this sort poses two requirements: (1) a criterion-referenced test, that is, a test that measures performance on objectives, and (2) a test that measures performance on objectives that were covered earlier in the sequence, going back as far as can be considered convenient for testing purposes. By looking back in the sequence and finding a minus score on an objective, the teacher may find the basis for a student's current difficulties. Failure to have acquired proficiency on a particular objective may have occurred during the preceding school year when the student had a different teacher from the current one. (Forms such as appear in

STANFORD Achievement Test
1973 Edition

INDIVIDUAL RECORD

for Brown Charlie

Teacher MISS L JONES

School SOUTH ELEMENTARY

System WESTERNER

Date of Testing 10/73

Grade 3

Number Right / Number Possible	Scaled Score	%ile Rank Local	%ile Rank Nat'l.	Grade Equiv.	TESTS	NATIONAL STANINE PROFILE
						1 2 3 Below Average / 4 5 6 Average / 7 8 9 Above Average
26/37	133		50	3.2	Vocabulary	–5–
43/45	148		80	4.2	Reading - Part A	–7–
44/48	151		84	4.4	Reading - Part B	–7–
87/93	148		84	4.4	Reading Comprehension	–7–
43/65	121		40	2.5	Word Study Skills	–5–
32/35	155		92	5.0	Math Concepts	–8–
28/37	141		72	3.5	Math Computation	–6–
21/28	142		68	3.7	Math Applications	–6–
40/43	158		92	5.3	Spelling	–8–
					Language	
15/27	118		16	2.1	Social Science	–3–
20/27	130		54	3.3	Science	–5–
43/50	151		90	4.9	Listening Comprehension	–8–
					AREA TOTALS	
130/158	138		60	3.5	Total Reading	–6–
81/100	143		82	4.0	Total Mathematics	–7–
69/87	139		74	4.0	Total Auditory	–6–
					BATTERY TOTAL	
355/442	139		72	3.8	COMPLETE BATTERY	–6–

SCORE DETAIL

Mental Age Yrs.	Mos.	Raw Score	Grade Norms PR	S	Age Norms %ile Rank Local	Age Norms %ile Rank Nat'l.	Dev. I.Q.	OTIS - LENNON MENTAL ABILITY TEST	1 2 3 Below Average / 4 5 6 Average / 7 8 9 Above Average
08	10	52	46	5		57	103	AGE NORM STANINE ---	–5–

OTHER PUPIL DATA:

Age 08 yrs. 10 mos.

Other Information

Pupil Number

TEACHER NOTES:

TEST INFORMATION:

	Level	Form	Norms Used
Stanford	PRIMARY 2	A	GRADE 3.2
Otis-Lennon	ELEMENT 1	J	GR 3 BEG

Local Norms based on _____ pupils.   Process No. 000-0000-000

See back for aids for interpretation.

Achievement Test Results for One Student, Charlie Brown, in Miss Jones' Class.* **Figure 15.4**

Figures 13.9 and 13.10 are used to report results on criterion-referenced tests.)[5]

In general, broad deficiencies or strengths can be diagnosed by means of published, norm-referenced tests while specific deficiencies are most easily identified using criterion-referenced tests that extend reasonably far back in a learning sequence.[6]

Prescribing Instruction

To the extent that the curriculum is not fixed, the teacher may prescribe specific instructional experiences for students. In most cases a large part of the curriculum is reasonably fixed with the remainder available for supplementary activities. In other cases, the sequence of instruction is fixed but the rate at which a student can progress may be varied.

To make prescriptive decisions, teachers can make good use of both their own tests and published tests. In the case of Charlie Brown, for example (cited in the preceding section based on Figure 15.4), his weakness in word study skills that showed up on his standardized test scores suggests that the teacher have him work with vocabulary cards or do dictionary assignments in conjunction with his reading. His teacher could use a diagnostic reading test in order to pinpoint areas in which additional instruction would be helpful.

Prescriptions for instruction can also be based on the results of teacher tests in conjunction with the recordkeeping form illustrated in Figure 15.2. The blanks in the form for a particular student indicate the objectives on which he or she has failed to demonstrate adequate proficiency. A teacher's tests should be considerably more than a mechanism for certifying progress; tests can be and should be a basic part of the mechanics for indicating supplementary or even primary instruction.

---

[5] The individual student report form shown in Figure 13.5 for a standardized test also reports performance in specific content categories and on individual items, thus offering the potential for use as a diagnostic test (that is, a measure of past deficiencies). However, interpretation of results on individual items poses serious problems in terms of reliability. For standardized tests to be used in a criterion-referenced way, interpretations would need to be based on specific content category scores. (See Figure 13.1 for a mapping of items to content categories on one such standardized achievement test and Figure 13.9 for criterion-referenced reporting on another standardized achievement test.)

[6] Information about specific tests designed exclusively for diagnostic purposes can be found in the *Mental Measurements Yearbook*. Also, tests useful for diagnosing reading difficulties were described in Chapter 13.

"Winston Churchill was also an underachiever."

Although tests are an excellent source of feedback for students, merely providing them with a score that tells only their overall level of performance may be more demoralizing than helpful. The most helpful feedback should be that which tells them which objectives they failed to master and the nature of their mistakes. Test feedback should provide the student with information to help him or her improve subsequent test performance; mere scores can be more of a frustration than a help. Witness the standardized test score report shown in Figure 15.4, a similar version of which was sent home with Charlie Brown, a third grader. How will the information on the individual record form help Charlie? Since it doesn't tell him exactly where his deficiencies lie, it may produce either frustration or a competitive sense of self-satisfaction (perhaps the latter because his scores are relatively high).

In order for achievement test results to serve a helpful feedback function for a student, the teacher must be able to point out to that student where his or her errors lie. The teacher cannot do this unless information at this level of detail is available (often not

Providing Student Feedback

the case with standardized test results).[7] Hence, standardized test results have the potential to assist teachers and thereby indirectly assist students (through prescriptive instruction) but not, under most circumstances, assist students directly. Therefore, the major source of student feedback is teacher-built tests. To maximize the feedback value of such tests, teachers should do the following.

(1) *Give a pretest* (i.e., the end-of-unit test itself or an alternate form of it prior to the instruction). If pretesting is not viable, at least present the objectives of instruction at the start of an instructional sequence.

(2) *Return the scored tests themselves, not just the scores.* The scores alone have the same shortcomings as most standardized test score reports, i.e., no actual feedback in terms of specific performance on objectives.

(3) *Return the tests quickly after they are given.* Otherwise students will forget the instructional goals.

(4) *Clearly indicate errors and bases for scoring on each student's test.* Feedback is based on the discrepancy between what is and what ought to be; your markings on the students' tests should tell them what "ought to be."

(5) *Test in a warm and accepting atmosphere* rather than a threatening one so that students will believe, accept, and use feedback in a constructive way rather than feel they must defend themselves against it. This usually means giving students at least a second chance to "pass" the test; it means always projecting the philosophy that tests should serve to help students improve rather than simply to evaluate their performance.

CLASSROOM APPLICATIONS OF TEST DATA

In addition to helping teachers interpret the learning and performance of individual students, test data can be used to help teachers improve upon their own instructional procedures. Let us consider how an examination of the collective test performance of students can be accomplished and how it can be useful.

[7] However, the Student Monitoring System, a published criterion-referenced test described in Chapter 13 on page 394 has the feature of built-in immediate feedback. Students mark their answer choice with a special crayon which reveals to them whether or not the choice is correct. If not, they make choices until the correct one is attained.

Consider the sample roster in Figure 15.2. While it was constructed originally to record and evaluate individual student performance, it can also help a teacher to evaluate his or her own performance. The last row of the roster presents the results on each objective accumulated across all the students in the class. By examining the accumulative results on each objective, the teacher can determine those objectives on which additional or different instructional procedures are needed. Suppose, for example, that approximately 80% of the students demonstrate adequate proficiency on all but five of the objectives. On these five, only 50% of the class at most perform at an acceptable level. The teacher must first examine the objectives themselves and the test items used to measure them to make sure they were not too difficult; but if they seem not to be, the teacher must conclude that the instruction provided for these five objectives was insufficient and provide further or alternative forms of instruction.

The important point is that student performance taken individually reflects upon individual learning but that individual performances can be considered collectively to help tell the teacher, empirically, whether his or her instruction is working as well as it should be.

Using Results of Teacher-built Tests

To be able to use standardized test scores to help evaluate classroom instruction, they must be reported for the classroom as a unit. For illustrative purposes, a class summary of scores is shown in Figure 15.5 for Miss Jones' third grade class. Based on this report, Miss Jones' third graders appear to be doing well in all tested areas. In no area are fewer than 30% of the third graders performing in the highest three stanines. The weakest areas are vocabulary and math computation, each with 37% performing below average. On the basis of these scores, Miss Jones should consider working more intensively with those small groups of 10 students each (not necessarily the same ones) who are performing below average in vocabulary and math computation and spending less time teaching spelling.

Published criterion-referenced tests can be used quite conveniently as the basis for a *classroom achievement monitoring* system. Level A of the Prescriptive Mathematics Inventory, for example, has 107 items. Let us assume that the teacher intends to cover all the objectives measured by these items in four segments. He or she can divide the test into four subtests (in this example, of 26,

Using Results of Published Tests

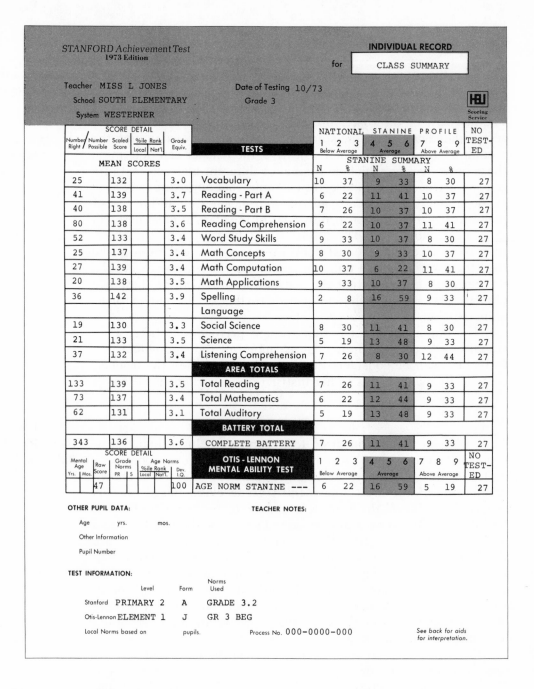

Number Right / Number Possible	Scaled Score	%ile Rank Local	%ile Rank Nat'l	Grade Equiv.	TESTS	1 2 3 Below Average N	%	4 5 6 Average N	%	7 8 9 Above Average N	%	NO TEST-ED
					MEAN SCORES							
25	132			3.0	Vocabulary	10	37	9	33	8	30	27
41	139			3.7	Reading - Part A	6	22	11	41	10	37	27
40	138			3.5	Reading - Part B	7	26	10	37	10	37	27
80	138			3.6	Reading Comprehension	6	22	10	37	11	41	27
52	133			3.4	Word Study Skills	9	33	10	37	8	30	27
25	137			3.4	Math Concepts	8	30	9	33	10	37	27
27	139			3.4	Math Computation	10	37	6	22	11	41	27
20	138			3.5	Math Applications	9	33	10	37	8	30	27
36	142			3.9	Spelling	2	8	16	59	9	33	27
					Language							
19	130			3.3	Social Science	8	30	11	41	8	30	27
21	133			3.5	Science	5	19	13	48	9	33	27
37	132			3.4	Listening Comprehension	7	26	8	30	12	44	27
					AREA TOTALS							
133	139			3.5	Total Reading	7	26	11	41	9	33	27
73	137			3.4	Total Mathematics	6	22	12	44	9	33	27
62	131			3.1	Total Auditory	5	19	13	48	9	33	27
					BATTERY TOTAL							
343	136			3.6	COMPLETE BATTERY	7	26	11	41	9	33	27

Figure 15.5 *Class Summary for Miss Jones' Third Grade Class.**

27, 27, and 27 items respectively), and administer them as shown in Figure 15.6. The class is divided into four equal groups, with each group taking one-quarter of the test during each testing time. At the first testing, for example, the group that takes items 1–26 will be taking an immediate posttest following instruction on these objectives. The other three groups will provide pretest data. By the second testing, the group taking items 1–26 will be taking a retention test. Now the second group of items (27–53) will constitute the immediate posttest. The remaining two groups of items, as yet untaught, still represent pretests. By the third testing time, only the last group of items is being pretested and by the fourth testing time, three of the four groups are being tested for retention.

Although each student takes each test item only once, under this system the teacher has a basis for determining whether adequate learning is taking place. *It is not a system for evaluating in-*

	testing time 1		testing time 2		testing time 3		testing time 4
Student Group 1	items 1-26 IPT		items 81-107 PrT		items 27-53 ReT		items 54-80 ReT
Student Group 2	items 27-53 PrT		items 54-80 PrT		items 1-26 ReT		items 81-107 IPT
(Teach Objectives)	*1-26*		*27-53*		*54-80*		*81-107*
Student Group 3	items 54-80 PrT		items 27-53 IPT		items 81-107 PrT		items 1-26 ReT
Student Group 4	items 81-107 PrT		items 1-26 ReT		items 54-80 IPT		items 27-53 ReT

IPT = immediate posttest
PrT = pretest
ReT = retention test

A System for Monitoring Achievement.   **Figure 15.6**

dividual performance but a system for evaluating instruction. If the gains from pretest to immediate posttest do not reflect adequate proficiency on all the objectives taught in that segment, then supplementary or additional instruction can be introduced. The goal is for all students to demonstrate acceptable levels of proficiency on all the objectives measured by the 107 items over the course of the semester or school year.

Box 15.1

___

TESTING: FOR WHOM AND WHAT?

There have been some recent instances of opposition from teacher organizations to testing programs. The professional organizations claim that the results of the testing programs will be used to evaluate teachers and that such evaluation is outside the terms of their contract. The latter point is usually indisputable; teachers have a right to negotiate the terms of their employment, and evaluation as a factor in job security is clearly one of the most important of these terms. Formally trying to change these terms through collective bargaining to include the application of classroom test data for the task of teacher evaluation may be imminent in public education.

It is the first point, the intent of these testing programs, that is the more critical at the moment. Those carrying out the testing program are typically interested in program or system evaluation and/or in providing teachers with useful feedback rather than evaluating them. Teachers are suspicious that such data may be otherwise used by their detractors and are right in protecting themselves from this unfair possibility. It must be pointed out that poor performance by students taken as a classroom group does not necessarily indicate poor teaching; poor performance also reflects on facilities, budgets, administrative support, and the characteristics of the students themselves. However, poor teaching does represent *one* of the potential causes of poor student performance (90% of school operating budgets is spent on teachers' salaries). Certainly school systems would benefit if teachers were responsive to collective student performance data as a source of feedback and basis for self-improvement and administrators and school boards were willing to allow teachers some margin for self-improvement rather than the two sides being in conflict over the testing issue.

PROGRAM AND SYSTEM APPLICATIONS OF TEST DATA

For purposes of measurement it is convenient to separate educational variables into *input, process, and output. Measurable educational inputs* are the givens of an educational system—school budget, facilities, community needs, and the characteristics that students and teachers bring with them into the school system. For students input would include prior learning and for teachers past experience. *Measurable educational processes* are the performance characteristics of the system itself—the teaching behaviors of teachers, the administering behavior of administrators, and the operation of the instructional program. Finally, we have *measurable educational outputs*, the area of greatest concern in measurement. These are learner achievements, attitudes, and behaviors, that when taken together reflect upon the inputs and processes of the school. These relationships are shown in Figure 15.7.

It is possible to use various types of instruments to measure school inputs, processes, and outputs. One way to measure input would be to measure in essence the static qualities of the schools or what they look like at 8:00 a.m. on Monday morning as the students and staff enter the buildings. What are the capacities, needs, and expectations of the teachers? How experienced is the superintendent? How well-equipped are the schools? How does the community feel about education? What programs are available in the schools for the students? What is the size of the school budget?

Examples of Input, Process, Output, and Their Relationship. **Figure 15.7**

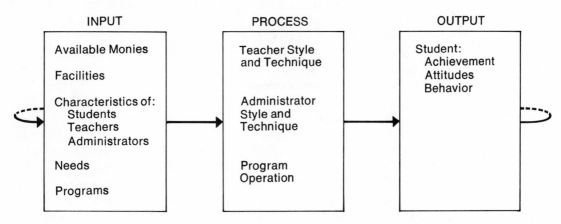

"It's nice to see a cheerful headline for a change."

What abilities do the students possess? How much have they already learned? As education proceeds, input is constantly changing.

Activities that go on in the school constitute process. The way that teachers handle disciplinary problems, the amount of individual attention students receive, the extent to which kits and other learning devices are used, the extent to which teachers are provided with suitable and constructive supervision, the using of math workbooks, the taking of nature walks—all these are manifestations of educational process.

The chief focus of educational measurement is on output. In a very real sense, the "products" of education are the students; thus it is important to measure their collective acquisition of skills, knowledges, attitudes, and behaviors. It is important, too, to measure the individual acquisition of these skills, knowledges, attitudes, and behaviors in order to evaluate, facilitate, and certify that growth and progress. Thus, we can distinguish for purposes of educational measurement individual effects and group effects (the latter being the sum of the former and thus representing tendencies) on school input, process, and output (see Figure 15.8).

Some Examples of Potentially Measurable Dimensions of the   **Figure 15.8**
Schools.

	INDIVIDUAL	GROUP
INPUT	How well-trained is teacher X? What is administrator Y's attitudes toward pupil control? How bright is Johnny?	What is the average amount of training of teachers in the system? What do the administrators believe is the best way to control students? How bright are the 1st graders in the school?
PROCESS	Does teacher X use individually designed workbooks? Does administrator Y have an open-door policy? Are students in teacher Z's class permitted to choose their own tasks?	How many teachers use individually designed workbooks? What is the policy of the administrative staff? In how many classes may students select their own tasks?
OUTPUT	What aspects of reading give Jane the most trouble? How does Emil feel about the rights of women? How well-mannered is Ethel toward adults in the school?	How well can the 2nd graders in the District read? How do children in the school feel about women's rights? How well-behaved are the students?

While it is difficult to be sure one way of doing something is better **Measuring**
than another, we can have considerable confidence in specifying, **Educational**
for example, that high reading performance is better than low **Output**
reading performance. In other words, it is easier to attach positive
values to outcomes than to processes. People may not be able to
agree on the best way to teach children to read but they can agree
that improving their reading skills is a goal of education. Thus,
educational outputs rather than processes are appropriate for
measuring and evaluating educational effects.

A second reason for focusing on outputs as measures of educational effectiveness is that we are far more adept at measuring output than we are at measuring process (that is, we are much more adept at measuring how students perform than how systems perform). Also, we are an output-oriented society with a tendency to value our processes only if we also value their products. In the final analysis we judge things (and people) by how well they "work."

Basic Subject Outputs. The first area of interest in examining the school's outputs includes the basic subjects: language arts, mathematics, social science, and science. The performance of students in these basic subjects can be measured by examining standardized test results such as those appearing in Figure 15.9. On the average, South Elementary School's third graders (whose results appear in Figure 15.9) are performing at or above grade level on all tests. A look at the "Below Average" stanine column reveals vocabulary to be the weakest area with 37% of the third graders performing below average.

To better evaluate results like those shown in Figure 15.9, it is helpful to make comparisons. Has the performance of students improved in any area from last year to this year? Has it worsened? Assume that the school was experimenting with a new mathematics workbook series that focused on computation. Achievement test results could be used to answer the following questions: (1) Have these third grade students improved their math computational skills during the course of the year while the experimental materials were in use? (2) Are this year's third graders, all of whom used the new workbook, performing better than last year's third graders, none of whom used the new workbook? (3) Are the third graders in South Elementary, all of whom used the new workbook, performing better than the third graders in North Elementary (an otherwise reasonably comparable school with a similar student population), none of whom used the new workbook? Thus, results on a standardized achievement test can be examined across schools, across districts (not illustrated here), across time (following the progress of a class), or across classes (comparing this year's class to last year's class) to make the results an interpretable reflection of system or program effects.

The results of teacher tests can also be used as a reflection of system or program effects when examined collectively across students and classes; that is, by keeping track of the percentage of students who acquire proficiency on each objective over the

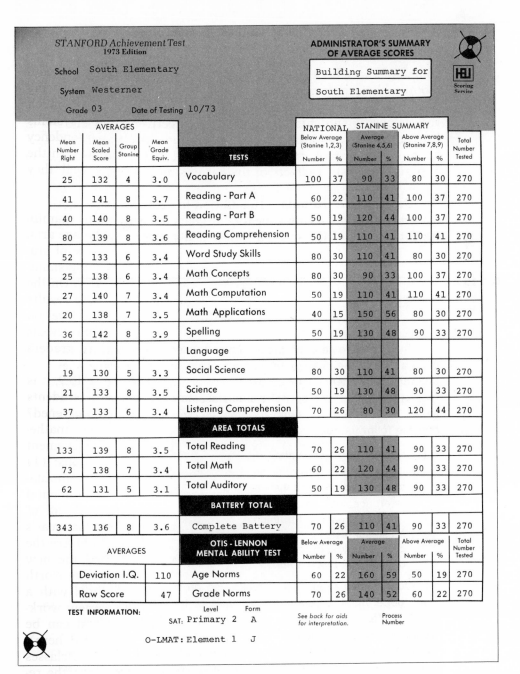

*Achievement Test Results for South Elementary School's Third Grade.** **Figure 15.9**

course of the school year. Thus, if the teacher uses Figure 15.2 to monitor the acquisition of individual student proficiency (for purposes of facilitating individual learning) and then sums up the results across students to monitor the effectiveness of classroom instruction, an administrator could sum up the classroom results for an entire school, grade level, or school district to arrive at an appraisal of system effects in the basic subject areas.

Broad-based Outputs.   In addition to goals for basic subjects, consider a broad set of educational goals such as those that appear in Figure 15.10. Note that these goals cover a wide variety of

Box 15.2

EVALUATION

The measurement of predetermined educational outputs has long been a part of the strategy of program evaluation, particularly when such programs are intended to be exemplary and are financed by state and federal funds. Perhaps school districts should evaluate their total offering as if it represented an exemplary program. To implement such an evaluation, the following resources may be helpful:

(1) testing expert(s) on staff
(2) consultants
(3) catalogs and test publishers, and
(4) reference sources and libraries, to
    a. direct in-service training
    b. select tests
    c. design test programs and evaluations
    d. interpret test results.

Output evaluation should make use on a classroom, school, grade level, department, or district-wide basis of teacher-built tests, published test batteries and programs, tests that come with curriculums, and tests from the research literature. Tests should be chosen on the basis of the five test criteria, and test results interpretation should include the identification of weaknesses in the testing program. Technical assistance will probably be most helpful in (1) determining goals, and (2) measuring output with respect to each goal, although local teachers and administrative staff should be asked to participate in determining and measuring goals.

---

learning areas, all of which are an important part of growing up but not all of which are covered in the schools.[8] While it has often been emphasized that reading and mathematics are the most critical areas of school responsibility, it is important to acknowledge the many areas of development at which schooling is and should be aimed. The list in Figure 15.10 represents an attempt at a broad and comprehensive list of such goals.

Ideally, each school district should generate its own list of goals (with teachers, parents, and students working cooperatively) and consider the attainment of those goals as the major purpose of the group school testing program. To build such a testing program, existing achievement and attitude scales can be combined and supplemented by new ones developed for that purpose. Certainly, a number of the tests described in Chapter 14 might be useful for this purpose. The prime advantage of using standardized instruments is to make possible comparisons across districts; the major disadvantage is the difficulty in expecting a single instrument to fit a variety of districts. Teacher-built measures may be used to supplement published tests but would have to be considered across classes.[9]

Measuring Educational Input

The matter of measuring input can be put into perspective by considering it in relation to the above discussion of output. To a large extent, educational input and output measures are the same except that input measurement occurs at the start of a sequence and output measurement at the conclusion. A school's proficiency can be based not on its final level of performance at one point in time but on the *degree of gain from input to output*. Input measurement as an essential part of the determination of proficiency can serve as the performance baseline from which gains are to be evaluated, that is, the basis for the detection of self-improvement. In addition, if learning gains are adjusted to reflect their individual financial cost, a district can determine unit costs. While this formulation should not be used to encourage educational miserliness, it may help districts make decisions about their best allocation of money.

---

[8] Indeed, some people will argue that such goals do not belong in the schools. As much as possible, a district should involve the community in goal setting but even so, it will be impossible to satisfy everyone.

[9] The use of teacher-built measures across districts is not recommended unless they can be shown to be of equally high appropriateness in each district used.

Figure 15.10 *List of Educational Goals.**

LEARN HOW TO BE A GOOD CITIZEN
A. Develop an awareness of civic rights and responsibilities.
B. Develop attitudes for productive citizenship in a democracy.
C. Develop an attitude of respect for personal and public property.
D. Develop an understanding of the obligations and responsibilities
   of citizenship.

**LEARN HOW TO RESPECT AND GET ALONG WITH PEOPLE WHO
THINK, DRESS AND ACT DIFFERENTLY**
A. Develop an appreciation for and an understanding of other people and
   other cultures.
B. Develop an understanding of political, economic, and social patterns
   of the rest of the world.
C. Develop awareness of the interdependence of races, creeds, nations
   and cultures.
D. Develop an awareness of the processes of group relationships.

**LEARN ABOUT AND TRY TO UNDERSTAND THE CHANGES
THAT TAKE PLACE IN THE WORLD**
A. Develop ability to adjust to the changing demands of society.
B. Develop an awareness and the ability to adjust to a changing world
   and its problems.
C. Develop understanding of the past, identify with the present, and the
   ability to meet the future.

DEVELOP SKILLS IN READING, WRITING, SPEAKING AND LISTENING
A. Develop ability to communicate ideas and feelings effectively.
B. Develop skills in oral and written English.

UNDERSTAND AND PRACTICE DEMOCRATIC IDEAS AND IDEALS
A. Develop loyalty to American democratic ideals.
B. Develop patriotism and loyalty to ideas of democracy.
C. Develop knowledge and appreciation of the rights and privileges
   in our democracy.
D. Develop an understanding of our American heritage.

LEARN HOW TO EXAMINE AND USE INFORMATION
A. Develop ability to examine constructively and creatively.
B. Develop ability to use scientific methods.
C. Develop reasoning abilities.
D. Develop skills to think and proceed logically.

UNDERSTAND AND PRACTICE THE SKILLS OF FAMILY LIVING
A. Develop understanding and appreciation of the principles of living
   in the family group.
B. Develop attitudes leading to acceptance of responsibilities as family
   members.
C. Develop an awareness of future family responsibilities and
   achievement of skills in preparing to accept them.

**LEARN TO RESPECT AND GET ALONG WITH PEOPLE
WITH WHOM WE WORK AND LIVE**
A. Develop appreciation and respect for the worth and dignity of individuals.
B. Develop respect for individual worth and understanding of minority
   opinions and acceptance of majority decisions.
C. Develop a cooperative attitude toward living and working with others.

DEVELOP SKILLS TO ENTER A SPECIFIC FIELD OF WORK
A. Develop abilities and skills needed for immediate employment.
B. Develop an awareness of opportunities and requirements related to
   a specific field of work.
C. Develop an appreciation of good workmanship.

LEARN HOW TO BE A GOOD MANAGER OF MONEY, PROPERTY AND RESOURCES

A. Develop an understanding of economic principles and responsibilities.
B. Develop ability and understanding in personal buying, selling and investment.
C. Develop skills in management of natural and human resources and man's environment.

DEVELOP A DESIRE FOR LEARNING NOW AND IN THE FUTURE

A. Develop intellectual curiosity and eagerness for lifelong learning.
B. Develop a positive attitude toward learning.
C. Develop a positive attitude toward continuing independent education.

LEARN HOW TO USE LEISURE TIME

A. Develop ability to use leisure time productively.
B. Develop a positive attitude toward participation in a range of leisure time activities—physical, intellectual and creative.
C. Develop appreciation and interests which will lead to wise and enjoyable use of leisure time.

PRACTICE AND UNDERSTAND THE IDEAS OF HEALTH AND SAFETY

A. Establish an effective individual physical fitness program.
B. Develop an understanding of good physical health and well being.
C. Establish sound personal health habits and information.
D. Develop a concern for public health and safety.

APPRECIATE CULTURE AND BEAUTY IN THE WORLD

A. Develop abilities for effective expression of ideas and cultural appreciation (fine arts).
B. Cultivate appreciation for beauty in various forms.
C. Develop creative self-expression through various media (art, music, writing, etc.).
D. Develop special talents in music, art, literature and foreign languages.

GAIN INFORMATION NEEDED TO MAKE JOB SELECTIONS

A. Promote self-understanding and self-direction in relation to student's occupational interests.
B. Develop the ability to use information and counseling services related to the selection of a job.
C. Develop a knowledge of specific information about a particular vocation.

DEVELOP PRIDE IN WORK AND A FEELING OF SELF-WORTH

A. Develop a feeling of student pride in his achievements and progress.
B. Develop self-understanding and self-awareness.
C. Develop the student's feeling of positive self-worth, security, and self-assurance.

DEVELOP GOOD CHARACTER AND SELF-RESPECT

A. Develop moral responsibility and a sound ethical and moral behavior.
B. Develop the student's capacity to discipline himself to work, study, and play constructively.
C. Develop a moral and ethical sense of values, goals, and processes of free society.
D. Develop standards of personal character and ideas.

GAIN A GENERAL EDUCATION

A. Develop background and skills in the use of numbers, natural sciences, mathematics, and social sciences.
B. Develop a fund of information and concepts.
C. Develop special interests and abilities.

Measuring Schools are encouraged to measure process in order (1) to deter-
Educational mine whether intended processes are being carried out, and (2) to
Process discover which processes produce the desired outcomes. If educators can measure the processes of teaching, of classroom and
school management, of school climates, of teacher morale, and so
on, the results of the measurement could be used to increase the
gains in student learning or reduce the costs of these gains or both.

An important aspect of educational process is the classroom
behavior of teachers and students. These behaviors can be recorded through the use of behavior rating scales as illustrated in
Chapter 7 (see Figures 7.7 and 7.8).

Box 15.3 ──

IMPLEMENTING THE SYSTEM TESTING PROGRAM

To use a school testing program to stimulate self-improvement, a
a district should first *specify its educational goals.* Secondly, a district
should *accept the principle of using the school testing program as the
measure of the attainment of these goals.* Tests must be viewed as having
value not only for the determination and facilitation of individual learning
but for the purpose of identifying school-wide and district-wide effects as
well.

The third step should be to *identify and administer appropriate test
batteries.* Criterion-referenced tests (particularly the published ones) have
the greatest potential.

The fourth step should be to *compare the performance on each goal
for students at different grade levels* and to compare student performance
to goals specific for their grade level. The purpose of this comparison is
to determine whether, and to what extent, growth or improvement is occurring over the course of the school years, and also whether goals are being
met in an absolute sense. Input and output comparisons are also useful
for this purpose.

As a final step a district should *make a chart indicating all the curricular or programmatic activities in each goal area.* Presumably, in those
areas where programmatic effort and expenditures are small, gains should
be slight or nonexistent while in the areas with greatest effort and investment, gains should be great. Linking educational experiences or processes
with gains (gains being the difference between performance outputs and
inputs) would help the district to evaluate specific programs and events.

──

Whether the purpose of testing is to monitor and improve individual, class, or system performance, the pattern of procedures is largely the same (and has basically served as the theme of this book). In all cases objectives must be specified and tests must be constructed or found to measure those objectives—tests that are appropriate, valid, reliable, interpretable, and usable. To determine the degree of proficiency that has been attained by the student, class, or system, the test results are compared to the objectives. Where proficiency levels are adequate, no additional evaluation is needed; but where performance is below acceptable levels, test results should be analyzed to provide intensified or alternative programs of instruction to attempt to raise performance to an acceptable level, and further evaluation will be necessary. To monitor, to diagnose, to provide feedback, to facilitate the achievement of proficiency, to certify—these then are the functions of tests in the schools, for the students, the teachers, and the administrators.

Additional Information Sources

Anderson, S. B. et al. *Encyclopedia of evaluation.* San Francisco: Jossey-Bass, 1974.

Bauernfeind, R. H. *Building a school testing program.* Boston: Houghton Mifflin, 1963.

Davis, F. B. *Educational measurements and their interpretation.* Belmont, Calif.: Wadsworth Publishing Co., 1964.

Findley, W. G. The impact and improvement of school testing programs. *Sixty-second yearbook of the National Society for the Study of Education, Part II.* Chicago: University of Chicago Press, 1963.

Glaser, R. & Nitko, A. J. Measurement in learning and instruction. In R. L. Thorndike (Ed.). *Educational measurement,* 2nd ed. Wash. D.C.: American Council on Education, 1971, Chap. 17.

Goldman, L. *Using tests in counseling.* N.Y.: Appleton-Century-Crofts, 1961.

Strong, R. *How to report pupil progress.* Chicago: Science Research Associates, 1961.

Tyler, R. W. Educational evaluation: New roles, new means. *The sixty-eighth yearbook of the National Society for the Study of Education, Part II.* Chicago: The University of Chicago Press, 1969.

Womer, F. B. & Wahl, N. K. Test use. In R. L. Ebel (Ed.). *Encyclopedia of educational research,* 4th ed. N.Y.: Macmillan, 1969, pp. 1461–1469.

Self-test of Proficiency

(1) You are trying to convince your colleagues to collaborate on the construction of a test item file. Cite three reasons you would use to convince them that the file is a good idea.

(2) Describe the steps in establishing a test item file.

(3) Individual test results can be very helpful to the classroom teacher. Give an example how the teacher can obtain and use test data to
   a. monitor and certify student progress.
   b. diagnose individual deficiencies.
   c. decide whether or not to prescribe additional instruction.
   d. provide feedback to students.

(4) Construct a sample roster for recording student's performance by objective.

(5) Consider the class summary of achievement test performance shown in the printout on pages 472–73.
   a. What is the area of greatest strength? How did you determine this?
   b. What is the area of greatest weakness? How did you determine this?
   c. Based on the print-out, what changes in instruction would you recommend the teacher make?

(6) Describe a system for classroom achievement monitoring.

(7) a. Describe a primary value of measuring educational input.
   b. Why are educational outputs more appropriate than processes for measuring and evaluating educational effects?
   c. Question b above notwithstanding, there are some uses to which the measurement of educational processes can be put. List two.

(8) Describe three ways to determine whether a new instructional procedure being used throughout the sixth grade of a school is effective.

COMBINATION
CLASS RECORD SHEET

CENTRAL   10/73
ANYTOWN   05.1
JONES LC   CA

NAME	A / B	LANGUAGE C/D	NON-LANGUAGE C/D	TOTAL C/D	READING VOCABULARY 1 / 3	2 / 4	COMPREHENSION 1 / 3	2 / 4	TOTAL 1 / 3	2 / 4
BELL ROBERT	10-07	121	113	120	56	61	53	53	56	58
	13-10	93	83	92	85-29		96-43		88-32	
BISHOP JANE	10-02	99	84	91	40	29	38	31	39	29
	8-10	42	16	26	48		44		47	
DEAN CATHY	10-06	124	118	124	79	89	65	68	72	80
	14-05	94	89	95	89		102-37		96-24	
FLYNN RUTH	10-01	94	72	80	23	6	25	8	22	5
	7-06	31	4	9	39-16		36-11		38-16	
HUNT EDWARD	10-02	102	118	109	49	46	44	41	48	45
	11-08	50	86	70	53		58		56	
LINDER AMY	10-05	86	99	92	36	22	26	11	31	15
	9-02	18	50	31	39		40-14		40	
NEWTON TAMMY	9-10	97	108	103	36	22	42	37	39	29
	10-03	34	64	48	50-14		50		51	
PHILLIPS FRAN	9-09	103	99	102	36	22	40	34	38	28
	9-11	46	41	44	50-14		51		51-13	
REED CYNTHIA	10-02	102	84	93	46	39	38	31	43	35
	9-02	50	16	31	49		47		49	
RICE JULIE	10-07	111	93	104	58	64	73	74	64	72
	11-03	78	36	64	66		70		68	
ROSS LYNN	10-09	111	116	115	68	77	65	68	67	74
	13-02	80	89	87	73		87		79	
SEARS MIKE	10-06	73	—	—	29	13	26	11	28	10
4		5								
		—	—	—	—	—	—	—	—	—
MEANS ** TOTAL CASES WITH OGE OR OSS	10-04 10-10	102	100	103	46		42		43	
		—	—	—	—		—		—	
CASES WITH AAGE OR AASS	—	—	—	—	47		44		45	
					57-10		59-15		58-13	

CHRON. AGE   A | C INTEL. QUOTIENT
MENTAL AGE   B | D NAT. PCT./GRADE

**Comprehensive Tests
of Basic Skills**

```
SHORT FORM TEST OF ACADEMIC
APTITUDE - LEVEL 3                                        12/18/73
CTBS-LEVEL 2, FORM S                    9395        001       1
```

LANGUAGE								MATHEMATICS/ARITHMETIC								*TOTAL BATTERY		REFR		SCIE		SOC ST	
MECHANICS		EXPRESSION		SPELLING		TOTAL		COMPUTA-TION		CONCEPTS		APPLICA-TIONS		TOTAL									
1	2	1	2	1	2	1	2	1	2	1	2	1	2	1	2	1	2	1	2	1	2	1	2
3	4	3	4	3	4	3	4	3	4	3	4	3	4	3	4	3	4	3	4	3	4	3	4
48	47	46	44	58	62	53	55	52	54	61	63	49	46	54	56	53	53	74	74	58	60	51	50
97	-49	100	-54	82		92	-39	69		80		83	-34	72	-18	81	-28	89		91	-33	98	-47
38	32	46	44	83	83	57	60	50	48	56	57	49	46	52	51	48	44	29	14	50	49	40	30
45		44		49	+34	46		46		37		39		42		45		42		38		44	
119	97	119	99	119	99	119	99	63	75	95	96	68	73	69	82	84	91	86	81	78	78	103	93
115		107	+12	100		105	+14	80		85		90		82		90		100		98		104	
25	12	20	5	17	4	20	3	20	1	31	17	16	2	18	1	19	1	44	38	19	4	26	8
36		34	-14	37	-20	34	-14	38	-18	30		33	-17	34	-16	36	-17	35		31	-12	36	
34	26	50	49	64	67	52	53	37	20	51	49	55	56	46	38	47	42	29	14	47	44	55	57
69	-35	63		54		57		62	-25	66		66		62	-16	58		59	-30	63		59	
42	39	37	31	73	75	52	53	52	54	31	17	29	13	43	32	42	31	58	59	33	20	53	54
49		39		47		44		50		42		43		48		44		44		39		43	
119	97	40	35	10	1	28	14	46	34	46	42	39	29	44	35	37	23	44	38	40	32	40	30
61	+58	55		56	-46	56	-28	52		48		48		51		51	-14	51		46		49	
38	32	40	35	53	54	46	43	53	58	51	49	52	51	54	56	46	40	44	38	47	44	44	36
55		52		54		53		52		47		48		51		51		50		46		50	
57	55	65	63	64	67	63	65	30	6	24	8	36	24	28	7	42	33	33	19	40	32	57	61
46		46		50		48		47	-17	39	-15	40		44	-16	47		44		40		47	
57	55	77	72	102	94	84	82	34	11	31	17	39	29	33	15	53	54	40	32	36	26	63	68
68		72		65	+37	68		52	-18	54	-23	53		54	-21	61		62		56	-20	67	
48	47	96	85	51	50	63	65	70	85	77	82	61	64	67	80	66	74	86	81	73	74	94	88
104	-56	95		85	-34	93	-30	74		77		79		74		79		91		83		91	
25	12	28	16	24	11	26	10	32	7	24	8	16	2	22	3	26	5	22	5	15	2	22	5
49		52		53		52		45		45		39		42		45		44		41		49	
54		56		55		55		46		48		42		45		47		47		44		53	
67	-13	63	-7	59	-4	60	-5	55	-9	54	-6	55	-13	55	-10	57	-10	58	-11	53	-9	57	-4

*TOTAL BATTERY INCLUDES READING,
LANGUAGE AND MATHEMATICS/ARITHMETIC
ONLY.

```
GRADE EQUIVALENT       1|2  NATIONAL PERCENTILE
ANTIC. GRADE EQUIV.    3|4  G. E. DIFFERENCE
```

Appendices

APPENDIX A   A GLOSSARY OF MEASUREMENT TERMS*

Academic Aptitude. The combination of native and acquired abilities that are needed for school learning; likelihood of success in mastering academic work, as estimated from measures of the necessary abilities. (Also called *scholastic aptitude*)

Achievement Age. The performance level or achievement test score expressed in terms of the chronological age group for which a particular performance level or achievement test score is average.

Achievement Test. A test that measures the extent to which a person has "achieved" something, acquired certain information, demonstrated proficiency in certain skills—usually as a result of instruction.

Acquiescence Response Bias. Responding to stimuli other than the test items themselves. This usually takes the form of responding

* Adapted from *A Glossary of Measurement Terms* (Test Service Notebook 13), prepared by Blythe C. Mitchell, distributed by Harcourt Brace Jovanovich, Inc., and reproduced by permission. It is introduced in part, by the following statement. "This glossary of terms used in educational and psychological measurement is primarily for persons with limited training in measurement, rather than for the specialist. The terms defined are the more common or basic ones such as occur in test manuals and educational journals. In the definitions, certain technicalities and niceties of usage have been sacrificed for the sake of brevity and, it is hoped, clarity. Where there is not complete uniformity among writers in the measurement field with respect to the meaning of a term, either these variations are noted or the definition offered is the one that writers judged to represent the 'best' usage." In addition to the HBJ glossary edited for use here, other measurement terms related to concepts developed in this book have been included.

in some systematic pattern such as marking *true* (yea saying) or *false* (nay saying) on every item.

Age Norms. Values representing typical, or average, performance for persons of various age groups.

Alternate-form Reliability. The closeness of correspondence, or correlation, between results on alternate (i.e., equivalent or parallel) forms of a test; thus, a measure of the extent to which the two forms are consistent or reliable in measuring whatever they do measure. (See *reliability, reliability coefficient*)

Appropriateness. On achievement tests, an indication of the extent to which the test items adequately represent the objectives that they have been written or selected to measure. It is best established by a comparison of test content with instructional objectives. (Also called *content validity*)

Aptitude. A combination of abilities and other characteristics, whether native or acquired, known or believed to be indicative of an individual's ability to learn or to develop proficiency in some particular area. Aptitude tests include those of general academic ability (commonly called *mental ability* or *intelligence* tests); those of special abilities, such as verbal, numerical, mechanical, or musical ability; those assessing "readiness" for learning; and prognostic tests, which measure both ability and previous learning and are used to predict future performance, usually in a specific field, such as foreign language, shorthand, or nursing.

Arithmetic Mean. The sum of a set of scores divided by their number. It is usually referred to as the *mean* or *average*.

Average. A general term applied to the various measures of central tendency. The three most widely used averages are the arithmetic mean (mean), the median, and the mode. When the term "average" is used without designation as to type, the most likely assumption is that it is the arithmetic mean.

Battery. A group of several tests standardized on the same sample population so that results on the several tests are comparable. (Sometimes loosely applied to any group of tests administered together, even though not standardized on the same subjects.) The most common test batteries are those of school achievement, which include subtests in the separate learning areas.

Behavior Rating Scale. An instrument used to record judgments about the incidence or nature of the behavior of a given individual or group. Such judgments will be influenced by subjective factors and should be tested for reliability.

Ceiling. The upper limit of performance measured by a test.

Checklist. A list of behaviors, observations, or characteristics, each of which is checked (or answered "yes") by the rater or observer when the item has been judged to have occurred satisfactorily and not checked (or answered "no") when judged not to have occurred satisfactorily.

Chronological Age. A person's age usually expressed in years and months.

Coefficient of Correlation. A measure of the degree of relationship or "going-togetherness" between two sets of measures for the same individuals. The correlation coefficient most frequently used in test development and educational research is that known as the Pearson, or *product-moment r*. Unless otherwise specified, "correlation" usually refers to this coefficient, but *rank, biserial* and others are used in special situations. Correlation coefficients range from .00, denoting a complete absence of relationship, to + 1.00, and to − 1.00, indicating perfect positive or perfect negative correspondence, respectively. (See *correlation*)

Completion Item. A short-answer test question calling for the filling in of an omitted word or phrase.

Concurrent Validity. See *validity*.

Construct Validity. See *validity*.

Content Outline. A specification of the content covered in a segment of instruction and of the importance of each piece of content. This outline serves as a basis for test item construction.

Content Validity. See *appropriateness*.

Correction for Guessing (correction for chance). A reduction in score for wrong answers, sometimes applied in scoring true–false or multiple choice questions. Such scoring formulas ($R - W$ for tests with 2-option response, $R - \frac{1}{2}W$ for 3-option response, $R - \frac{1}{3}W$ for 4, etc.) are intended to discourage guessing and to yield more accurate rankings of test takers in terms of their true knowledge. They are used much less today than in the early days of testing.

Correlation. Relationship, or "going-togetherness," between two sets of scores or measures; tendency of one score to vary concomitantly with the other, as the tendency of students of high IQ to be above average in reading ability. The existence of a strong relationship— i.e., a high correlation—between two variables does not necessarily indicate that one has any causal influence on the other. (See *coefficient of correlation*)

Criterion. A standard by which a test or test performance may be judged or evaluated; a set of scores, ratings, etc., that a test is designed to measure, predict, or correlate with. (See *validity*)

Criterion-referenced Test. Term used to describe tests designed to provide information on the specific knowledge or skills possessed by a student. Such tests are designed to measure the objectives of instruction. Their scores have meaning in terms of *what* the student knows or can do, rather than in their relation to the scores made by some comparison or norm group.

Criterion Validity. See *validity*.

Culture-fair Test. Culture-fair tests attempt to provide an equal opportunity for success by persons of all cultures and life experiences. Their content must therefore be limited to that which is assumed to be equally common to all cultures, or to material that is entirely unfamiliar and novel for all persons whatever their cultural background.

Decile. Any one of the nine percentile points (scores) that divide a distribution into ten parts, each containing one-tenth of all the scores or cases; every tenth percentile. The first decile is the 10th percentile, the second the 20th, the eighth the 80th percentile, etc.

Deviation. The amount by which a score differs from a designated reference value, such as the mean, the norm, or the score on some other test.

Deviation IQ (DIQ). An age-based index of general mental ability. It is based upon the difference, or deviation, between a person's score and the typical, or average, score for persons of the same chronological age. Deviation IQs from most current mental ability measures are standard scores with a mean of 100 and a standard deviation of 16 for each defined age group. (See *intelligence quotient*)

Diagnostic Test. A test used to locate specific areas of weakness or strength, to determine the nature of weaknesses or deficiencies, and to yield measures of the components or subparts of a larger body of information or skill. Diagnostic tests are most commonly prepared for reading and mathematics.

Difficulty Index. The percentage of a specified group, such as students of a given age or grade, who answer a test item correctly.

Discriminability Index. The ability of a test item to differentiate between persons possessing much or little of a certain trait, skill, or proficiency. It is usually derived from the number passing the item in the highest third of the group (on total score) and the number passing in the lowest third.

Distractor. Any of the incorrect choices, or options, in a multiple choice or matching short-answer test item.

Distribution (frequency distribution). A tabulation of the scores of a group of individuals showing the number of individuals obtaining each score, or the number of individuals within the range of each interval.

Domain-referencing. Systematically constructing items to be representative of the full range of possible conditions set forth in the objective for which the items are intended to be a measure.

Equivalent Form. Any of two or more forms of a test that are closely parallel with respect to the nature of the content and the number and difficulty of the items included, and that will yield very similar average scores and measures of variability for a given group. (Also called *alternate, comparable,* or *parallel form*)

Error of Measurement. See *standard error of measurement*.

Essay-type Item. An item that provides test takers with the opportunity to structure and compose their own responses within relatively broad limits. Scoring of an essay-type item often involves the subjective judgment of the scorer, in contrast to a short-answer item, which structures or even includes the correct response, making scoring quite objective.

Extrapolation. In general, any process of estimating values of a variable beyond the range of available data. As applied to test norms, the process of extending a norm line into grade or age levels not tested in the standardization program, in order to permit interpretation of extreme scores. Since this extension is usually done graphically rather than empirically or according to a given mathematical function, considerable judgment is involved. Extrapolated values are thus to some extent arbitrary; for this and other reasons, they have limited meaning.

Face Validity. Refers to the acceptability of the test and test situation by the examinee or user, in terms of apparent uses to which the test is to be put. A test has face validity when it appears to measure the variable or objectives to be tested.

Factor. In mental measurement, a hypothetical trait, ability, or component of ability that underlies and influences performance on two or more tests and hence causes scores on the tests to be correlated. The term "factor" strictly refers to a theoretical variable, derived by a process of factor analysis from a table of intercorrelations among tests. However, it is also used to denote the psychological interpretation given to the variable—i.e., the mental trait assumed to be represented by the variable, as *verbal ability, numerical ability*, etc.

Factor Analysis. Any of several methods of analyzing the intercorrelations among a set of variables such as test scores. Factor analysis attempts to account for the interrelationships in terms of some underlying "factors," preferably fewer in number than the original variables, and it reveals how much of the variation in each of the original measures arises from, or is associated with, each of the hypothetical factors. Factor analysis has contributed to an understanding of the organization or components of intelligence, aptitudes, and personality; and it has pointed the way to the development of "purer" tests of the several components.

Faking. Giving a test response on an affective test that is an intended distortion in an attempt to create an impression. It is more likely to occur when the test taker feels pressure to respond in a particular way, such as when taking an employment test.

Forced-choice Item. Broadly, any multiple choice item in which the examinee is required to select one or more of the given choices. The term is most often used to denote a special type of multiple choice item used in personality tests in which the options are (1) of equal "preference value," i.e., chosen equally often by a typical group, and are (2) such that one of the options discriminates between persons high and low on the factor that this option measures, while the other option measures another factor.

Frequency Distribution. See *distribution.*

Grade Equivalent (GE). The grade level for which a given score is the real or estimated average. Grade-equivalent interpretation, most appropriate for elementary level achievement tests, expresses obtained scores in terms of grade and month of grade, assuming a 10-month school year (e.g., 5.7). Since such tests are usually standardized at only one (or two) point(s) within each grade, grade equivalents between points for which there are data-based scores must be "estimated" by interpolation. (See *extrapolation, interpolation*)

Grade Norm. The average test score obtained by typical pupils classified at a given grade placement. (See *grade equivalent, norms, percentile rank, stanine*)

Group Test. A test that may be administered to a number of individuals at the same time by one examiner.

Individual Test. A test that can be administered to only one person at a time.

Intelligence Quotient (IQ). Originally, the ratio of a person's mental age to his or her chronological age, MA/CA, multiplied by 100 to eliminate the decimal. More precisely—and particularly for adult ages, at which mental growth is assumed to have ceased—the ratio of mental age to the mental age normal for chronological age. This quotient IQ has been gradually replaced by the deviation IQ concept. (See *deviation IQ*)

Interpolation. In general, any process of estimating intermediate values between two known points. As applied to test norms, it refers to the procedure used in assigning interpretive values (such as grade equivalents) to scores between the successive average scores actually obtained in the standardization process. Also, in reading norm tables it is necessary at times to interpolate to obtain a norm value for a score between two scores given in the table; e.g., in the table shown here, a percentile rank of 83 (from 81 + ⅓ of 6) would be assigned, by interpolation, to a score of 46; a score of 50 would correspond to a percentile rank of 94 (obtained as 87 + ⅔ of 10).

Score	Percentile Rank
51	97
48	87
45	81

Interpretability. An indication of what the scores on a test mean and how their meaning is derived or determined. Test interpretation is either *criterion-referenced* or *norm-referenced.*

Inventory Test. An achievement test that attempts to cover rather thoroughly some relatively small unit of specific instruction or training. An inventory test, as the name suggests, is in the nature of a "stock-taking" of an individual's knowledge or skill, and is often administered prior to instruction. Inventories are also used to measure personality traits, interests, attitudes, problems, motivation, etc. (See *personality test*)

Item. A single question or exercise in a test.

Item Analysis. The process of evaluating single test items by determining the difficulty value and the discriminating power of the item, and often its correlation with some criterion.

Kuder-Richardson Formula(s). Formulas for estimating the reliability of a test that are based on inter-item consistency and that require only a single administration of the test. The one most used, *formula 21*, requires information based on the number of items in the test, the variance, and the test mean. Kuder-Richardson formulas are not appropriate for use with speed tests, that is, tests which measure rate of performance, nor with tests whose items cannot be scored as either right or wrong.

Likert Scale. An attitude scale in which the test taker is given a series of attitude statements and responds by choosing one of given choices: *strongly agree, agree, undecided* (this choice is not always used), *disagree,* or *strongly disagree.*

Matching Item. A short-answer test item in which the student must associate an entry in one list with one in another.

Mean. See *arithmetic mean.*

Median. The middle score in a distribution or set of ranked scores; the point (score) that divides the group into two equal parts; the 50th percentile. Half of the scores are below the median and half above it.

Mental Ability. Skills including reasoning, verbal comprehension and fluency, numerical or quantitative ability, and figural comprehension that are influenced by or relate to a learning environment which reinforces or requires them. More traditionally, this has been called *intelligence.*

Mental Age (MA). The age for which a given score on an intelligence or mental ability test is average or normal. If the average score made by an unselected group of children 6 years, 10 months of age is 55, then a child making a score of 55 is said to have a mental age of 6-10. (See *achievement age, chronological age*)

Mode. The score, or value, that occurs most frequently in a distribution.

Multiple Choice Item. A test item in which the test taker's task is to choose the correct or best answer from several given answers, or options.

N or n. The symbol commonly used to represent the number of cases or observations in a distribution.

Nominations. The procedure of naming choices or preferences. It is often used to identify friendship choices in which case its results are diagrammed as a *sociogram.*

Nonverbal Test. A test that does not require the use of words in the item or in the response to it. (However, oral directions may be included in the formulation of the task.) A test cannot be classified as nonverbal simply because it does not require reading on the part of the test taker.

Normal Distribution. A distribution of scores or measures that in graphic form has a distinctive bell-shaped appearance. The graph of a normal distribution is known as a *normal curve.* In a normal distribution, scores or measures are distributed symmetrically about the mean, with as many cases at various distances above the mean as at equal distances below it. Cases are concentrated near the mean and decrease in frequency the farther one departs from the mean. The assumption that mental and psychological characteristics are distributed normally has been useful in much test development work.

Norming Group. Sample on which norms or comparison scores are obtained as part of the process of test standardization. (Also called a *norm group* or *standardization sample*)

Norm-line. A smooth curve drawn to best fit (1) the plotted mean or median scores of successive age or grade groups, or (2) the successive percentile points for a single group.

Norm-referenced Test. Term used to describe tests designed to provide information on the performance of test takers relative to one another. Usually norms for interpretation are obtained from a *norming group.* This type of test is contrasted to a *criterion-referenced test,* which is interpreted on an absolute rather than a relative basis.

Norms. Statistics that supply a frame of reference by which meaning may be given to obtained test scores. Norms are based upon the actual performance of pupils of various grades or ages in the standardization group for the test. Since norms represent average or typical performance, they should not be regarded as standards or as universally desirable levels of attainment. The most common types of norms are *deviation IQ, percentile rank, grade equivalent,* and *stanine.* Reference groups are usually those of specified age or grade.

Objective. An intended outcome of instruction stated in such a way that its attainment can be observed and measured. Objectives serve as the basis for constructing test items. (Also called *behav-*

ioral, instructional, measurable, learner, or *performance* objectives) (See *appropriateness*)

Omnibus Test. A test (1) in which items measuring a variety of mental operations are all combined into a single sequence rather than being grouped together by type of operation, and (2) from which only a single score is derived, rather than separate scores for each operation or function. Omnibus tests make for simplicity of administration, since one set of directions and one overall time limit usually suffice.

Other Two-choice Item. A short-answer item other than *true–false* that requires the test taker to classify or categorize objects into one of two categories (such as: a capitol city, not a capitol city).

Parallel-item Agreement. A reliability procedure for use with criterion-referenced tests in which performances on the items that were written to measure the same objective are compared and an indication of similarity or dissimilarity in these performances noted. Lack of agreement can then become the basis for item revision.

Percentile. The percent of cases falling at or below a given or indicated point in the distribution. Thus a score coinciding with the 35th percentile (P_{35}) is regarded as equaling or surpassing that of 35 percent of the persons in the group, and such that 65 percent of the performances exceeds this score.

Percentile Rank (PR). The expression of an obtained test score in terms of its position within a group of 100 scores; the percentile rank of a score is the percent of scores equal to or lower than the given score in its own group or in an external reference (i.e., norm) group.

Performance Test. A test usually involving some motor or manual response on the test taker's part, generally a manipulation of concrete equipment or materials as contrasted to a paper-and-pencil test. The term "performance" is also used to denote a test that is actually a work sample; in this sense it may include paper-and-pencil tests, as, for example, a test in bookkeeping, in shorthand, or in proofreading, where no materials other than paper and pencil may be required, and where the test response is identical with the behavior about which information is desired.

Personality Test. A test intended to measure one or more of the non-intellective aspects of an individual's mental or psychological make-up; an instrument designed to obtain information on the affective characteristics of an individual—emotional, motivational, attitudinal, etc.—as distinguished from his or her abilities. Personality tests include (1) personality and adjustment inventories that seek to measure a person's status on such traits as dominance, sociability, introversion, etc., by means of self-descriptive responses to a series of questions; (2) rating scales that call for rating, by one's self or another, the extent to which a subject possesses certain traits; and (3) opinion or attitude inventories.

More specifically, category (1) may be called tests of personality orientation, category (2), self-concept, and category (3), attitude scales.

Power Test.   A test intended to measure level of performance unaffected by speed of response; hence one in which there is either no time limit or a very generous one. Items are usually arranged in order of increasing difficulty.

Practice Effect.   The influence of previous experience with a test on a later administration of the same or a similar test; usually an increased familiarity with the directions, kind of questions, etc. Practice effect is greatest when the interval between testings is short, when the content of the two tests is identical or very similar, and when the initial test taking represents a relatively novel experience for the subjects.

Predictive Validity.   See *validity.*

Product-moment Coefficient   (*r*). Also known as the *Pearson r.* (See *coefficient of correlation*)

Proficiency Test.   A test designed to determine whether a pupil has acquired proficiency on a given unit of instruction or a single knowledge or skill; a test whose results give information on what a pupil knows, rather than on how his or her performance relates to that of some norm-reference group. Such tests are usually referred to as criterion-referenced tests.

Profile.   A graphic representation of the results on several tests, for either an individual or a group, when the results have been expressed in some uniform or comparable terms (standard scores, percentile ranks, grade equivalents, etc.). The profile method of presentation permits identification of areas of strength or weakness.

Prognosis (prognostic) Test.   A test used to predict future success in a specific subject or field.

Projective Technique (projective method).   A method of personality study in which the subject responds as he or she chooses to a series of ambiguous stimuli, such as ink blots, pictures, unfinished sentences, etc. It is assumed that under this free-response condition the subject "projects" manifestations of personality characteristics and organization that can, by suitable methods, be scored and interpreted to yield a description of his or her basic personality structure. The Rorschach (ink blot) Technique, and the Murray Thematic Apperception Test are commonly used projective methods.

Quartile.   One of three points that divide the cases in a distribution into four equal groups. The lower quartile (Q_1), or 25th percentile, sets off the lowest fourth of the group; the middle quartile (Q_2) is the same as the 50th percentile, or median, and divides the second fourth of cases from the third; and the third quartile (Q_3), or 75th percentile, sets off the top fourth.

r.   See *coefficient of correlation.*

Random Sample.   A sample of the members of a specified total population drawn in such a way that every member of the population has an equal chance of being included—that is, in a way that precludes the operation of bias or selection. The purpose in using a sample free of bias is, of course, the requirement that the cases used be representative of the total population if findings for the sample are to be generalized to that population. In a stratified random sample, the drawing of cases is controlled in such a way that those chosen are "representative" also of specified subgroups of the total population. (See *representative sample*)

Range.   The difference between the highest and the lowest score on a test by a group of test takers.

Raw Score.   The first quantitative result obtained in scoring a test; for example, the number of right answers, time required for performance, number of errors, or a similar direct, unconverted, uninterpreted measure.

Readiness Test.   A test that measures the extent to which an individual has achieved a degree of maturity or has acquired certain skills or information needed for successfully undertaking a particular new learning activity. Thus a reading readiness test indicates whether a child has reached a developmental stage where he or she may profitably begin formal reading instruction.

Recall Item.   A type of item that requires the test taker to supply the correct answer from memory or recollection, as contrasted with a *recognition* item, in which he or she need only identify the correct answer. For example:

Columbus discovered America in the year _____ is a *recall* item. Both *completion* and *unstructured* items are recall items.

Recognition Item.   An item that requires the examinee to recognize or select the correct answer from among two or more given answers (options). For example:

Columbus discovered America in
    a. 1425   *b.* 1492   *c.* 1520   *d.* 1546
is a recognition item. All short-answer item formats other than completion or unstructured require recognition. (See *recall item*)

Regression Effect.   The tendency for students who make extremely high or extremely low scores on a test to make less extreme scores, i.e., scores closer to the mean, on a second administration of the same test or on some predicted measure.

Reliability.   The extent to which a test is consistent in measuring whatever it does measure; accuracy, dependability, stability, trustworthiness, relative freedom from errors of measurement. Reliability is usually expressed by a reliability coefficient or by the standard error of measurement derived from it.

Reliability Coefficient.   The coefficient of correlation between two forms of a test, between scores on two administrations of the same test, or between halves of a test (corrected by Spearman-Brown formula). The three measure somewhat different aspects of reliability, but all are properly spoken of as reliability coefficients. (See *alternate-form reliability, split-half reliability coefficient, Spearman-Brown formula, test-retest reliability coefficient, Kuder-Richardson formula(s)*; see also *parallel-item agreement*)

Representative Sample. A sample that corresponds to or matches the population of which it is a sample with respect to characteristics important for the purposes under investigation. In an achievement test norm sample, such significant aspects might be the proportion of cases from various types of schools, different geographical areas, and so on.

Scale. A continuum marked off into numerical units that can be applied to some object or state in order to measure a particular property of it.

Scholastic Aptitude. See *academic aptitude*.

Semantic Differential. A bipolar adjective scale used for measuring attitudes toward a given object or stimulus. Scales are labeled with an adjective and its opposite at each end with seven points between as shown below

interesting ___: ___: ___: ___: ___: ___: ___ boring

to reflect the test taker's judgment of the "goodness" (evaluation), potency, activity, or some other more specific property of the given stimulus.

Short-answer Item. An item for which the correct responses or scoring key may be set up in advance so that scores are unaffected by the opinion or judgment of the scorer. Such an item is contrasted with an essay-type item to which different persons may assign different scores, ratings, or grades.

Skewed Distribution. A distribution that departs from symmetry, or balance around the mean, i.e., from normality. Scores pile up at one end and trail off at the other.

Social Desirability Response Bias. Giving a presumably unconsciously distorted test response that conforms to the test taker's expectation of what is the most "normal" or socially acceptable response.

Spearman-Brown Formula. A formula giving the relationship between the reliability of a test and its length. The formula permits estimation of the reliability of a test lengthened or shortened by any amount from the known reliability of a test of specified length. Its most common application is the estimation of reliability of an entire test from the correlation between its two halves. (See *split-half reliability coefficient*)

Split-half Reliability Coefficient. A coefficient of reliability obtained by correlating scores on one half of a test with scores on the other half, and applying the Spearman-Brown formula to adjust for the doubled length of the total test. Generally, but not necessarily, the two halves consist of the odd-numbered and the even-numbered items.

Standard Deviation (σ, s, S.D.). A measure of the variability or dispersion of a set of scores based on the square of the deviation of each score from the mean. The more the scores cluster around the mean, the smaller the standard deviation. For a normal distribution, approximately two thirds (68.3 percent) of the scores are within the range from one S.D. below the mean to one S.D. above the mean. The square of the standard deviation is called the *variance*.

Standard Error of Measurement (S.E.M.). Estimate of the magnitude of "error" present in an obtained score, whether (1) an individual score, or (2) a group measure, as a mean or a correlation coefficient. It is the standard deviation of the difference between obtained scores and corresponding true scores.

Standard Score. A general term referring to any of a variety of "transformed" scores, in terms of which raw scores may be expressed for reasons of convenience, comparability, ease of interpretation, etc. The simplest type of standard score, known as a z-score, is an expression of the deviation of a score from the mean score of the group in relation to the standard deviation of the scores of the group. Thus:

$$\text{standard score } (z) = \frac{\text{raw score } (X) - \text{mean } (\overline{X})}{\text{standard deviation (S.D.)}}$$

Adjustments may be made in this ratio so that a system of standard scores having any desired mean and standard deviation may be set up. The use of such standard scores does not affect the relative standing of the individuals in the group or change the shape of the original distribution. *T*-scores have a mean of 50 and an S.D. of 10. Deviation IQs are standard scores with a mean of 100 and a chosen S.D., most often 16. Standard scores are useful in expressing the raw scores of two forms of a test in comparable terms in instances where tryouts have shown that the two forms are not identical in difficulty; also, successive levels of a test may be linked to form a continuous standard-score scale, making across-battery comparison possible.

Standardized Test. A test designed to provide a systematic sample of individual performance, administered according to prescribed directions, scored in conformance with definite rules, and interpreted in reference to certain normative information. We can further restrict the usage of the term "standardized" to those tests for which the items have been chosen on the basis of experimental evaluation, and for which data on reliability and validity are provided. Typically such tests are commercially published. (See *norm-referenced test*)

Stanine. One of the steps in a nine-point scale of standard scores. The stanine (short for standard-nine) scale has values from 1 to 9, with a mean of 5 and a standard deviation of 2.

Structured Item. Any of a number of short-answer items where the correct answer is provided and the test taker must recognize it. (See *recognition item, matching item, multiple choice item, other two-choice item,* and *true–false item*)

Survey Test.   A test that measures general achievement in a given area, usually with the connotation that the test is intended to assess group status, rather than to yield precise measures of individual performance.

T-**score.**   A standard score scale using a mean of 50 and a standard deviation of 10.

Taxonomy.   An embodiment of the principles of classification; a survey, usually in outline form, such as a presentation of the objectives of education. Two taxonomies are those of the cognitive and affective domains.

Test-retest Reliability Coefficient.   A type of reliability coefficient obtained by administering the same test a second time, after a short interval, and correlating the two sets of scores.

True–False Item.   A test question in which the test taker is given a statement and asked whether it is true or false.

True Score.   A score entirely free of error; hence, a hypothetical value that can never be obtained by testing, because testing always involves some measurement error. A true score may be thought of as the average score from an infinite number of measurements from the same or exactly equivalent tests, assuming no practice effect or change in the test taker during the testings. The standard deviation of this infinite number of "samplings" is known as the *standard error of measurement.*

Unstructured Item.   A short-answer question that can be answered by a word, phrase, or number. It is similar to a completion item except without the blank contained within the item. For example: Who is the author of *Catch-22*? (See *completion item* and *recall item*)

Usability.   An indication of the suitability or practicality of a test as it relates to its intended use. For teachers, this would be classroom use.

Validity.   The extent to which a test does the job for which it is used, that is, measures what it is supposed to measure.

    Concurrent Validity.   The extent to which different tests of the same property are in agreement. Such validity might be evidenced by concurrent measures of academic ability and of achievement, by the relation of a new test to one generally accepted as or known to be valid, or by the correlation between scores on a test and criteria measures that are valid but are less objective and more time consuming to obtain than a test score would be.

    Construct Validity.   The extent to which two tests or measures of different but conceptually related properties agree. Tests of personality, verbal ability, mechanical aptitude, critical thinking, etc., are validated in terms of their construct and the relation of their scores to pertinent external data.

Criterion Validity. The extent to which a group already proficient or experienced in the quality measured by a test scores higher on that test than before they acquired proficiency or higher than a nonproficient or inexperienced group. For the validation of performance tests, trained groups are compared to untrained groups or groups are compared before and after training.

Predictive Validity. The accuracy with which a test (such as an aptitude, prognostic, or readiness test) indicates future outcomes (for example, learning success) in a particular area, as evidenced by correlations between scores on the test and future criterion measures (e.g., the relation of score on an academic aptitude test administered in high school to grade point average over four years of college).

Variance. A measure of dispersion of a set of scores from the mean: the square of the standard deviation.

z-score. A standard score expressed in standard deviation units having a mean of 0 and a standard deviation of 1.

APPENDIX B   PREPARING TEST ITEM SPECIFICATIONS

After you have written your objectives but before you write the test items, it is advisable to prepare test item specifications. A simple way to carry out this intermediate step is to use index cards, either 5″ × 8″ or 4″ × 6″. At the top of the card, write the objective, and below the objective make a table consisting of three parts: the conditions, the action, and the criteria.

Following are some examples. Note that the specifications provide information about the range and kind of conditions that are suitable for measuring the objective, the specific action or performance required of the student, and the criteria for evaluation of the performance.

Example A

Objective: Given a map of New Jersey, the student will plot the natural and human-made boundaries, the capital and major cities.

CONDITIONS	ACTION	CRITERIA
An outline map of New Jersey with water and human-made boundaries	a. Label each body of water and human-made boundary that separates New Jer-	Correct labeling of Delaware River, Delaware Bay, Arthur Kill, Upper New

marked; and three dots, one in position of Trenton, one Newark, and one Atlantic City.	sey from its neighbors. *b.* Each of these dots represents a city. Label each by name and indicate which is the capital.	York Bay, Hudson River, and human-made boundary with New York State. Cities labeled correctly and Trenton marked as capital.

Example B

Objective: Given a pair of numbers, the student will list their common factors and choose the greatest common factor.

CONDITIONS	ACTION	CRITERIA
Two numbers between 2 and 100 that have no fewer than two and no more than four common factors other than 1, e.g., 24 and 8.	*a.* State all common factors. *b.* State the greatest common factor.	E.g., states all common factors, 8, 4, and 2; designates largest, 8.

Example C

Objective: Given a copy of a personal letter that has commas omitted, the student will demonstrate proper placement of all necessary commas.

CONDITIONS	ACTION	CRITERIA
Personal letter of 3 or 4 paragraphs, including a heading, salutation, and closing. The body of the letter will contain compound sentences, introductory adverbial clauses, words in series, and at least one appositive.	Write in all necessary commas and no unnecessary ones.	Places commas in heading, after salutation and closing. Uses a comma to separate the two parts of a compound sentence; after the adverbial clause; before the word connecting the last two elements in a series of three or more; and to set off an appositive.

Example D

Objective: Given the equipment and directions, the student will set up the equipment and conduct an electrical experiment in accordance with the instructions.

CONDITIONS	ACTION	CRITERIA
All equipment and directions to do an unfamiliar experiment in electricity, e.g., wiring a circuit to light a bulb. (Note, however, that the student should be familiar with the equipment and its use.)	Carry out the experiment in accordance with the directions to produce the results called for.	All equipment is used properly (safely and as called for in the directions). All procedures that are called for are followed. Experiment produces desired result, e.g., the bulb lights.

Writing specifications is an important step because it insures that the item will measure the objective and that the range of conditions suitable for the objective will not be exceeded. In preparing the specifications, do not repeat the wording of the objective; the point is to increase the level of detail preparatory to writing the items. At the same time, specifications should be broad enough to cover two items unless (as in Example A) one item would exhaust all possibilities. The final step is, of course, writing the items themselves and entering them on the back of the index card.

APPENDIX C   AN EXAMPLE OF STANDARDIZING SCORES

Consider the distribution of 30 test scores (raw scores) shown below.

99	88	80	75	70	57
97	85	79	75	68	54
95	83	76	74	65	50
92	82	76	72	63	47
90	80	75	70	60	43

These 30 scores have been plotted in groups of 5-point ranges as shown in Figure C-1. Note that the plot of the 30 scores approximates a normal distribution (that is, it is highest in about the middle). For illustrative purposes, each of the above 30 scores have been converted into a (1) z-score, (2) T-score, (3) percentile score, and (4) stanine score. These scores are shown in Figure C-2. (The mean of the distribution of the 30 scores is 74.0; the standard deviation is 14.6) The standard deviation was computed using the formula:

$$\text{s.d.} = \sqrt{\frac{N\Sigma X^2 - (\Sigma X)^2}{N(N-1)}}$$

We can now convert the 30 raw scores into both z-scores and T-scores using the following *standard score formula*:

$$\text{STANDARD SCORE (SS)} = M + S \left(\frac{X - \overline{X}}{\text{s.d.}}\right)$$

where M = predesignated standard score mean
S = predesignated standard score standard deviation
X = raw score
$\overline{X}$ = mean of raw scores
s.d. = standard deviation of raw scores

(Remember that the z-score has a predesignated mean of 0 and standard deviation of 1 while the T-score has a predesignated mean of 50 and standard deviation of 10.) Note that if the z-scores are algebraically summed, the result is approximately zero, actually -0.1 in this case because of rounding errors.

Frequency Distribution of 30 Test Scores.   **Figure C-1**

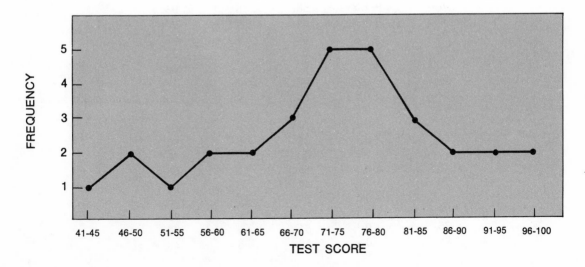

Percentiles were calculated based on the *percentile formula* given below.

$$\text{PERCENTILE} = \frac{100(\text{no. of scores exceeded})}{\text{Total number of scores}}$$

Note the recurring pattern: 0,3,7—except in the cases of ties where adjustments were made in the denominator. Other than for ties, any set of 30 scores, once rank-ordered, would receive the same percentiles, regardless of the individual raw scores, because the percentile is based *only on relative position* or standing and not at all on the absolute magnitude of the raw score.

The *stanine scores* represent the top and bottom 4%, the next top and bottom 7%, the next top and bottom 12%, the next top and bottom 17%, and middle 20% of the scores. Note that the stanine score conversion results in as many as six raw scores having the same stanine score—a decided disadvantage of the stanine score. This is somewhat compensated for by not having large jumps in rank scores for small jumps in raw score in the middle of the distribution. Moreover, for ease of interpretation, there is an obvious advantage to having a possibility of only nine scores as opposed to a number equal to the number of students taking the test (in this case, 30).

Figure C-2   *The Conversion of 30 Raw Scores on a Test to z-Scores, T-Scores, Stanine Scores, and Percentiles.*

RAW SCORE	z-SCORE	T-SCORE	STANINE SCORE	PERCENTILE
99	+1.7	67	9	97
97	+1.6	66	8	93
95	+1.4	64	8	90
92	+1.2	62	7	87
90	+1.1	61	7	83
88	+1.0	60	7	80
85	+0.8	58	7	77
83	+0.6	56	6	73
82	+0.5	55	6	70
80	+0.4	54	6	65
80	+0.4	54	6	65
79	+0.3	53	6	60
76	+0.1	51	5	55
76	+0.1	51	5	55
75	+0.1	51	5	46
75	+0.1	51	5	46
75	+0.1	51	5	46
74	0	50	5	40

72	−0.1	49	4	37
70	−0.3	47	4	31
70	−0.3	47	4	31
68	−0.4	46	4	27
65	−0.6	44	4	23
63	−0.8	42	3	20
60	−1.0	40	3	17
57	−1.2	38	3	13
54	−1.4	36	3	10
50	−1.6	34	2	7
47	−1.8	32	2	3
43	−2.1	29	1	0

APPENDIX D   DIRECTORY OF TEST PUBLISHERS

American Guidance Service, Inc.
Publishers' Bldg., Circle Pines, Minn. 55014

The Bobbs-Merrill Co., Inc.
4300 W. 62d St., Indianapolis, Ind. 46206

Bureau of Educational Measurements
Kansas State Teachers College, Emporia, Kansas 66801

Bureau of Educational Research and Service
University of Iowa, Iowa City, Iowa 52240

California Test Bureau/McGraw-Hill Book Co., Inc.
Del Monte Research Park, Monterey, Calif. 93940

Consulting Psychologists Press, Inc.
577 College Ave., Palo Alto, Calif. 94306

Counselor Recording and Tests
Box 6184 Acklen Station, Nashville, Tenn. 37212

Educational and Industrial Testing Service
P.O. Box 7234, San Diego, Calif. 92107

Educational Testing Service (and the ERIC Clearinghouse on Tests, Measurement, and Evaluation)
Princeton, N.J. 08540

Harcourt Brace Jovanovich, Inc.
757 Third Avenue, New York, N.Y. 10017

Harper & Row, Publishers
10 E. 53rd St., New York, N.Y. 10022

Houghton Mifflin Company
2 Park St., Boston, Mass. 02107

Institute for Personality and Ability Testing
1602 Coronado Dr., Champaign, Ill. 61820

Instructional Objectives Exchange
Box 24095, Los Angeles, Calif. 90024

Personnel Press
20 Nassau St., Princeton, N.J. 08540

The Psychological Corporation
757 Third Avenue, New York, N.Y. 10017

Psychological Test Specialists
Box 1441, Missoula, Montana 59801

Psychometric Affiliates
1743 Monterey, Chicago, Ill. 60643

Science Research Associates, Inc.
259 E. Erie St., Chicago, Ill. 60611

Sheridan Supply Co.
P.O. Box 837, Beverly Hills, Calif. 90213

Stanford University Press
Stanford, Calif. 94305

Western Psychological Services
Box 775, Beverly Hills, Calif. 90213

Answers

Chapter 1

(1) *b*
(2) False
(3) To decide what it is you want to measure.
(4) *c*
(5) appropriateness
(6) *d*

Chapter 2

(1) An intended outcome stated in such a way that its attainment can be determined; to state desired outcomes, to plan strategies for and produce the desired outcomes, to measure to what extent desired outcomes are being achieved.
(2) To store food, to store eating and cooking implements, to prepare meals, to serve meals, to clean eating and cooking implements, to provide a social setting.
(3) Instruction, construction of achievement tests.
(4) By helping you to know what is expected of you; by providing a basis for judging if you are meeting the expectations.
(5) *c*
(6) False
(7) To be correct, an action verb must have been used and all three parts of the objective provided. E.g., *given a map of the United States, the student shall identify by pointing to the longest river system; he or she shall point to the Mississippi-Missouri River.*
(8) E.g., *Given five addition problems, each with two 3-digit numbers, the student shall compute the correct answer for at least four.*
(9) *b*
(10) In proper relation to prior, concomitant, and subsequent objectives. Determined by seeing if students who fail it also fail those objectives for which it is a prerequisite or an objective that is prerequisite to it.
(11) *d*
(12) *c*

Chapter 3

(1) *a. iii; b. iv; c. i.*
(2) *c*
(3) *c*
(4) *a.* False
   b. True
(5) application
(6) affective domain

(7) *State the names of your state's two senators.*

(8) *Create an accompaniment for a familiar melody.*

(9) E.g., using a jack, removing a tire, putting on a tire, tightening bolts.

(10) E.g., defining fascism and democracy, presenting examples of fascist governments (or describing principles of fascism), presenting examples of democratic governments (or describing examples of democracy), discussing advantages and disadvantages of fascism in comparison with democracy.

Chapter 4

(1) *a.* state

   b. identify

(2) A *iii*; B *iv*; C *ii.*

(3) *b*

(4) *a.* True

   b. False

   c. False

(5) • Name the first three presidents of the United States in order.

   • The first, second, and third presidents of the United States were _____, _____, and _____.

   • Washington, Adams, and Jefferson were the first three presidents of the United States in that order.   TRUE   FALSE

   • Circle the names of those people who were United States presidents.

         J. Adams

         A. Burr

         P. Henry

         T. Jefferson

         G. Washington

         A. Hamilton

   For those circled, indicate which was first, second, and third.

   • Which represents the first three presidents of the United States in the proper order?

   a. Washington, Jefferson, Adams

   b. Washington, Jefferson, Madison

   c. Washington, Adams, Jefferson

   d. Adams, Washington, Jefferson

   e. Adams, Washington, Madison

   • Match the categories on the left with names on the right.

         first president   Adams

         second president   Madison

         third president   Hamilton

                                  Washington

                                  Jefferson

(6) • What is the result of adding 7 and 3?

   • 7 + 5 = _____

   • 3 + 2 = 6   TRUE   FALSE

- Circle the correct additions:

$2 + 1 = 3$	$9 + 6 = 16$
$3 + 5 = 7$	$8 + 2 = 11$
$4 + 4 = 8$	$5 + 6 = 11$

- Which one of the following results when 5 and 6 are added?
  - *a.* 9
  - *b.* 10
  - *c.* 11
  - *d.* 12
  - *e.* 13
- Match the number on the right which, when added to the number on the left, gives 13 as the result.

1. 4	*a.* 8
2. 6	*b.* 6
3. 9	*c.* 9
4. 5	*d.* 7
	e. 4

(7) *c*

(8) *a*

Chapter 5

(1) *a. iv;   b. v;   c. i;   d. ii.*

(2) True

(3) E.g., *on occasion, often with little forwarning, certain commodities become short in supply (for example, gasoline in the spring of 1974). What effect do such shortages have on prices? Name at least two possible reasons for such shortages.*

(4) E.g., *describe five ways that moles, opossums, beavers, and wood-chucks are similar and one way that they are different. Use no more than one sentence for your description of each similarity or difference.*

(5) E.g., *in 300 words or less describe how to use carrots and celery to make a device that tells time. Be as specific as possible.*

(6) E.g., *evaluate the Treaty of Versailles as a means of solving the problems of aggression. Specify at least five criteria and apply to the treaty in an essay of 400–500 words.*

(7) Organization, content accuracy, accuracy of solution, completeness, internal consistency, originality.

(8) *b; c; e; f; h.*

Chapter 6

(1) E.g., students will enjoy coming to school; students will feel that school is helping them learn.

(2) E.g., students will work cooperatively; students will respect one another's privacy.

(3) *a. iv;   b. v;   c. ii;   d. i.*

(4) semantic differential

(5) *a; b; d; g; h.*

(6) *a.* Because this is a purely factual statement, students would have no basis for agreement or disagreement.

b. Because this statement contains two thoughts, a teacher would not know which one the student was responding to.

(7) E.g., liking for the subject matter, liking for the presentation, relevancy, practical value.   *Uaal* *Usagl*

(8) E.g., relevancy, interest value, convenience, expense, first-hand learning. *motivation*

(9) • Field trips add relevancy to the learning process.

   SA   A   U   D   SD

• Field trips are really interesting to take.

   SA   A   U   D   SD

• Field trips provide a good basis for first-hand learning.

   SA   A   U   D   SD

• Field trips are too expensive and inconvenient.

   SA   A   U   D   SD

• Field trips are a waste of time.

   SA   A   U   D   SD

• I would rather stay in school than go on a field trip.

   SA   A   U   D   SD

(10) • *Semantic Differential*

FIELD TRIPS

pleasant ____:____:____:____:____:____:____ unpleasant

irrelevant ____:____:____:____:____:____:____ relevant

• *Adjective Checklist*

Field trips are   _____ pleasant

(check all that apply)   _____ irrelevant

• *Nominations*

1. Name your three favorite educational activities.

2. Name the two ways you most enjoy learning about different industries and the jobs they provide.

(11) *d*

(12) E.g., use or adapt existing measures where possible, try the measure on your colleagues, do not require names on papers, let students decide what information to share, do a briefing and a debriefing, be sensitive to students' fears, be responsive to student feedback.

Chapter 7

(1) See the list of criteria on pages 179–80.

(2) E.g., *given an analytical balance and a sample substance, demonstrate a procedure for determining the weight of the substance. Given tools, materials, and a plan, construct a bird feeder.* Reason: Each objective calls for a real performance or product.

(3) E.g., *given a piece of construction paper, compass, and pencil, construct an exact equilateral right triangle.*

(4) *a.* Uses compass to lay off equal sides. _____

b. Uses compass to construct the perpendicular properly. _____

c. Resulting triangle has equal sides and contains a right angle. _____

d. Work is neat and construction lines removed. _____

(5) E.g., *given a ruler, graph paper, and colored pencils, draw the layout of this floor of the school.*

(6) E.g.,

   a. Drawing contains all areas of this floor of the school. _____

   b. All spaces are proportional to actual size. _____

   c. All spaces are correctly located with respect to one another. _____

   d. All spaces are accurately labeled. _____

   e. Drawing is neat. _____

(7) Student motivation

   a. Comes on time.

   b. Volunteers for activities.

   c. Completes assignments.

   d. Asks questions.

   e. Shows enthusiasm.

(8) Student:

	NEVER	RARELY	OCCA-SION-ALLY	FRE-QUENTLY	ALWAYS
Comes to class on time.	N	R	O	F	A
Volunteers for activities.	N	R	O	F	A
Completes assignments.	N	R	O	F	A
Asks questions.	N	R	O	F	A
Shows enthusiasm.	N	R	O	F	A

(9) E.g., the teacher will show well-preparedness in teaching a lesson.

   1. Has a prepared lesson plan.

   2. Is familiar with what he/she wants to do.

   3. Proceeds in a smooth fashion.

   4. Is well-organized.

   5. Knows the content.

   6. Is able to answer questions.

(10) Teacher:

	BEHAVIOR ABSENT				BEHAVIOR PRESENT
Has a prepared lesson plan.	1	2	3	4	5
Is familiar with what he/she wants to do.	1	2	3	4	5
Proceeds in a smooth fashion.	1	2	3	4	5
Is well-organized.	1	2	3	4	5
Knows the content.	1	2	3	4	5
Is able to answer questions.	1	2	3	4	5

(11) Affective objectives that deal with such behaviors as cooperativeness and involvement should not be neglected; as part of overall student evaluation, rating of such behaviors would be useful.

(12) As values are clarified and change, student behavior should also change. (For example, students might become more cooperative or more involved.) Measurement of student behavior would help to determine whether the experimental program was stimulating positive changes in the behavior of students.

Chapter 8

(1) *c*

(2) Does it fit my objective? Does it reflect the action verb? Does it utilize the conditions? Does it employ the criteria?

(3) *a.* List the three objectives.
    b. Determine how many items you want to write for each based on its relative importance.
    c. Draw the map indicating the number of items per objective.
    d. Follow the map to construct items.

(4)

OBJECTIVES	UNITS OF IMPORTANCE			
	1	2	3	4
1	◉	◉		
2	◉	◉	◉	◉
3	◉	◉	◉	◉
4	◉	◉		

(5) two

(6) *a. i; b. iv; c. ii; d. v.*

(7) Items 1 & 2 are appropriate for measuring objective 1; items 3 & 4 are appropriate for measuring objective 2; item 5 is inappropriate (no objective); items 6 & 7 are appropriate for measuring objective 3; and no items among the first seven measure objective 4.

(8) *d*

(9) False

(10) *a, d, e*

(11) *a. ii; b. iv; c. v.*

Chapter 9

(1) *b*

(2) external

(3) *d*

(4) B

(5) *a. ii; b. v; c. i; d. iii.*

(6) *a.* criterion; *b.* construct; *c.* concurrent; *d.* predictive.

(7) *a.* Relate scores on the test to scores on a subsequent test of achievement in electronics or to ratings of successful performance in electronics.

   b. Compare the scores of people employed in the electronics field (that is, people trained in electronics) with scores of people employed in another field (that is, people untrained in electronics).

(8) *a.* Ask students how much they like school and see if those who say they like it score higher on the test than those who say they don't like it.

   b. See if there is a relationship between scores on the test and the presumed causes of these scores, such as warmth of the teacher, attitudes of the teacher toward students, or number of successful experiences of the student, or between liking for school and its manifestations or by-products, such as attendance, deportment, or school performance.

(9) Compare students' test scores to your own ratings of their artistic ability; have another art teacher examine and rate representative samples of each student's work, then compare those ratings with the test scores; compare students' test scores to their own ratings of their artistic ability.

(10) Solicit the judgment of professional colleagues; see if students do better on them after taking the course or reading the book than before; see if professionals in the field do better on them than students; see if persons who rate themselves higher on knowledge and experience in the field do better on them than persons who rate themselves lower.

Chapter 10

(1) *c*

(2) True

(3) *d*

(4) False

(5) *a. v; b. i; c. iv; d. ii; e. iii.*

(6) *a.* split-half

   b. parallel-item

   c. Kuder-Richardson 21

   d. test-retest

   e. alternate forms

son to group data, makes conclusions based on test scores somewhat independent of the failings or weaknesses of the test.

Disadvantages: norms become dated and no longer reflect the types of performances of which people are capable, an emphasis on the relative interpretation of tests tends to obscure the relation between the content of those tests and any bearing on the past or future (i.e., real capabilities) of the the test takers.

(7) *a.* skill-testing

b. intrinsic

(8) *a, c, d*

(9) *a.* Report the names of each objective that each student has "passed" rather than reporting simply the total number of items right on the total test.

b. Consider a student to have "passed" an objective if he or she gets both of the items right that were written to measure proficiency on each objective.

(10) *a.* Make a table displaying the number of students showing proficiency per objective versus the number not showing proficiency; where the percentage showing proficiency dips below 50 percent, the instruction for that objective must be considered less than completely effective.

b. Rank order all the test scores (that is, total number of items right) and divide them up in segments such as fifths or pentiles; give each student a number score (1–5), which represents his or her pentile.

(11) *a.* Practical for classroom use.

b. Students can comprehend and relate to it.

c. Short enough to avoid tedium.

d. Standard procedures for administration.

(12) *a.* Show a copy of each picture to the class as a whole on a projector and then have them write their test answers to questions based on the one being observed.

b. Make the big words smaller so that students can understand them (unless it's a vocabulary test).

c. Cut down on the number of test items per objective or measure fewer objectives or give the test in more than one sitting.

d. Write down all the procedures for test administration.

Chapter 12

(1) *a. v; b. ix; c. vi; d. vii; e. viii; f. i; g. iv; h. ii.*

(2) False

(3) *c, f, g, i, j*

(4) It refers to where intelligence comes from and where it leads. It means that intelligence is derived in part by experiencing an environment that reinforces it and can be successfully applied to an environment that requires its application for success.

(5) *c*

(6) *a*

(7) *a.* mental; *b.* chronological; *c. ratio.*

(8) *a.* IQ=101; *b.* M.A.=11 years, 3 months.

(9) *b*

(10) *d*

(11) *b, c*

(12) *a. ii, iii, iv, vi, vii, ix, x*

    b. i, v, viii

    c. i, vii

    d. ii

    e. ix

    f. iv

(13) *e*

(14) Make up a number of responses, or answers, to given problems or situations that are novel or imaginative as well as fitting the situation or solving the problem.

(15) Supply a word related (as a mediating link) to each of three given words.

(16) *c*

(17) *b*

(18) *e*

Chapter 13

(1) *d*

(2) *a.* application; *b.* computation; *c. concepts.*

(3) Appropriateness because teachers can build test to fit their own objectives whereas standardized achievement tests are built around a general content outline.

(4) Reliability because revision based on item analysis allows for the elimination of inconsistent items.

(5) False

(6) 1. *e;* 2. *c;* 3. *a;* 4. *b;* 5. *d.*

(7) In order to maintain constancy across test conditions from administration, to administration tests must be administered the same way each time. Only familiarity with administrative procedures makes this possible. Some tests have practice tests that are administered in advance. Without familiarizing yourself with these and other procedures, you are likely to overlook an instruction or a stop in the testing procedure.

(8) Make sure all students have everything they need to take the test and no more. Make sure each student fills in all information called for in the Pupil Information Box. Clearly give all instructions as called for in the directions. Adhere to time limits exactly. Make sure that all students know how to take the test. Monitor test taking from various points in the room. Make sure students take the testing seriously.

(9) *a. ii; b. v; c. i; d. viii; e. iv; f. vii; g. iii.*

(10) *a. i.* grade-equivalent score   *ii.* percentile rank   *iii.* raw score   *iv.* standard score   *v.* stanine score
  b. ii.
(11) You would know how much mathematics the student knows relative to other students at his or her grade level; you would not know exactly what math objectives the student is or is not proficient in.
(12) On a criterion-referenced test 85 percent means that the student has shown proficiency on 85 percent of the objectives or, if the test was of a single objective, on 85 percent of the items. On a norm-referenced test, 85th percentile means that the student has gotten more items right than 85 percent of the students in the norming group at the same grade level.
(13) Time to completion, number of subtests, number of scores, types of scores, number of levels, age range covered.
(14) *a.* either the Davis or Nelson-Denny
  b. Gates-MacGinitie
  c. Iowa Silent Reading Test

Chapter 14

(1) *a.* SDS;   *b.* Kuder;   *c.* OVIS;   *d.* Strong;   *e.* CMI.
(2) *Scoring*: The Strong is scored by comparing responses to successful people in different fields. The Kuder is scored by tallying the number of items chosen which fit each of 10 different interest orientations. The OVIS is scored on 24 predetermined categories that reflect emphases on data, people, and things.
  Interpretation: The Strong tells you how much the student's interests resemble those of successful people in different fields. The Kuder tells you about the student's relative interest in each of 10 orientations that themselves can be logically related to different occupational fields. The OVIS tells you specific occupations to which the student is oriented based on his or her relative emphasis on data, people, and things.
(3) *a.* School Sentiment Index;   *b.* Tennessee;   *c.* Self-appraisal.
(4) *self: a, b, d, f; school: c, e, g, h.*
(5) *a.* Scale of Values;   *b.* CPI;   *c.* EFT;   *d.* EPPS;   *e.* CTP.
(6) *a.* A;   *b.* P;   *c.* V;   *d.* P;   *e.* N;   *f.* A.
(7) Increasing students' self-awareness, aiding students in making career decisions, evaluating the effectiveness of classroom activities aimed at the affective domain.
(8) *As an example*: Administer the School Sentiment Index before and after trying out a set of activities in the classroom to see if the use of these activities makes students' attitudes toward school more positive.
  Another example: Administer the Scale of Values to students and have them score the test themselves as a way of becoming aware of their own values.

Chapter 15

(1) Teacher-built tests constitute a major portion of the school testing program so it is obviously important to improve them; a test is a resource like a curriculum and hence should be reused; a test item file results in tests that are more valid and reliable.

(2) *a.* Teacher prepares test items to fit instructional objectives.
   b. Teacher uses items in classroom testing.
   c. Teacher uses test results to evaluate items in terms of the five criteria.
   d. Teacher discards poor items, retains good ones.

(3) *a.* Make sure the test is appropriate for measuring the objectives of instruction. Record the date proficiency on an objective is acquired and the degree of proficiency attained.
   b. Select a test that measures objectives in sequence within a wide range, in particular covering objectives that should have been mastered prior to instruction. Examine the student's performance on this test to identify prior objectives on which the student has not acquired proficiency.
   c. Determine from test results whether there are any objectives that a particular student has failed to acquire proficiency on (or any students who have failed to acquire proficiency on a particular objective) and provide additional instruction appropriate to that objective.
   d. Give a pretest or at least precede instruction by presenting the objectives; give a posttest and return scored tests with minimal delay; clearly indicate errors and bases for scoring; test in a warm and accepting atmosphere.

(4) See Figure 15.2, page 446.

(5) Greatest strength: spelling (52 percentile).
   Greatest weakness: math applications (42 percentile).
   Instructional recommendation: spend more time teaching math applications and less time teaching spelling.

(6) Divide the test of all objectives to be covered into subtests and the class into the same number of subgroups as subtests for testing purposes. Give each subgroup a different subtest at each testing time so that after all the objectives have been covered each subgroup will have taken each subtest. Using this procedure, pretest, immediate posttest, and retention data will be provided for the different subgroups as a basis for evaluating the results of instruction.

(7) *a.* Education input can serve as a baseline from which to measure gains in performance.
   b. We are more adept at measuring how students perform (output) than at measuring how systems work (process). We are an output-oriented society and, in the final analysis, judge things and people by how well they "work."
   c. To determine whether intended processes are being carried out and to discover which processes produce the desired outcomes.

(8) Compare the 6th graders using the new instruction before and after to see how much they improve. Compare the end results on this year's 6th graders—who have used the new instruction—with last year's (in the same school) who have not. Compare the end results on this year's 6th graders—who have used the new instruction—with the end results for 6th graders in a comparable school in the district not using the new instruction.

References

American Association for the Advancement of Science. *An evaluation model and its application.* Washington, D.C.: AAAS Commission on Science Education, 1965.

American Educational Research Association, American Psychological Association, National Council on Measurement in Education. *Standards for educational and psychological tests.* Washington, D.C.: American Psychological Association, 1974.

Amidon, E. J. and Hough, J. B., eds. *Interaction analysis: Theory, research, and application.* Reading, Mass.: Addison-Wesley, 1967.

Ammons, M. Objectives and outcomes. In R. L. Ebel, ed. *Encyclopedia of Educational Research*, 4th ed. New York: Macmillan, 1969, 908–14.

Anastasi, A. *Psychological testing*, 3rd ed. New York: Macmillan, 1968.

Anderson, H. Acquiescence response bias to difficult achievement-type true–false tests of male high school students exhibiting rule breaking or rule obeying behavior. Unpublished doctoral dissertation, Rutgers University, New Brunswick, N.J., 1969.

Anderson, S. B. et al. *Encyclopedia of evaluation.* San Francisco: Jossey-Bass, 1974.

Anghoff, W. H. Scales, norms, & equivalent scores. In R. L. Thorndike, ed. *Educational measurement*, 2nd ed. Washington, D.C.: American Council on Education, 1971, Chap. 15.

Armstrong, R. J. et al. *Development and evaluation of behavioral objectives.* Belmont, Calif.: Charles A. Jones Publishing Co., 1970.

Asch, S. E. Effects of group pressure upon the modification and distortion of judgments. In E. E. Maccoby, T. M. Newcomb and E. L. Hartley, eds. *Readings in social psychology*, 3rd ed. New York: Holt, Rinehart and Winston, 1958, 174–83.

Ashburn, R. R. An experiment in the essay-type question. *Journal of Experimental Education*, 1938, 7, 1–3.

Backman, M. and Tuckman, B. W. A review of the *Remote Associates Test. Journal of Educational Measurement*, 1972, 9, 161–162.

Barclay, J. R. *Controversial issues in testing.* Boston: Houghton Mifflin, 1968.

Barron, F. The measurement of creativity. In D. K. Whitla, ed. *Handbook of measurement and assessment in behavioral sciences.* Reading, Mass.: Addison-Wesley, 1968, 348–66.

Barton, K. Recent data on the *Culture Fair Scales. Information Bulletin No. 16.* Champaign, Ill.: Institute for Personality and Ability Testing, 1973.

Bauernfeind, R. H. *Building a school testing program.* Boston: Houghton Mifflin, 1963.

Beatty, W. H., ed. *Improving educational assessment and an inventory of measures of affective behavior.* Washington, D.C.: Association for Supervision and Curriculum Development, NEA, 1969.

Bennett, G. K., Seashore, H. G., and Wesman, A. G. *Differential Aptitude Tests,* 4th ed. Manual, Forms M & L. New York: The Psychological Corporation, 1966.

Berg, H. D. Evaluation in social science. In P. L. Dressel, ed. *Evaluation in higher education.* Boston: Houghton Mifflin, 1961, Chap. 4.

Binet, A. *Les Idées modernes sur les enfants.* Paris: E. Flamarion, 1909.

———. *The development of intelligence in children,* translated by E. S. Kite. Baltimore: Warwick & York, 1916.

Binet, A. and Simon, T. Le Développement de l'intelligence chez les enfants. *L'Année psychologique,* 1908, *14,* 1–94.

Blanton, W., Farr, R., and Tuinman, J. J. *Reading tests for the secondary grades: A review and evaluation.* Newark, Del.: International Reading Association, 1972.

Bloom, B. S. *Taxonomy of educational objectives.* Handbook I: Cognitive domain. New York: David McKay, 1956.

———. *Stability and change in human characteristics.* New York: Wiley, 1964.

Bloom, B. S., Hastings, J. T., and Madaus, G. F. *Handbook on formative and summative evaluation of student learning.* New York: McGraw-Hill, 1971.

Bonjean, C. M., Hill, R. J., and McLemore, S. D. *Sociological measurement: An inventory of scales and indices.* San Francisco: Chandler Publishing Co., 1967.

Boring, E. G. Intelligence as the tests test it. *New Republic,* 1923, *34,* 35–37.

———. *A history of experimental psychology.* New York: Appleton-Century-Crofts, 1950.

Boyd, R. D. and De Vault, M. V. The observation and recording of behavior. *Review of Educational Research,* 1966, *36,* 529–51.

Brown, W. The development and testing of a behavioral-reference groups model for evaluation of vocational education pilot programs. New Jersey State Department of Education: Occupational Research Development Monograph No. 4, 1970.

Buros, O. K., ed. *Reading tests and reviews.* Highland Park, N.J.: Gryphon Press, 1968.

———, ed. *Personality tests and reviews.* Highland Park, N.J.: Gryphon Press, 1970.

———, ed. *The seventh mental measurements yearbook.* Highland Park, N.J.: Gryphon Press, 1972.

Campbell, D. P. Stability of interests within an occupation over 30 years. *Journal of Applied Psychology,* 1966, *50,* 51–56. (a)

————. Stability of vocational interests within occupations over long ing Research and Development Center, University of Pittsburgh, Report No. BR-5-0253, 1966.

Crites, J. O. Interests. In R. L. Ebel, ed. *Encyclopedia of educational research*, 4th ed. New York: Macmillan, 1969, 678–86.

————. *Vocational psychology*. New York: McGraw-Hill, 1971.

Cronbach, L. J. Validation of educational measures. *Proceedings of the 1969 Invitational Conference on Testing Problems*. Princeton, N.J.: Educational Testing Service, 1969, 35–52.

————. *Essentials of psychological testing*, 3rd ed. New York: Harper & Row, 1970.

————. Test validation. In R. L. Thorndike, ed. *Educational measurement*, 2nd ed. Washington, D.C.: American Council on Education, 1971, Chap. 14.

Cureton, E. E. Measurement theory. In R. L. Ebel, ed. *Encyclopedia of educational research*, 4th ed. New York: Macmillan, 1969, 785–804. time spans. *Personnel and Guidance Journal*, 1966, *44*, 1012–19. (b)

————. *Manual for Strong Vocational Interests Blanks for men and women*, rev. ed. Stanford, Calif.: Stanford University Press, 1966. (c)

Carter, H. D. The development of vocational attitudes. *Journal of Consulting Psychology*, 1940, *4*, 185–91.

Carver, R. P. Two dimensions of tests: psychometric and edumetric. *American Psychologist*, 1974, *29*, 512–18.

Cattell, J. McK. Mental tests and measurements. *Mind*, 1890, *15*, 373–81.

Cattell, R. B. and Warburton, F. W. *Objective personality and motivation tests: A theoretical introduction and practical compendium.* Urbana, Ill.: University of Illinois Press, 1967.

Chauncey, H. and Dobbin, J. E. *Testing: Its place in education today.* New York: Harper & Row, 1963.

Churchman, C. W. *The systems approach.* New York: Delacorte Press, 1969.

Coffman, W. E. Achievement tests. In R. L. Ebel, ed. *Encyclopedia of educational research*, 4th ed. New York: Macmillan, 1969, 7–17.

————. Essay examinations. In R. L. Thorndike, ed. *Educational measurement*, 2nd ed. Washington, D.C.: American Council on Education, 1971, Chap. 10.

Coleman, W. and Cureton, E. E. Intelligence and achievement: The "jangle fallacy" again. *Educational and Psychological Measurement*, 1954, *14*, 347–51.

Comrey, A. L., Backer, T. E., and Glaser, E. M. *A sourcebook for mental health measures.* Los Angeles: Human Interaction Research Institute, 1973.

Cox, R. and Vargas, J. S. A comparison of item selection techniques for norm-referenced and criterion-referenced tests. Pittsburgh: Learn-

Davis, F. B. *Educational measurements and their interpretation.* Belmont, Calif.: Wadsworth Publishing Co., 1964.

D'Costa, A. G. and Winefordner, D. W. A cubistic model of vocational interests. *Vocational Guidance Quarterly,* 1969, *17,* 242–49.

Dewey, J. What psychology can do for the teacher. [1895]. In Archambault, ed. *J. Dewey on education.* New York: Modern Library, 1963.

Dick, W. and Hagerty, N. *Topics in measurement: Reliability and validity.* New York: McGraw-Hill, 1971.

Doppelt, J. E. How accurate is a test score? *Test Service Bulletin No. 50.* New York: The Psychological Corporation, 1956.

Dunn, L. M. *Manual for the Peabody Picture Vocabulary Test.* Circle Pines, Minn.: American Guidance Service, 1965.

Ebel, R. L. Obtaining and reporting evidence on content validity. *Educational and Psychological Measurement,* 1956, *16,* 269–82.

———. Standardized achievement tests: Uses and limitations. *National Elementary School Principal,* 1961, *40,* 29–32.

———. Measurement and the teacher. *Educational Leadership,* 1962, *20,* 20–24.

———. Some limitations of criterion-referenced measurement. Paper presented at the American Educational Research Association, Minneapolis, 1970.

Educational Testing Service. *Making the classroom test. A guide for teachers.* Princeton, N.J.: Educational Testing Service, Evaluation & Advisory Service Series No. 4, 1959.

———. *Graduate Record Examination scores for basic reference groups.* Princeton, N.J.: Educational Testing Service, 1960.

———. *Multiple-choice questions: A close look.* Princeton, N.J.: Educational Testing Service, 1963.

———. *Anchor test study. Equivalence and norms tables for selected reading achievement tests* (Grades 4, 5, 6). Washington, D.C.: U.S. Government Printing Office (stock no. 1780-01312), 1974.

Edwards, A. L. *Techniques of attitude scale construction.* New York: Appleton-Century-Crofts, 1957.

———. *The measurement of personality traits.* New York: Holt, Rinehart, and Winston, 1970.

Farr, R. and Anastasiow, N. *Tests of reading readiness and achievement: A review and evaluation.* Newark, Del.: International Reading Association, 1969.

Farr, R., Tuinman, J. J., and Blanton, B. E. How to make a pile in performance contracting. *Phi Delta Kappan,* 1972, *53,* 367–69.

Feuerstein, R. A procedure to improve the intellective performance of young children. Paper presented at Rutgers University, New Brunswick, N. J., 1968.

Findley, W. G. The impact and improvement of school testing programs. *Sixty-Second yearbook of the National Society for the Study of Education*, Part II. Chicago: University of Chicago Press, 1963.

Flanders, N. A. *Analyzing classroom interaction.* Reading, Mass.: Addison-Wesley, 1969.

Freeman, F. S. *Theory and practice of psychological testing*, rev. ed. New York: Holt, Rinehart, and Winston, 1955.

————. *Theory and practice of psychological testing*, 3rd ed. New York: Holt, Rinehart, and Winston, 1962.

Fry, E. Judging readability of books. *Teacher Education*, 1964, *5*, 34–39.

Gagné, R. M. *The conditions of learning.* New York: Holt, Rinehart, and Winston, 1965.

————. *The conditions of learning*, 2nd ed. New York: Holt, Rinehart, and Winston, 1970.

————. *Essentials of learning for instruction.* Hinsdale, Ill.: The Dryden Press, 1974.

Galton, F. *Inquiries into human faculty and its development.* London: Macmillan & Co., 1883.

Gardner, E. F. Interpreting achievement profiles—uses and warnings. *NCME measurement in education: A series of special reports of the National Council on Measurement in Education, 1* (2), 1970.

Gerberich, J. R. *Specimen objective test items.* New York: Longmans, Green & Co., 1956.

Gerberich, J. R., Greene, H. A., and Jorgensen, A. N. *Measurement and evaluation in the modern school.* New York: David McKay, 1962.

Gerhard, M. *Effective teaching strategies with the behavioral outcomes approach.* Nyack, N.Y.: Parker Publishing, 1971.

Getzels, J. W. and Jackson, P. W. *Creativity and intelligence: Explorations with gifted students.* New York: Wiley, 1962.

Glaser, R. Instructional technology and the measurement of learning outcomes. *American Psychologist*, 1963, *18*, 519–21.

Glaser, R. and Nitko, A. J. Measurement in learning and instruction. In R. L. Thorndike, ed. *Educational measurement*, 2nd ed. Washington, D.C.: American Council on Education, 1971, Chap. 17.

Goldman, L. *Using tests in counseling.* New York: Appleton-Century-Crofts, 1961.

Graham, M. *Modern elementary mathematics.* New York: Harcourt Brace Jovanovich, 1970.

Granger, C. H. The hierarchy of objectives. *Harvard Business Review*, 1964, May–June, 63–74.

Green, J. A. *Teacher-made tests.* New York: Harper & Row, 1963.

Guilford, J. P. *The nature of human intelligence.* New York: McGraw-Hill, 1967.

Harvey, O. J., Hunt, D. E., and Schroder, H. M. Conceptual systems and personality organization. New York: Wiley, 1961.

Hawes, G. R. *Educational testing for the millions: What tests really mean for your child.* New York: McGraw-Hill, 1964.

Heron, A. The effects of real-life motivation on questionnaire response. *Journal of Applied Psychology*, 1956, *40*, 65–68.

Hively, W. et al. Domain-referenced curriculum evaluation: A technical handbook and a case study from the Minnemast Project. Los Angeles: Center for the Study of Evaluation, UCLA Graduate School of Education, CSE Monograph Series in Evaluation No. 1, 1973.

Hoepfner, R. and Klein, S. *CSE elementary school test evaluation.* Los Angeles: Center for the Study of Evaluation, UCLA Graduate School of Education, 1970.

Hoepfner, R. et al., eds. *CSE-RBS test evaluations: Tests of higher order cognitive, affective, and interpersonal skills.* Los Angeles: Center for the Study of Evaluation, UCLA Graduate School of Education, 1972.

Hopkins, K. D. and Bracht, G. H. The stability and change of language and non-language IQ scores. Final Report, Project No. 0-H-024. Washington, D.C.: Office of Education, Bureau of Research, U.S. Department of Health, Education & Welfare, 1971.

Instructional Objectives Exchange. *English literature 10–12 objectives.* Los Angeles: Instructional Objectives Exchange, 1970.

———. *Mathematics 7–9 objectives.* Los Angeles: Instructional Objectives Exchange, 1970.

———. *Reading K–3 objectives.* Los Angeles: Instructional Objectives Exchange, 1970.

———. *Attitude toward school K–12*, rev. ed. Los Angeles: Instructional Objectives Exchange, 1972.

———. *Measures of self-concept K–12*, rev. ed. Los Angeles: Instructional Objectives Exchange, 1972.

Jackson, R. Developing criterion-referenced tests. Princeton, N.J.: ERIC Clearinghouse on Tests, Measurement, & Evaluation, Educational Testing Service, 1970.

Jensen, A. R. Social class, race, & genetics: Implications for education. *American Educational Research Journal*, 1968, *5*, 1–42.

———. How much can we boost IQ and scholastic achievement? *Harvard Educational Review*, 1969, *39*, 1–123.

Johnson, O. G. and Bommarito, J. W. *Tests and measurements in child development: A handbook.* San Francisco: Jossey-Bass, Inc., 1971.

Johnson, R. A., Kast, F. E., and Rosenzweig, J. E. *The theory and management of systems*, 2nd ed. New York: McGraw-Hill, 1967.

Katz, M. *Selecting an achievement test: Principles and procedures*, 2nd ed. Princeton, N.J.: Educational Testing Service (Evaluation and Advisory Service Series, No. 3), 1961.

Kibler, R. J., Barker, L., and Miles, D. *Behavioral objectives and instruction.* Boston: Allyn & Bacon, 1970.

Kohlberg, L. The contribution of developmental psychology to education—examples from moral education. *Educational Psychologist*, 1973, *10*, 2–14.

Krathwohl, D. R., Bloom, B. S., and Masia, B. B. *Taxonomy of educational objectives*. Handbook II: Affective domain. New York: David McKay, 1964.

Krathwohl, D. R. and Payne, D. Defining and assessing educational objectives. In R. L. Thorndike, ed. *Educational measurement*, 2nd ed. Washington, D.C.: American Council on Education, 1971, Chap. 2.

Krech, D., Crutchfield, R. S., and Ballachey, E. L. *Individual in society*. New York: McGraw-Hill, 1962.

Kriege, J. W. Behavioral objectives: 10 ways to make them count. *Grade Teacher*, 1971, Sept., 138–43.

Lake, D. G., Miles, M. B., and Earle, R. B. *Measuring human behavior: Tools for the assessment of social functioning*. New York: Teachers College Press, 1973.

Lennon, R. T. Assumptions underlying the use of content validity. *Educational and Psychological Measurement*, 1956, *16*, 294–304.

———. Scores and norms. In R. E. Ebel, ed. *Encyclopedia of educational research*, 4th ed. New York: Macmillan, 1969, 308.

Levine, A. S. Aptitude versus achievement tests as predictors of achievement. *Educational and Psychological Measurement*, 1958, *18*, 517–25.

Lien, A. J. *Measurement and evaluation of learning*. Dubuque, Iowa: Wm. C. Brown, 1967, Chap. 6.

Light, R. J. Issues in the analysis of qualitative data. In R. M. Travers, ed. *Second handbook of research on teaching*. Chicago: Rand McNally, 1973, 318–81.

Lord, F. M. The relation of the reliability of multiple-choice tests to the distribution of item difficulties. *Psychometrika*, 1952, *17*, 181–94.

Lyman, H. B. *Test scores and what they mean*. Englewood Cliffs, N.J.: Prentice-Hall, 1963.

Mager, R. F. *Preparing instructional objectives*. Palo Alto, Calif.: Fearon Publishers, 1962.

———. *Measuring instructional intent*. Palo Alto, Calif.: Fearon Publishers, 1973.

Malcolm D. D. Which interest inventory should I use? *Journal of Educational Research*, 1950, *44*, 91–98.

Mallinson, G. G. and Crumrine, W. M. An investigation of the stability of interests of high school students. *Journal of Educational Research*, 1952, *45*, 369–83.

McAshan, H. H. *Writing behavioral objectives*. New York: Harper & Row, 1970.

McClelland, D. Testing for competence rather than for "intelligence." *American Psychologist*, 1973, *28*, 1–14.

McNemar, Q. Lost: Our intelligence. Why? *American Psychologist*, 1964, *19*, 871–82.

Michael, W. B. Prediction. In R. L. Ebel, ed. *Encyclopedia of educational research*, 4th ed. New York: Macmillan, 1969, 982–93.

Miller, D. C. *Handbook of research design and social measurement*, 2nd ed. New York: David McKay, 1970.

Millman, J. Passing scores and test lengths for domain-referenced tests. *Review of Educational Research*, 1973, *43*, 205–16.

Myers, S. S. and Delon, F. G. *Mathematics tests available in the United States*. Washington, D.C.: National Council of Teachers of Mathematics, 1968.

Nelson, M. J. Intelligence and special aptitude tests. In R. L. Ebel, ed. *Encyclopedia of educational research*, 4th ed. New York: Macmillan, 1969, 667–77.

Osgood, C. E., Suci, G. J., and Tannenbaum, P. H. *The measurement of meaning*. Urbana, Ill.: University of Illinois Press, 1957.

Page, E. B. How we all failed at performance contracting. *Phi Delta Kappan*, 1972, *54* (2), 115–17.

Payne, D. A. *The specification and measurement of learning outcomes*. Waltham, Mass.: Blaisdell Publishing Co., 1968.

Pemberton, C. The closure factors related to other cognitive processes. *Psychometrika*, 1952, *17*, 267–88.

Piaget, J. *The psychology of intelligence*. New York: Harcourt Brace, 1950.

———. *The origins of intelligence in children*. New York: W. W. Norton, 1952.

Popham, W. J. Probing the validity of arguments against behavioral goals. Paper presented at meeting of American Educational Research Association, Chicago, 1968.

Popham, W. J. and Baker, E. *Writing tests which measure objectives*. Englewood Cliffs, N.J.: Prentice-Hall, 1973.

Robinson, J. P. et al. *Measures of political attitudes*. Ann Arbor, Mich.: Institute for Social Research, University of Michigan, 1968.

———. *Measures of occupational attitudes and occupational characteristics*. Ann Arbor, Mich.: Institute for Social Research, University of Michigan, 1969.

Robinson, J. P. and Shaver, P. R. *Measures of social psychological attitudes*. Ann Arbor, Mich.: Institute for Social Research, University of Michigan, 1969.

Rosen, P., ed. *Test collecting bulletin*. Princeton, N.J.: Educational Testing Service, 1967 to present.

Rosenthal, R. and Jacobson, L. *Pygmalion in the classroom*. New York: Holt, Rinehart, & Winston, 1968.

Sattler, J. M. Analysis of the functions of the 1960 Stanford-Binet Intelligence Scale, Form L-M. *Journal of Clinical Psychology*, 1965, *21*, 173–79.

Scheier, I. H. What is an "objective" test? *Psychological Reports*, 1958, *4*, 147–57.

Schoer, L. A. *Test construction: A programmed guide*. Boston: Allyn & Bacon, 1970.

Seibel, D. W. Measurement of aptitude and achievement. In D. K. Whitla, ed. *Handbook of measurement and assessment in behavioral sciences*. Reading, Mass.: Addison-Wesley, 1968, Chap. 8.

Shaw, M. E. and Wright, J. M. *Scales for the measurement of attitudes*. New York: McGraw-Hill, 1967.

Simon, A. and Boyer, E. G., eds. *Mirrors for behavior: An anthology of classroom observation instruments*. Philadelphia: Research for Better Schools, 1967–70.

Solomon, R. J. Improving the essay test in the social studies. In H. D. Berg, ed. *Evaluation in social studies*. Washington, D.C.: National Council for Social Studies, 1965, 137–53.

Spearman, C. *The abilities of man*. New York: Macmillan, 1927.

Stalnaker, J. M. The essay type of examination. In E. F. Lindquist, ed. *Educational measurement*. Washington, D.C.: American Council on Education, 1951.

Stanley, J. C. Reliability. In R. L. Thorndike, ed. *Educational measurement*, 2nd ed. Washington, D.C.: American Council on Education, 1971, Chap. 13.

Stefflre, B. The reading difficulty of interest inventories. *Occupations*, 1947, *26*, 95–96.

Stewart, N. AGCT scores of Army personnel grouped by occupation. *Occupations*, 1947, *26*, 5–41.

Stoddard, G. D. *The meaning of intelligence*. New York: Macmillan, 1943.

Strang, R. *How to report pupil progress*. Chicago: Science Research Associates, 1961.

Strong, E. K., Jr. *Vocational interests of men and women*. Stanford, Calif.: Stanford University Press, 1943.

Strong-Campbell Interest Inventory, The. Stanford, Calif.: Stanford University Press, 1974.

Super, D. E. et al. *Vocational development: A framework for research*. New York: Teachers College, Columbia University, Bureau of Publications, 1957.

Super, D. E. and Crites, J. O. *Appraising vocational fitness*, rev. ed. New York: Harper & Row, 1962.

Tarczan, C. *An educator's guide to psychological tests: Descriptions and classroom implications*. Springfield, Ill.: Charles C Thomas, 1972.

Terman, L. *The measurement of intelligence*. Boston: Houghton Mifflin, 1916.

Thorndike, R. L. *Personnel selection*. New York: Wiley, 1949.

———. Reliability. In *Proceedings of 1963 Invitational Conference on Testing Problems*. Princeton, N.J.: Educational Testing Service, 1964.

Thorndike, R. L. and Hagen, E. *Examiner's manual. Cognitive Abilities Test* (Multi-Level Edition). Boston: Houghton Mifflin, 1971.

Thurstone, L. L. *Primary mental abilities.* (Psychometric Monograph No. 1.) Chicago: University of Chicago Press, 1938.

————. Comment. *American Journal of Sociology,* 1946, *52,* 39–50.

Thurstone, L. L. and Thurstone, T. G. *The Chicago Tests of Primary Mental Abilities. Manual of instructions.* Chicago: Science Research Associates, 1943.

Tiegs, E. W. and Clark, W. W. *Test coordinator's handbook: California Achievement Tests.* Monterey, Calif.: California Test Bureau/McGraw-Hill, 1970 a.

————. *Bulletin of technical data number 1: California Achievement Tests.* Monterey, Calif.: California Test Bureau/McGraw-Hill, 1970 b.

Tinkelman, S. N. Planning the objective test. In R. L. Thorndike, ed. *Educational measurement,* 2nd ed. Washington, D.C.: American Council on Education, 1971.

Triggs, F. O. A further comparison of interest measurement by the Kuder Preference Record and the Strong Vocational Interest Blank for Men. *Journal of Educational Research,* 1944, *37,* 538–44.

Tuckman, B. W. Development and testing of an evaluation model. New Brunswick, N.J.: Rutgers University (U.S. Office of Education, Final Report; OE6-8355), 1967. (ERIC retrieval no.: ED 016 083).

————. The psychology of the culturally deprived. In B. W. Tuckman & J. L. O'Brian, eds. *Preparing to teach the disadvantaged.* New York: The Free Press, 1969, 3–20.

————. The study of curriculums for occupational preparation and education. New Brunswick, N.J.: Rutgers University (U.S. Office of Education, Final Report; OE8-0334), 1970. (ERIC retrieval no.: ED 044 525).

————. *Conducting educational research.* New York: Harcourt Brace Jovanovich, 1972.

————. Second year evaluation of Project: Open Classroom. Wayne, N.J.: Project: Open Classroom, Wayne Board of Education, 1973.

————. Teaching: The application of psychological constructs. In R. H. Hyman, ed. *Teaching: Vantage points for study,* 2nd ed. Philadelphia: Lippincott, 1974.

Tuckman, B. W. and Bierman, M. Beyond Pygmalion: Galatea in the schools. Paper given at New York meeting of American Educational Research Association, 1971.

Tuckman, B. W., Cochran, D., and Travers, E. Evaluating the open classroom. *Journal of Research and Development in Education,* 1974, *8,* 14–19.

Tuckman, B. W. and Corman, M. N. Measuring IA competencies. A review of ETS Cooperative Tests of Industrial Arts. *Journal of Educational Measurement,* 1971, *8,* 341–42.

Tuckman, B. W. and Edwards, K. J. A systems model for instructional design and management. *Educational Technology*, 1971, *11*, 21–26.

Tuddenham, R. D. Intelligence. In R. L. Ebel, ed. *Encyclopedia of educational research*, 4th ed. New York: Macmillan, 1969, 654–64.

Tyler, R. W. Educational evaluation: New roles, new means. *The sixty-eighth yearbook of the National Society for the Study of Education, Part II*. Chicago: The University of Chicago Press, 1969. (a)

———. The purposes of assessment. In W. H. Beatty, ed. *Improving educational assessment and an inventory of measures of affective behavior*. Washington, D.C.: Association for Supervision and Curriculum Development, NEA, 1969. (b)

Vargas, J. *Writing worthwhile behavioral objectives*. New York: Harper & Row, 1972.

Varon, E. J. Development of Alfred Binet's psychology. *Psychological Monographs, 46*, No. 3, 1935.

Walker, D. K. *Socioemotional measures for preschool and kindergarten children: A handbook*. San Francisco: Jossey-Bass, Inc., 1973.

Wallach, M. A. and Kogan, N. *Modes of thinking in young children: A study of the creativity–intelligence distinction*. New York: Holt, Rinehart, and Winston, 1965.

Webb, E. J. et al. *Unobtrusive measures: Nonreactive research in the social sciences*. Chicago: Rand McNally, 1966.

Wechsler, D. *The measurement of adult intelligence*. Baltimore: Williams & Wilkins, 1944.

Weick, K. E. Systematic observational methods. In G. Lindzey and E. Aronson, eds. *Handbook of social psychology*, Vol. 2, 2nd ed. Reading, Mass.: Addison-Wesley, 1968, 357–451.

Wesman, A. G. Writing the test item. In R. L. Thorndike, ed. *Educational measurement*, 2nd ed. Washington, D.C.: American Council on Education, Chap. 4.

Witkin, H. A. Individual differences in ease of perception of embedded figures. *Journal of Personality*, 1950, *19*, 1–15.

Witkin, H. A. et al. *Personality through perception: An experimental and clinical study*. New York: Harper & Row, 1954.

———. *Psychological differentiation*. New York: Wiley, 1962.

Wodtke, K. H. Some data on the reliability and validity of creativity tests at the elementary school level. *Educational and Psychological Measurement*, 1964, *24*, 399–408.

Womer, F. B. *Test norms: Their use and interpretation*. Washington, D.C.: National Association of Secondary School Principals, 1965.

Womer, F. B. and Wahl, N. K. Test use. In R. L. Ebel, ed. *Encyclopedia of educational research*, 4th ed. New York: Macmillan, 1969, 1461–69.

Wood, D. A. *Test construction: Development and interpretation of achievement tests*. Columbus, Ohio: Charles E. Merrill, 1960.

Worthen, B. R. and Clark, P. M. Toward an improved measure of remote associational ability. *Journal of Educational Measurement,* 1971, *8,* 113–23.

Worthen, B. R. and Sanders, J. R. *Educational evaluation: Theory and practice.* Worthington, Ohio: Charles A. Jones, 1972.

Wylie, R. C. *The self-concept: A critical survey of pertinent research literature.* Lincoln, Neb.: University of Nebraska Press, 1961.

Yamamoto, K. Creative writing and school achievement. *School and Society,* 1963, *91,* 307–308.

index of authors[*]

[*]Page numbers in italics refer to figures and boxes, *n* refers to footnotes.

index of subjects and tests*

*Page numbers in italics refer to figures and boxes, *n* refers to footnotes.

(7) *a.* lasting and general characteristics—reading ability
    b. lasting and specific characteristics—knowledge required by particular test items
    c. temporary and general characteristics—fatigue
    d. temporary and specific characteristics—luck (For more examples, see Figure 10.3 on page 263.)

(8) *a. T; b. E; c. T; d. E; e. E.*

(9) *a, b, c, e, g*

(10) longer

(11) *a.* Separate the tests of the high scorers and low scorers and compare the performance of each group on each item. Take those items on which the two groups had about the same success rate and revise or replace them with ones that correspond more closely to the content of the unit.
    b. Identify those items that the majority of students got wrong and find the answer choices that were selected more often than the ones you designated as correct; see if these choices are possibly correct. If they could be considered correct, change them to improve the items.
    c. Identify in advance the ideas that must be presented for each item in order to earn different amounts of credit; determine the point allocation per essay response for the different features (e.g., organization, creativity); do not look at student names; score one-fifth of the responses twice.

(12) This test was designed to measure six objectives with two items per objective; students' performance on each pair of items per objective can be examined and those pairs where half or more of the students got one member of the pair right and one wrong identified; a close examination of the items in these nonparallel item pairs can form the basis for a revision or replacement of at least one member of the pair.

Chapter 11

(1) scores or performance

(2) *a.* Information about the performance (that is, test results) of a specific group of people on which subsequent test score interpretation is based.
    b. The specific group of people on whose test scores interpretation is based.

(3) *a.* percentile rank
    b. grade-equivalent score
    c. standard score
    d. stanine score

(4) *a.* 5; *b.* 50; *c.* average.

(5) *b, d, e*

(6) Advantages: enables individual scores to be interpreted by compari-